FOCUS 4

SECOND EDITION

B2/B2+

STUDENT'S BOOK

Live and learn

Educating the mind without educating the heart is no education at all.
Aristotle

LEARNING A NEW SKILL

1 Watch the BBC video.
For the worksheet, go to page 132.

1.1 VOCABULARY

Education • phrasal verbs • describing teachers and students • collocations

I can talk about further education, university courses and educational issues.

SHOW WHAT YOU KNOW

1 Match the words to make collocations.

1 university/bachelor's/master's [b]
2 attend/have/skip [ ]
3 communication/language/people [ ]
4 fail/pass/take [ ]
5 further/higher/private [ ]
6 long/rewarding/successful [ ]

a career
b degree
c education
d exams
e lessons
f skills

2 Write two true sentences and a false one using collocations in Exercise 1. Can your partner guess which one is false?

I'd like to do a master's degree in Business Studies.

3 SPEAKING Look at some traditional fields of study on the signpost. What are the three most/least appealing subjects? Which way would you go? Discuss your ideas with a partner.

4 Read the information on the webpage. Which degree would you like to do the most?

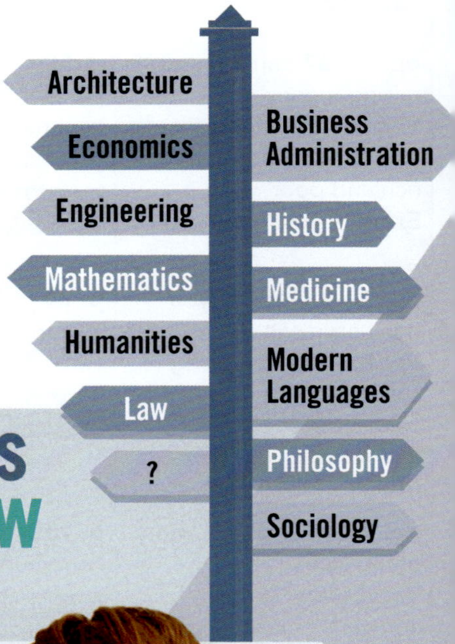

DEGREE COURSES YOU DIDN'T KNOW EXISTED

Is this you?

You're keen to **go on to** higher education. But none of the traditional subjects appeal. Don't worry, these days you can get a degree in most things. You like baking? You can **major in** baking technology management. More inclined towards fashion? How about writing a dissertation on handbag and accessories design? If you have a passion for something, you can usually find a course that specialises in your area. Here are three courses you never knew existed.

5 1.2 **Listen to a father and daughter discussing the webpage. What does the daughter find out about her father?**

6 1.2 **Listen again and choose the correct option. Use a dictionary if necessary.**

1 The daughter is *gifted* / *weak*.
2 The daughter is *lazy* / *a swot* compared to her father.
3 The father couldn't ***settle down*** / *make friends* in class.
4 The father was *disruptive* / *self-disciplined*.
5 The father nearly *got expelled* / *got a scholarship*.
6 The father had *lenient* / *strict* teachers.
7 The father's teachers ***gave up on*** / *supported* him.
8 The father was *dyslexic* / *a bully*.
9 The father *did well* / ***fell behind*** at school.
10 The father ***scraped through*** / *failed* his exams.

7 SPEAKING **What do you know about your parents' education? Discuss your ideas with a partner.**

1 THE SCIENCE OF SUPERHEROES
University of California, USA

This course is a new, creative way to learn physics. Through studying heroes and villains, you'll learn the answers to important real-life questions such as what the chemical composition of Captain America's armour is. In other words, you'll attend lectures on the real principles of physics, but they'll be given in a more engaging and accessible way.

2 SURF SCIENCE AND TECHNOLOGY
University of Plymouth, UK

The university website warns that 'You will not be taught how to surf, and it is important to realise that this is an academic course.' That means you don't graduate because you can catch a good wave – you have to sit exams here! Core modules include ecology and scientific aspects of health, fitness and sports nutrition.

3 THE BEATLES, POPULAR MUSIC AND SOCIETY
Liverpool Hope University, UK

If you enrol on this course, you'll deepen your knowledge of the band's music as well as how it was influenced by the city of Liverpool. The Beatles not only changed the world of music, but they also had a big impact on youth culture and fashion. This course will be of interest to those working in the field of cultural studies and if you want to go into the music industry.

Go to WORD STORE 1 page 3

WORD STORE 1A Phrasal verbs

8 1.3 **Complete WORD STORE 1A with the base form of the phrasal verbs in red in the text and in Exercise 6. Then listen, check and repeat.**

9 SPEAKING **Complete the questions with the prepositions in WORD STORE 1A. Ask and answer the questions.**

1 How often do you only just scrape ______ exams?
2 Have you ever given ______ anything that was important to you?
3 Have you ever fallen ______ at school because of illness or some other issue?
4 If you go ______ university, what subjects do you think you will major ______ ?
5 In what subject or lesson do you find it most difficult to settle ______ and concentrate?
6 What profession would you like to go ______ ?

WORD STORE 1B Describing teachers and students

10 1.4 **Complete WORD STORE 1B with the underlined words in Exercise 6. Use definitions 1–8 to complete the crossword and find the mystery word. Then listen, check and repeat. Which words are used more often to describe a student and which ones to describe a teacher?**

11 **Complete the sentences with the words in WORD STORE 1B.**

1 Mr Morris is a ____________ teacher. He doesn't mind if you hand your homework in late.
2 Jackie is a ____________ . She spends all her time studying and always gets top marks.
3 Miss Nelmes is very ____________ . She demands absolute silence in her lessons.
4 May is musically ____________ . She can play almost any instrument and has a beautiful voice.
5 Barry is quite ____________ in class. He shouts out and generally causes problems.
6 Mike is very ____________ . He always does his homework as soon as he gets home.

WORD STORE 1C Collocations

12 1.5 **Complete WORD STORE 1C with the base form of the verbs highlighted in the text and in Exercise 6. Then listen, check and repeat.**

13 **Complete the sentences with a suitable noun in WORD STORE 1C. Do you agree or disagree with them?**

1 Don't enrol on a university ____________ unless you have a ____________ for it.
2 Sitting ____________ is much more stressful than writing a ____________ .
3 Getting a ____________ to study at a foreign university is an impossible dream.
4 Working in the ____________ of science and technology is better than being an artist.
5 You don't have to attend ____________ to deepen your ____________ . Just google everything.

1.2 GRAMMAR

Present and past habits

I can talk about present and past habits.

1 **Read about Gillian Lynne's education. What do you think Gillian did when her mum and the psychologist left the room?**

2 1.6 SPEAKING **Listen to two friends talking about Gillian's story and check your ideas in Exercise 1. Discuss what this story teaches us about educating children.**

3 **Read the GRAMMAR FOCUS. Complete the examples in the table using the verb forms in blue in the text in Exercise 1.**

GRAMMAR FOCUS

Present and past habits

- You can use the **Present Simple** and the **Past Simple** to talk about habits. You also use the Past Simple to talk about single past actions.
- You can use ***used to*** to talk about regular past actions that don't happen any more or past states that are no longer true.
  She [1] *used to fail* *all her exams.*
  Life [2] ____________ *so good.*
- You can use ***will*** (present) or ***would*** (past) to talk about characteristics or predictable actions. You don't use them to talk about states.
  She [3] ____________ *and move around instead of listening to the teacher.*
  Her teachers [4] ____________ *about her disruptive behaviour.*
  Note: You don't usually ask questions with this use of *will* and *would*.
- You can use the **Present Continuous** or **Past Continuous** with ***always*** to stress the repetitiveness of an action or to show your annoyance.
  She [5] ____________ *people.*
  She [6] ____________ *and handing in her homework late.*

4 **Complete the sentences with the correct form of the verbs in brackets. Use *would* where possible. If *would* is not possible, use *used to*. If *used to* is not possible, use the Past Simple.**

1 This school *used to be* (be) smaller than it is now.
2 Mum ____________ (take) me to school every day.
3 I ____________ (not like) going to school.
4 I ____________ (hate) having school lunches.
5 I ____________ (go) swimming every week.
6 I ____________ (go) on a school trip to England.

5 SPEAKING **Ask and answer questions based on the sentences in Exercise 4. Use *used to* or the Past Simple.**

1 Did this school use to be smaller than it is now?

The right education

Ken Robinson is an educationalist. In his book, *The Element*, he interviews people who have made a successful living doing what they love. This is Gillian Lynne's story.

Gillian had a successful career in the theatre, but life **didn't use to be** so good. When she was eight her schoolwork was a disaster, her handwriting was awful, and she **used to fail** all her exams. Her teachers **would complain** about her disruptive behaviour: she **was always fidgeting** and handing in her homework late. They told her mother that she had a learning disorder. So Gillian's mother took her to see a psychologist and listed some of the problems: she never pays attention in class – she**'ll get up** and move around instead of listening to the teacher; she**'s always disturbing** people and her homework's always late. Finally, the doctor turned to Gillian and said, 'Gillian, I need to speak to your mother privately now. Don't worry. We won't be long.' As they left the room, he turned on the radio on his desk ...

6 **Write sentences comparing your routine at primary school and now. Compare your sentences with a partner. Who has changed the most?**

	Primary school	Now
1 For breakfast	I'd ______	I'll ______
2 Before setting off for school	I'd ______	I'll ______
3 At break time	I'd ______	I'll ______
4 At lunchtime	I'd ______	I'll ______
5 After school	I'd ______	I'll ______
6 Before going to bed	I'd ______	I'll ______

1 For breakfast, I'd have cereal with milk in primary school, but now I'll just have a piece of toast.

7 **Complete the sentences about annoying habits. Use one verb from the box to complete both sentences in each example. Use the Present and Past Continuous with *always*.**

check ~~chew~~ lose talk tell

1 Before, Tim *was always chewing* the end of his pen.
Now, he*'s always chewing* gum.
2 Before, Julie ____________ her make-up.
Now, she ____________ her phone.
3 Before, Sam ____________ about himself.
Now, he ____________ about his new friends.
4 Before, Dave ____________ his temper.
Now, he ____________ his keys.
5 Before, Mary ____________ lies.
Now, she ____________ people what to do.

8 **List the habits in Exercise 7 from the least to the most annoying. Compare your ideas with a partner. Do you know people who had or have any of these habits?**

FOCUS VLOG **About daily routines**

3 **Watch the Focus Vlog. For the worksheet, go to page 133.**

Grammar page 148

1.3 LISTENING

Matching

I can identify specific information in a detailed spoken dialogue about memory.

1 **SPEAKING Discuss how good you are at remembering the different things in the box.**

dates and times · English words · faces · items on a shopping list · names · song lyrics

2 **1.7 Read about two methods of memorising a shopping list. Choose the best heading for each method. There are three extra headings. Then listen and check.**

A Use your imagination
B Make up a dramatic narrative
C Learn how to give a speech
D Imagine what each item tastes like
E Visualise the items in a familiar place

MEMORY TIPS

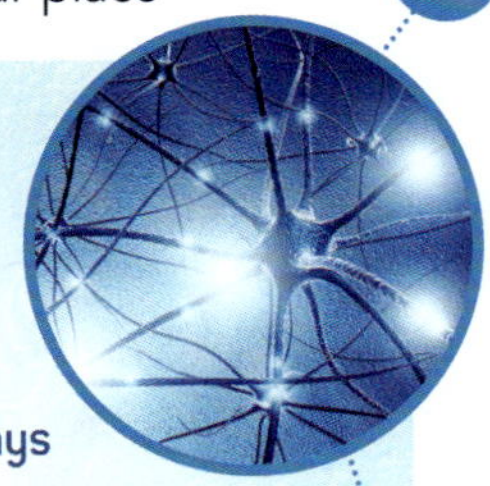

Greek philosopher Socrates famously said 'Learning is remembering'. So, how can we improve our memory? The key is to use your imagination. Here are two ways of remembering a shopping list of eight items.

1 ___ First, imagine a huge loaf of bread, and suddenly, coffee squirts out of the top and makes a fountain of dark brown liquid. After a few seconds, the dark brown changes to white yoghurt. The yoghurt forms a river and it goes under a bridge – the bridge is a steak. Some black and green olives are crossing the bridge and some big brown eggs are chasing them. The olives hide behind a big carton of orange juice. You lift an olive to your mouth to eat and it turns into an onion which tastes horrible. That's it. You've reached the end.

2 ___ Think of your home and get a mental image of the rooms in your house. Then, put the items on the list, one by one, in specific places in the rooms. For instance, you imagine the bread on the doormat as you come in the door. Then you go into the living room and the coffee is in front of the television, the yoghurt is on the sofa and the steak is stuck to the mirror on a wall. And so on, it's all about making personal associations … you get the idea. This method isn't just useful for memorising shopping lists. Some famous people have used it to give a speech without using notes.

3 **SPEAKING Test your partner's memory. Follow the instructions to complete the task.**

- Write down a shopping list of eight items and give it to your partner.
- Study your partner's list for sixty seconds using one of the methods in Exercise 2.
- Take it in turns to recall your list. Did the tip help?

EXAM FOCUS Matching

4 **1.8 Listen to four people talking about memory. Match statements A–E with speakers 1–4. There is one extra statement.**

Speaker 1: ☐ Speaker 2: ☐ Speaker 3: ☐ Speaker 4: ☐

The speaker …
A refers to someone who is incapable of forgetting anything.
B wanted a family member to confirm whether his/her memory was correct.
C disagrees with someone about how they keep a good memory.
D wishes they could forget witnessing a crime.
E can identify someone after seeing them for a short while.

5 **1.8 Listen again and answer the questions.**

1 What is Speaker 1's earliest memory?
2 Does Speaker 2's grandfather have trouble remembering things?
3 Can Speaker 3 remember names and faces well?
4 Does Speaker 4 have a good memory?

WORD STORE 1D Memory

6 **1.9 Complete WORD STORE 1D with the words in the box. Then listen, check and repeat.**

7 **SPEAKING Complete the questions with the words in WORD STORE 1D. Then ask and answer the questions.**

1 What's the most ___________ memory you have from your childhood? Why do you think you remember it so well?
2 Do you have a photographic ___________ ? Would you like to?
3 Have you ever heard about anyone who's ___________ their memory and couldn't remember anything?
4 If people can't remember certain events, are there ways to ___________ their memory and help them remember?
5 What do you have the most terrible memory ___________ ? Names? Phone numbers? Anything else?
6 Do you know anyone who has a memory like a ___________ ? Is it difficult to be around such people?

PRONUNCIATION FOCUS

8 **1.10 Listen and repeat the words in the box. Do any of the words have the same vowel sound?**

bread · clear · learn · mean · steak · wear

9 **1.11 Add the words from Exercise 8 to the table. Then listen, check and repeat.**

Sound	Typical spelling	Occasional spelling
/iː/	need detail [1] *mean*	piece
/ɪə/	here career [2] ________	
/ɜː/	reserved squirt turn	[3] ________
/e/	egg	[4] ________
/eɪ/	made detail pay	[5] ________
/eə/	pair rare	[6] ________

1.4 READING

Gapped text

I can infer unstated information and understand relationships between ideas in a descriptive text.

1 SPEAKING How much do you know about your brain? Do the quiz on page 9 and discuss your ideas with a partner.

2 1.12 Listen and check your answers.

3 Read the text and answer the questions.

1 What hidden talents did the five people discover?
2 What caused them to discover their hidden talents?
3 How do some experts explain the phenomenon?

EXAM FOCUS Gapped text

4 Read the text again. Complete gaps 1–4 with sentences A–E. There is one extra sentence.

A After a year, he realised he had acquired extraordinary memory skills and could recall the day of the week of any given date.

B Some of us are athletic, some of us mathematical, some of us artistic, and others musical; some of us are just good, while some are exceptional.

C We even know where many of the different brain functions, such as memory, sight and smell, are located.

D However, their existence has led some researchers to argue that there is an undiscovered genius within all of us.

E Soon afterwards, he noticed that his vision had changed. He also realised that he had developed remarkable mathematical abilities.

WORD STORE 1E Collocations

5 1.14 Complete WORD STORE 1E with the base form of the verbs in blue in the text. Explain the difference, if any, between the pairs of collocations. Then listen, check and repeat.

6 Complete the questions with the correct form of the verbs in WORD STORE 1E. Then answer the questions.

1 What aspects of the human brain ____________ a mystery?
2 Where was Jason Padgett when he was attacked and ____________ unconscious?
3 How common is it for savants to lose the new skills they have ____________?
4 Why did Ben McMahon ____________ a coma?
5 What was Orlando Serrell doing when he ____________ a head injury?
6 Where was Tony Cicoria when he ____________ by lightning?
7 When did Heather Thompson first ____________ an urge to paint?
8 Did she lose ____________ when it happened?

7 SPEAKING If you could discover your hidden talent, what would you like that talent to be? Discuss your ideas with a partner.

8 1.15 Complete the expressions with the words in the box. Use a dictionary if necessary. Then listen, check and repeat.

~~behind~~ on rack have

1 **be the brains** *behind* **sth** = be responsible for inventing or organising sth
2 **brainstorm sth** = discuss (new) ideas
3 **brainy** = very intelligent (informal)
4 ______ **a brainwave** = suddenly think of a good idea
5 **have sth** ______ **the brain** = keep thinking constantly about sth
6 ______ **your brains** = try very hard to remember or to solve sth

9 Complete the text about Tim Berners-Lee with the expressions in Exercise 8. Why isn't he a multi-billionaire?

Tim Berners-Lee

Tim Berners-Lee is proof that you don't have to be a savant to do amazing things. Berners-Lee, a modest engineer and computer scientist is [1]____________ the World Wide Web. In 1989 he was working for CERN, the European Organisation for Nuclear Research, in Switzerland. An essential part of his job was to [2]____________ ideas with his colleagues and then share information with researchers in different geographical locations. It was while he was [3]____________ for ways to improve the communication process that he [4]____________ – he could use hypertext, a language for sharing text electronically, to allow computers all over the world to talk to each other – through the Internet. The World Wide Web was born! But Tim Berners-Lee did not have money [5]____________! Had he been a more materialistic man, he could have become a multi-billionaire by charging royalties for his invention. Instead, he gave it to the world for free.

10 SPEAKING Which scientist, inventor or thinker do you most admire? Decide on your top three and give reasons. Compare your ideas with other people in the class.

THE HUMAN BRAIN QUIZ

fact or fiction?

1. A larger brain is smarter than a smaller brain.
2. On average a person has 70,000 thoughts each day.
3. The brain's storage capacity is practically unlimited.
4. The brain produces enough electricity to power a small light bulb.
5. Most people only use 10 percent of their brain.

HIDDEN TALENTS

1.13

Despite some recent advances, there is still a great deal about the human brain that **remains a mystery**. We know it is made up of about 100 billion nerve cells, called neurons, connected like wires in a giant telephone exchange. We know messages pass down them like electrical signals and jump from one neuron to the next when chemicals known as neurotransmitters are released. [1]___ But what we don't fully understand are things like consciousness, intelligence and creativity.

Much of our knowledge comes from studying brain functions when things go wrong. There are some fascinating cases of where a bang on the head has brought about changes in personality or caused a person to become talented in a way they weren't at all before the injury.

A famous case was Jason Padgett, a furniture salesman from Washington, who was mugged by two men after leaving a karaoke bar. He survived the attack, but **was left unconscious**. [2]___ Padgett began to see patterns in everything he looked at, and to draw complex geometric figures. He seemed to understand the mathematical nature of the universe despite the fact that he had little formal academic training. The man who had barely scraped though his school exams ended up pursuing a career in mathematics as a number theorist.

Padgett's is a case of acquired savant syndrome, a condition in which brain damage of some kind unlocks extreme mental abilities. All cases of acquired savant syndrome involve a head injury and the special abilities are typically in the fields of maths, languages, music or art. Having **acquired the new skill**, it is extremely rare for a savant to lose it. The change is permanent.

Another example of this syndrome is twenty-four-year-old Ben McMahon from Australia, who **fell into a coma** after a car crash. A week later he woke up speaking Mandarin Chinese. He had studied Chinese at school, but had never been fluent until the accident. McMahon works now as a Chinese-speaking tour guide in Australia.

Orlando Serrell **suffered a head injury** when he was knocked out in a baseball game at the age of ten. When he regained consciousness, he felt OK and finished the game. [3]___ He has never made a mistake. For instance, ask him about 11 February 1983 and he says 'Friday. It was raining that day. I had a pizza – pepperoni sausage.'

Some knocks on the head are more dramatic than others. Tony Cicoria, an orthopaedic surgeon, **was struck by lightning** as he was leaving a public payphone. Luckily there was a nurse nearby and she saved his life. Several weeks after the accident, Cicoria developed a strong desire to listen to classical piano music and play the piano even though he'd never wanted to play a musical instrument before. He is now a successful pianist and composer.

Although cases of female savants are not as common as those of males, there are some examples. Heather Thompson, a successful businesswoman from Washington, was loading her supermarket shopping into her car when the boot door crashed down onto her head. Although she never **lost consciousness**, the accident changed her life. Soon afterwards she **felt an urge** to paint, and overnight she became a talented abstract artist. She explained that her hands simply knew how to use colour and white spaces – it felt natural to her to paint.

There is no single theory to explain each case, but many researchers believe that acquired savant syndrome happens when the right side of the brain compensates for an injury to the left side. The condition is rare – fewer than one hundred cases have been identified. [4]___ The challenge is how to access that hidden knowledge and skill without experiencing a bang on the head.

1.5 GRAMMAR

Verb patterns

I can use a wide range of different verb patterns

1 1.16 **Listen to Part 1 of a podcast about being left-handed. What jobs seem to be more suited to 'lefties'?**

2 1.16 **Listen to the podcast again. Are statements 1–4 true (T) or false (F)?**

1 No one knows what **makes someone use** their right or left hand. ☐
2 Left-handers **tend to choose** creative professions. ☐
3 Dominance of the left hemisphere **enables left-handers to be** better at 3D perception. ☐
4 Rafa Nadal **keeps winning** because he is naturally left-handed. ☐

3 Read GRAMMAR FOCUS I and complete it using the verb forms in blue in Exercise 2.

GRAMMAR FOCUS I

Verb patterns

1 **verb + *to* + infinitive:** *tend to choose*
2 **verb + object + *to* + infinitive:** __________
3 **verb + object + infinitive without *to*:** __________
4 **verb + *-ing*:** __________

4 Match the verbs in the box with verb patterns 1–4 in GRAMMAR FOCUS I. Check the lists on page 149 if you are not sure.

advise ☐ allow ☐ arrange ☐ avoid ☐
can't afford ☐ can't help ☐ can't stand ☐ cause ☐
decide ☐ encourage ☐ expect ☐ fancy ☐
force ☐ imagine ☐ intend ☐ let ☐ manage ☐
offer ☐ refuse ☐ remind ☐ seem ☐
spend/waste time ☐ urge ☐ warn (not) ☐

5 1.17 **Complete Part 2 of the podcast with the correct form of the verbs in brackets. Then listen and check. How many left-handed people do you know?**

6 Read GRAMMAR FOCUS II. Find examples of verb patterns with *remember*, *stop*, *hear* and *see* in Exercise 5. Explain the changes in meaning.

GRAMMAR FOCUS II

Verb patterns – change in meaning

- You can use ***remember***, ***forget***, ***stop*** and ***try*** with the *-ing* form or a *to* + infinitive, but with a change in meaning.

  *I **remember doing** my homework. Sadly, I **didn't remember to hand** it **in**.*

  *Jim **will never forget going** on that school trip. He **forgot to take** any money.*

  *'I've **stopped eating** chocolate.' 'Really? Why **did you stop to buy** some on the way home?'*

  *I **tried to convince** Jane but she doesn't want my advice. Why don't you **try talking** to her?*

- You use ***feel***, ***hear***, ***see***, ***watch*** **+ object + *-ing*** to describe ongoing actions or the same verbs **+ object + infinitive without *to*** to describe finished actions.

  *I **watched Dan playing** football and **saw him score** the winning goal.*

7 Complete the sentences with the correct form of the verbs in brackets. Which sentences are true for you? Compare with a partner.

1 I often forget *to bring* (bring) my pens to school.
2 I'll never forget __________ (meet) my best friend.
3 I don't remember __________ (learn) how to swim.
4 I always remember __________ (switch) my phone off in lessons.
5 I stopped __________ (take) piano lessons a while ago.
6 I usually stop __________ (buy) sweets on my way.
7 If my laptop freezes, I try __________ (turn) it off and on again.
8 I tried __________ (work), but I was tired.
9 I've never seen my father __________ (lose) his temper.
10 I often see my neighbour __________ (drive) to work.

Grammar page 149

So that's the good news about being left-handed. The bad news is that manufacturers don't remember to make tools and machinery for left-handers. Society [1]__________ (force/us/use) objects that are designed for right-handed people and this [2]__________ (make/us/look) clumsy.

As a child I don't remember deciding that I was left-handed. But when my primary school teacher saw me using my left hand for writing and drawing she [3]__________ (encourage/me/swap) hands. She didn't [4]__________ (manage/change) my natural inclination, and I didn't stop writing with my left hand. Why [5]__________ (waste time/try) to change someone's natural handedness? Just [6]__________ (let/them/use) the hand they feel comfortable with – you can't [7]__________ (expect/people/do) what isn't natural to them!

I once heard someone say that left-handed people were strange. But when you stop to think about famous historical figures who were left-handed, you can't [8]__________ (avoid/conclude) that they were brilliant! I'm sure Leonardo da Vinci, Mahatma Gandhi, Albert Einstein, Winston Churchill and Marie Curie would agree!

1.6 SPEAKING

Describing a photo

I can describe a photo and speculate about hypothetical situations.

1 SPEAKING **Look at the adjectives in the box. Tell your partner about the last time you experienced these feelings while you were learning something.**

confused determined enthusiastic frustrated relieved terrified thrilled

The last time I felt really confused was when I was trying to understand when to use the Present Perfect tense in English! But, fortunately, I understand it now …

2 SPEAKING **Take turns to describe and speculate about photo A.**

- Say what the photo shows.
- Speculate about the people and their feelings.
- Speculate about the situation just before and/or just after the photo was taken.

SPEAKING FOCUS

Speculating about people

Based on …, I'd say he's/she's/it's …
Judging by …, I (don't) think …
It looks/seems as if/as though …
He/She/It appears/doesn't appear to be …
The chances are (that) he's/she's/it's …

Showing certainty

Clearly, (there's a problem/something is wrong).
It's obvious/clear (from the expression on his/her face) that …
He/She/It is definitely/certainly (not) …

Showing uncertainty

It's hard to be sure (whether/if …)
It's not easy to say (whether/if …)
I can't really tell (whether/if …)

Speculating about the situation

He/She could/might have ('ve) just + *Past Participle (recent past)*
He/She could/might be + *-ing (present)*
He/She could/might be about to + *infinitive (near future)*

A

B

3 1.18 **Listen to someone describing photo A. Does the speaker have the same ideas about the situation as you?**

4 1.18 **Read the SPEAKING FOCUS. Complete the description of photo A with one word in each gap. Then listen again and check.**

This is a photo of a teenage girl driving a car. It's [1]____________ to be sure whether she's having a driving lesson or taking her driving test. The middle-aged man sitting in the passenger seat to her left has got some official looking papers and a pen, so the [2]____________ are he's an examiner rather than an instructor. [3]____________ on his body language, I'd say they might be [4]____________ to crash! [5]____________ , something is wrong. It looks [6]____________ if he's absolutely terrified. He's covering his face and hiding behind his papers. He could've [7]____________ seen a car pull out in front of them or, even worse, a pedestrian step out into the road. The girl doesn't [8]____________ to be as scared as him, so maybe she hasn't noticed the problem yet. Hopefully, she'll be able to stop in time. [9]____________ by the examiner's reaction, I don't think she's going to pass her driving test this time!

5 SPEAKING **Take turns to describe and speculate about photo B. Use the SPEAKING FOCUS to help you.**

6 1.19 **Listen to a teenager answering a question. Which of these questions has she been asked?**

1 Which school subject do you feel is the most useful and why?
2 Is it important for you to learn to drive? Why?/ Why not?
3 In your opinion, what qualities should a good teacher or instructor have?
4 Given the choice, which new subjects or skills would you like to learn and why?

7 1.19 **Listen again. Which phrases do you hear?**

Personally, I think …
In my opinion …
Actually …
To be honest …
I intend to …
For this reason, I feel …
That's why I think …

8 SPEAKING **Ask and answer the questions in Exercise 6. Use the phrases in Exercise 7 to help you.**

1.7 USE OF ENGLISH

Register

I can use formal and informal language appropriately.

1 SPEAKING **Read UK TODAY. Discuss why you think fewer UK students are studying foreign languages these days. What is the situation in your country?**

UK TODAY

International exchange trips

- Young people can experience life with a host family and at a local high school, new places, customs and people.
- 62 percent of UK students decided to study languages at university after an exchange trip, but …
- Only 30 percent of state secondary schools organise international exchange trips these days and …
- Fewer than 8 percent of UK students study a foreign language until age eighteen and the numbers are falling.

2 **Read Texts 1 and 2 and answer the questions.**

1 What is happening at Stoneberry School?
2 What is the purpose of Text 1 and Text 2?
3 Which text is formal/informal? Why?

3 **Complete the LANGUAGE FOCUS with the examples in blue in Texts 1 and 2.**

Text 1

To: Jill Duncan (Head of English)
From: Angie Dalton (School Exchange Organiser)

Hi Jill,

I've been thinking about having a welcome party for the Swiss exchange students. They can come to a get-together in the main hall. Make sure all your staff come along and also could you say a few words? – you know, say hello and tell the visitors a bit about the school and the town. We'll follow this with a bit of food (menu TBC). They can come in through the main entrance and we can get our students to say hello and then they can show the exchange students around the school.

BTW, I've already posted a map and directions on the website.

Thanks, Jill 🙂

Angie

Text 2

Stoneberry School

You are invited to attend a reception in honour of the exchange group from Switzerland.

The reception will be held in the school assembly hall from 5 p.m. to 6:30 p.m.

All English teaching staff will be present and in addition the Head of English will give a welcome speech.

This will be followed by light refreshments. A map and directions have been posted on the website.

Please enter through the front entrance where student representatives will greet you.

Visitors will be given a guided tour of the school.

4 **There are twelve more underlined examples of formal and informal equivalents in Texts 1 and 2. Write them down in a new formal/informal table.**

LANGUAGE FOCUS

Register – formal and informal language

Formal language is more common in written English, e.g. in official documents, business letters and invitations. It is also used in certain spoken contexts such as announcements, presentations or speeches. Informal language is more common in spoken English. It's also used in some written contexts, e.g. in informal emails, blogs or postcards.

Formal	Informal
No contractions or abbreviations: *I have been thinking …* *To be confirmed*	**Contractions and abbreviations:** [1] *I've been thinking …* [2] ________
Greater use of the Passive: [3] ________	**Less use of the Passive:** *We'll follow this …*
More use of indirect questions: *Do you think you could say a few words?*	**More use of direct questions:** [4] ________ ?

Formal	Informal
More complex noun phrases: *light refreshments*	**Simpler noun phrases:** [5] ________
More verbs of Latin origin: [6] ________	**More phrasal verbs:** *come in*
Complex prepositional phrases: *a reception* [7] ________ *the exchange group*	**Simple prepositions:** *a welcome party for the exchange students*
More formal linkers: [8] ________ *incidentally*	**Neutral linkers:** *also* *BTW (by the way)*

5 Read an email from one of the Swiss exchange students to the student in her English host family. Choose the correct option.

[1]*Dear Miss Natalie Brown, / Hi Natalie,*

[2]*Sorry for not writing earlier / I apologise for the delay in writing to you*, but [3]*I've been up to my eyes in / I have been extremely busy with my* school work. [4]*I am delighted to be invited / Thanks for inviting me* to stay in your house for three weeks.

[5]*I'd like / Please allow me* to tell you a bit about myself. [6]*I was raised / I grew up* in Basel and I have quite a big family. [7]*There are / It consists of* three children – two girls and a boy. [8]*In addition / Also*, we have two dogs.

[9]*BTW / Incidentally*, have you ever [10]*considered / thought about* learning German? You could come and stay with me in Basel.

[11]*Anyway / In conclusion*, my train [12]*gets in to / arrives in* London at 2:30 p.m. and [13]*so / consequently* I should be at your house by 3:30 p.m. I hope [14]*that is acceptable / that's OK.*

[15]*CU soon, / Yours sincerely,*

Annika

6 Rewrite the sentences in the Passive using the more formal equivalents of the underlined phrasal verbs. Use the verbs in the box.

address demolish omit postpone reject reprimand ~~tolerate~~

1 I will not <u>put up with</u> bad behaviour.
Bad behaviour will not be tolerated.
2 You can <u>leave out</u> question 7.
____
3 I'll <u>deal with</u> those issues tomorrow.
____
4 They are <u>pulling down</u> the old hall next week.
____
5 Unfortunately, the city council <u>turned down</u> our proposal.
____
6 We've <u>put off</u> the decision till next week.
____
7 I've <u>told</u> him <u>off</u> twice already.
____

7 Complete the more formal version of each question.

1 Is there a swimming pool at the school?
I was wondering ____________________ .
2 Are we going to London?
Do you know ____________________ ?
3 Where can I change some money?
Could you tell me ____________________ ?
4 What time does school start in the morning?
I'd like to know ____________________ .
5 Are we allowed to wear trainers to school?
Do you think ____________________ ?

8 USE OF ENGLISH Complete the second sentence so that it has a similar meaning to the first. Use between two and five words including the word in capitals. Do not change the word given.

1 It's fantastic you've chosen our school for your exchange trip. **DELIGHTED**
We ____________ chosen our school for your exchange trip.
2 You must wear school uniform at all times during school hours. **WORN**
____________ at all times during school hours.
3 What is your favourite school subject? **IS**
I'd like to know what ____________ .
4 Turn off your mobile phones, otherwise we will take them away from you. **CONFISCATED**
Turn off your mobile phones, otherwise ____________ .
5 A meeting for parents is planned so that we can provide them with the necessary information. **ORDER**
A meeting for parents is planned ____________ provide them with the necessary information.

9 USE OF ENGLISH Read about the Tower of London and use the information to complete the informal email. Sometimes more than one answer is possible.

Visit the
TOWER OF LONDON
Guided tours every day

Visitors will be given a guided tour. You will be accompanied by a Beefeater who will recount stories of the history of the Tower. Prepare to be dazzled by the Crown Jewels. This will be followed by the Ceremony of the Keys.

We recommend allowing a minimum of three hours to complete your visit.

The tours start at 9 a.m. The last tour commences at 2:30 p.m. in winter and 3:30 p.m. in summer. Please be aware that in poor weather conditions, the tour will be given in the Chapel.

Hi Annika,
I think visiting the Tower of London is a great idea. They [1]____________ us a guided tour of the Tower, and we can [2]____________ our tour any time in the morning. We need at [3]____________ three hours to see everything. A Beefeater will take us around the Tower and he'll [4]____________ stories about its history. We'll start with the Crown Jewels – they're amazing! And [5]____________ we'll see the Key Ceremony. If the weather's [6]____________ , the tour will be in the Chapel. If you want to know anything else, we can just [7]____________ it up on the website.
Cheers,
Natalie

10 SPEAKING Discuss your own experiences or views about international exchange trips.

1 What are the pros and cons?
2 What countries would you most like to have an exchange with?
3 Where would you take an exchange student in your area?

Use of English page 150

1.8 WRITING

A CV and a covering email

I can write a CV and covering letter to describe my skills, education and work experience.

1 SPEAKING Discuss the questions.

1 What kind of part-time or summer jobs do students in your country do?
2 Have you ever applied for a part-time or summer job?
3 Have you got a CV? How are CVs different from covering letters/emails?

2 Read Sigrid's CV and covering email. What position is she applying for? Which skills and experience make her an appropriate candidate for the job?

SIGRID HALVERSON

14 Cherry Tree Drive,
Chatfield, CH17 3QP.
DOB: 23.10.02

Mob: 1101 351 191
s.halverson3@mymail33.com

1 ______

Bright and responsible sixth-former with **practical experience of** caring for young children and a **proven ability to** work well in a team.

2 ______

- **well-developed** communication skills
- **excellent command of** Danish and Spanish
- **competent user of** Microsoft Office

3 ______

Currently: Queen Anne's College, Chatfield
Level 3 NVQ Childcare

2012–2019 Stoneferry School, Chatfield
GCSEs Maths (C), English (B), Spanish (A), Combined Science (B), History (C), Geography (B), Art and Design (A), English Literature (B)

4 ______

Summer 2019 Work experience: Chatfield Kindergarten, Childcare Assistant

- **dedicated member of** care team assisting learning through play
- relevant knowledge of health and safety regulations

2017–2019 Babysitting two preschoolers for family friends

5 ______

Art and design, mountain biking, cross-training, animals

6 ______

Mrs C. Waters
Manager, Chatfield Kindergarten
c.waters@cfk.com

Mrs D. Sommer
Course Coordinator (Childcare)
Queen Anne's College, Chatfield
d.sommer@qac.co.uk

3 Complete the headings in Sigrid's CV with the phrases in the box.

Education and qualifications   Interests
Employment history   Personal profile
Referees   Skills and achievements

4 Discuss the questions. Then read WRITING FOCUS I and check.

1 How long is Sigrid's CV and how has she made it easy to follow?
2 Why does she avoid using full sentences, e.g. *~~I have a~~ good command of English?*
3 How are her referees linked to her experience?

From: s.halverson3@mymail33.com
Subject: Sigrid Halverson – summer work application
Attachments: Sigrid Halverson CV

Dear Ms Laver,

I am writing in response to your online advertisement seeking staff for Chatfield Zoo's summer activities programme. I wish to apply for the position of children's activity coordinator.

I am an eighteen-year-old childcare student and I am passionate about working with children. I intend to pursue a career as a kindergarten teacher when I finish my education. With this in mind, I hope to gain as much relevant experience as possible while I am still a student. I would welcome the opportunity to work with and learn from a successful organisation such as Chatfield Zoo.

I gained considerable work experience at a local kindergarten last summer. During my work placement there, I worked alongside teachers, contributed to classes and supervised the children at break times. I also sat in on staff meetings and coordinated a very successful sports day. Additionally, as a keen athlete and artist, I feel confident I possess relevant skills and would be well suited to the position.

I would be delighted to attend an interview at your convenience and have attached my CV for your consideration. Please do not hesitate to contact me if you require any further information.

Yours sincerely,
Sigrid Halverson

WRITING FOCUS I

Organising a CV

- A CV should be one to two pages long.
- Save space and make your CV concise by avoiding full sentences.
- Use headings and bullet points to organise your CV logically.
- Use positive language to describe your skills and experience.
- Choose referees linked to your education and work experience.
- Check whether a photo is required in the country where you are applying for a job.

5 **Read WRITING FOCUS II. Find examples of each point in Sigrid's covering email. Has she followed all the advice?**

WRITING FOCUS II

Organising a covering email

- Use full sentences and a variety of positive language.
- Say why you are writing and which job you are applying for.
- Give details about yourself and explain why you want the job.
- Explain more about your relevant skills and experience (don't just repeat what's on your CV).
- Mention availability for interview and any attachments you are sending e.g. your CV.

6 **Complete the examples in LANGUAGE FOCUS I with information from Sigrid's CV.**

LANGUAGE FOCUS I

Use these phrases to give concise information on your CV. Avoid full sentences.

1 competent user of *Microsoft Office*
2 dedicated member of ____________
3 excellent command of ____________
4 practical experience of ____________
5 proven ability to ____________
6 well-developed ____________

7 **Complete the list of skills with phrases from LANGUAGE FOCUS I.**

1 ____________ meet deadlines
2 ____________ leading a team
3 ____________ image editing software
4 ____________ leadership skills
5 ____________ Mandarin Chinese
6 ____________ school athletics team

8 **Make a similar list of your skills and abilities. Compare your list with a partner. Which of your skills and abilities might help you get the job Sigrid is applying for?**

9 **Read LANGUAGE FOCUS II and complete the examples with the underlined verbs in Sigrid's email. Then match the verbs with their meanings.**

LANGUAGE FOCUS II

Use these phrases to explain more about your work experience in a covering email. Use full sentences.

1 I *gained* considerable work experience. ☐
2 I ____________ teachers. ☐
3 I ____________ to classes. ☐
4 I ____________ the children at break times. ☐
5 I ____________ staff meetings. ☐
6 I ____________ a sports day. ☐

a attended but didn't take part in
b helped to organise
c got
d gave my ideas, time and effort
e watched/checked
f worked together with

10 **Complete the extracts from covering emails with words from LANGUAGE FOCUS II.**

1 Two classmates and I ____________ the end-of-term party for our year at school.
2 While volunteering at the animal hospital, I ____________ valuable knowledge of common pet illnesses.
3 I ____________ a group of younger students during a field trip to a museum.
4 During my work placement at the theatre, I ____________ rehearsals and watched the director.
5 I am proud to say I ____________ to some ideas that the company used in their marketing campaign.
6 I learned a lot because I ____________ some of the most experienced members of staff.

11 **Find other useful phrases in Sigrid's covering letter.**

12 SPEAKING **Make notes on your ideal summer job. What is it? What skills and experience would be helpful? Discuss your ideas with a partner.**

SHOW WHAT YOU'VE LEARNT

13 **Do the writing task. Use the ideas in WRITING FOCUS I and II, LANGUAGE FOCUS I and II and Exercise 12 to help you.**

Write a one-page-long CV and a covering email to apply for your ideal summer job.

Part 1 – CV

- Use the headings from Sigrid's CV.
- Invent any necessary details.
- Check that the CV is one-page long.

Part 2 – Covering email

- Use Sigrid's email as an example.
- Give more details of your skills and experience than in the CV.

1.1 Vocabulary 4.1

accessible /ək'sesəbəl/
appeal /ə'piːl/
appealing /ə'piːlɪŋ/
armour /'ɑːmə/
attend a lecture /əˌtend ə 'lektʃə/
be of interest to /ˌbi əv 'ɪntrəst tə/
bully /'bʊli/
chemical composition /ˌkemɪkəl ˌkɒmpə'zɪʃən/
core /kɔː/
deepen your knowledge /ˌdiːpən jə 'nɒlɪdʒ/
design /dɪ'zaɪn/
disruptive /dɪs'rʌptɪv/
dyslexic /dɪs'leksɪk/
engaging /ɪn'geɪdʒɪŋ/
enrol on a course /ɪnˌrəʊl ɒn ə 'kɔːs/
fall behind /ˌfɔːl bɪ'haɪnd/
get a degree /ˌget ə dɪ'griː/
get a scholarship /ˌget ə 'skɒləʃɪp/
get expelled (from school) /ˌget ɪk'speld (frəm ˌskuːl)/
get top marks /ˌget tɒp 'mɑːks/
gifted /'gɪftɪd/
give a lecture /ˌgɪv ə 'lektʃə/
give up on /ˌgɪv 'ʌp ɒn/
go into /ˌgəʊ 'ɪntə/
go on to /ˌgəʊ 'ɒn tə/
graduate /'grædʒueɪt/
have a passion for /ˌhæv ə 'pæʃən fə/
have an impact on /ˌhæv ən 'ɪmpækt ɒn/
hero /'hɪərəʊ/
inclined towards /ɪn'klaɪnd təˌwɔːdz/
keen to do sth /ˌkiːn tə 'duː ˌsʌmθɪŋ/
lenient /'liːniənt/
major in /'meɪdʒə(r) ɪn/
management /'mænɪdʒmənt/
music industry /'mjuːzɪk ˌɪndəstri/
nutrition /njuː'trɪʃən/
principle /'prɪnsəpəl/
scrape through /ˌskreɪp 'θruː/
self-disciplined /ˌself 'dɪsɪplɪnd/
settle down /ˌsetl 'daʊn/
sit an exam /ˌsɪt ən ɪg'zæm/
strict /strɪkt/
swot /swɒt/
villain /'vɪlən/
work in the field of /ˌwɜːk ɪn ðə 'fiːld əv/
write a dissertation /ˌraɪt ə ˌdɪsə'teɪʃən/
youth culture /'juːθ ˌkʌltʃə/

1.2 Grammar 4.2

annoying /ə'nɔɪ-ɪŋ/
complain about /kəm'pleɪn əˌbaʊt/
disturb /dɪ'stɜːb/
educationalist /ˌedjʊ'keɪʃənəlɪst/
fidget /'fɪdʒət/
hand in /hænd 'ɪn/
handwriting /'hændˌraɪtɪŋ/
learning disorder /'lɜːnɪŋ dɪsˌɔːdə/
lose your temper /ˌluːz jə 'tempə/
make a successful living /ˌmeɪk ə səkˌsesfəl 'lɪvɪŋ/
pay attention in class /ˌpeɪ əˌtenʃən ɪn 'klɑːs/

1.3 Listening 4.3

accurately /'ækjərətli/
association /əˌsəʊsi'eɪʃən/
chase /tʃeɪs/
earliest memory /ˌɜːliəst 'meməri/
give a speech /ˌgɪv ə 'spiːtʃ/
have a clear memory of /ˌhæv ə ˌklɪə 'meməri əv/
have a distant memory of /ˌhæv ə ˌdɪstənt 'meməri əv/
have a good memory for /ˌhæv ə ˌgʊd 'meməri fə/
have a memory like a sieve /ˌhæv ə 'meməri laɪk ə ˌsɪv/
have a photographic memory /ˌhæv ə ˌfəʊtəˌgræfɪk 'meməri/
have a terrible memory for /ˌhæv ə ˌterəbəl 'meməri fə/
have a vague memory of /ˌhæv ə ˌveɪg 'meməri əv/
have a vivid memory of /ˌhæv ə ˌvɪvəd 'meməri əv/
improve your memory /ɪmˌpruːv jə 'meməri/
jog your memory /ˌdʒɒg jə 'meməri/
lose your memory /ˌluːz jə 'meməri/
make up /ˌmeɪk 'ʌp/
memorise /'meməraɪz/
narrative /'nærətɪv/
squirt /skwɜːt/
visualise /'vɪʒuəlaɪz/
witness /'wɪtnəs/

1.4 Reading 4.4

a great deal /ə 'greɪt diːl/
academic training /ˌækə'demɪk ˌtreɪnɪŋ/
acquire a skill /əˌkwaɪə(r) ə 'skɪl/
advance /əd'vɑːns/
bang on the head /ˌbæŋ ɒn ðə 'hed/
be found unconscious /bi ˌfaʊnd ʌn'kɒnʃəs/
be hit by lightning /bi ˌhɪt baɪ 'laɪtnɪŋ/
be left unconscious /bi ˌleft ʌn'kɒnʃəs/
be made up of /bi ˌmeɪd 'ʌp əv/
be struck by lightning /bi ˌstrʌk baɪ 'laɪtnɪŋ/
be the brains behind sth /bi ðə 'breɪnz bɪˌhaɪnd ˌsʌmθɪŋ/
boot /buːt/
brainstorm /'breɪnstɔːm/
brainy /'breɪni/
bring about /ˌbrɪŋ ə'baʊt/
charge royalties /ˌtʃɑːdʒ 'rɔɪəltiz/
come out of a coma /ˌkʌm ˌaʊt əv ə 'kəʊmə/
compensate for /'kɒmpənseɪt fə/
complex /'kɒmpleks/
develop a desire /dɪˌveləp ə dɪ'zaɪə/
essential part /ɪ'senʃəl ˌpɑːt/
fall into a coma /ˌfɔːl ˌɪntʊ ə 'kəʊmə/
feel an urge /ˌfiːl ən 'ɜːdʒ/
geometric pattern /ˌdʒiːəˌmetrɪk 'pætən/
get an urge /ˌget ən 'ɜːdʒ/
have a brainwave /ˌhæv ə 'breɪnweɪv/
have sth on the brain /ˌhæv ˌsʌmθɪŋ ɒn ðə 'breɪn/
knock sb out /ˌnɒk ˌsʌmbɒdi 'aʊt/
lose consciousness /ˌluːz 'kɒnʃəsnəs/
modest /'mɒdəst/
nerve cell /'nɜːv sel/
neurotransmitter /ˌnjʊərəʊtrænz'mɪtə/
number theorist /'nʌmbə ˌθɪərəst/
overnight /ˌəʊvə'naɪt/
payphone /'peɪfəʊn/
personality /ˌpɜːsə'næləti/
rack your brains /ˌræk jə 'breɪnz/
recall /rɪ'kɔːl/
recover from an injury /rɪˌkʌvə frəm ən 'ɪndʒəri/
regain consciousness /rɪˌgeɪn 'kɒnʃəsnəs/
release /rɪ'liːs/
remain a mystery /rɪˌmeɪn ə 'mɪstəri/
remarkable /rɪ'mɑːkəbəl/
savant syndrome /'sævənt ˌsɪndrəʊm/
sharpen a skill /ˌʃɑːpən ə 'skɪl/
solve a mystery /ˌsɒlv ə 'mɪstəri/
suffer an injury /ˌsʌfər ən 'ɪndʒəri/
telephone exchange /ˌteləfəʊn ɪks'tʃeɪndʒ/
unlock /ʌn'lɒk/
vision /'vɪʒən/
wire /waɪə/

1.5 Grammar 4.5

clumsy /'klʌmzi/
enable /ɪ'neɪbəl/
fancy /'fænsi/
handedness /'hændɪdnəs/
hemisphere /'heməsfɪə/
left-handed /ˌleft 'hændɪd/
left-hander /ˌleft 'hændə/
natural inclination /ˌnætʃərəl ˌɪŋklə'neɪʃən/

perception /pə'sepʃən/
swap /swɒp/
tend to do sth /'tend tə ˌduː ˌsʌmθɪŋ/
urge sb to do sth /'ɜːdʒ ˌsʌmbɒdi tə ˌduː ˌsʌmθɪŋ/

1.6 Speaking 4.6

appear /ə'pɪə/
based on /'beɪst ɒn/
certainly /'sɜːtnli/
certainty /'sɜːtnti/
clearly /'klɪəli/
confused /kən'fjuːzd/
definitely /'defɪnətli/
determined /dɪ'tɜːmənd/
enthusiastic /ɪnˌθjuːzi'æstɪk/
expression /ɪk'spreʃən/
hard to be sure /'hɑːd tə bi ˌʃɔː/
intend to /ɪn'tend tə/
judging by /'dʒʌdʒɪŋ baɪ/
obvious /'ɒbviəs/
pedestrian /pə'destriən/
pull out /ˌpʊl 'aʊt/
relieved /rɪ'liːvd/
thrilled /θrɪld/
uncertainty /ʌn'sɜːtnti/

1.7 Use of English 4.7

address /ə'dres/
announcement /ə'naʊnsmənt/
assembly hall /ə'sembli ˌhɔːl/
be up to your eyes in /bi 'ʌp tə jə ˌaɪz ɪn/
chapel /'tʃæpəl/
consist of /kən'sɪst əv/
custom /'kʌstəm/
confiscate /'kɒnfɪskeɪt/
dazzle /'dæzl̩/
deal with /'diːl wɪð/
delighted /dɪ'laɪtəd/
demolish /dɪ'mɒlɪʃ/
exchange student /ɪks'tʃeɪndʒ ˌstjuːdənt/
exchange trip /ɪks'tʃeɪndʒ ˌtrɪp/
get-together /'get təˌgeðə/
greet /griːt/
guided tour /ˌgaɪdɪd 'tʊə/
hold /həʊld/
host family /'həʊst ˌfæməli/
in honour of /ɪn 'ɒnər əv/
incidentally /ˌɪnsə'dentəli/
leave sth out /ˌliːv ˌsʌmθɪŋ 'aʊt/
omit /əʊ'mɪt/
postpone /pəʊs'pəʊn/
pull down /ˌpʊl 'daʊn/
put sth off /ˌpʊt ˌsʌmθɪŋ 'ɒf/
put up with /ˌpʊt 'ʌp wɪð/
reception /rɪ'sepʃən/
refreshments /ri'freʃmənts/
reject /rɪ'dʒekt/
reprimand /'reprəmɑːnd/
require /rɪ'kwaɪə/
tell sb off /ˌtel ˌsʌmbədi 'ɒf/
the Crown Jewels /ðə ˌkraʊn 'ʤuːəlz/
turn sb down /ˌtɜːn ˌsʌmbɒdi 'daʊn/
welcome party /'welkəm ˌpɑːti/
welcome speech /'welkəm ˌspiːtʃ/

1.8 Writing 4.8

apply for a position /əˌplaɪ fər ə pə'zɪʃən/
at your convenience /ət jə kən'viːniəns/
be passionate about /bi 'pæʃənət əˌbaʊt/
childcare /'tʃaɪldkeə/
competent user of /ˌkɒmpɪtənt 'juːzər əv/
considerable /kən'sɪdərəbəl/
contribute to /kən'trɪbjuːt tə/
coordinate /kəʊ'ɔːdəneɪt/
covering letter /ˌkʌvərɪŋ 'letə/
dedicated member of /ˌdedɪkeɪtɪd 'membər əv/
excellent command of /ˌeksələnt kə'mɑːnd əv/
gain work experience /ˌgeɪn wɜːk ɪk'spɪəriəns/
health and safety regulations /ˌhelθ ən 'seɪfti ˌreɡjuˌleɪʃənz/
image editing software /ˌɪmɪdʒ 'edɪtɪŋ ˌsɒftweə/
in response to /ɪn rɪ'spɒns tə/
kindergarten /'kɪndəgɑːtn/
lead a team /ˌliːd ə 'tiːm/
leadership skills /'liːdəʃɪp ˌskɪlz/
meet deadlines /ˌmiːt 'dedlaɪnz/
part-time job /ˌpɑːt 'taɪm 'dʒɒb/
practical experience of /ˌpræktɪkəl ɪk'spɪəriəns əv/
preschoolers /priː'skuːləz/
proven ability to /ˌpruːvən ə'bɪləti tə/
pursue a career /pəˌsjuː ə kə'rɪə/
relevant /'reləvənt/
sit in /sɪt 'ɪn/
staff /stɑːf/
summer job /'sʌmə dʒɒb/
supervise /'suːpəvaɪz/
valuable /'væljuəbəl/
volunteer /ˌvɒlən'tɪə/
welcome an opportunity /ˌwelkəm ən ˌɒpə'tjuːnəti/
well suited /ˌwel 'suːtɪd/
well-developed /ˌwel di'veləpt/
work alongside /'wɜːk əˌlɒŋˌsaɪd/
work placement /'wɜːk ˌpleɪsmənt/

MY WORD LIST

STUDYING

MEMORY AND THE BRAIN

OTHER

FOCUS REVIEW 1

VOCABULARY AND GRAMMAR

1 Match the verbs in box A with the prepositions in box B to make phrasal verbs, then complete the sentences with the phrasal verbs.

A fall go major settle scrape

B behind down in into through

1 After the lunch break, the kids were excited and took time to ___________.
2 Maths wasn't my best subject and I just managed to ___________ the exam.
3 If you miss a few classes, it's easy to ___________. Then it's hard to catch up.
4 He enjoys working with kids and he'd like to ___________ teaching as a career.
5 She wants to ___________ Biology at university, then get a job at a nature reserve.

2 Choose the correct option.

1 Many students can't afford to go to university unless they get a *degree / scholarship / dissertation*.
2 I have a very *vague / clear / photographic* memory of my first day at school – I remember it really well.
3 Amy fainted, but thankfully after just a few seconds she *remained / lost / regained* consciousness.
4 George got bored quickly and his teachers complained he was *disruptive / gifted / expelled* in class.
5 Our sports coach is pretty *lenient / self-disciplined / strict*; she makes us work really hard in training.
6 You can't possibly be hungry again – you always have food *on / in / inside* the brain!

3 Complete the text with one word in each gap.

THE SCHOOL REUNION

Last week I went to a school reunion and I was amazed how different the school looks now. The building where we [1]________ to have PE classes has been demolished and a new sports centre has been built instead.

I clearly remember how we [2]________ beg our sports teacher to allow us to play games in the old building! Then I bumped into Caroline who I [3]________ always having arguments with. I hardly recognised her. She didn't [4]________ to look so glamorous. But one thing hasn't changed about her. She [5]________ always talking about others behind their back. It's so unpleasant. The reunion also reminded me of the importance of punctuality that the school head teacher talked about so often. I got used to certain things so much that even now I [6]________ arrive at meetings at least fifteen minutes earlier than necessary!

4 Complete the sentences with the correct form of the verbs in brackets.

1 If you need more details, try ___________ (look) online for information. Maybe you'll find something.
2 The Music Academy exam board first listened to us all ___________ (sing) and then they announced who was admitted.
3 I'm sorry, sir. I forgot ___________ (check) if my essay is within the word limit you required.
4 Do you think our Chemistry teacher will let us ___________ (use) the lab to carry out our own experiments?
5 We were warned ___________ (not/touch) any of the exhibits.

USE OF ENGLISH

5 Read the text. Choose the correct answer, A, B, C or D.

New research suggests that having a smartphone on your desk when you are studying tends [1]___ a negative effect on your ability to concentrate. It [2]___ that in IQ tests where candidates had a smartphone nearby, even when they did not actively use it, they [3]___ less well than those without. It is thought that we have become accustomed to being alert to updates and notifications on our mobile devices. Thus, just having a smartphone in sight may be enough to [4]___ our attention from the task at hand.

1 A to having B you to have C have had D to have
2 A has been shown B was showing C is shown D has shown
3 A made B got on C performed D got through
4 A put off B distract C omit D mess with

6 Complete the second sentence using the word in capitals so that it has a similar meaning to the first. Use up to four words in each gap, but do not change the word in capitals.

1 So, did you get that email I sent you about the new course? **WONDERING**
I was ___________ that email I sent you about the new course.
2 Teachers are typically more aware of dyslexia now than they were in the past. **TEND**
Teachers ___________ aware of dyslexia now than they were in the past.
3 Our English teacher often took us to the cinema to watch foreign films. **WOULD**
Our English teacher ___________ to the cinema to watch foreign films.
4 My best friend has a very irritating habit of chewing gum loudly. **ALWAYS**
My best friend ___________ loudly.
5 I'm not sure if I've told my parents about the school trip. **REMEMBER**
I ___________ my parents about the school trip.

READING

7 Read the text. Complete gaps 1–5 with sentences A–F. There is one extra sentence.

NEW YORK

BROOKLYN FREE SCHOOL

A school with no grades, no homework, no tests and no obligation to attend classes. That's the Brooklyn Free School, a learning institution that follows a 'free' education philosophy. Neither the school's head teacher nor the teaching staff, who are known as advisers, tell the students what to do. [1]___ This is based on the school's belief that learning only happens when it is self-directed and not imposed by others.

The school is open to students from three to eighteen years of age. It encourages them to get involved in everything that concerns the school. In order to do so, students attend a Democratic Meeting where they have equal votes with the staff. This get-together is at the heart of the school's philosophy. [2]___ Announcements are made, issues are raised and everyone cooperates for the well-being of the school. Attendance at the weekly meeting is one of the few school rules. Though some of the younger students don't pay much attention, preferring to read or draw instead, they must be present.

A typical school day is different for every student. They can paint, play video games or work on laptops. Some prepare for the school's annual play by rehearsing or building stage sets. In the kitchen, others might be baking a cake or sorting rubbish for recycling. Traditional classroom lessons are also available if students wish to attend. [3]___ By offering these choices, the school accommodates all needs. Being part of a group of classes on a regular basis fits some students best, while doing individual projects is what suits others.

The school's philosophy is a radical one. Parents hope it will make their children independent thinkers and problem solvers. However, the school's system has its share of opponents. [4]___ This is due to the enormous freedom students have, which can lead to laziness and lack of discipline. Furthermore, they believe that students whose families cannot afford to hire private tutors have fewer chances of gaining college entry. It's believed that the school's academic preparation is inadequate. This seems to be supported by the fact that there are parents who have had to hire help to make sure their children learn the basics. [5]___ Since then, however, enrolments have increased and people are regaining confidence in the idea of self-regulated education and the school's mission.

A Also, in its first academic year, a third of the original students left, as did the teachers.
B These are best for students who prefer a structured day along with a weekly timetable.
C Many students go there to escape the stress and exam pressures of conventional schools.
D Taking place every Wednesday, it gives staff and students an opportunity to be heard.
E Their main criticism is that it does not, in fact, adequately prepare students for real life.
F It's entirely up to them to choose what they learn and how they wish to learn it.

LISTENING

8 1.20 Listen to four people talking about classes they attend. Match the speakers with the statements. There is one extra sentence. You will hear the recording twice.

Speaker 1: ☐
Speaker 2: ☐
Speaker 3: ☐
Speaker 4: ☐

The speaker …

A is looking to develop a professional goal.
B is struggling with the amount of work on the course.
C is motivated by feedback from the tutor.
D is thinking of quitting the course.
E is surprised by the attitude of the tutor.

SPEAKING

9 Look at photos where people are learning new things at different ages. Discuss when it's more difficult to learn new things: when you're a child or an elderly person. Why?

A

B

WRITING

10 Read the writing task and write a covering email.

Your town is going to host an international sport event during the summer holidays. The organisers are looking for English-speaking volunteers to assist the participants. Write a covering email for this post. Explain why you would like to do this job and why you are well-suited for it.

2

Human nature

We are what we repeatedly do. Excellence, then, is not an act, but a habit.
Aristotle

BBC

NATURE OR NURTURE?

5 Watch the BBC video.
For the worksheet, go to page 134.

VOCABULARY 2.1

People • personality adjectives • compound adjectives • describing personality

I can talk about people and describe their personalities.

SHOW WHAT YOU KNOW

1 **Write positive and negative adjectives for each noun in the box.**

ambition friendliness honesty kindness patience politeness responsibility sensitivity

ambition, ambitious, unambitious

2 SPEAKING **Discuss the qualities in Exercise 1 that you admire most/least and the qualities you think you possess.**

KNOW YOURSELF

PERSONALITY TEST

How well do you really know yourself? Read each sentence carefully and circle the symbol next to it if you feel it truly describes the real you.

1 I learn new things fast.
2 I feel others' emotions.
3 I do jobs straight away.
4 I like being alone.
5 I have a vivid imagination.
6 I make people feel relaxed.
7 I like telling funny stories.
8 I know myself well.
9 I pay attention to detail.
10 I love partying.
11 I come up with new ideas.
12 I make new friends easily.
13 I prefer small groups of people.
14 I have a soft heart.
15 I usually start conversations.
16 I love helping others.
17 I enjoy the arts.
18 I keep my things tidy.
19 I think before I speak.
20 I plan things in advance.

KEY

The symbols represent five different personality types. How many of each symbol did you choose?

♥ __ ★ __ ■ __ ▲ __ ● __

3 **Do the personality test and then read the key.**

4 **SPEAKING Write a short sentence that summarises your results. Compare your results with a partner and then discuss the questions.**

I am quite deep and fairly conscientious.

1 How accurate do you think this personality test is?
2 Why do you think people like doing personality tests?
3 Can you learn more about a person from a fifteen-minute personality test or a fifteen-minute chat?

AGREEABLE

You're kind-hearted and sensitive to the needs of others. Being relaxed, trusting and laid-back, you work well with others. In difficult situations, you're tactful and avoid hurting people. In fact, you're very good at making people feel at ease. You're affectionate and show your feelings. You're good-natured, friendly and popular.

IMAGINATIVE

You're artistic and creative and so you have the ability to think outside the box. You're daring and you're not afraid to do adventurous things. You're also quite perceptive and intellectual and have a love of learning.

ORGANISED

You're thorough – you like to plan things carefully. Being quite strong-willed, you usually get what you want. You're level-headed and you think things through carefully. In future, you will excel in leadership positions.

DEEP

You're a deep thinker and you're not comfortable with small talk. You're not insecure, but you are quite humble, and you can be a little self-conscious or even self-critical at times. You enjoy your own company, but you're not a loner – you like being with close friends. Above all, you're fair-minded and if you feel strongly about something, you're not afraid to speak up.

SOCIABLE

You're the life and soul of the party and love being the centre of attention. People enjoy your company because you're witty and spontaneous. You're larger than life and good fun to be around. However, on bad days you can be moody and short-tempered. Also, there are times when you appear a little self-centred and full of yourself.

Go to WORD STORE 2 page 5

WORD STORE 2A Personality adjectives

5 **1.21 Complete WORD STORE 2A with the adjectives in red in the quiz. Use a dictionary if necessary. Then listen, check and repeat.**

6 **Read the descriptions and choose the correct option. Use WORD STORE 2A to help you.**

1 Megan is brave enough to say things that shock people. She's quite *daring / insecure*.
2 Janet understands difficult concepts and enjoys debating serious topics. She's *intellectual / witty*.
3 Tom is diplomatic and is unlikely to upset or embarrass people. He's very *thorough / tactful*.
4 Sue has a very gentle, loving nature. She's extremely *perceptive / affectionate*.
5 Rick never talks about his achievements. He's very *humble / moody*.
6 Harry believes that most people are good and honest. He's very *spontaneous / trusting*.

WORD STORE 2B Compound adjectives

7 **1.22 Complete WORD STORE 2B with the underlined words in the quiz. Then listen, check and repeat.**

8 **Match each comment with an appropriate compound adjective in WORD STORE 2B.**

1 'Everyone seems really stressed. I'm cool. No problem.'
2 'I'm not going to change my mind, I'm determined.'
3 'I'm happy to fit in with what everybody else thinks.'
4 'I was hopeless. I should have done so much better.'
5 'I can see both sides of the argument.'

9 **Which compound adjectives in WORD STORE 2B are positive and which are negative? Which describe you?**

Kind-hearted and good-natured are positive, but short-tempered and self-centred are negative.
I think I'm strong-willed, and sometimes self-critical.

WORD STORE 2C Describing personality

10 **1.23 Complete WORD STORE 2C with the highlighted expressions in the quiz. Then listen, check and repeat.**

11 **SPEAKING Replace the underlined phrases with an expression in WORD STORE 2C. Which statements do you agree with and why? Discuss with a partner.**

1 It's up to teachers, not parents, to inspire and encourage a desire for knowledge in children.
2 Computers will never replace humans because they can't view things creatively.
3 People often perform better in oral exam situations when they feel comfortable.
4 People who have a really high opinion of themselves rarely make good friends.
5 Everybody would like to be entertaining on social occasions.

2.2 GRAMMAR

Past Perfect Simple and Continuous

I can talk about a past action or situation that took place before another past action or situation.

1 Read the story. Why did Amelie and Steve wait seventeen years to get married?

It was meant to be

Amelie was studying English in the UK when she met Steve. It was love at first sight and they spent a wonderful summer together. Amelie returned to France after her course finished. They tried to keep a long-distance relationship going, but they drifted apart.

A few years later, Steve wrote to Amelie, but Amelie's mother put the letter on the mantelpiece, forgot to tell Amelie, and it slipped down the back of the fireplace. Many years later, a builder was removing the fireplace when he found the letter. It had been there for ten years.

During that time, Amelie had remained single and had never forgotten the love of her life. Meanwhile, Steve had been working in a factory in his home town. He had been thinking about Amelie too, but he assumed she had got married to somebody else.

When she finally read the letter, Amelie was too nervous to call as so much time had passed. But she finally plucked up courage and they arranged to meet.

They got married seventeen years after they had first met.

2 Read the GRAMMAR FOCUS. Match the underlined examples in the story in Exercise 1 with rules 1–4.

GRAMMAR FOCUS

Past Perfect Simple and Continuous

You use the **Past Perfect** to make it clear that an activity took place before the main events in a story.

1. You use the **Past Perfect Simple** to describe a completed action.
2. You use the **Past Perfect Continuous** to describe an activity in progress.
3. You use the **Past Perfect Simple** (NOT ~~Continuous~~) with state verbs (*be, have, know*, etc.).
4. You don't have to use the **Past Perfect** if a time expression (i.e. *before* or *after*) makes the order of events clear.

3 Find other examples of the Past Perfect in the story and discuss why the simple or continuous forms have been used.

4 Choose the correct option.

1. Amelie didn't know that Steve *wrote / had written* to her.
2. Steve didn't know that Amelie *had never received / had never been receiving* his letter.
3. Steve thought Amelie *had got / got* married to somebody else.
4. Amelie found the letter and realised it *was lying / had been lying* behind the fireplace for ten years.
5. Amelie was nervous about calling Steve because they *hadn't seen / didn't see* each other for a long time.

5 USE OF ENGLISH Complete the sentences with the correct form of the words in brackets. Make any changes necessary, but do not change the order of the words.

1. The roads were wet this morning. *It had been raining* (it/rain) all night.
2. Yesterday I was tired. I ____________ (not/sleep) well the previous night.
3. I went to the doctor last week because I ____________ (not/feel) well.
4. I ____________ (have/same/phone) for ages so I got a new one last month.
5. I didn't understand yesterday's homework because I ____________ (not/listen/teacher) in class.
6. By the time I arrived, ____________ (lesson/already/start).

6 Are any sentences in Exercise 5 true for you? Write three of your own sentences using Past Perfect forms.

7 Complete the story with the Past Perfect Simple or Continuous form of the verbs in the box. Why did Eric and Vilma wait forty years to get married?

grow hear ~~know~~ live make meet move search see work

Eric and Vilma
40 YEARS ON

Vilma was my wife's best friend. They [1] *had known* each other since childhood. When Vilma moved away we lost touch, but she [2]____________ a big impression on me. So when my wife and I separated, I decided to ask my friends if anyone [3]____________ from her, but no one had. Vilma was a very compassionate person so I imagined that she [4]____________ to Tibet and [5]____________ for a charity for a few years. Finally, my niece called to say she [6]____________ Vilma's profile on Facebook. I rang her and found that she [7]____________ in Paris, so I [8]____________ in the wrong place! We met up and when we saw one another it was magical. We [9]____________ older, but that didn't matter. She was widowed and didn't have children. I proposed immediately. Forty years after we [10]____________ for the first time, we got married.

8 Write questions about the story from the prompts. Then answer the questions.

1. How long / Eric's ex-wife / know / Vilma?
   How long had Eric's ex-wife known Vilma?
2. any of Eric's friends / hear / from Vilma / after she / move away?
3. Why / Eric / think / Vilma / move / to Tibet?
4. Where / Vilma / live / since Eric / lose touch / with her?
5. Vilma / have / any children / with her late husband?

Grammar page 151

2.3 LISTENING

Multiple choice

I can understand the details of an extended radio interview with a neuroscientist.

1 SPEAKING **'What is love?' is one of the most popular searches on Google. Match the people 1–4 with their definition of love in the memes A–D. Which definition do you like best? Why?**

1 A novelist
2 A charity worker
3 A parent
4 A neuroscientist

2 1.24 **Listen to an interview with a neuroscientist and answer the questions.**

1 What does she specialise in?
2 How does she define love?
3 Does her research affect her own feelings about love?

EXAM FOCUS Multiple choice

3 1.24 **Listen to the interview again. For questions 1–5, choose the correct answer A–D.**

1 Dr Ruby Niverton studies how
A emotions influence the brain.
B chemical reactions in the brain affect us.
C data about the brain can be collected.
D the brain is linked to the heart.

2 According to Dr Niverton, romantic love
A is linked to hunger and thirst.
B isn't very powerful.
C is like an addiction.
D is a characteristic of all addicts.

3 The scanner showed that when someone is in love
A there is only activity in one area of the brain.
B the strength of their passion has no effect on brain activity.
C two parts of the brain are activated.
D their brain activity is similar to when they think about chocolate.

4 Experiments found that when a person is heartbroken, the love-related activity in their brain
A stops completely.
B is significantly reduced.
C continues in a different part of the brain.
D can be increased.

5 Dr Niverton's findings demonstrate that strong romantic emotions
A are usually of shorter duration than hunger.
B are not always related to brain activity.
C cause brain reactions that can be scientifically measured.
D rarely lead to obsession.

WORD STORE 2D Relationship phrases

4 1.25 **Complete WORD STORE 2D with the words in the box. Then listen, check and repeat.**

5 Match the phrases in WORD STORE 2D with their definitions. Can you put these possible stages in a relationship in a logical order?

1 fancy sb = ____________
2 adore sb = ____________
3 end a relationship = ____________
4 fall in love with sb = ____________
5 start seeing sb = ____________
6 worship sb = ____________

6 In pairs, write a short love story. Use phrases from Exercise 5. Read the love stories written by other students. Decide which is the best one.

When Harry met Sally …

PRONUNCIATION FOCUS

7 1.26 **Listen and repeat the words in the box. Write pairs of words with the same consonant sound.**

~~church~~ confusion courage ~~feature~~
Japan measure official pressure

church – feature

8 1.27 **Complete the table with the words from Exercise 7. Then listen, check and repeat.**

Sound	Typical spelling	Example
/ʃ/	*sh* *ti + vowel* *ci + vowel* *ss*	shrine worship attention emotional [1] *official* passionate [2] ____________
/ʒ/	*s + ion* *s + ure*	[3] ____________ decision [4] ____________ pleasure
/tʃ/	*ch* *t + ure*	[5] ____________ match [6] ____________ picture
/dʒ/	*j* *g*	[7] ____________ journey [8] ____________ marriage

2.4 READING

Multiple choice

I can find specific information in a long text.

1 Look at the book genres in the box. Which books do you often (✔)/sometimes (?)/never (✘) read? Compare with a partner.

adventure ☐ (auto)biographies ☐ crime ☐
fantasy ☐ historical fiction ☐ horror ☐
mystery ☐ romance ☐ science fiction ☐

2 SPEAKING Look at the screenshots from a film based on the book *Me Before You* by Jojo Moyes and discuss the questions with a partner.

1 What kind of a story do you think it is?
2 What is the relationship between the two characters?

3 Read the information about Jojo Moyes and the extract. Check your ideas in Exercise 2 and match the characters with the adjectives.

1 Mrs Traynor ☐
2 Lou Clark ☐
3 Nathan ☐
4 Will ☐

a level-headed, responsible, professional
b strange, short-tempered, dependent
c neurotic, worried, formal
d shocked, self-conscious, nervous

EXAM FOCUS Multiple choice

4 Read the extract again. For questions 1–5, choose the correct answer, A, B, C or D.

1 Mrs Traynor was hoping that
A Lou would make an effort with her clothes.
B Lou and she would become friends.
C Lou could be good company for Will.
D Lou could help Will use his digital devices.

2 After she spoke to Mrs Traynor and before she went in to meet Will, Lou thought that
A she had nothing in common with him.
B Will was into Hollywood comedies.
C she could develop a friendship with Will.
D Will was like her other disabled friends.

3 When Mrs Traynor opened Will's door, Lou saw
A a spacious elegantly furnished room.
B a small room with colourful furniture.
C a room with a glass door that was open.
D a room with a sheepskin on the floor.

4 When Lou entered Will's room,
A Will was the first to speak.
B Lou spoke to Will confidently.
C Lou shook hands with Will.
D Will ended up greeting her politely.

5 The passage shows
A Lou's ability to be a good carer to Will.
B the challenges facing Will in his day-to-day life.
C what sort of relationship Will has with his mother.
D what kind of situation Lou is getting herself into.

5 🔊 1.29 Complete the definitions with the base form of the verbs and phrases in blue in the text. Then listen, check and repeat.

1 bend low = crouch down
2 appear for a short time (e.g. on a face) = ______
3 react suddenly = ______
4 move an arm from side to side = ______
5 make an ugly face = ______
6 hold firmly = ______
7 pause nervously = ______
8 make a low sound of pain = ______
9 handle or control sth = ______
10 make a movement as if drink is going down your throat = ______

6 Complete the questions with the correct forms of the verbs from Exercise 5. Then answer the questions.

1 Why does Will find it hard to ______ the remote control and ______ it?
2 Why did Mrs Traynor ______ before knocking on Will's door?
3 Who was ______ to adjust Will's feet on the wheelchair?
4 How did Mrs Traynor react when Will ______ a ______ ?
5 Why did Lou try not to ______ when Will was ______ and crying out?
6 Why did Lou ______ instead of shaking Will's hand?
7 When did a smile ______ Will's face?

WORD STORE 2E Ways of looking

7 🔊 1.30 Complete WORD STORE 2E with the words *glance*, *gaze* and *stare* from the extract. Then listen, check and repeat.

8 Choose the more likely verbs to complete these example sentences from the *Longman Dictionary of Contemporary English*.

1 We *peeped / gazed* through a crack in the fence and saw Mrs Finley talking to a strange-looking man.
2 He *stared / glanced* over his shoulder, the man was coming towards him, pushing through the crowd.
3 I lay back on the sand and *glanced / gazed* at the stars above.
4 From the corner of my eye, I *glimpsed / stared at* a man running out of the store.
5 She sat there *staring / peeping* into space.
6 Roger *peered / gazed* into the dark corridor to see what was making the noise.

9 SPEAKING Tell your own story with a partner.

1 Say a sentence including at least one word or phrase from WORD STORE 2E or Exercise 5.
2 Your partner says another sentence to continue the story.
3 Take turns to develop and conclude the story in up to eight sentences.
4 Compare your story with other pairs.

From me before you

by Jojo Moyes

1.28

Mrs Traynor looked at my clothes, as if for the first time. I was wearing the very shaggy waistcoat thing that Dad says makes me look like an emu. I tried to smile. It seemed like an effort.

'Obviously I would hope that you could … get on with each other. It would be nice if he could think of you as a friend rather than a paid professional.'

'Right. What does he … um … like to do?'

'He watches films. Sometimes he listens to the radio, or to music. He has one of those digital things. If you position it near his hand, he can usually **manipulate** it himself. He has some movement in his fingers, although he finds it hard to **grip**.'

I felt myself brightening. If he liked music and films, surely we could find some common ground? I had a sudden picture of myself and this man laughing at some Hollywood comedy, me running the Hoover around the bedroom while he listened to his music. Perhaps this was going to be okay. Perhaps we might end up as friends. I had never had a disabled friend before – only Treen's friend David, who was deaf, but would put you in a head-lock if you suggested that meant disabled.

'Do you have any questions?'

'No.'

'Then let's go and introduce you.' She glanced at her watch. 'Nathan should have finished dressing him now.' We **hesitated** outside the door and Mrs Traynor knocked. 'Are you in there? I have Miss Clark to meet you, Will.'

There was no answer.

'Will? Nathan?'

A broad New Zealand accent. 'He's decent, Mrs T.' She pushed open the door. The annexe's living room was deceptively large, and one wall consisted entirely of glass doors that looked out over open countryside.

A wood burner glowed quietly in the corner, and a low beige sofa faced a huge flat-screen television, its seats covered by a wool throw. The mood of the room was tasteful, and peaceful – a Scandinavian bachelor pad.

In the centre of the room stood a black wheelchair, its seat and back cushioned by sheepskin. A solidly built man in white collarless scrubs was **crouching down**, adjusting a man's feet on the footrests of the wheelchair. As we stepped into the room, the man in the wheelchair looked up from under shaggy, unkempt hair. His eyes met mine and after a pause, he **let out a** bloodcurdling **groan**. Then his mouth twisted, and he let out another unearthly cry.

I felt his mother stiffen.

'Will, stop it!'

He didn't even glance towards her. Another prehistoric sound emerged from somewhere near his chest. It was a terrible, agonizing noise. I tried not to **flinch**. The man was **grimacing**, his head tilted and sunk into his shoulders as he stared at me through contorted features. He looked grotesque, and vaguely angry. I realized that where I held my bag, my knuckles had turned white.

'Will! Please.' There was a faint note of hysteria in his mother's voice. 'Please, don't do this.'

Jojo Moyes

is an English journalist, novelist and screenwriter. She was a journalist for ten years before becoming a full-time novelist in 2002. She's written numerous best-selling novels, and her book *Me Before You* won several awards and has gone on to sell over eight million copies worldwide. *Me Before You* is a love story between Will Traynor, paralysed after a motorcycle accident, and Louisa Clark, his new carer. The film based on the book was also a huge box-office success. Jojo lives and writes on a farm in Essex, England, with her husband and their three children.

Oh God, I thought. I'm not up to this. I **swallowed**, hard. The man was still staring at me. He seemed to be waiting for me to do something.

'I – I'm Lou.' My voice, uncharacteristically tremulous, broke into the silence. I wondered, briefly, whether to hold out a hand and then, remembering that he wouldn't be able to take it, **gave a** feeble **wave** instead. 'Short for Louisa.'

Then to my astonishment his features cleared, and his head straightened on his shoulders.

Will Traynor gazed at me steadily, the faintest of smiles **flickering across** his face. 'Good morning, Miss Clark,' he said. 'I hear you're my latest minder.'

GRAMMAR

2.5

Relative clauses

I can identify and use different types of relative clauses.

1 SPEAKING **Discuss the advantages or disadvantages of being the firstborn child in a family.**

2 **Read Part 1 of a text about birth order. Are any of the things you discussed in Exercise 1 mentioned?**

WHAT BIRTH ORDER SAYS ABOUT YOU

Part 1

Birth order is the key [1]that can unlock your personality. Here are some generalisations that have come out of research [2]carried out over the years.

The firstborn

Parents [3]learning to bring up their first child tend to be extremely attentive and protective. Firstborn children, [4]who have their parents' undivided attention, are responsible, reliable and well-behaved. Firstborns tend to be perfectionists bursting with confidence, [5]which makes it hard for them to admit when they're wrong.

3 **Read the GRAMMAR FOCUS. What types of clauses are examples 1–5 in blue in Part 1 of the text?**

GRAMMAR FOCUS

Relative clauses

- In **defining relative clauses** you can leave out *who*, *which* or *that* when it is the object of the verb.
  Olga is the girl who sits next to me. ('who' is the subject of 'sit')
  Olga is the girl (who) I sit next to. ('who' is the object of 'sit')
- In **non-defining relative clauses,** *who*, *which*, *where* or *whose* always come after a comma and you cannot leave them out.
  Eva is friends with Sam, who I can't stand. (= 'I can't stand Sam.')
- In **reduced relative clauses** (defining and non-defining) you use a Present Participle for active verbs and a Past Participle for passive verbs.
  There's a new teacher teaching Year Four. ('who is teaching')
  Josh, taught by the new teacher, is delighted. (= 'who is taught')
- In **comment clauses** you refer to the whole of the main clause using ***which***.
  Eva is friends with Sam, which I can't stand. (='I can't stand the situation.')

Part 2

The middle child

Middle children, [1]*which have been / [Ø]* given less attention by their parents, are more independent. Middle children [2]*which / whose* older siblings boss them around feel life is unfair. They often believe their other siblings get all the attention, [3]*which / that* can make them feel left out.

The baby of the family

Parents [4]*which are / [Ø]* bringing up their youngest children are more lenient, [5]*which / what* means that last-borns are rarely told off. Youngest children, [6]*that / who* have fewer responsibilities, are carefree and easy-going. The baby of the family, [7]*whose / who* is used to having things done for them, tends to be bad at making decisions.

The only child

Only children have many of the same qualities as the oldest child, [8]*that / which* is not surprising. Only children, [9]*which / who* spend more time with adults, will often act older than their age. The typical only child likes being the centre of attention, [10]*which / whose* sometimes makes them appear self-centred.

4 **Read Part 2 of the text and choose the correct option.**

5 SPEAKING **What about your family? Discuss the comments in Parts 1 and 2. Which statements do you agree with?**

6 **Rewrite the sentences using reduced relative clauses. Tick the statements you agree with.**

1 Siblings who share a bedroom tend to be less selfish.
Siblings sharing a bedroom tend to be less selfish.
2 Children who have been brought up as the baby of the family are often fussy eaters.
3 Firstborns, who are accustomed to accepting rules, are better behaved at school.
4 Middle-born children, who grow up with a younger and older sibling, can be argumentative.
5 Only children who spend a lot of time alone tend to be very creative.
6 The youngest child, who is used to being the centre of attention, is usually sociable and good fun to be around.

7 **Complete the sentences with *who*, *which*, *that*, *where*, *whose* or Ø (no pronoun). Which sentences are true for you? Compare with a partner.**

1 My sister is always leaving her clothes on the floor, *which* is very annoying!
2 In my family, the person ______ cooks the most delicious food is my grandmother.
3 I'm jealous of people ______ parents let them do whatever they want.
4 The only place ______ I can get some peace at home is in the bathroom.
5 My mother, ______ thinks I'm still a baby, worries when I go out late.
6 I've got several cousins ______ living in the same town as me.
7 We live in a house ______ built over 100 years ago.

FOCUS VLOG About important people

8 **Watch the Focus Vlog. For the worksheet, go to page 135.**

Grammar page 152

2.6 SPEAKING

Telling a personal anecdote

I can tell a personal anecdote about a memorable day out.

1 SPEAKING **Look at the extract from a website. Discuss which activities you find the most/the least attractive and why.**

Home | Events | News | Archives

memorableday.com

Are you tired of doing the same old things with your friends? Why not try something different with one of our alternative days out?

- Go mountain biking
- Visit an art gallery or photo exhibition
- Sing karaoke
- Rent a rowing boat or kayak
- Attend a workshop (e.g. dancing or DJing)
- Go go-kart racing
- Visit an aquarium or zoo

2 SPEAKING **Describe the photo in Exercise 1 and discuss the questions with a partner.**

1 What might the people be thinking and feeling?
2 In your opinion, what factors make a memorable day out?

3 **Order the parts of an anecdote about a memorable day out.**

a Where and when the day took place, and other background information ☐
b Who was involved in the day ☐
c Why the day was so memorable ☐
d What the anecdote is going to be about ☐
e What happened step by step ☐

4 1.31 **Listen to someone describing a memorable day out and check your ideas in Exercise 3. Try to retell the anecdote with a partner.**

5 1.31 **Complete the SPEAKING FOCUS with the words in the box. Then listen again and check.**

All As As soon as blue doubt Funnily Initially ~~place~~

SPEAKING FOCUS

Introducing the anecdote

(Right, so) I'm going to tell you about (a great day out).
(OK, so) this is a story about (a day I'll never forget).
This took [1]*place* about (a month ago).

Sequencing events in the anecdote

[2]__________/When/Just after (we got there, the sun came out).
[3]__________/To begin with, (we were the only people there …)
As/While (we were sitting there …)
Suddenly/[4]__________ of a sudden, (the weather changed).

Describing events vividly

Predictably/[5]__________ expected (other people soon started …)
Unexpectedly/Out of the [6]__________, (it started pouring with rain).
Luckily/Fortunately, (after it stopped raining, the sun came out again).

Finishing the anecdote

Without a [7]__________, it was (one of the best days I've had in ages).
When I look back (on that day) now, I feel …
It turned out to be (an unforgettable day out).
Strangely/[8]__________ enough, (the best days are often the ones you don't really plan).

6 1.32 **Read the anecdote and choose the correct option. Then listen and check.**

Right, so this [1]*took place / is a story* about a day I'll never forget. I've always loved music and last month my friend and I went to a DJing workshop. [2]*To begin with / Just after*, we learnt about the equipment. We can't afford our own stuff yet but, [3]*fortunately / out of the blue*, we were able to use the decks, mixers and laptops at the centre. [4]*When / While* we had understood the basics, it was time to have a go. [5]*Strangely / Predictably*, it was really difficult at first, but after a while I started to get the hang of it. It feels and sounds fantastic when you get it right. It turned out to be an [6]*unexpected / unforgettable* day. I can't wait for the next workshop.

7 SPEAKING **Follow the instructions below. Take turns to be Student A and Student B.**

Student A: Tell a personal anecdote about a memorable day out. Use the SPEAKING FOCUS to help you.
Student B: Listen to your partner's anecdote and think of a question to ask them when they have finished.

USE OF ENGLISH 2.7

Collocations

I can recognise and use common collocations.

1 SPEAKING Read Lisa's post and comment on her last sentence. Discuss whether you could share a flat with Lisa. Give reasons for your answer.

Home | New posts | Friends | Profile

Lisa is looking for a flatmate

Message | Send invitation

I'm a twenty-one-year-old student with a spare room to rent. It's a big room with a bed, a wardrobe and a desk. The flat has two bedrooms, a living room, a kitchen and a bathroom. Only people who meet the requirements below should apply.

You need to be on a full-time course because I don't want you hanging around the flat in the daytime.

I lead a healthy lifestyle. I'm a vegan and I don't like people cooking meat in my kitchen. It's equally important that there are no cooking smells during the weekend.

If you expect me to be your friend, you'll be **bitterly disappointed**. I'm painfully shy and I can't stand being the **centre of attention**. I don't need a soulmate, I just want a quiet life.

I **sleep badly**, so I don't want you to binge-watch TV programmes or roar with laughter late at night. Lights go out here at 11 p.m. Basically, I'd like you to use your common sense. If I've gone to bed, I expect you to **keep quiet**.

Friends are okay, but if more than three **guests turn up**, it's too much.

I set **high standards** of cleanliness here. I like people who are **neat and tidy**. When you move in, we can **reach an agreement** about how we share the cleaning.

I'm quite easy-going.

2 Read the LANGUAGE FOCUS and complete it with the examples in blue in Lisa's post.

LANGUAGE FOCUS

Collocations

- A collocation is a central feature of any language. It refers to typical, frequently occurring combinations of words. For example, you can have *strong feelings*, but not *~~tough feelings~~. You might *burst into tears*, but not *~~explode into tears~~.
- The strength of a collocation can vary. *Have a laugh* is quite weak because you can also *have a day off*, *have a shower* or *have a baby*. *Shrug your shoulders* is strong. You can't really *shrug* anything else!
- Different types of collocations:

  adjective + noun = ***nasty habit, vivid imagination***, [1]*high standards*

  verb + noun = ***share an interest, break the law***, [2]________

  noun + verb = ***accidents happen***, [3]________

  noun + (*of*/*and*) noun = ***sense of humour***, [4]________

  verb + adjective = ***look miserable***, [5]________

  adjective + adjective = ***loud and clear***, [6]________

  verb + adverb = ***smile politely***, [7]________

  adverb + adjective = ***perfectly normal***, [8]________
- Choosing the right collocation will make your English sound more natural.

3 Look at the underlined collocations in Lisa's post. What type of collocation are they? Add them as examples in the LANGUAGE FOCUS box.

4 USE OF ENGLISH Read the posts from Anna and Martin and complete the texts with one word in each gap. Which person would be more suitable to share a flat with Lisa?

Home | New posts | Friends | Profile

Anna's looking for a room

Message | Send invitation

I'm sociable, so I'd love to live with like-minded people. I hope we may [1]__________ the same interests. I have an excellent sense of [2]__________ and I like to [3]__________ a laugh. I don't have any nasty [4]__________ and I've never [5]__________ the law. My private life is perfectly [6]__________ .

Martin's looking for a room

Message | Send invitation

I'm a medical student, so I work long hours at the hospital. I usually go back to my home town to visit my parents two weekends a month or whenever I [7]__________ a day off. I eat out a lot because I can't cook. I'd like to live with somebody who has [8]__________ standards of cleanliness and is [9]__________ and tidy like me. Please get in touch if you like my profile.

5 1.33 Match a word from box A with a word from box B to make six common collocations. Then listen to the conversation between Lisa and Dave and check your answers.

A

~~casual~~ deeply free good highly supremely

B

~~acquaintance~~ company confident depressed intelligent spirit

casual acquaintance

6 SPEAKING Discuss the ideal qualities for somebody to share a flat with. Use the collocations from Exercise 5.

I would/wouldn't like to live with someone who is (a/an) …

7 Choose the correct option, A, B, C or D. Which sentences are true for you?

1 Dad says it's important to set __________ standards for yourself.
A fine B tall C high D big

2 My sister has a __________ imagination and draws incredible pictures.
A vivid B detailed C sharp D strong

3 The last film I saw was rubbish. I was __________ disappointed.
A totally B absolutely C bitterly D completely

4 Most of my online friends are best described as __________ acquaintances.
A occasional B casual C nearby D relaxed

5 I eat well and try to lead a __________ lifestyle.
A strong B fit C wise D healthy

8 Complete the questions with one word in each gap.

1 Do you sometimes doubt yourself or are you always __________ confident?

2 Are you messy or __________ and tidy?

3 Are you shy or do you like being the __________ of attention?

4 Are you a good citizen? Have you ever __________ the law?

5 Are you emotional? How likely are you to __________ into tears?

6 Can you remember the last time you __________ with laughter?

9 SPEAKING Ask and answer the questions in Exercise 8. Give reasons for your answers.

SHOW WHAT YOU'VE LEARNT UNITS 1–2

10 USE OF ENGLISH Complete the second sentence so that it has a similar meaning to the first. Use between two and five words including the word in capitals. Do not change the word given.

1 People describe me as independent or rebellious. **FREE**
People describe me as __________ .

2 Students at our school don't have to wear school uniform. **REQUIRED**
Students at our school __________ to wear school uniform.

3 My best friend is very shy and hates it when everybody looks at her. **ATTENTION**
My best friend is very shy and hates __________ .

4 Someone's posted a funny video on the school website. **BEEN**
A funny video __________ on the school website.

5 If my parents shouted at me when I was younger I used to start crying. **INTO**
If my parents shouted at me when I was younger I used to __________ .

6 My last exam results were extremely disappointing. **BITTERLY**
I __________ my last exam results.

Use of English page 153

2.8 WRITING

An article

I can write an article attracting the reader's attention using participle clauses.

1 Look at the photos. Which aspects of adolescence do they illustrate?

2 SPEAKING Read *Last week's competition* on the *Psychology Magazine* website and discuss the questions with a partner.

1 Why is adolescence described as a 'roller coaster ride'?
2 What are the best things about being a young adult?
3 What new challenges do you face as a young adult?

3 Read the winning article on the magazine website and discuss the questions with a partner.

1 Did the author mention any of the pleasures or challenges you discussed in Exercise 2?
2 What is the author's conclusion? Do you agree?

Psychology Magazine

Home | Latest news | Competitions | Near you | Photos Search

Have Your Say

Last week's competition

The journey from teenager to adult can bring joy and pain, success and failure, friendship and heartbreak. If you are riding the roller coaster of adolescence right now, then *Psychology Magazine* wants to hear from you.

Send us an article in which you describe some of the very best things about coming of age and discuss the most challenging aspects of life for people living through these 'in-between' years.

As usual, a selection of articles will be published in an upcoming edition of *Psychology Magazine*.

The winning article:

Adolescence: Pain and Pleasure in Equal Measure

by Josh Payne

Remember when you were little and school summer holidays seemed to go on forever? Being children, most of us lived carefree and happy lives. Sadly, this does not last and we must all grow up. I can reliably report that the process brings pain and pleasure in equal measure.

First, there is the pain. Adolescence is a time of huge physical and emotional change. For many of us this change is accompanied by feelings of self-doubt, envy and embarrassment. Apparently, we are neither children nor adults; asked to act like 'grown ups' in certain situations, but not in others. 'Be responsible and act your age … but be home by 9 p.m.!' These mixed messages can be hard to deal with. Add to this the pressure of schoolwork, and it is no wonder we sometimes feel unable to cope.

Thankfully, alongside the pain, there is also pleasure. Though we have to study, few of us need to worry about bills or housework. As a result, whether it is playing sport or online games, we have time to enjoy ourselves. On top of this, we have our friends. Pleasure and pain alike, can be shared with those who know exactly how we feel.

Despite the challenges, as far as I am concerned, the pleasure of being a young adult outweighs the pain. Although it may not always seem so now, perhaps in the future we will look back on adolescence as 'the best days of our lives'.

This week's competition

There are many unfair gender-based stereotypes concerning the interests and attitudes of adolescents. Write an article of 200–250 words in which you describe some of these common stereotypes and challenge them by explaining why they are untrue or unfair. As usual, a selection of articles will be printed in an upcoming edition of *Psychology Magazine*.

4 **Read the WRITING FOCUS and look at the article again. Decide which techniques the author used for writing the title, the introduction and the conclusion.**

WRITING FOCUS

An article

Title

Attract the reader's attention from the start:

1 ask a question (*Are These the Best Days of Our Lives?*)

2 use vivid adjectives (*Adolescence: Thrilling and Terrifying*)

3 summarise the topic (*The Pains and Pleasures of Adolescent Life*)

4 use rhyme/wordplay (*Top Ten Tips for Troubled Teens*)

Introduction

Define the topic and hold the reader's attention:

5 ask a question

6 tell a short anecdote

7 give an interesting or surprising fact or figure

8 give a quotation

Main paragraphs

Develop the topic and discuss all the issues mentioned in the question.

Conclusion

Give your personal opinion and leave the reader with something to think about:

9 ask a question

10 refer to the future

11 make an appeal or suggestion

12 return to the idea in the title or the introduction

Note: Articles tend to be written in a formal or semi-formal style. In a formal article avoid: informal phrases (~~*I think*~~ = *As far as I am concerned …*), colloquial language (~~*Most parents reckon that*~~ … = *In most parents' opinions …*) and contractions (~~*don't*~~ = *do not*).

5 **Read the example article introductions and conclusions. Decide which techniques 5–12 in the WRITING FOCUS the authors used.**

Introductions:

a It's easy to forget that 100 percent of adults alive today were once teenagers like us. As a young man, my 'sensible' father was a real rebel. He rode a motorbike and got a tattoo at the age of sixteen.

b In his famous book, American author John Gray said that 'Men are from Mars, women are from Venus'. Does this also apply to adolescents? Are younger men and women really so different from each other?

Conclusions:

c As I began by saying, men and women differ in many ways, but individuals also differ regardless of their gender. We should be wary of stereotyping, respect each other and cooperate to use our strengths for a common good.

d So, as a regular teenage girl, am I really that different from the boy sitting opposite me in class? Perhaps not. Whether we will become more or less alike in later life remains to be seen.

6 **Read the LANGUAGE FOCUS and rewrite the underlined fragments using participle clauses.**

1 <u>Because they want to look stylish</u>, many adolescent boys also enjoy shopping for clothes.

2 <u>Because they attend mixed schools</u>, most adolescent boys and girls receive the same education.

3 <u>Because I grew up with three sisters</u>, I know something about the differences between boys and girls.

4 <u>Because they are stereotypes</u>, such statements do contain an element of truth, of course.

5 <u>Because I have always got on well with boys</u>, I think I understand some of their attitudes.

LANGUAGE FOCUS

Participle clauses to express reason

You can use **participle clauses** in formal writing to express the **reason** for a statement made in the main clause.

- Use a **Present Participle (verb + *ing*)** when states or actions occur at the same time.
  Being children, *most of us lived carefree and happy lives.*
  = *Because we were children* (past), *most of us lived carefree and happy lives.* (past)
- Use a **Perfect Participle (*having* + Past Participle)** when one state or action occurs before another.
  Having grown physically, *many adolescents expect to be treated as adults.*
  = *Because they have grown physically* (past), *many adolescents expect to be treated as adults.* (present)

7 SPEAKING **Read the statements and decide if they are stereotypes about adolescent girls or boys. Do they reflect reality? Discuss in groups.**

- They find it difficult to talk about their feelings.
- They are always gossiping.
- They love fashion and shopping.
- They love sports and gadgets.
- They are kind and considerate.
- They are rude and aggressive.

SHOW WHAT YOU'VE LEARNT

8 **You are going to reply to *This week's competition* on the *Psychology Magazine* website. Look at page 30, read the topic on the website and think about the following:**

- Where will your article appear and who will read it?
- Choose two or three gender-based stereotypes you think are untrue or unfair (see Exercise 7 for ideas). Note down reasons to support your views.
- Select techniques from the WRITING FOCUS to help you attract and hold the reader's attention.
- Make sure you use a formal or semi-formal style.

9 **Complete the writing task from the website. Include at least one participle clause to express a reason. Use the WRITING FOCUS and LANGUAGE FOCUS to help you.**

2.1 Vocabulary 4.9

adventurous /əd'ventʃərəs/
affectionate /ə'fekʃənət/
agreeable /ə'griːəbəl/
daring /'deərɪŋ/
excel in /ɪk'sel ɪn/
fair-minded /ˌfeə 'maɪndɪd/
feel strongly about sth /ˌfiːl 'strɒŋli əˌbaʊt ˌsʌmθɪŋ/
(be) full of oneself /(bi) fʊl əv wʌn'self/
good-natured /gʊd 'neɪtʃəd/
have a love of learning /ˌhəv ə lʌv əv 'lɜːnɪŋ/
honest /'ɒnəst/
hopeless /'həʊpləs/
humble /'hʌmbəl/
imaginative /ɪ'mædʒənətɪv/
insecure /ˌɪnsɪ'kjʊə/
intellectual /ˌɪntə'lektʃuəl/
kind-hearted /ˌkaɪnd 'hɑːtəd/
laid-back /ˌleɪd 'bæk/
larger than life /'lɑːdʒə ðən ˌlaɪf/
level-headed /ˌlevəl'hedɪd/
make sb feel at ease /meɪk ˌsʌmbədi ˌfiːl ət 'iːz/
moody /'muːdi/
party /'pɑːti/
pay attention to detail /ˌpeɪ ˌə'tenʃən tə 'diːteɪl/
perceptive /pə'septɪv/
plan in advance /ˌplæn ɪn əd'vɑːns/
self-centred /ˌself 'sentəd/
self-conscious /ˌself 'kɒnʃəs/
self-critical /ˌself 'krɪtɪkəl/
short-tempered /ˌʃɔːt 'tempəd/
small talk /'smɔːl tɔːk/
sociable /'səʊʃəbəl/
speak up /ˌspiːk 'ʌp/
spontaneous /spɒn'teɪniəs/
strong-willed /ˌstrɒŋ 'wɪld/
tactful /'tæktfəl/
the life and soul of the party /ðə ˌlaɪf ən ˌsəʊl əv ðə 'pɑːti/
think outside the box /'θɪŋk aʊt'saɪd ðə 'bɒks/
thorough /'θʌrə/
trusting /'trʌstɪŋ/
witty /'wɪti/

2.2 Grammar 4.10

assume /ə'sjuːm/
compassionate /kəm'pæʃənət/
drift apart /ˌdrɪft ə'pɑːt/
late /leɪt/
long-distance relationship /ˌlɒŋ ˌdɪstəns rɪ'leɪʃənʃɪp/
lose touch /ˌluːz 'tʌtʃ/
love at first sight /ˌlʌv ət ˌfɜːst 'saɪt/
make an impression /ˌmeɪk ən ɪm'preʃən/
mantelpiece /'mæntlpiːs/
pluck up the courage /ˌplʌk ʌp ðə 'kʌrɪdʒ/
propose to sb /prə'pəʊz tə ˌsʌmbɒdi/
remain /rɪ'meɪn/
separate from sb /'sepəreɪt frəm ˌsʌmbɒdi/
slip down /slɪp daʊn/
widowed /'wɪdəʊd/

2.3 Listening 4.11

addiction /ə'dɪkʃən/
adore /ə'dɔː/
be attracted to /bi ə'træktɪd tə/
confusion /kən'fjuːʒən/
fall for /ˌfɔːl 'fə/
fall in love with /ˌfɔːl ɪn 'lʌv wɪð/
fancy /'fænsi/
feature /'fiːtʃə/
generosity /ˌdʒenə'rɒsəti/
go out with /ˌgəʊ 'aʊt wɪð/
heartbroken /'hɑːtˌbrəʊkən/
(be) madly in love with /(bi) ˌmædli ɪn 'lʌv wɪð/
measure /'meʒə/
novelist /'nɒvəlɪst/
(be) obsessed with /(bi) əb'sest wɪð/
passionate /'pæʃənət/
pleasure /'pleʒə/
pressure /'preʃə/
reduced /rɪ'djuːst/
relationship /rɪ'leɪʃənʃɪp/
see sb /'siː ˌsʌmbɒdi/
self-sacrifice /ˌself 'sækrɪfaɪs/
shrine /ʃraɪn/
split up with /ˌsplɪt 'ʌp wɪð/
unconditional /ˌʌnkən'dɪʃənəl/
worship /'wɜːʃɪp/

2.4 Reading 4.12

adjust /ə'dʒʌst/
agonizing /'ægənaɪzɪŋ/
astonishment /ə'stɒnɪʃmənt/
bachelor pad /'bætʃələ ˌpæd/
be up to sth /bi 'ʌp tə ˌsʌmθɪŋ/
bend /bend/
bloodcurdling /'blʌdˌkɜːdlɪŋ/
box-office success /ˌbɒks ˌɒfɪs sək'ses/
brighten /'braɪtn/
broad accent /ˌbrɔːd 'æksənt/
carer /'keərə/
chest /tʃest/
collarless /'kɒlələs/
confidently /'kɒnfɪdəntli/
contorted /kən'tɔːtɪd/
crack /kræk/
crouch down /'kraʊtʃ ˌdaʊn/
cushioned /'kʊʃənd/
deaf /def/
decent /'diːsənt/
deceptively /di'septɪvli/
dependent /dɪ'pendənt/
disabled /dɪs'eɪbəld/
emerge /ɪ'mɜːdʒ/
entirely /ɪn'taɪəli/
face a challenge /ˌfeɪs ə 'tʃæləndʒ/
faint /feɪnt/
feeble /'fiːbəl/
fence /fens/
find common ground /ˌfaɪnd ˌkɒmən 'graʊnd/
firmly /'fɜːmli/
flicker across /'flɪkər əˌkrɒs/
flinch /flɪntʃ/
footrest /'fʊtrest/
from the corner of your eye /frəm ðə ˌkɔːnər əv jɔːr 'aɪ/
furnished /'fɜːnɪʃt/
gaze /geɪz/
get yourself into /ˌget jɔːˌself 'ɪntə/
give a wave /ˌgɪv ə 'weɪv/
glance /glɑːns/
glimpse /glɪmps/
grimace /'grɪməs/
grip /grɪp/
have nothing in common /ˌhæv ˌnʌθɪŋ ɪn 'kɒmən/
hesitate /'hezəteɪt/
keyhole /'kiːhəʊl/
knuckle /'nʌkəl/
let out a groan /ˌlet aʊt ə 'grəʊn/
make an effort /ˌmeɪk ən 'efət/
manipulate /mə'nɪpjəleɪt/
minder /'maɪndə/
neurotic /njʊ'rɒtɪk/
passage /'pæsɪdʒ/
peaceful /'piːsfəl/
peep /piːp/
peer /pɪə/
position /pə'zɪʃən/
push through /ˌpʊʃ 'θruː/
put sb in a head-lock /pʊt ˌsʌmbɒdi ɪn ə 'hed lɒk/
screenwriter /'skriːnˌraɪtə/
scrubs /skrʌbz/
shaggy /'ʃægi/
sheepskin /'ʃiːpˌskɪn/
solidly built /ˌsɒlɪdli 'bɪlt/
spacious /'speɪʃəs/
stare /steə/
steadily /'stedəli/
stiffen /'stɪfən/
straighten /'streɪtn/
swallow /'swɒləʊ/
tasteful /'teɪstfəl/
tilt /tɪlt/
tremulous /'tremjələs/
twist your mouth /ˌtwɪst jə 'maʊθ/
uncharacteristically /ʌnˌkærɪktə'rɪstɪkli/
unearthly /ʌn'ɜːθli/
unkempt /ˌʌn'kempt/
wonder /'wʌndə/
wood burner /'wʊd ˌbɜːnə/
wool throw /ˌwʊl 'θrəʊ/

2.5 Grammar 4.13

accustomed to /ə'kʌstəmd tə/
argumentative /ˌɑːgjə'mentətɪv/

attentive /ə'tentɪv/
boss sb around /ˌbɒs ˌsʌmbɒdi ə'raʊnd/
bursting with confidence /ˌbɜːstɪŋ wɪð 'kɒnfɪdəns/
carefree /'keəfriː/
carry out research /ˌkæri ˌaʊt rɪ'sɜːtʃ/
(be) the centre of attention /(bi) ðə ˌsentər əv ə'tenʃən/
feel left out /ˌfiːl 'left ˌaʊt/
firstborn /'fɜːstbɔːn/
fussy eater /ˌfʌsi 'iːtə/
protective /prə'tektɪv/
reliable /rɪ'laɪəbəl/
sibling /'sɪblɪŋ/
undivided attention /ˌʌndɪˌvaɪdəd ə'tenʃən/
well-behaved /ˌwel bi'heɪvd/

2.6 Speaking 4.14

all of a sudden /ˌɔːl əv ə 'sʌdn/
attend a workshop /əˌtend ə 'wɜːkʃɒp/
funnily /'fʌnəli/
get the hang of /ˌget ðə 'hæŋ əv/
have a go /ˌhəv ə 'gəʊ/
initially /ɪ'nɪʃəli/
memorable /'memərəbəl/
out of the blue /ˌaʊt əv ðə 'bluː/
pour with rain /ˌpɔː wɪð 'reɪn/
predictably /prɪ'dɪktəbli/
unexpectedly /ˌʌnɪk'spektɪdli/

2.7 Use of English 4.15

accidents happen /'æksɪdənts ˌhæpən/
binge-watch /'bɪndʒ wɒtʃ/
bitterly disappointed /ˌbɪtəli ˌdɪsə'pɔɪntəd/
break the law /ˌbreɪk ðə 'lɔː/
burst into tears /ˌbɜːst 'ɪntə 'tɪəz/
casual acquaintance /ˌkæʒuəl ə'kweɪntəns/
common sense /ˌkɒmən 'sens/
deeply depressed /ˌdiːpli dɪ'prest/
deeply disappointed /ˌdiːpli ˌdɪsə'pɔɪntəd/
equally important /ˌiːkwəli ɪm'pɔːtənt/
free spirit /ˌfriː 'spɪrət/
full-time course /ˌfʊl taɪm 'kɔːs/
go out /ˌgəʊ 'aʊt/
good company /ˌgʊd 'kʌmpəni/
hang around /ˌhæŋ ə'raʊnd/
have a baby /ˌhæv ə 'beɪbi/
have a day off /ˌhæv ə 'deɪ ɒf/
have a laugh /ˌhæv ə 'lɑːf/
have a shower /ˌhæv ə 'ʃaʊə/
healthy lifestyle /ˌhelθi 'laɪfstaɪl/
high standards /ˌhaɪ 'stændədz/
highly intelligent /ˌhaɪli ɪn'telədʒənt/
keep quiet /ˌkiːp 'kwaɪət/
like-minded /ˌlaɪk 'maɪndɪd/
look miserable /ˌlʊk 'mɪzərəbəl/
loud and clear /ˌlaʊd ən 'klɪə/
meet the requirements /ˌmiːt ðə rɪ'kwaɪəmənts/
miserable /'mɪzərəbəl/
nasty habit /ˌnɑːsti 'hæbɪt/
neat and tidy /ˌniːt ən 'taɪdi/
painfully shy /ˌpeɪnfəli 'ʃaɪ/
perfectly normal /ˌpɜːfɪktli 'nɔːməl/
post a video /ˌpəʊst ə 'vɪdiəʊ/
quiet life /'kwaɪət ˌlaɪf/
reach an agreement /ˌriːtʃ ən ə'griːmənt/
roar with laughter /ˌrɔː wɪð 'lɑːftə/
roommate /'ruːmˌmeɪt/
sense of humour /ˌsens əv 'hjuːmə/
set high standards /set ˌhaɪ 'stændədz/
share an interest /ˌʃeər ən 'ɪntrəst/
shrug your shoulders /ˌʃrʌg jə 'ʃəʊldəz/
sleep badly /ˌsliːp 'bædli/
smile politely /ˌsmaɪl pə'laɪtli/
soulmate /'səʊlmeɪt/
spare room /ˌspeə 'ruːm/
strong feeling /ˌstrɒŋ 'fiːlɪŋ/
supremely confident /sʊˌpriːmli 'kɒnfədənt/
turn up /ˌtɜːn 'ʌp/
vivid imagination /ˌvɪvəd ɪˌmædʒə'neɪʃən/

2.8 Writing 4.16

apparently /ə'pærəntli/
attract sb's attention /əˌtrækt ˌsʌmbədiz ə'tenʃən/
come of age /ˌkʌm əv 'eɪdʒ/
cope with /'kəʊp wɪð/
differ /'dɪfə/
embarrassment /ɪm'bærəsmənt/
envy /'envi/
for the common good /fər ðə ˌkɒmən 'gʊd/
gender-based stereotype /ˌdʒendə ˌbeɪst 'steriətaɪp/
gossip /'gɒsɪp/
heartbreak /'hɑːtbreɪk/
hold sb's attention /ˌhəʊld ˌsʌmbədiz ə'tenʃən/
in equal measure /ɪn ˌiːkwəl 'meʒə/
outweigh /aʊt'weɪ/
regardless of /rɪ'gɑːdləs əv/
roller coaster ride /'rəʊlə ˌkəʊstə ˌraɪd/
self-doubt /ˌself 'daʊt/

MY WORD LIST

PERSONALITY	ACTIONS OF THE BODY	OTHER

FOCUS REVIEW 2

VOCABULARY AND GRAMMAR

1 Complete the sentences with words from the unit. The first and last letter of each word is given.

1 The hero in action films is traditionally **d**______**g** and prepared to take risks.
2 She plays the type of detective who's especially **p**______**e** and notices the smallest of details.
3 My favourite character is the brother because he's very **l**______**–**______**k**. When everyone else is getting stressed, he doesn't seem worried.
4 I didn't like the main character because she's so **s**______**–**______**d**. Everything's about her and she doesn't care how it affects the others.
5 There's a scene where the uncle points out the problems with Joe's plan. He's really **t**______**l** though and does it without discouraging his nephew.
6 When Billy first dances in front of an audience, he's really **s**______**–**______**s**, but over time, he gains confidence.

2 Choose the correct option.

1 It's important that an interviewer makes the candidate feel *at ease / eased / at rest*.
2 She's confident, but not too *filled with / full of / full with* herself. She'll always acknowledge when she doesn't know something.
3 When my uncle saw his future wife for the first time, he was immediately attracted *with / to / at* her.
4 When Mum saw my new haircut, a look of shock *hesitated / grimaced / flickered* across her face.
5 I only briefly *glimpsed / glanced / gazed* the message on her phone, but I'm sure it was from Bianca.

3 Complete the sentences with the Past Perfect Simple or Past Perfect Continuous forms of the words in brackets.

1 Joshua ____________ (already/be) married twice before he met Carol.
2 I asked Martha and Sue to organise my wedding because they ____________ (prepare) quite a few before.
3 Stewart was really exhausted because he ____________ (look) after the twins the whole afternoon.
4 Dad, how long ____________ (you/date) Mum before you got engaged?
5 I stopped talking to my brother after we ____________ (have) a serious argument for the third time that week.
6 When I saw Jane, I could see she ____________ (cry), but I didn't know why.

4 Complete the sentences with one word in each gap.

1 Maria accepted Niko's invitation to the cinema, ____________ made him really happy.
2 Last week I bumped into the Smiths, ____________ son used to be in my class at school.
3 Would you like to meet my cousin ____________ I told you about yesterday?
4 Here are some lovely photos from Greece ____________ on our honeymoon.

USE OF ENGLISH

5 Complete the text with the correct form of the words in the box. There are two extra words.

deep	equal	full	health	perfect	polite

In parks around the world, it's become [1]____________ normal to come across hundreds of people gathering every Saturday morning to run their weekly five kilometres. Since it started in 2004, parkrun has become a global phenomenon with events taking place in hundreds of locations in more than twenty countries across the world. Parkruns attract people of all ages and for a whole range of different reasons. Most participants see running as part of a [2]____________ lifestyle. For many, the social side of the events is [3]____________ important. People who start off as casual acquaintances nodding to each other and smiling [4]____________, can end up as firm friends.

6 Choose the correct answer, A, B or C.

1 Let me introduce you to the woman ____________ husband originally set up the gallery.
  A who
  B whose
  C that
2 ____________ the village where she grew up, my granny enjoyed living in the city.
  A Leaving
  B Had left
  C Having left
3 When we got to the reception, we realized that we ____________ the present for the newlyweds at home. We felt extremely embarrassed.
  A had left
  B left
  C have left
4 How long ____________ for a reply to his email before he realized he wasn't going to get a response?
  A Tom waited
  B did Tom wait
  C has Tom waited
5 Mark says he never has time to make his bed in the morning, ____________ me a lot. He should get up earlier.
  A which irritates
  B who irritates
  C that irritates

7 Complete the second sentence using the word in capitals so that it has a similar meaning to the first. Use up to five words in each gap, but do not change the word in capitals.

1 First we went for a meal and then we went to the cinema. **BEEN**
After we ____________ , we went to the cinema.

2 Dan wasn't at the party and Cathy's parents were extremely upset. **BITTERLY**
Cathy's parents ____________ Dan wasn't at the party.

3 I first met Sally at the restaurant over there. **WHERE**
That's the restaurant ____________ Sally.

4 After working for ages, I decided to take a break. **SO**
I'd ____________ I decided to take a break.

LISTENING

8 1.34 **You will hear a talk with a psychologist Adam Martins. Listen and complete the notes with information from the talk. Use a word or a short phrase. You will hear the recording twice.**

1 The reporter asks if it is true that twins have a special mental and emotional ____________ .

2 Some reports suggest that the special psychic bond is shared mostly by ____________ .

3 However, the existence of psychic powers has not been ____________ .

4 When Adam and ____________ were fifteen, they drew very similar pictures while sitting on opposite sides of a classroom.

5 According to studies, some twins tend to be a bit ____________ than regular siblings or only children.

6 During childhood, twins compete with each other mostly for ____________ .

7 Studying different subjects, at different universities often in different countries is one way in which twins try to establish a greater ____________ .

8 Research shows that the most important factor responsible for our psychological characteristics is ____________ .

SPEAKING

9 Do the task in pairs.

A

B

Student A

Look at photo A. Describe the photo and answer the questions.

- What do you think is going to happen next? Why?
- Do you get on better with boys or girls in your family? Why?
- Tell me about a situation in which you or someone you know was involved in a family argument.

Student B

Look at photo B. Describe the photo and answer the questions.

- How do you think the man is feeling? Why?
- What's the most challenging thing about living on your own? Why?
- Tell me about the household chores that you or somebody you know had to do when you were a child.

WRITING

10 Read this announcement on an international students' website and write an article in reply.

Do parents and teenagers in your country always have the same opinion about different topics?

Write an article about the most common things teenagers and parents in your country disagree about. We'll put the best articles on the website next month!

3

Living spaces

A city is not a concrete jungle, it is a human zoo.

Desmond Morris

BBC

SMOG-FREE MEXICO CITY

9 Watch the BBC video.
For the worksheet, go to page 136.

VOCABULARY 3.1

Landscape features • prepositions describing location • describing places • in the city

I can describe cities and talk about city life.

SHOW WHAT YOU KNOW

1 Which of these townscape and landscape features can you find near your school? Discuss with a partner.

a breathtaking view   a bridge   a canal   a fast-flowing river   a historic monument   a housing estate   a market square   a shopping centre   a waterfront restaurant   slums

2 Discuss how far you would need to go to see features in Exercise 1 that are *not* near your school.

3 SPEAKING A city in Spain has banned cars from the city centre. Discuss the possible advantages and disadvantages. Then read the text and compare your ideas. Use the text to make a final list of good and bad points.

A SMALL CITY WITH BIG IDEAS

Pontevedra, located on the northwest coast of Spain, is a small city surrounded by rolling hills. The **picturesque** old town of Pontevedra comes alive at night and the **vibrant** atmosphere continues well into the early hours.

So far, it sounds like any Spanish city. But this one is different – I'm standing in the city centre and I can't hear any cars!

The mayor of Pontevedra was determined to preserve the historic centre of the city with its **bustling** squares, Gothic architecture and **quaint** backstreets, and limit **urban** development.

4 2.1 **Read the questions and make sure you understand the meaning of the underlined collocations. Then listen to a phone-in programme and answer the questions.**

1 How has Ryan's daily commute changed?
2 According to Jack, what can a reliable network of buses replace?
3 Where does Sarah want planners to put in cycle lanes?
4 Why is Julia's home town very popular with tourists?
5 Why can't ancient cobbled streets have cycle lanes, according to Julia?

5 SPEAKING **Think about your own local town or city. Discuss the questions:**

1 How doable/desirable would it be to ban all cars from the centre?
2 What changes would have to be made before the ban and in what order?
3 Compare the advantages and disadvantages. Use the list in Exercise 3 to help you. Which list is longer?

So he banned cars – completely! He transformed the **medieval** centre into a pedestrian zone. He felt that the historical centre was dead. It was a city in decline, polluted, with a lot of traffic accidents. He got rid of on-street parking and opened underground car parks on the outskirts of the city within walking distance of the centre. With pedestrianisation, the **shabby** city centre got a facelift: roundabouts replaced traffic lights and pavements, drainage systems, public lighting and street furniture were all renovated.

The benefits of all these changes are numerous: deaths in traffic accidents in the city centre have dropped to zero and CO_2 emissions are down by 70 percent. The city centre is growing with 12,000 new inhabitants who have moved there while other cities in the region are getting smaller. By not allowing big shopping malls to be built in the centre, small businesses have flourished. Noise pollution has been replaced with the tweeting of birds and the sound of human voices.

Go to WORD STORE 3 page 7

WORD STORE 3A Prepositions describing location

6 2.2 **Complete WORD STORE 3A with the prepositions in the box. Then listen, check and repeat.**

7 **Complete the sentences with the prepositions in WORD STORE 3A. Name an example for each sentence. Compare your answers with a partner.**

Name…
1 a big city located ______ the coast.
2 a café ______ walking distance of where you are.
3 a famous monument ______ the city centre of your capital city.
4 a town located ______ the border of your country.
5 a school, a shopping centre or a sports centre located ______ the suburbs of a nearby city.
6 a park or play area ______ easy reach of your house.

WORD STORE 3B Describing places

8 2.3 **Complete WORD STORE 3B with the adjectives in red in the text. Then listen, check and repeat.**

9 SPEAKING **Replace the words in bold in the description of Norwich with an adjective from WORD STORE 3B. Would you like to visit Norwich? Discuss with a partner.**

NORWICH – *a cathedral city*

Visit Norwich, one of England's most [1]**beautiful** cathedral cities. During the middle ages Norwich was England's second city and there are some spectacular examples of [2]**12th–15th century** architecture in the city. See the cathedral, of course, but don't miss the [3]**nice, old-fashioned** backstreets behind it. Norwich is also famed for its huge, [4]**busy and noisy** open-air food market as well as its [5]**exciting** nightlife. Less than two hours from the capital, Norwich should definitely become your next destination.

WORD STORE 3C In the city

10 2.4 **Complete WORD STORE 3C with the underlined collocations and compound nouns in the text and in Exercise 4. Then listen, check and repeat.**

11 SPEAKING **Complete the sentences with the collocations or compound nouns in WORD STORE 3C. Would such measures improve your home town? Discuss with a partner.**

1 All ___________ should be replaced by smooth modern surfaces like tarmac.
2 ___________ should be limited to residents only.
3 ___________ should be for people on foot only. No cycling!
4 There should be more ___________ to take cars off the street.
5 There should be a lot more ___________ to encourage people to use bikes.
6 Anybody causing ___________ should be heavily fined.

3.2 GRAMMAR

Future forms including the Future Perfect Continuous

I can use a variety of forms to talk about the future.

1 SPEAKING **Look at the pairs of sentences. Which alternative is more likely? Discuss with a partner. Give reasons for your answers.**

In three years' time …

1 a I'll still be living at home with my parents.
  b I won't be living at home with my parents.
2 a I'll have moved to another part of the country.
  b I won't have moved to another part of the country.
3 a I'll have been studying at university for a year.
  b I won't have been studying at university for a year.

2 **Read the GRAMMAR FOCUS and do the task.**

1 Translate example sentences 1–3 into your own language.
2 Discuss the difference in meaning between the sentences.
3 Look at Exercise 1 and name the future verb forms in blue.

GRAMMAR FOCUS

Future forms

- You use the **Future Continuous** to talk about unfinished actions in progress at a time in the future. It often refers to future events that are fixed or expected.
  1 *At 11 a.m. tomorrow, I'll be doing an exam.*
- You use the **Future Perfect Simple** to talk about an action that will be completed before a certain time in the future.
  2 *By 11 a.m. tomorrow, I'll have done an exam.*
- You use the **Future Perfect Continuous** to talk about how long an action will have been in progress before a certain time in the future.
  3 *By 11 a.m. tomorrow, I'll have been doing an exam for an hour.*

3 **Read Part 1 of the story about the Franklin family plans. Complete the text with *'ll, be, been* or *have*. Then discuss the questions.**

1 What problems do the children predict?
2 Which child seems more positive about the voyage?

THE VOYAGE OF A LIFETIME

Part 1

In a few weeks' time, the Franklin family will [1] *be* embarking on a three-year sailing voyage. We asked the children how they felt about the adventure. Mandy (aged seventeen) said, 'We'll [2] ______ missing a lot of school, but I think that by the end of this trip we'll [3] ______ learnt more than in a classroom. We'll have [4] ______ travelling for three years and we [5] ______ have seen places with our own eyes. We won't [6] ______ just read about them in books.'

Mandy had a few worries: 'The worst thing is that I'll [7] ______ spending three years in a small space with my untidy brother.'

Jake (twelve years old) was less keen than his sister: 'By the time we go, I'll have [8] ______ playing basketball for my school team for two years, and I want to become a professional in the future. I'll [9] ______ practising whenever I can, but it's not easy on a boat.'

4 **Complete Part 2 with the correct form of the verbs in brackets. Use the Future Continuous, Future Perfect Simple or Future Perfect Continuous. Would you like to go on a voyage like this? Why?/Why not?**

Part 2

Eileen Franklin told us 'We're not in a hurry, so after leaving San Francisco we [1] *will be travelling* (travel) down the coast of Mexico for a few weeks. After that, we [2] ______ (sail) across the Pacific and we [3] ______ (end) our journey in Indonesia. It's a long voyage, but by the time we leave we [4] ______ (plan) for several years, so I think we're as prepared as we can be.'

'Yes', added Bob. 'And by the time we set off, we [5] ______ (do) everything possible to make this a safe trip: Jake [6] ______ (improve) his swimming and Eileen [7] ______ (do) an advanced first-aid course. On the boat, we [8] ______ (use) top-of-the-range technology to chart our route. It's the trip of a lifetime, so we [9] ______ (not take) any chances!'

5 **Read REMEMBER THIS. Then rewrite questions 1–6 using the Future Continuous to make them more polite.**

REMEMBER THIS

You can also use the **Future Continuous** to make polite enquiries. Compare:
Will you be staying in tonight? = I just want to know. (polite)
Are you going to stay in tonight? = I'd like a decision. (more direct)

1 Are you going home straight after school?
2 Are you doing anything interesting this evening?
3 Who do you plan to see at the weekend?
4 When will you go on your next holiday?
5 Are you going to have a party for your eighteenth birthday?
6 Do you think you'll leave home permanently before you're twenty-five?

6 SPEAKING **Ask and answer the questions you have rewritten in Exercise 5.**

FOCUS VLOG About dreams

11 **Watch the Focus Vlog. For the worksheet, go to page 137.**

Grammar page 154

3.3 LISTENING

Multiple choice

I can identify specific information in a detailed spoken dialogue about places to live.

A Freedom Ship

B Co-housing

C Smart home

1 Match photos A–C with descriptions 1–3. Use the photo captions to complete the texts.

1 In the ___________ of the future, all appliances will be connected through wireless networking systems. The house and car would use power that is collected through solar panels and stored.

2 ___________ is a housing development where each household has a self-contained house or flat. People have the opportunity to eat together and meet regularly in a large communal house.

3 The ___________ is designed to be twenty-five storeys high. If the concept became reality, it would feature a casino, an art gallery, a park, a shopping centre and accommodation for 80,000 people. It would cost $12 billion to build.

2 SPEAKING Discuss which house in Exercise 1 you would most/least like to live in. Give reasons for your answers.

3 2.5 Listen to three recordings. In which order are places A–C in Exercise 1 mentioned?

1 ☐ 2 ☐ 3 ☐

EXAM FOCUS Multiple choice

4 2.5 Listen again. For questions 1–3, choose the correct answer A–C.

1 Which statement is an opinion and NOT a fact?
  A Over a third of British people don't know their neighbours.
  B In Denmark, tens of thousands of people live in co-housing developments.
  C The neighbourly relations at Springhill will be 100 percent better.

2 The speakers think that the Freedom Ship project is
  A unlikely to happen.
  B not big enough for 80,000 people.
  C a good investment opportunity.

3 Choose the most appropriate headline for this news report.
  A SMART HOMES MEAN LESS SHOPPING
  B SMART HOMES SAVE TIME AND MONEY
  C SMART HOMES NEED SMART PHONES

WORD STORE 3D Collocations and compound nouns

5 2.6 Complete WORD STORE 3D only with vowels. Use these definitions to help you. Then listen, check and repeat.

1 a task to be done regularly at home, such as cleaning, washing, etc.
2 an electrical device you have at home which helps you do the cooking, vacuuming, etc.
3 a number of houses or flats built close together at the same time
4 a car park consisting of several levels
5 a district where people live
6 an additional house, e.g. a holiday home
7 a flat which has all the necessary facilities needed for living, e.g. a kitchen, bathroom, toilet, etc.
8 a tall building divided into separate flats or offices

6 Complete the collocations with the words in WORD STORE 3D. Then complete the sentences to make them true for you. Compare with a partner.

1 My least favourite ___________ **chore** is …
2 The nearest ___________ **car park** is …
3 The one ___________ **appliance** I couldn't live without is …
4 The newest ___________ **development** in my neighbourhood is …
5 The tallest ___________ **block** in my city is …
6 The ___________ **area** I'd most like to live in is …
7 I'd love to have a ___________ **home** in …
8 I'd prefer to live in a small ___________ **flat** than …

PRONUNCIATION FOCUS

7 2.7 Listen and complete the chants in section A. Listen again. Repeat, paying attention to the rhythm.

A ■ ▪ ▪ ▪ ■
What *will* *you* *be* doing?
What ______ ______ ______ seen?
Where ______ ______ ______ going?
Where ______ ______ ______ been?

B ▪ ■ ▪ ▪ ▪ (▪) ■
How long ______ ______ ______ ______ learning?
How much ______ ______ ______ learnt?
How long ______ ______ ______ ______ earning?
How much ______ ______ ______ earned?

8 2.7 Complete the chants in section B with *you* and correct auxiliary verbs. Then listen and check. Repeat, paying attention to the rhythm.

3.4 READING

Gapped text

I can infer unstated information and understand relationships between ideas in a descriptive text.

1 **2.8** **Look at the list of words and phrases. Which ones would you use to describe your house or flat? Use a dictionary if necessary. Then listen and repeat.**

A house has …

1 a canvas camp bed ☐
2 central heating ☐
3 an en suite bathroom ☐
4 a fireplace ☐
5 a fitted kitchen ☐
6 running water ☐

A house is …

7 cramped ☐
8 damp ☐
9 draughty ☐
10 inaccessible ☐
11 minimalist ☐
12 snug ☐

2 **Complete the table with the words from Exercise 1. Add six words of your own. Then compare your ideas with a partner.**

House of my dreams!	House of my nightmares!

3 **Look at the photo of Zeki and the map. Which words from Exercise 1 would you use to describe his 'house'?**

4 **Read the article and check your ideas in Exercise 3. Then answer the questions.**

1 Where does Zeki come from?
2 Who taught him to live in the wilderness?
3 Where is he living at the moment?
4 What is he studying?
5 What is his daily routine?
6 Does he miss his friends?
7 What does he like about his lifestyle?
8 What would you like/hate most about Zeki's lifestyle?

I am 16 and live alone in the wilderness

2.9

I live alone on the Isle of Skye in a tipi almost impossible to find without detailed directions. It might seem unusual for someone of sixteen, but I love my own company and I'm passionate about preserving wild spaces. I grew up with my mum, Ghillie, and older sister, Yazzie, in a remote and sometimes inaccessible home in the Scottish mountains, using cross-country skis to drag food and supplies to the house.

Mum, a cookbook writer, taught us about possible dangers and how to cope with them, then let us **run wild** from an early age. 1 ________ . I spent so much time with tribes who rely on the land that this **became second nature to me**. When I gained a place at the School of Adventure Studies on the Isle of Skye last year, I decided to live in a tipi, **practising what I preach**.

I sleep on an ancient canvas camp bed my grandfather gave me, with two old army blankets and some skins I tanned myself for warmth. I have an open fire and spend my evenings tanning animal and fish skins, and carving wood. I store clothes and books in an old metal trunk of my mum's – it's covered in stickers from her travels. I wash my clothes in the river and dry them in the wind or in the heat from the fire. I have a bush shower using water from the river.

EXAM FOCUS Gapped text

5 Read the article again. Complete gaps 1–4 in the text with sentences A–E. There is one extra sentence.

A A few people were exhausted and had to be taken off the mountain by the leaders, but I feel comfortable in the mountains and enjoyed the challenge.

B We also travelled abroad regularly, visiting remote tribes and cultures, where we lived for weeks as Mum studied food and recipes to write about.

C I'd like to see more people look after the land and not be scared of getting outside, getting wet, learning how to survive. When my studies are over, I'll move the tent back to Mum's house.

D Eating things in nature is not something to play around with – if you make a mistake it can be quite a serious one. I sometimes eat too much of something and I get a stomach ache.

E There's usually some fire left from the previous day, so the fire is soon blazing while I have cereal for breakfast. I collect wood for later in the day, then I wash at the river.

I wake at 6 a.m. and get the fire on straight away using flints and steel. [2]______ . Sometimes I just jump in, especially when there's frost on the ground. When I rush back to the tipi, it's like a sauna. I get my backpack organised, including any food and kit I need for the day, cover the fire to keep it low, but alive and walk thirty minutes to the school. There are twelve of us on the course, of all ages, and we've just finished mountaineering. We're about to start whitewater kayaking.

I've **had a few hairy moments**. Once I was on the hills when the weather turned bad and I became disoriented, but thanks to Mum's training, I knew I had to **keep a cool head**. My classmates and I recently had a two-day test in horrible weather. [3]______ . However, I'm aware that I need to **keep my wits about me** and be prepared.

My friends used to love coming to our home and running wild with me, so they are used to the way I live. I hope some of them will visit me soon. People ask if I miss the Internet, but I never used to use it much, or watch television. I am sociable, but I have always **enjoyed my own company**. I use my mobile every few weeks to catch up with friends and my mum, who I usually see once a month.

What I'm doing **isn't everyone's cup of tea**, but it makes me happy. [4]______ . Until then, I'm happiest sitting by the flickering fire, carving a spoon in perfect silence and watching the stars through the open tipi door.

WORD STORE 3E Idiomatic expressions

6 2.10 Complete WORD STORE 3E with the expressions in blue in the text. Then listen, check and repeat.

7 Which of the expressions in WORD STORE 3E does Zeki use to describe …

1 … something he was allowed to do as a child?
2 … the reason why he decided to live in a tipi?
3 … his feelings about being on his own?
4 … the long-lasting effect that visiting remote tribes had on him?
5 … something that doesn't suit everybody?
6 … the state of being alert and prepared for any new situation?
7 … the ability to stay calm in a stressful situation?
8 … some of the frightening experiences he has had?

8 Rewrite the questions by replacing the underlined phrases with the appropriate form of the expressions in WORD STORE 3E.

1 When was the last time you experienced something really frightening or dangerous?
2 When you were a child, did your parents allow you to behave exactly as you wanted to?
3 Are there times when you like being by yourself more than being with others?
4 When do you have to be alert and focussed in your daily life?
5 When was the last time you did something that you advise other people to do?
6 What kind of everyday actions do you do easily without having to think about them?
7 Are you capable of staying calm in stressful situations or do you panic?
8 Is camping in the wild something that appeals to you?

9 SPEAKING Ask and answer the questions in Exercise 8 with a partner. Give reasons for your answers.

3.5 GRAMMAR

Quantifiers

I can use a range of different quantifiers correctly.

1 SPEAKING **Describe your bedroom to a partner. On a scale of 1–10 (1=extremely tidy, 10=extremely untidy), what score is your bedroom?**

2 2.11 **Read and listen to Part 1 of a vlog post. Why does the vlogger want to tidy her room?**

Part 1

Welcome fellow teens to my video blog. Today's vlog is called 'How to tidy your room in ten minutes!' I'm sure all of you know what I'm talking about – your room's a total nightmare. It looks as if a bomb has exploded. There's loads of dirty washing – in fact the whole floor is covered. There's no space anywhere. You have plenty of clothes, but you don't wear half of them because you can't find them. Most of them are in a pile because there are not enough drawers to put them in. You've had a number of opportunities to tidy your room but you haven't, and now the very cool new friend you like is coming round. Very few of your friends know what a slob you are and you want to keep it like that. You don't have much time, so here are a few speed-cleaning tips.

3 **Read the GRAMMAR FOCUS. Then find more examples in blue of rules 1–3 in the text.**

all of you = rule 2

GRAMMAR FOCUS

Quantifiers

You can use a wide range of different expressions to talk about quantity:

Countable nouns	Uncountable nouns	Both
every, each many a number of*, several a few (very) few both, a couple of* either neither	much, a great deal of* a little (very) little	all most a lot of*, lots of*, loads of*, plenty of* some no, none of*

1 Use quantifiers without *of* before nouns: *most people*
2 Use quantifiers with *of* before determiner + noun: *most of the people*, and before pronouns: *most of them*
3 *Always use these quantifiers with *of*: *a lot of people*

Note: *all the people* and *all of the people* are possible. You can't use *of* after *no* and *every*. Use *none of* and *every one of*.

4 2.12 **Read Part 2 of the vlog post and choose the correct option. Then listen and check.**

Part 2

- Find a laundry basket and put [1]*all / each* the clothes on the floor into it. Too [2]*much / many* clothes? OK, get [3]*a couple / a few* of bin bags and put the rest in there. Then hide [4]*both / either* of the bags in the wardrobe. If the cool friend sees [5]*plenty / either* of the bags, just say it's [6]*a few / few* things you're collecting for charity.
- The whole place smells of snacks, so take [7]*every / some* half-empty drink and stale half-eaten crisp packet to the kitchen immediately. There's a big difference between messy and disgusting.
- There are [8]*a number / several* of things that would give the wrong impression, things like your huge pink teddy bear … Hide them.
- Make the bed. There's [9]*no / none* excuse for an unmade bed.
- Open [10]*plenty / all* the windows – now!

You're ready!

5 **Discuss with a partner in which sentences *of* is necessary. Then make the sentences true for you by using other quantifiers if necessary. Compare your sentences.**

1 A couple ______ my friends are quite tidy.
2 Some ______ classmates are very untidy.
3 Several ______ people I know share a bedroom.
4 Very few ______ my neighbours have big gardens.
5 Many ______ the buildings in my street are old.
6 Every ______ room in my house has Wi-Fi.
7 None ______ my friends have a TV in their room.
8 Most ______ rooms in my house have paintings on the walls.

6 **Write one false and two true sentences about yourself. Use a different word in the box in each sentence.**

all couple every little loads lots most none plenty

All of my music is on my phone.

7 **Work with a partner. Read your sentences from Exercise 6 to each other. Guess which sentence is false.**

Grammar page 155

3.6 SPEAKING

Organising a place to live

I can justify my views when suggesting, agreeing to and objecting to a course of action.

1 Put these factors in order of importance when looking for a flat to share with friends.

decoration/furniture location privacy rent security size

2 SPEAKING Discuss your ideas in Exercise 1 with other classmates. Agree on the final order.

3 2.13 Listen to a conversation between two friends who are talking about a flat to share. Which two factors from Exercise 1 are not mentioned?

4 2.13 Read the SPEAKING FOCUS and complete the conversation with one word in each gap. Then listen again and check.

Zoe: I can't believe we've both been accepted into the same university!
Amy: Isn't it great? I'm so excited! And we'll be living together.
Zoe: I know. I can't wait!
Amy: What do you think [1]__________ living in halls of residence? To be honest, I'm not sure.
Zoe: No, me neither. Do you know Jay?
Amy: Yep, why?
Zoe: Well, his brother studies there and he says the halls are really old and noisy. Maybe we ought to just look for a place of our own.
Amy: You're [2]__________ right.
Zoe: The question is do we want to share with other people. It would probably be cheaper.
Amy: Well yeah, but [3]__________ it be better to get our own place? Obviously, it depends how much it costs, but if we could find the right flat at the right price, I think I'd prefer not to share.
Zoe: I know what you mean, but I'm not [4]__________ we'll be able to afford it. Why don't we [5]__________ halfway and look for shared accommodation, but in a place where we could have our own rooms?
Amy: I suppose that could [6]__________ . That way we might even be able to afford something near the university. Given the choice, I'd [7]__________ be within walking or cycling distance, and you?
Zoe: Totally. I don't even mind if it's a small room, as long as it's close to the campus.
Amy: That's [8]__________ then. So, let's have a look online and see what we can find.

SPEAKING FOCUS

Suggesting a course of action
What do you think about (+ *-ing*)?
Maybe we ought to (just) …
What would you say if we (+ Past Simple)?
Given the choice, I'd rather … , and you?

Objecting
No way!/Absolutely not!/You must be joking! (informal)
Fair? I think it's completely unfair.
(Well yeah, but) wouldn't it be better to …?
I know/see what you mean/what you're saying, but …
I'm not convinced (we'll be able to afford it/that's a good idea/that'll work).

Compromising
If you agree to (pay more), I'll (take the smaller room).
We could (split the cost/go halves/share).
Why don't we compromise/meet halfway (and agree that …)?
I guess so./I suppose that could work.
OK, that seems like a fair compromise.

Agreeing
True./Right./Absolutely./Totally. You are absolutely right.
I fully/completely agree. OK, that's settled then.

5 SPEAKING Read the situation and discuss the questions with a partner.

You and a friend are moving into a flat together for your first year at university. The flat is unfurnished and needs decorating, but you don't have a great deal of money.

- What furniture/household appliances do you think are the most important to buy?
- What colours would you like in the flat (walls, curtains, carpets etc.)?
- Who will get the bigger bedroom?
- Who will do the decorating?

6 Prepare a dialogue in which you discuss the questions in Exercise 5. Try to get what you want, but also be ready to compromise. Use the SPEAKING FOCUS to help you.

7 Practise the dialogue and act it out.

ROLE-PLAY Organising a place to live

13 Watch the video and practise. Then role-play your dialogue.

3.7 USE OF ENGLISH

Determiners

I can use **all, both, each, every, whole, another, other, others** *correctly.*

1 Read a review of the Hobbiton movie set and answer the questions.

- Where is it located?
- What did the tourists think of it?
- Would you like to go there?

A hobbit fan's PARADISE

If you're a fan of *The Hobbit* movies, you'll love this Hobbiton tour. I was on a family holiday with my parents and my sister in New Zealand. **The whole family** are fans of *The Hobbit* movies and we've seen **every one of them**, so we went to visit the Hobbiton movie set which is located on a sheep farm. It's a popular tourist spot – **all the tourists** take hundreds of photos, and so did we! There are forty-four Hobbit holes, and I think we visited **all of them**. **Each Hobbit hole** is different and has a round brightly painted door. A team of four gardeners keep the village looking neat and tidy. There were two places to eat and drink: The Shire's Rest Café and The Green Dragon Inn, and we stopped at **both places**! In fact, the tour ended at the Green Dragon Inn. It was exactly like in the film and **the whole time** we were there, we were expecting Bilbo Baggins to walk in! My sister and I had ginger lemonade. There were **other drinks** like tea and hot chocolate, but we were really thirsty. Mum and Dad had tea and cookies. Mum was so hungry she wanted **another cookie**, but we didn't have time.

2 Read and complete the LANGUAGE FOCUS with the examples in blue from the text.

LANGUAGE FOCUS

both, each, every* and *all*; *all* and *whole*; *another, other, others, each other* and *one another

	+ noun	+ of + my/the etc. + noun	+ pronoun
both = *2 things or people*	*both* [1]*places*	*both of the places*	*both of them*
each = *2 or more things or people*	*each* [2]______	*each (one) of the Hobbit holes*	*each (one) of them*
every = *3 or more things or people*	*every Hobbit movie*	*every one of* The Hobbit *movies*	*every* [3]______
all = *3 or more things or people*	*all the* [4]______	*all (of) the tourists*	*all* [5]______

each, every* and *all

- *Each, every* and *all* have similar meanings. You use *each* when you want to emphasise that you are thinking about individual people or things separately:
  Each Hobbit hole had a slightly different door and I took a selfie in front of each one.
- You can use *every* and *all* (NOT *each*) with adverbs like *almost, nearly, practically.*
  I've visited practically every country in Asia.

all* and *whole

- You can use *all (of) the* or *the whole (of the)* to talk about 100 percent of something. You don't use *the whole …* with plural nouns for this meaning.
  all the tourists NOT ~~*the whole tourists*~~
  all the time and the [6]______
  all the family and the [7]______

another, other, others, each other* and *one another

- *another* [8]______ means 'a different cookie' or 'an additional cookie'.
- *other* [9]______ means 'different drinks', but not usually '~~additional drinks~~'. (Use *more drinks*.)
- *the other(s)* and *the other one(s)* refers to the second of two people or things or to the rest of people or things in a group.
  I'll carry this bag. Can you carry the other one?
  I can see Tom. Where are the others?
- *each other* and *one another* mean the same thing.
  My sister and I took photos of each other. = She took a photo of me and I took a photo of her.

3 Complete the questions with the words in the box. Then ask and answer.

all (x2)   both   each (x2)   every   whole (x2)

1 Can you write your name with __________ hand?
2 Have you got earrings in __________ ears?
3 Do __________ your relatives look like you?
4 What film has almost __________ student in your class already seen?
5 Are you off school for the __________ month of August?
6 Do __________ your friends live near you?
7 Can you kick a ball with __________ foot?
8 When you eat an apple, do you eat the __________ thing?

4 Read about the *Mamma Mia* film locations. Choose the correct option.

Profile   Holidays   Messages   Log out

Posted yesterday

My fantastic *Mamma Mia* trip

If you love Abba, Meryl Streep and picturesque places, you'll love ¹*every / all* minute of the *Mamma Mia* films. I've seen practically ²*each / every* film with Meryl Streep in it and I don't know how she manages to be so different in ³*each / all the* role she plays. I loved *Mamma Mia* and I've just seen *Mamma Mia: Here We Go Again*. ⁴*Both / Every* of the films are equally good.

For my eighteenth birthday, my parents took me on a trip to Greece to visit the film locations for *Mamma Mia*. There are two main locations: the islands of Skopelos and Skiathos. ⁵*Both / Each* of the islands are stunning, just like in the films. You can't see ⁶*every one / all* the places in the films because some of them were built just for the shoot – for instance, Villa Donna, the hotel owned by Meryl Streep, was filmed in studios in the UK. But I wanted to see the church where Sophie gets married. We had to climb 199 steps, but once we got there the view was breathtaking. The ⁷*all / whole* trip was fantastic – a dream come true! Next year my parents are taking me to Croatia where *Mamma Mia: Here We Go Again* was filmed.

Share   Like   Comment

5 SPEAKING Discuss your favourite films and make a list of the top three film locations you would like to visit.

6 Match sentences 1–2 with meanings a–b.

A 1 Have **another** biscuit. ☐
2 Have **the other** biscuit. ☐
a There is one biscuit available.
b There are several biscuits available.

B 1 Here's one photo, where's **the other**? ☐
2 Here's one photo, where are **the others**? ☐
a There's one photo missing.
b There are several photos missing.

C 1 Could I have **another** coffee? ☐
2 Could I have **the other** coffee? ☐
a I'd like the same coffee again.
b I'd like the alternative coffee you offered.

7 USE OF ENGLISH Complete the second sentence so that it has a similar meaning to the first. Use between two and five words including the word in capitals. Are the sentences true for you?

1 I've seen nearly all of the James Bond films. **ONE**
I've seen __________ the James Bond films.
2 I saw the first *Harry Potter* film, but I haven't seen any of the others. **OTHER**
I saw the first *Harry Potter* film, but I haven't seen __________ .
3 I think each of *Pirates of the Caribbean* movies is worth seeing. **EVERY**
I think __________ *Pirates of the Caribbean* movies is worth seeing.
4 I saw the film twice and I enjoyed it each time. **BOTH**
I saw the film twice and I enjoyed it __________ .
5 I've never found a film that is fun for all the family. **WHOLE**
I've never found a film that is fun __________ .
6 I'd like to see *Mission Impossible* in a different cinema – a bigger one. **ANOTHER**
I'd like to see *Mission Impossible* __________ – a bigger one.

SHOW WHAT YOU'VE LEARNT UNITS 1–3

8 USE OF ENGLISH Complete the sentences with the correct forms of the words in brackets. Use up to five words in each gap.

1 On arrival yesterday, visitors __________ (*be/give*) a guided tour of the movie set.
2 You are reminded that taking photographs __________ (*be/strict/forbid*).
3 Quiet please! Are you going to __________ (*chat/another*) during the whole visit?
4 Most people enjoyed the experience, but I __________ (*be/bitter/disappoint*).
5 One person thought the guide was so amusing that he __________ (*keep/roar/laughter*).
6 At the end, __________ (*almost/every*) the visitors gave the guide a tip.
7 My brother and I love films. __________ (*both/we/go*) to the cinema as often as we can.
8 The last film I saw was so sad. At the end everybody __________ (*burst/tears*).
9 I was wondering whether you __________ (*able/come*) tomorrow.

Use of English page 156

3.8 WRITING

A 'for and against' essay

I can write a 'for and against' essay using formal language and expressions of concession.

1 SPEAKING Read UK TODAY. How similar or different do you think the situation in your country is?

UK TODAY

Halls of Residence

- Most UK universities provide accommodation for first-year students in university-owned halls of residence, on or near the campus.
- There is often a supervisor, whose job it is to maintain order and support students with everyday issues.
- Rooms in these halls are generally small but private, and in most cases, bills are included in the rental price. Kitchen facilities are usually shared.
- In 2018/19 the average cost of renting a room in halls of residence in the UK was about £140 per week.

2 Read the comments made by first-year university students. Decide if they refer to advantages or disadvantages of living in halls of residence. Then compare with a partner.

1 Freedom! (Ammar, Newcastle)
2 It's impossible to get any studying done. (Ian, Edinburgh)
3 I'm exhausted. There are parties every night. (Nick, Hull)
4 There's a supervisor we can talk to if we have any problems. (Emma, Durham)
5 Rules, rules, rules! Keep quiet, clean up, no visitors. (Ollie, Oxford)
6 We all help each other out. I've made so many new friends. (Abigail, Liverpool)
7 Someone stole my sausages! (Jason, Manchester)
8 Our halls are on campus. I fall out of bed and into my lectures. (Anahita, London)
9 My room is OK but it's tiny. (Richard, Nottingham)

3 Read the essay on living in halls of residence. In pairs, decide which advantages and disadvantages from Exercise 2 the author mentions. Which one is NOT included?

Some university students prefer to live with their families until they graduate and can earn their own living. However, it is also very common for young people beginning university to choose to live together with other students in halls of residence. Although there are several potential **downsides** to this communal way of living, there are also numerous benefits.

One of the most **convincing** arguments for halls of residence is that they allow students to experience independent living in a safe place with a strong sense of community. Having never lived alone, most new students appreciate this supportive environment. In the same **way**, the presence of an official supervisor is likely to be reassuring for students and their parents. **Yet** another plus is that halls of residence are usually very convenient because they are located on or close to university campuses. This allows residents to save time and money.

Despite these clear advantages, there are also considerable drawbacks. The first downside is that the rooms tend to be very small and bathrooms may sometimes have to be shared. Being full of young people, halls can also be very noisy. This can make them difficult places in which to study. **Likewise**, parties and late nights are common, and can interfere with students' academic progress. Other **minuses** are that food can 'go missing' from shared fridges and cupboards, and communal kitchens are often busy, and sometimes dirty.

All things **considered**, there are pros and cons to living in halls. Certainly, residents need to be self-disciplined in order to successfully balance study and social life. Personally, I **imagine** the benefits of living closely with other students outweigh the drawbacks.

4 SPEAKING **Discuss the questions.**

1 What is the author's opinion of halls of residence?
2 Would you like to live in this type of student accommodation? Why?/Why not?

5 **Complete the WRITING FOCUS. Use the words and expressions in purple in the text.**

WRITING FOCUS

A 'for and against' essay

Introduction

- Begin with general or factual comments on the topic.
  Many young people beginning university choose to live in halls of residence.
- End with a statement that mentions both sides of the issue.
  Although there are several potential [1] downsides to … , there are also numerous benefits.

Main paragraphs

- Present *arguments for* in one paragraph and *arguments against* in another.
  The first/One/A further/Another/ [2] ___________ another benefit/plus/drawback/ downside of …
  There are numerous/potential/clear/considerable pluses/[3] ___________ to …
  One of the most [4] ___________ /most persuasive/ strongest arguments for/against … is …
- Develop and support some of your arguments with additional comments or examples.
  This allows residents to save time and money.
- Make comparisons.
  In the same [5] ___________ , …
  Similarly,/Equally,/[6] ___________ , …

Conclusion

- Make a summarising statement.
  All things [7] ___________ ,/All in all,/On balance, there are pros and cons to …
- End with your personal opinion.
  Personally, I think/feel/believe/[8] ___________ …

6 **Read the sentences and choose the correct option.**

1 One of the most *persuasive / potential* arguments for living at home is the amount of money that can be saved.
2 There are also several *numerous / clear* upsides to living independently while at university.
3 The daily commute is one of the drawbacks *of / for* living a long way from the university campus.
4 Living alone, students learn to cook and clean for themselves. *On balance / Equally*, they gain experience in managing their money.
5 *All in all / Personally*, there are pluses and minuses to remaining in the family home while at university.

7 **Read the LANGUAGE FOCUS and then find two sentences in the essay which express concession.**

LANGUAGE FOCUS

Expressing concession

You can increase the variety in your written English by including sentences that express concession.

- ***Although/Even though* + clause**
  Although halls of residence are not always the cheapest option, *many students prefer them.*
  Many students prefer halls of residence ***even though they are not always the cheapest option.***
- ***In spite of/Despite* + noun or *-ing***
  In spite of the cost, *many students prefer halls of residence.*
  Many students prefer halls of residence ***despite the cost.***
  Despite living *cheaply, many students still find themselves short of money.*

8 USE OF ENGLISH **Rewrite the sentences so that they have a similar meaning. Use the words in capitals.**

1 Although there are numerous arguments for living with your parents while at university, there are also considerable drawbacks. **DESPITE**
Despite the numerous arguments for living with your parents while at university, there are also considerable drawbacks.
2 Many students live at home with their parents, even though there are minuses. **SPITE**
3 In spite of the cooking facilities in halls of residence, students often survive on fast food only. **ALTHOUGH**
4 Although some student accommodation offers good value for money, it is still likely to be cheaper for students to live with their parents. **DESPITE**
5 Many teenagers have plenty of freedom despite living with their parents. **THOUGH**

SHOW WHAT YOU'VE LEARNT

9 **Do the writing task. Use the WRITING FOCUS, the LANGUAGE FOCUS and the points below to help you.**

Many young people who enter higher education choose to study in their hometown and continue living with their parents throughout their university years.
Write an essay in which you present arguments for and against this arrangement.

- What general or factual comments could you make on the topic?
- Write down arguments for and against the topic and choose the ones you want to use. Which argument(s) will you develop and support and how?
- What is your personal opinion on the topic? Where will you include it?
- Choose sentences from Exercises 6 and 8 to adapt for your essay.

3.1 Vocabulary 4.17

ancient /ˈeɪnʃənt/
at the roundabout /ət ðə ˈraʊndəbaʊt/
at the town hall /ət ðə ˈtaʊn ˌhɔːl/
at the traffic lights /ət ðə ˈtræfɪk ˌlaɪts/
ban /bæn/
bustling /ˈbʌsəlɪŋ/
cobbled street /ˈkɒbəld ˌstriːt/
cycle lane /ˈsaɪkəl ˌleɪn/
daily commute /ˌdeɪli kəˈmjuːt/
destination /ˌdestəˈneɪʃən/
determined /dɪˈtɜːmɪnd/
drainage system /ˈdreɪnɪdʒ ˌsɪstəm/
early hours /ˈɜːli ˈaʊəz/
emission /ɪˈmɪʃən/
famed for /ˈfeɪmd fə/
fine sb /faɪn ˌsʌmbədi/
flourish /ˈflʌrɪʃ/
get a facelift /get ə ˈfeɪslɪft/
home town /ˌhəʊmˈtaʊn/
in decline /ɪn dɪˈklaɪn/
in the city centre /ɪn ðə ˌsɪti ˈsentə/
in the park /ɪn ðə ˈpɑːk/
in the suburbs /ɪn ðə ˈsʌbɜːbz/
inhabitant /ɪnˈhæbɪtənt /
limit /ˈlɪmət/
mayor /meə/
medieval /ˌmediˈiːvəl/
noise pollution /ˈnɔɪz pəˌluːʃən/
on the border /ɒn ðə ˈbɔːdə/
on the coast /ɒn ðə ˈkəʊst/
on the outskirts /ɒn ði ˈaʊtskɜːts/
on-street parking /ɒn striːt ˈpɑːkɪŋ/
open-air market /ˌəʊpənˌeə ˈmɑːkət/
pavement /ˈpeɪvmənt /
pedestrian zone /pəˌdestriən ˈzəʊn/
pedestrianisation / pəˈdestriənaɪzeɪʃən/
picturesque /ˌpɪktʃəˈresk/
popular with /ˈpɒpjələ wɪð/
preserve /prɪˈzɜːv/
quaint /kweɪnt/
reliable network /rɪˌlaɪəbəl ˈnetwɜːk/
replace /rɪˈpleɪs/
rolling hills /ˌrəʊlɪŋ ˈhɪlz/
scenery /ˈsiːnəri /
shabby /ˈʃæbi/
smooth /smuːð/
surface /ˈsɜːfəs/
street furniture /ˈstriːt ˌfɜːnɪtʃə/
surround /səˈraʊnd/
tarmac /ˈtɑːmæk/
tweet /twiːt/
underground car park /ˌʌndəgraʊnd ˈkɑː pɑːk/
urban /ˈɜːbən/
urban development /ˌɜːbən dɪˈveləpmənt/
vibrant /ˈvaɪbrənt/
vibrant colour /ˌvaɪbrənt ˈkʌlə/
within 500 metres /wɪðˌɪn faɪv ˌhʌndrəd ˈmiːtəz/
within easy reach /wɪðˌɪn ˌiːzi ˈriːtʃ/
within walking distance /wɪðˌɪn ˌwɔːkɪŋ ˈdɪstəns/

3.2 Grammar 4.18

chart /tʃɑːt/
embark on /ɪmˈbɑːk ɒn/
first aid course /ˌfɜːst ˈeɪd kɔːs/
route /ruːt/
set off /ˌset ˈɒf/
take a chance /ˌteɪk ə ˈtʃɑːns/
top-of-the-range /ˌtɒp əv ðə ˈreɪndʒ/
voyage of a lifetime /ˌvɔɪ-ɪdʒ əv ə ˈlaɪftaɪm/

3.3 Listening 4.19

affordable /əˈfɔːdəbəl/
casino /kəˈsiːnəʊ /
co-housing /kəʊ ˈhaʊzɪŋ/
communal /ˈkɒmjənəl/
communal house /ˌkɒmjənəl ˈhaʊs/
disposable income /dɪˌspəʊzəbəl ˈɪŋkʌm/
dock /dɒk/
domestic chore /dəˌmestɪk ˈtʃɔː/
homeowner /ˈhəʊmˌəʊnə/
household /ˈhaʊshəʊld/
household appliance /ˌhaʊshəʊld əˈplaɪəns/
housing development /ˌhaʊzɪŋ dɪˈveləpmənt/
light fixture /ˈlaɪt ˌfɪkstʃə/
multi-storey car park /ˌmʌltɪ-ˌstɔːri ˈkɑː pɑːk/
neighbourly /ˈneɪbəli/
profitable /ˈprɒfətəbəl/
provider /prəˈvaɪdə/
resident /ˈrezɪdənt/
residential area /ˌrezəˌdenʃəl ˈeəriə/
run low on sth /ˈrʌn ləʊ ɒn ˌsʌmθɪŋ/
second home /ˌsekənd ˈhəʊm/
self-contained flat /ˌself kənˌteɪnd ˈflæt/
smart house /ˌsmɑːt ˈhaʊs/
social housing /ˈsəʊʃəl ˌhaʊzɪŋ/
solar panel /ˌsəʊlə ˈpænl/
sustainable /səˈsteɪnəbəl/
store /stɔː/
tower block /ˈtaʊə blɒk/
well-established /ˌwel ɪˈstæblɪʃt/
wireless /ˈwaɪələs/

3.4 Reading 4.20

alert /əˈlɜːt/
be/become second nature to sb /biˌ/bɪˌkʌm sekənd ˈneɪtʃə tə ˌsʌmbɒdi/
blanket /ˈblæŋkət/
blazing /ˈbleɪzɪŋ/
canvas camp bed /ˌkænvəs ˌkæmp ˈbed/
carve wood /ˌkɑːv ˈwʊd/
central heating /ˌsentrəl ˈhiːtɪŋ/
cramped /kræmpt/
damp /dæmp/
directions /dəˈrekʃənz/
drag /dræg/
draughty /ˈdrɑːfti/
en suite bathroom /ɒn ˌswiːt ˈbɑːθrʊm/
enjoy your own company /ɪnˌdʒɔɪ jər əʊn ˈkʌmpəni/
fireplace /ˈfaɪəpleɪs/
fitted kitchen /ˌfɪtəd ˈkɪtʃən/
flickering fire /ˌflɪkərɪŋ ˈfaɪə/
flint and steel /ˈflɪnt ən ˌstiːl/
have a hairy moment /ˌhæv ə ˌheəri ˈməʊmənt/
inaccessible /ˌɪnəkˈsesəbəl/
keep a cool head /ˌkiːp ə ˈkuːl ˌhed/
keep your wits about you /ˌkiːp jə ˈwɪts əˌbaʊt jə/
kit /kɪt/
minimalist /ˈmɪnɪməlɪst/
not be everyone's cup of tea /nɒt bi ˌevriwʌnz ˌkʌp əv ˈtiː/
practise what you preach /ˌpræktɪs wɒt jə ˈpriːtʃ/
rely on /rɪˈlaɪ ɒn/
remote /rɪˈməʊt/
run wild /ˈrʌn ˌwaɪld/
running water /ˌrʌnɪŋ ˈwɔːtə/
sauna /sɔːnə/
snug /snʌg/
supplies /səˈplaɪz/
tan a skin /ˌtæn ə ˈskɪn/
tribe /traɪb/
trunk /trʌŋk/
wilderness /ˈwɪldənəs/

3.5 Grammar 4.21

bin bag /ˈbɪn ˌbæg/
disgusting /dɪsˈgʌstɪŋ/
drawer /drɔː/
excuse /ɪkˈskjuːz/
laundry basket /ˈlɔːndri ˌbɑːskət/
nightmare /ˈnaɪtmeə/
pile /paɪl/
slob /slɒb/
stale /steɪl/

3.6 Speaking 4.22

agree /ə'griː/
compromise /'kɒmprəmaɪz/
course of action /ˌkɔːs əv 'ækʃən/
go halves /ˌgəʊ 'hɑːvz/
hall of residence /ˌhɔːl əv 'rezədəns/
meet halfway /ˌmiːt ˌhɑːf'weɪ/
object /əb'dʒekt/
privacy /'prɪvəsi/
rent /rent/
security /sɪ'kjʊərəti/
share a room /ˌʃeər ə 'ruːm/
split the cost /ˌsplɪt ðə 'kɒst/

3.7 Use of English 4.23

breathtaking /'breθˌteɪkɪŋ/
inn /ɪn/
movie set /'muːvi ˌset/
shoot /ʃuːt/
stunning /'stʌnɪŋ /
tourist spot /'tʊərɪst ˌspɒt/

3.8 Writing 4.24

all in all/all things considered /ˌɔːl ɪn 'ɔːl/ˌɔːl θɪŋz kən'sɪdəd/
appreciate /ə'priːʃieɪt/
argue for/against sth /'ɑːgjuː fə / əˌgenst ˌsʌmθɪŋ/
average cost /ˌævərɪdʒ 'kɒst/
balance /'bæləns/
benefit /'benəfɪt/
bills /bɪlz/
common /'kɒmən/
convenient /kən'viːniənt/
convincing /kən'vɪnsɪŋ/
downside/drawback /'daʊnsaɪd / 'drɔːbæk/
equally /'iːkwəli/
experience /ɪk'spɪəriəns/
go missing /gəʊ 'mɪsɪŋ/
interfere /ˌɪntə'fɪə/
kitchen facilities /ˌkɪtʃən fə'sɪlɪtiz/
likewise /'laɪk-waɪz/
maintain order /meɪn'teɪn ˌɔːdə/
on balance /ɒn 'bæləns/
potential /pə'tenʃəl/
persuasive /pə'sweɪsɪv/
pros and cons /ˌprəʊz ən 'kɒnz/
rental price /ˌrentl 'praɪs/
sense of community /ˌsens əv kə'mjuːnəti/
supervisor /'suːpəvaɪzə/
supportive /sə'pɔːtɪv/

MY WORD LIST

LANDSCAPES	LIVING CONDITIONS	OTHER

VOCABULARY AND GRAMMAR

1 Complete the sentences with the words in the box. There is one extra word.

bustling daily fitted medieval rolling running shabby

1 I'll never forget walking through the ________ market in the centre of Marrakesh, through crowds of people in-between the maze of stalls.
2 Some parts of the city are clearly in need of investment with ________ buildings sitting empty and covered in graffiti.
3 The Alhambra Palace dates back to the thirteenth century and is an example of ________ architecture.
4 The landscape south of the town is quite flat, but to the north there are ________ hills.
5 When the office moved to the outskirts of the city, Luke's ________ commute increased by thirty minutes.
6 She grew up in a remote mountain village without electricity or ________ water.

2 Choose the correct option.

1 Our hotel was *at / with / within* walking distance of the beach.
2 My family live in a fairly quiet *domestic / housing / residential* area in the suburbs.
3 We'd all like to spend less time on *domestic / home / residential* chores like cooking and cleaning.
4 The downhill sections of the path are slippery, so you need to *get / keep / run* your wits about you.
5 The conference venue is *at / in / on* the outskirts of the city close to the motorway.
6 I'm afraid opera isn't my cup of *coffee / tea / water.*

3 Complete the sentences with the Future Continuous, Future Perfect Simple and Future Perfect Continuous form of the verbs in brackets.

1 Ann and Tim feel so excited. This time next week they ________ (move) into their new home.
2 How many more places do you want to view today? By teatime we ________ (view) six flats!
3 ________ (you/put) in new bathroom fittings next weekend?
4 I hope that by the time Olivia starts living on her own, she ________ (learn) to cook.
5 I'm truly exhausted. By next week I ________ (renovate) our house for a month.
6 By tomorrow the plumber ________ (fix) the tap.

4 Choose the correct option.

1 I've asked six people to help me move. Unfortunately, *no / none / neither* of them will have time tomorrow.
2 I always have *plenty / a few / a little* snacks in the fridge in case friends drop round.
3 I'm sure we had two new light bulbs. But now, when I need them, I can't find *either / both / all* of them.
4 Apparently, the electricity was off for *few / several / loads* hours after the storm.
5 I've noticed that *a great deal / a number / couple* of furniture has been delivered next door.
6 There's only *a few / a little / a couple of* paint left. Do you think it will be enough?

USE OF ENGLISH

5 Complete the text with one word in each gap.

BRITAIN'S NEW TOWNS

At the end of the nineteenth century, Sir Ebenezer Howard became renowned for what he called 'garden cities': self-contained communities surrounded by a 'green belt', which would provide the best of city and country living. They were thought to be the answer to the overcrowding of Victorian cities. Letchworth and Welwyn Garden Cities were the only two towns based on his vision, [1] ________ of them in Hertfordshire, just north of London.

After World War II, the need for inexpensive housing [2] ________ easy reach of larger industrial towns became an urgent matter. In 1945, the British government created a committee to investigate building new self-sufficient towns. The first wave of new towns were mostly located near to London, [3] ________ one with its mix of residential development and green space. Later, more new towns were built to cope with housing demand from other major cities including Birmingham and Liverpool. In total by 1970, the committee had created twenty-one new towns spread across the [4] ________ of England.

And now, more than a century after Howard's manifesto, Britain is facing [5] ________ housing crisis. According to current demographic trends, by 2050 at least another 10 million people will [6] ________ moved to Britain. That means that 6 million new houses will need to be built to accommodate all those people.

6 Complete the sentences with the correct form of the words in brackets. Use up to five words in each gap and make any changes necessary.

1 By Saturday, Rob (design/new) ________ kitchen for us.
2 Despite (take out/loan) ________, they still don't have enough money to renovate their house.
3 I asked (every/one/friends) ________ to put me up for the night, but none of them was able to do so.
4 This house has been for sale for a year now (spite/be) ________ relatively cheap.
5 There is (deal/accommodation) ________ for rent, but you have to start looking well before the academic year begins.
6 Don't call tomorrow afternoon because we (paint/walls) ________ in my parents' house.

READING

7 Read the text and answer the questions.

A MODERN CAVE MAN

People have lived in caves since the dawn of time. But if you're picturing a cold, damp and cramped space, you'll need to think again. In Spain, thousands of modern day cave-dwellers call a hole in the ground their home and it's a better home than you thought. There are a large number of luxurious houses carved into the Andalucian mountains which offer more comfort than you might imagine. Why choose to live in a cave? To begin with, cave houses are affordable, easy to heat in the winter and stay cool in the summer. Being carved into stone, their temperature does not fluctuate much but rather a steady 20 degrees Celsius is maintained throughout the year. Each home is unique and, if you purchase a property which is licensed to be modified, it's easy enough to carve yourself out an extra shelf in the wall or even a whole new room. The largest cave home boasts as many as forty rooms and can be had for as little as 200,000 euros.

You don't need such a spacious cavern to feel the charm of a cave home, however. Even those of a much more modest size seem surprisingly open – there is no sense of being underground or feeling locked up. Cave houses bring a warmth and cosiness which is a unique selling point for many buyers: sound is gently muffled and the amount of light seems to ignore common logic. Most cave homes face southward to allow for natural light to enter through the windows cut into the rock face. But due to the ingenious layout of many homes and the white walls, light is easily transmitted throughout. In areas further back, modern builders often use a system of ordinary mirrors to reflect natural light around the interior.

Cave dwelling is also surprisingly safe. They are not prone to fires or earthquakes and they do not tend to collapse, however, while deciding to opt for this accommodation, you have to take into consideration a few factors. Ventilation is important, as a cave home needs to breathe and excess moisture can become problematic and in extreme cases even trigger asthma attacks. Electricity is generally preferred over gas – although when gas fittings are provided, these tend to be closer to the front of the cave for safety reasons.

As cave communities tend to be in small villages, a car is essential for getting around and nightlife is hard to find. Such homes are very much for those who prefer a quiet rural lifestyle, quaint cobbled backstreets and breathtaking views.

1 How many people live in cave houses in Spain?
2 Why are the houses easy to heat?
3 What factors contribute to the cosiness of cave houses?
4 Why are cave houses safe to live in?
5 What sort of people would appreciate living in such homes the most?

SPEAKING

8 Look at the diagram. It shows different aspects which might be problematic for people when they move to a big town or city. In pairs, follow these steps.

- Talk to each other about why these things might be problematic.
- Say which problem would be most difficult for you.

9 Ask and answer the questions.

1 Would you prefer to live in a town, a city or in the countryside? Why?
2 Do you think it's a good idea for children to live and study in cities? Why?/Why not?
3 Some cities attract a lot of tourists. Do you think this is a good thing for the people who live there? Why?/Why not?
4 How important is it to keep old traditional buildings in our cities and towns and not knock them down? Why?
5 Which city in the world would you like to live in for a short time? Why?

WRITING

10 Read the writing task and write an essay.

Currently many families are deciding to move from the city centre to the suburbs. Write an essay in which you present arguments for and against this decision.

4 Shopping around

Wealth consists not in having great possessions, but in having few wants.

Epictetus

BBC

YOUNG ENTREPRENEURS

14 Watch the BBC video.
For the worksheet, go to page 133.

4.1 VOCABULARY

Shopping • phrasal verbs • shopping collocations • verb phrases

I can talk about shops and buying clothes.

SHOW WHAT YOU KNOW

1 Complete the sentences with *for, in, on, to* or *up* and tick the ones that are true for you. Compare with a partner.

1 I only buy clothes that are **reduced** or ______ **special offer**.
2 I pay more attention ______ **price** than **fashion**.
3 I often buy clothes ______ **charity shops** or **vintage shops**.
4 I buy **designer clothes** and **brands** are important ______ me.
5 I never manage to **pick** ______ **a bargain** in the **sales**.
6 I look for clothes that are **good quality** and will **last** ______ **ages**.

2 Think about all the clothes you have in your wardrobe. Write sentences with *too few, enough* and *too many*.

I have too few smart shirts, enough pairs of jeans, too many T-shirts.

6 WAYS to buy clothes responsibly

Most young people are on a limited budget, so it's tempting to go bargain-hunting. When you do, you should consider these six ways to shop more responsibly.

1 Shop locally

You may have to pay out a bit more for local brands but it's good to support local producers. Large international chain stores can sell the latest fashion at bargain prices because they employ people in poor working conditions and pay them low salaries. You can check up on a brand's employment policies and avoid those that have a bad reputation.

2 Support brands that promote ethical values

Not all chain stores are bad! Shop around for stores that encourage recycling. There are new companies that have sprung up with more responsible attitudes and environmentally-friendly policies – these are the shops you should opt for.

3 Make a list

When you go shopping, cut down on impulse purchases by making a list of clothes you really need. Then, when you feel like treating yourself to another T-shirt, pause before you enter your PIN and look at your list. If it's not on the list, don't buy it … or at least ask the shop assistant to put the T-shirt aside while you think about it.

Go to WORD STORE 4 page 9

3 SPEAKING Read the FACT FILE. Do you think textile waste is a big problem in your country?

4 Read the rest of the text. Mark the six ways to buy clothes responsibly as follows: ✓ (I do this already), ? (I'm not sure) and ! (good idea).

FACT FILE

- The clothing industry is one of the largest polluters in the world.
- Since 2000, global clothes production has more than doubled. The average person now buys 60 percent more clothes every year.
- We live in a throw-away society! Every year the US generates 15 million tonnes of used textile waste – double the amount twenty years ago.
- The average life expectancy of garments today is less than three years.
- Synthetic fabrics can take hundreds of years to decompose – basically, they're like plastic.

4 Think about how you shop

When you shop online, you may think that you are cutting down on carbon emissions by not travelling to the shops by car or bus. But online shopping can also mean more vehicles on the road for delivery and pick-up when you want to send something back.

5 Choose natural materials

Synthetic fabrics (e.g nylon, acrylic, polyester) are bad news for the environment. Go for organic versions of natural materials. If you buy sportswear, look out for labels that use recycled products.

6 Go for second-hand goods

If you shop in charity or vintage shops, not only will you reduce your environmental impact, but you'll get something original, unlike the mass-produced products on the high street.

WORD STORE 4A Phrasal verbs

5 2.14 Complete WORD STORE 4A with the particles in the phrasal verbs in red in the text. Then listen, check and repeat.

6 Replace the underlined word or phrase with the correct form of a phrasal verb in WORD STORE 4A. Then answer the questions about the text.

1 Why is it worth spending more on local brands?
2 Why should finding information about employment policies influence where you shop?
3 Why is it a good idea to look in different shops for places that recycle?
4 Why might you ask a shop assistant to reserve an item for you?
5 Why don't you reduce carbon emissions when you shop online?
6 Why should you look carefully for sports clothes made from recycled materials?

It's good to pay out for local brands to support local producers, who do not employ people in poor working conditions.

WORD STORE 4B Shopping collocations

7 2.15 Complete WORD STORE 4B with the underlined words in the text. Then listen, check and repeat.

8 Complete the statements with your own ideas. Compare your ideas with a partner.

1 My favourite chain store is …
2 A synthetic fabric I am wearing at the moment is …
3 Impulse purchases are not a good idea because …
4 We live in a throw-away society because …
5 The last time I did some online shopping I bought …
6 A shop near here that always has bargain prices is …

I don't have a favourite chain store. I usually buy online or in small local shops.

WORD STORE 4C Verb phrases

9 2.16 Complete WORD STORE 4C with the highlighted verb phrases in the text. Then listen, check and repeat.

10 Complete the sentences with the correct form of the verbs in WORD STORE 4C. Are the sentences true for you? Compare with a partner.

1 I'm not good at ________ on a limited budget.
2 When I get birthday money, I like to ________ myself to something nice.
3 I agree with the idea of ________ local producers.
4 I can't be bothered to ________ bargain-hunting.
5 I don't think chain stores care if they ________ a bad reputation.
6 I'm always very cautious when I ________ my PIN in public.

11 SPEAKING Discuss which clothing industry problem is the most serious. Can it be dealt with by e.g. the government? What action could be taken?

GRAMMAR 4.2

Question tags and reply questions

I can use question tags and reply questions.

1 🔊 2.17 **Listen to a conversation between Laura and her mum. What is Laura's mum concerned about?**

2 🔊 2.17 **Read GRAMMAR FOCUS I and complete the examples from the conversation with auxiliary verbs. Then listen again and check.**

GRAMMAR FOCUS I

Question tags

- You normally add a negative tag to a positive statement and a positive tag to a negative statement.
  You know it's risky buying tickets online, [1] *don't* *you?*
  He hasn't passed his driving test, [2] ___________ *he?*

Special cases:

- *I am … → aren't I? Let's … → shall we?*
  I'm always careful when I borrow your things, [3] _________ *I?*
  *Let's go, **shall we**?*
- Negative words such as *never, no, nobody, hardly, rarely,* etc. → positive tag
  But you never wear them, [4] ___________ *you?*
- Imperatives → *will/would/can/could you?*
  Negative imperative → *will you?*
  *Sit down, **will you**?* (= tell sb to do sth)
  *Open the door, **would you**?* (= ask sb to do sth)
  Don't lose them, [5] ___________ *you?*
- With *everybody, somebody, nobody*, etc. use *they*.
  With *something, nothing* and *this/that* use *it*.
  *That's Jamie at the door, **isn't it**?*
  *Everybody's having a good time, **aren't they**?*

3 🔊 2.18 **Complete the conversation between Laura (L) and Jamie (J) with appropriate question tags. Then listen and check. What was Laura concerned about?**

J: This is the place. He said he'd meet me at the main entrance.
L: Did he? So why are we waiting at the staff entrance?
J: Oh no, you're right. Come on, we'd better hurry.
L: Let's call him, [1] *shall we*? You took his phone number, [2] ___________?
J: No, but he's got mine. He'll call me, [3] ___________?
L: Yes – I suppose he wants his cash. Don't lose it, [4] ___________?
J: What cash?
L: For the tickets. You haven't paid him yet, [5] ___________?
J: Yes, I have – I transferred the money to his account online.
L: Did you? Oh, hey, that's him over there, [6] ___________?
J: Is it? How do you know?
L: He's holding up a piece of paper with your name on it.

4 🔊 2.19 **Complete some things Jamie said at the concert with question tags. Then listen and check.**

1 We can go in now, *can't we*?
2 Let's get closer to the stage, ___________?
3 Look after my coat for a minute, ___________?
4 This is a great concert, ___________?
5 Everybody's dancing, ___________?
6 Don't forget where we're sitting, ___________?
7 Excuse me, nobody's seen a silver earring, ___________?

5 **Read GRAMMAR FOCUS II. Find three reply questions in the conversation in Exercise 3.**

GRAMMAR FOCUS II

Reply questions

You use reply questions to react to what somebody has said and to show interest. They usually have rising intonation.

Positive statement + positive reply question
*'We're going to a concert.' **'Are you?'*** ↗

Negative statement + negative reply question
*'Beyoncé hasn't played here before.' **'Hasn't she?'*** ↗

6 **Write true sentences about yourself from the prompts. Student A: read your sentences. Student B: react with a suitable reply question.**

1 I / need / a new phone.
A: I don't need a new phone. B: Don't you?
2 Dad / give / me money for my last birthday.
3 I / go / shopping recently.
4 I / think / I'm a very lucky person.
5 Mum / usually / do / the shopping online.
6 I / have got / a credit card.

7 **Write four more true sentences about yourself and read them out. Your partner reacts with a suitable reply question.**

A: I'm saving up to buy a laptop. B: Are you?

8 **SPEAKING Prepare and act out a dialogue between a teenager and a parent. Use the situations in the box or your own ideas. Include at least five question tags and/or reply questions.**

The teenager wants to …

dye their hair pink | form a band
get more pocket money
give up a sport or a musical instrument
go abroad with friends

Grammar page 157

4.3 LISTENING

Multiple choice

I can understand the main points of a radio interview about market trading.

1 SPEAKING Read UK TODAY and discuss the questions.

1 Do you have similar types of market in your nearest town or city?
2 When did you last go to a market? What did you buy?
3 Do you sometimes buy things in online auctions?

2 2.20 Listen to an interview on the Shopping Programme. What does Martin do for a living?

EXAM FOCUS Multiple choice

3 2.20 Listen to the interview again. For questions 1–5, choose the correct answer A–D.

1 This episode of the programme is about
A things that you can buy and sell at airports.
B markets where Martin sells second-hand items.
C the growing number of bags that are lost at airports.
D the increased activity in the used goods trade.

2 How does Martin get hold of the second-hand goods he sells?
A He goes to the market.
B He buys them from the owners.
C He bids for them at an auction.
D He claims them from the airport.

3 What kind of things can Martin find in the suitcases he buys?
A Designer clothes.
B Electrical goods.
C Rotten food.
D Shoes.

4 The thing that surprises Martin most is that people
A lose so many bags.
B check in bags in advance.
C forget baby items.
D come to the airport at the last minute.

5 What is Martin most likely to say about the way he earns his living?
A It makes me feel sad.
B It's just how he makes money.
C It's a risky job.
D It's shocking.

WORD STORE 4D Noun phrases

4 2.21 Complete WORD STORE 4D with the words in the box. Then listen, check and repeat.

UK TODAY

Where do British people go to buy and sell second-hand/pre-owned goods?

- **Flea markets** – Camden market is the biggest one in London. It sells second-hand clothes and reasonably-priced new fashion.
- **Antiques markets** – London's Portobello Market is located in the fashionable Notting Hill. It specialises in antiques and bric-a-brac (old-fashioned ornaments).
- **Car boot sales** – Every weekend thousands of people take their unwanted domestic clutter to car boot sales around the country. One person's rubbish is another person's treasure.
- **Online auctions** – More than 17 million people log on to sites like eBay each month to bid for a bargain.

5 Complete the sentences with the noun phrases in WORD STORE 4D. Then put the sentences in the correct order to explain what happens to unclaimed lost luggage at Heathrow Airport.

A Unclaimed ________ property goes to ________ houses where market stall holders bid for them. ☐
B That's how ________ belongings end up as ________ goods on ________ stalls. ☐
C Thousands of ________ bags go missing at Heathrow Airport every month. ☐

6 SPEAKING Discuss your ideas about buying pre-owned or second-hand goods. What sort of items would/wouldn't you buy second-hand?

PRONUNCIATION FOCUS

7 2.22 Listen and repeat the words in the box. Then put them in the correct column depending on the vowel sound.

~~auction~~ boot bought could gone goods lose put rotten stall through watch

1 /ɔː/	2 /ɒ/	3 /uː/	4 /ʊ/
auction	________	________	________
________	________	________	________
________	________	________	________

8 2.23 Listen, check and repeat.

4.4 READING

Matching

I can scan a set of related texts in order to find specific information.

1 SPEAKING Discuss the questions. Have you ever …

a sold clothes online?
b been to an auction?
c raised money for charity?

2 Read the list of weirdest things sold at an auction. Which one is not true?

- a ghost in a jar
- the meaning of life
- a grandmother
- Justin Timberlake's half-eaten French toast
- New Zealand
- the tea leaves from the bottom of Queen Elizabeth's teapot

3 2.24 Listen and check your ideas in Exercise 2. In your opinion, which thing on the list is the weirdest?

4 SPEAKING Read the titles of texts A–C and look at the photos. Discuss what you think the texts are about. Then read and check your ideas.

EXAM FOCUS Matching

5 Read the texts again. Match texts A–C with statements 1–4. One text has two matching statements.

In which case do people make or raise money …
1 by understanding young people's consumer behaviour? ☐
2 by getting something different than they paid for? ☐
3 by appealing to both the rich and the poor? ☐
4 by using auctions on the Internet and social media? ☐

6 2.26 Complete the phrases with the base form of the correct verbs in blue in the texts. Then listen, check and repeat.

1 *bid* for sth (in an auction)
2 ________ up for auction
3 ________ for charity
4 ________ an auction
5 ________ (your) earnings
6 ________ a fortune
7 ________ a profit

7 Replace the underlined phrases with phrases in Exercise 6. Then answer the questions.

1 How much did someone pay for *Girl with Balloon* when it became available for auction?
2 Who offered money for the artwork and what happened as soon as it was sold?
3 How are young people earning a lot of money?
4 How much money did Scarlett earn on top of what she spent on an on-trend backpack?
5 How does Lydia use social media to make more money from selling online?
6 Which television channel collects money for children who need help?
7 As well as organising auctions, what other things do people do for Children in Need?

WORD STORE 4E Being rich and poor

8 2.27 Complete WORD STORE 4E with the base forms of the underlined phrases in Text C. Then listen, check and repeat.

9 Complete the sentences and compare with a partner.

1 In my city, people who are rolling in money live in …
2 If I had money to burn, I'd buy …
3 If my friends and I are short of money and we want to go out, we …
4 The government helps families who are living from hand to mouth by …
5 I think people who are extremely well-off should …
6 When I'm broke, I earn some money by …
7 Even if I were loaded, I would never …
8 A good idea to save money if you find it hard to make ends meet is to …

10 SPEAKING Reflect on the three texts and discuss the questions.

1 How do you explain the large sums of money people spend on works of art?
2 At what age is it OK for young people to start making money?
3 Which causes or charities would you like to fundraise for? How would you raise money?

2.25

A

PAINTING WORTH MORE AS DAMAGED GOODS

Banksy's famous *Girl with Balloon* has been voted the UK's best loved work of art. It first appeared as graffiti on a wall in East London and the true identity of the artist has never been revealed. When a framed painting of *Girl with Balloon* **came up for auction** at the famous auction house, Sotheby's in London, it sold for £1.04 million. But then something extraordinary happened – shortly after it was sold, the painting began to pass through a shredder hidden in the frame.

Banksy posted an image on Instagram of the shredded painting, saying that he'd secretly built a shredder into the frame of the painting in case it ever came up for auction.

The auction house refused to reveal the identity of the buyer who successfully **bid for** the artwork, but suggested that the media attention would increase the value of the painting. 'This is now part of art history in its shredded state and we'd estimate Banksy has added a minimum 50 percent to its value.'

B

TEENS BUILD BUSINESS EMPIRES FROM THEIR BEDROOMS

Enterprising teens are selling stuff online and **making a fortune**! They're buying popular items from streetwear brands and reselling them on Depop, an auction app aimed at young people. Reselling limited edition goods can earn them up to several thousand pounds a month.

Scarlett was fourteen when she started recycling used clothes by selling them online. 'When I didn't wear something any more, I thought I may as well sell it on,' says Scarlett, now fifteen.

These days she buys products from hyped sports labels with a cult following, from boutiques and clothes markets in London and sells them online. She recently bought an on-trend backpack for £120 and sold it for £180, **making** her **a** nice **profit** of £60.

She finds out which products are in-demand by checking streetwear-focused social media groups. She earns around £100 a month. 'Wherever I go, I look out for products to resell. My dad is always asking what I've sold. He thinks it's cool.'

Seventeen-year-old Lydia also caught the bug for selling clothes online. She spends about two hours a day reselling and makes about £1,000 profit every month. To create more publicity and **increase her earnings**, she models the clothes on Instagram.

C

BBC RAISE MONEY FOR A GOOD CAUSE

BBC Children In Need Telethon is a televised event that **fundraises for charity**. The Telethon has raised millions of pounds for young people in the UK since it was first broadcast in 1980. The charity supports families who are short of money, or where there's a child with a disability or serious illness. For example, if a family is already living from hand to mouth and they can't afford to buy their disabled child a new wheelchair, Children in Need will step in.

The annual Children in Need Telethon features performances from top entertainers who encourage people to donate money online or on the phone. But it's not only wealthy people with money to burn who donate. Leading up to the telethon, schools all over the UK raise money in different ways: selling cakes, hosting a quiz or film night, **holding auctions** or simply getting people to guess how many sweets there are in a jar. Another popular way to raise money is to take on a challenge and ask friends' parents – especially those who are rolling in money! – to sponsor them. This means that everyone can contribute, from people who are well-off and can afford to donate, to those who may find it hard to make ends meet themselves, but have raised money in creative ways.

4.5 GRAMMAR

Present and past modal structures

I can give advice, criticise past actions and talk about past necessity.

1 2.28 **Listen to James talking to his sister Ellie. What is James's problem?**

2 2.28 **Listen again and choose the advice that Ellie gives. What reasons does she give?**

1 You *shouldn't / should* buy her clothes.
2 With a bracelet you *need to / needn't* worry about giving the wrong message.
3 You *ought to / ought not to* get her concert tickets in advance.
4 You *mustn't / must* buy her the same perfume as Mum.
5 You *had better / had better not* ask her friends for advice.

3 **SPEAKING Take turns to say the sentences with the affirmative or negative form of the words in brackets. Discuss whether you agree with the advice and why.**

1 You ___shouldn't___ (should) leave present buying till the last minute.
2 You ___________ (ought to) buy a present unless you are sure about it.
3 You ___________ (must) give your credit card details to a stranger.
4 You ___________ (need to) check if you can take the item back.
5 You ___________ (had better) remember your dad's birthday this year!

4 2.29 **Read and listen to a second conversation between James (J) and Ellie (E). Did James choose a good birthday present for his girlfriend?**

E: How was the birthday?
J: Oh, a bit of a disaster actually. I **should have listened** to your advice, but I didn't. I got a bracelet. I thought it was such a bargain – €15 for a gold bracelet. I **ought to have asked** if it was real gold.
E: You should have realised you couldn't get real gold for €15. But anyway, didn't she like it?
J: She's allergic to metal – she can only wear real gold. She put it on and got a big rash on her arm. We **had to go** to the doctor's.
E: Oh dear, did you have to take the bracelet back?
J: Yes, but I **needn't have bothered**. They refused to exchange it because I didn't have the receipt. Here you are – you can have it.
E: Ooh, thanks!

5 **Complete the GRAMMAR FOCUS with the past modal structures in blue in Exercise 4.**

GRAMMAR FOCUS

Past modal structures

- You can use ***should/shouldn't have*** + **Past Participle** or ***ought to/ought not to have*** + **Past Participle** to criticise a past action or show regret.
  I [1]*should have listened* *to your advice.*
  I [2]___________ *if it was real gold.*
- You use ***had to/didn't have to*** + **infinitive** to say a past action was necessary/unnecessary.
  We [3]___________ *to the doctor's.*
- You can also use ***didn't need to*** + **infinitive** or ***needn't have*** + **Past Participle** to say a past action was unnecessary.
  There is a difference in meaning:
  I didn't need to bother = I didn't bother, because it wasn't necessary.
  I [4]___________ = I bothered, but it wasn't necessary.

6 **Choose the phrase (a or b) that has a similar meaning to the underlined words in each sentence.**

1 I <u>needn't have revised</u> last night, my exam was cancelled.
 a I revised. b I didn't revise.
2 I <u>didn't need to buy</u> a phone – I've got one.
 a I bought a phone. b I didn't buy a phone.
3 I'm tired. I <u>should have gone</u> to bed earlier last night.
 a I went to bed early. b I didn't go to bed early.
4 I <u>ought not to have spent</u> so much money yesterday.
 a I spent a lot. b I didn't spend much.
5 It's a lovely day. I <u>needn't have brought</u> my coat.
 a I brought my coat. b I didn't bring my coat.

7 **USE OF ENGLISH Complete the second sentence so that it has a similar meaning to the first. Use up to four words including the word in capitals. Do not change the word given.**

1 It's a pity we didn't stay at home. **SHOULD**
 We ___________ at home.
2 It's a shame he didn't tell her. **TO**
 He ___________ her.
3 It was unnecessary to do what he said. **HAVE**
 You ___________ do what he said.
4 That was a silly thing for me to say. **SHOULD**
 I ___________ that.
5 It wasn't necessary for her to come. **BOTHERED**
 She ___________ coming.

8 2.30 **Listen to three conversations. Which sentence from Exercise 7 completes each conversation best?**

A ☐ B ☐ C ☐

9 **SPEAKING Choose a sentence from Exercise 7 and prepare your own conversation with a partner. Then practise and act out your conversation.**

Grammar page 158

4.6 SPEAKING

Making and justifying choices

I can evaluate options and justify choices with relevant arguments.

1 SPEAKING **Look at two different ways of shopping for food and answer the questions.**

1 What are the pluses and minuses of each option?
2 If you were university students doing your own food shopping, which option would you prefer? Why?

1

2

2 2.31 **Listen to Emma and Oscar discussing the options above. Do they mention any of the pluses and minuses you discussed in Exercise 1?**

3 2.31 **Complete the SPEAKING FOCUS with the words in the box. Then listen again and check.**

~~but~~ choice choose compare likely opt reason simply

SPEAKING FOCUS

Comparing and contrasting options

X (Going to the market) is … [1]*but* Y (shopping online) is …
X is the only one/option that …
When you [2]___________ the two/X and Y …
It is (much) more [3]___________ that …
X is definitely the cheaper/better/more suitable choice.

Choosing an option and justifying the choice

That's why I'd [4]___________ for X.
… and therefore, X is probably/clearly the best [5]___________.
The main/Another [6]___________ ((why) X would be my choice) is that …
I prefer X mainly/[7]___________ because …
This option is (clearly) the most/least + *adjective* … because …

Explaining reasons for rejecting other options

X might (require less effort), but I wouldn't [8]___________ it because …
X isn't the best choice if you consider …
The reason I wouldn't go for/pick/choose X is because …

4 **Complete the second sentence so that it has a similar meaning to the first. Use the words in brackets.**

1 There's a bigger chance that people will remember this one.
It is ___________ (likely) this one.
2 This one looks very stylish. That one looks a bit cheap.
This one ___________ (but) a bit cheap.
3 I'd choose this one because it gives more information.
It gives more information. That's ___________ (why/opt) this one.
4 I like this one because it's more eye-catching.
I ___________ (prefer/simply) more eye-catching.
5 This one is no good as it doesn't tell you anything about the shop.
I really don't think ___________ (suitable/because) about the shop.
6 I wouldn't choose this one because I think it's poorly designed.
The ___________ (reason/pick) poorly designed.

5 **Look at the leaflets advertising a clothes shop. In your answers to Exercise 4, replace the phrases 'this one' and 'that one' with 'leaflet 1' or 'leaflet 2'. Compare your ideas with a partner.**

Leaflet 1

Leaflet 2

6 SPEAKING **Look at the leaflets again. Your cousin owns a small shop which sells fashionable clothes for young people. She has asked you to help her to advertise the shop.**

- Choose the leaflet in Exercise 5 which, in your opinion, is most appropriate and give reasons.
- Explain why you have rejected the other option.

Use the SPEAKING FOCUS to help you.

ROLE-PLAY Making and justifying choices

17 **Watch the video and practise. Then role-play your dialogue.**

4.7 USE OF ENGLISH

Modality – alternative structures

I can use a range of alternative structures to express modality.

1 SPEAKING Are you 'a saver' or 'a spender'? Do the quiz and discuss the answers with a partner. Do you agree with the results?

2 Read the article about Jordon Cox. Answer the questions.

1 How did Jordon travel from Sheffield to Shenfield? Why?
2 Why were Jordon and his mother unable to afford to go out?
3 What gave Jordon the idea for saving money through coupons?
4 Why did he change his mind about going to university?
5 What is Jordon saving for now?
6 How is Jordon's attitude to money different from yours?

News Sport Weather Politics Health Education

Money-saving teen Jordon Cox: From blogging to Berlin

Teenage blogger Jordon Cox claims he **was able to save** £7.72 on his train journey from Sheffield in the north of England to Shenfield in south-east England – by taking a plane via Berlin. He **was supposed to be** getting the train from Sheffield to Shenfield, but found that it was cheaper to fly from Sheffield to Berlin and from Berlin to Shenfield. He then blogged about his journey on his money-saving blog, and immediately gained 7,000 Twitter followers.

So how did Jordon become an expert in saving money? His story started when his father and mother split up. This meant that he and his mother **were obliged to live** on much less money. Jordon **wasn't allowed to work** because he was too young, and consequently, they **were unable to go out** and enjoy the kind of things they used to do, such as going out for meals or trips.

Then Jordon saw a programme on TV called 'Extreme Couponing' – the reality TV series follows shoppers who **are required to buy** the most shopping for the least money by using money-off vouchers or coupons. Jordon was inspired by the programme and that week he went out and **succeeded in saving** £10 on shopping.

Once he had started saving money, Jordon decided to share his tips on a Facebook page. One of his most impressive 'shopping trips' was when he **managed to acquire** shopping worth £500 for 4p, giving it all away to a charity for disadvantaged families. A few months later he was running money-saving seminars.

A few years ago, Jordon thought he **was likely to go** to university when he was eighteen, but now he's happy to have a job and financial security and is planning to continue spreading his money-saving message. He thinks that if he saves for three years, he **is sure to have** enough to buy a house. Not bad for a teenager!

Me and Money Quiz

1) Where do you keep your money?
A) In my wallet.
B) In a bank account.

2) You get your allowance every Friday. What do you do with it?
A) I go shopping.
B) I put most of it in the bank.

3) When you buy something expensive how much time do you spend comparing prices?
A) None – I know what I want.
B) Days or weeks – I want to make sure I get the best deal.

4) You've just won millions in the lottery. What would be the first thing you'd do?
A) Buy something luxurious – a car or a house.
B) Go to a financial advisor for guidance.

5) Which of these statements about money do you most agree with?
A) You can't take it with you.
B) A penny saved is a penny earned.

Mostly As: You're a spender! You need to learn how to save for a rainy day.

Mostly Bs: You're a saver! Are your parents bank managers?!

3 Read and complete the LANGUAGE FOCUS with the base form of the phrases in blue in the article.

LANGUAGE FOCUS

Modality – alternative structures

As well as using modal verbs, you can express modality with adverbs (*perhaps*, etc.), adjectives or participles (*she's sure to, he's obliged to*, etc.) or with other verbs (*we managed to*, etc.)

MODAL VERBS	ALTERNATIVE STRUCTURES
probability can, could, may, might, must	be [1]*likely*/be unlikely to do/that … be bound to do … be [2]______ to do … be certain to do …
ability can, can't, could	be [3]______/be [4]______ to do … [5]______ to do … [6]______ in doing …
permission can, could, may	be allowed to do … be permitted to do …
prohibition can't, couldn't, may not, shouldn't, mustn't	not be [7]______ to do … be forbidden to do/from doing … be banned from doing …
obligation should, must	have to do … need to do … ought to do … be [8]______ to do … be [9]______ to do … be [10]______ to do … be meant to do …

4 Choose the correct option. Then tick the sentences that are true for you and compare with a partner.

1 My parents *succeed in / are banned from* using my phone under any circumstances.
2 I'm *supposed / certain* to change passwords regularly when I shop online, but I don't.
3 I can't find my wallet, but it's *bound / permitted* to turn up sooner or later.
4 I *managed / was forbidden* to save up for a new phone recently. I'm ordering one tomorrow.
5 My mum says I'm *allowed / certain* to use her credit card to buy things online.

5 Rewrite the sentences using the word in capitals to replace the underlined phrases.

1 My online delivery is late. It should be here by now. **MEANT**
My online delivery is late. It's meant to be here by now.
2 Janet couldn't persuade her parents to lend her any more money. **SUCCEED**
3 Terry should have called me last night, but he forgot. **SUPPOSED**
4 Everybody must show their ID when they open a bank account. **REQUIRED**
5 Tom will probably waste all his money on new clothes. You know what he's like. **BOUND**
6 You can spend up to €100 a day on this store card. **PERMITTED**

6 USE OF ENGLISH Complete the dialogue between Ron (R) and Eve (E) with a different word in each gap. Sometimes more than one answer is possible.

R: Let's go and have a coffee.
E: I can't afford it! You know me – I never [1]______ to get to the end of the week without spending all my pocket money.
R: What happens if you need [2]______ buy something big like a jacket or a new phone?
E: I've got my savings. My parents give me 10 euros a week, but I'm not [3]______ to spend all of it. I [4]______ to put 30 percent into a savings account. Then, I'm [5]______ to use the money I've saved for those things.
R: So what about money you earn doing babysitting?
E: I [6]______ supposed to save 30 percent of everything I earn, but recently I've been lending it all to my sister. She wants a new phone, but my parents have [7]______ her from using her savings, because she lost the last one. She loses things a lot. If she gets a new phone, she's [8]______ to lose it quickly.
R: So it's a waste of money!
E: Not for me – she's paying me interest on the loan!

SHOW WHAT YOU'VE LEARNT UNITS 1–4

7 USE OF ENGLISH Read the text and choose the correct answer, A, B, C or D.

THREE MONEY-SAVING TIPS

ONE Don't [1]___ an opportunity to get a discount on [2]___ your online purchases. Look for either a coupon or a code … or both! You can get a reduction in the price, and you're also [3]___ to get free delivery. In shops, buy things when they're on offer, or just smile and say, 'Excuse me, [4]___ have a small discount please?' It might work!
TWO [5]___ way to save money is to have a present drawer. Buy presents and birthday cards when they're on special offer. If you [6]___ buy something at the last minute, you're unlikely to get a bargain, but if you have a stock of presents, whenever there's a birthday you just open the drawer.
THREE Leave your wallet at home. It's a good idea to have days when [7]___ to spend any money. You'll avoid [8]___ purchases!

1 A fail B miss C let D pass
2 A the whole B every C each D all of
3 A likely B possible C banned D permitted
4 A can I B do you think could I C do you think I can't D why can't I
5 A Every B The others C Other D Another
6 A manage B are bound to C have to D succeed in
7 A you're not allowed B you're certain C your banned D you're sure
8 A wishful B impulse C reflex D reactive

FOCUS VLOG About money

18 Watch the Focus Vlog. For the worksheet, go to page 139.

Use of English page 159

4.8 WRITING

A formal email

I can describe an incident and make a complaint about it in writing.

1 SPEAKING Would you hang out with your friends in the places mentioned in the box? Why?/Why not?

coffee shop empty building park
fast-food restaurant shopping centre
skate park street corner

2 Read Jude's post on the *Youth City News* (YCN) website. Do you think he and his friends were treated unfairly? What is the advice given by the YCN?

3 Read Jude's email below and answer the questions.

1 Are the main events described in the email the same as those in Jude's message to YCN?
2 How does the style of the email differ from the style of the message?
3 How do you think the Centre Manager will react?

Dear Sir or Madam,

I am writing on ¹__________ of myself and my friends to ²__________ your attention to an incident that **took place** at the Queen Plaza Shopping Centre last Saturday. I would like to ³__________ a formal complaint about the way we were treated by staff at the centre.

Last Saturday, some friends and I met in the centre at Plaza Café. We had bought some drinks and were enjoying ourselves when the manager of the café **approached** our table and **accused** us of being too noisy. When we tried to **reason with** him, he immediately called security. A moment later, two guards arrived and forced us to leave the café and the shopping centre. To make ⁴__________ worse, they **threatened** to call the police and told us not to return in the future.

We are particularly upset because the ⁵__________ is we were no noisier than some of the other people in the café. To be honest, we are amazed that the centre security guards are allowed to treat customers in this way. Without doubt, the worst ⁶__________ of this whole incident was being thrown out of the busy shopping centre like criminals. We were so **humiliated** that we decided to contact you and complain.

As the manager of the centre, we ⁷__________ you to reconsider your policies towards teenage customers. It is simply unfair to discriminate against young people in this way. We have contacted the local media about the incident and look forward to your response.

Yours faithfully,

Jude Seaborne

YCN *Youth City News*

YCN Message Board

Got comments? Need advice? This is the place ...

Jude: Last Saturday, my friends and I were kicked out of Queen Plaza Shopping Centre for ... no good reason! We were having a coffee in Plaza Café when the manager came over and told us to be quiet. We honestly weren't being that loud and my friend said this to the manager. Next thing, two security guards arrived and told us to leave or they'd call the police! They walked us to the exit and told us not to come back. It was so embarrassing and a total overreaction. What can we do?

YCN: If you really weren't disturbing anyone, then it does seem unfair, Jude. Why don't you write to the centre management and explain the situation? Be sure to let us know their reaction.

4 Read the WRITING FOCUS below. Which words complete Jude's email correctly? Sometimes more than one answer is possible.

WRITING FOCUS

A formal email – describing an incident and making a complaint

Introduction

- Say why you are writing and summarise your complaint.
  I am writing on behalf of myself and my friends ...
  I am writing to draw your attention to ...
  I would like to make a formal complaint about ...

Main paragraphs

- Use narrative tenses to describe the incident you are complaining about.
- Give your reaction to the incident.
  We are particularly upset because ...
  To make matters worse, ...
  The truth/fact is (that) ...
  Without (a) doubt, the worst part of this whole incident was ...
  ... I/we decided to contact you and complain.

Conclusion

- Say what you would like to happen.
  I/We urge you to (reconsider your policies ...)
  I/We ask/demand that you (investigate the matter ...)
- Make a final statement.
  It is simply unfair to discriminate against young people in this way.
- Mention that you expect a reply.
  I/We look forward to your response.

5 Complete the sentences with the appropriate words or phrases in purple from the email. Use the definitions in brackets to help you.

I am writing to complain about an incident that [1] ___________ (happened) last night at Skybowl bowling alley.

a We told her we had paid and tried to [2] ___________ her (persuade her to be more sensible). ☐
b She [3] ___________ us (said that we had done something bad) of trying to leave without paying for our drinks. ☐
c My friends and I had finished our game and were about to leave when a waitress [4] ___________ (came towards) us. ☐
d All the other customers heard her shouting and we felt really [5] ___________ (ashamed or embarrassed). ☐
e However, she started shouting at us and [6] ___________ (promised to do something bad) to call the police. ☐

In the end, the manager checked the computer and found that it was the waitress's mistake. The worst part of this whole event was that nobody apologised.

6 Put sentences a–e in Exercise 5 in the correct order to form an extract from an email.

7 SPEAKING Read the LANGUAGE FOCUS and rewrite the questions with *so* or *such a/an/Ø* (no article). Then ask and answer.

When was the last time …
1 you were ___________ angry that you shouted at someone?
2 you had ___________ good time hanging out with your friends that you didn't want the day to end?
3 you felt ___________ humiliated that you went red in the face?
4 you received ___________ terrible service that you complained or told someone else about it?
5 you had to deal with ___________ rude people that you felt offended?

LANGUAGE FOCUS

Expressing cause and result

You can make your writing more varied by using ***so/such* + *that* clause** to give information about a cause, and link it to a result:

- ***so* + adjective + *that* clause**
  We were ***so*** *humiliated* ***that we decided to contact you and complain.***
- ***such* + *a/an/Ø* + (adjective) + noun + *that* clause**
  It was ***such a*** *humiliating situation* ***that we decided to contact you and complain.***

8 You are going to write an email of complaint about an incident. Imagine you experienced one of the situations described below. Make notes about:

- The details of the incident (what happened and how you felt/reacted)
- What you want the manager (of the place/company) to do.

1 A bus driver refused to let you and four friends onto a bus late at night. He said he recognised you and that you had caused trouble on the bus the week before. None of you had been on the bus the week before.
2 You and your friends were asked to leave the cinema after a member of staff accused you of throwing popcorn around. It was actually some young children sitting a few rows in front of you.
3 You were leaving a supermarket when the security alarm went off. The security guards were very aggressive and searched all your bags. After keeping you there for half an hour, they found there was a fault with the alarm.

SHOW WHAT YOU'VE LEARNT

9 Choose one of the situations in Exercise 8 and complete the writing task. Use your notes from Exercise 8, the WRITING FOCUS and LANGUAGE FOCUS to help you.

Write a formal email complaining about the way you were treated.
- Describe the incident.
- Say what actions you expect the recipient of the email to take.

4.1 Vocabulary 4.25

average /'ævərɪdʒ/
bargain price /'bɑːgən ˌpraɪs/
be on a limited budget /bi ɒn ə 'lɪmɪtɪd 'bʌdʒət/
carbon emission /'kɑːbən ɪˌmɪʃən/
cautious /'kɔːʃəs/
chain store /'tʃeɪn stɔː/
check up on /ˌtʃek 'ʌp ɒn/
clothing industry /'kləʊðɪŋ ˌɪndəstri/
cut down on /ˌkʌt 'daʊn ɒn/
decompose /ˌdiːkəm'pəʊz/
delivery /dɪ'lɪvəri/
double /'dʌbəl/
enter your PIN /'entə jə 'pɪn/
ethical values /ˌeθɪkəl 'væljuːz/
employment policy /ɪm'plɔɪmənt ˌpɒləsi/
environmental impact /ɪnˌvaɪrənˌmentl 'ɪmpækt/
garment /'gɑːmənt/
generate /'dʒenəreɪt/
go bargain-hunting /ˌgəʊ ˌbɑːgən 'hʌntɪŋ/
have a bad reputation /ˌhæv ə bæd ˌrepjə'teɪʃən/
high street /'haɪ striːt/
impulse purchase /'ɪmpʌls ˌpɜːtʃəs/
latest /'leɪtɪst/
life expectancy /laɪf ɪk'spektənsi/
local brands /'ləʊkəl brændz/
look out for /'lʊk aʊt fə/
mass-produced product /ˌmæs prə'djuːst ˌprɒdʌkt/
online shopping /ˌɒnlaɪn 'ʃɒpɪŋ/
opt for /'ɒpt fə/
pay out /ˌpeɪ 'aʊt/
pick-up /'pɪk ʌp/
polluter /pə'luːtə/
put sth aside /pʊt ˌsʌmθɪŋ ə'saɪd/
responsible attitude /rɪˌspɒnsəbəl 'ætətjuːd/
responsibly /rɪ'spɒnsəbli/
send sth back /ˌsend ˌsʌmθɪŋ 'bæk/
shop around /ˌʃɒp ə'raʊnd/
shop locally /ˌʃɒp 'ləʊkəli/
sportswear /'spɔːtsweə/
spring up /ˌsprɪŋ 'ʌp/
support local producers /səˌpɔːt ˌləʊkəl prə'djuːsəz/
synthetic fabric /ˌsɪn'θetɪk 'fæbrɪk/
tempting /'temptɪŋ/
textile waste /ˌtekstaɪl 'weɪst/
throw-away society /ˌθrəʊ ə'weɪ səˌsaɪəti/
treat yourself to /'triːt jɔːˌself tə/

4.2 Grammar 4.26

be concerned about /bi kən'sɜːnd əˌbaʊt/
dye your hair /ˌdaɪ jɔː 'heə/
form a band /ˌfɔːm ə 'bænd/
hold sth up /ˌhəʊld ˌsʌmθɪŋ 'ʌp/
risky /'rɪski/
staff entrance /ˌstɑːf 'entrəns/
stage /steɪdʒ/
transfer money /ˌtræns'fɜː 'mʌni/

4.3 Listening 4.27

antiques market /æn'tiːks ˌmɑːkət/
auction house /'ɔːkʃən haʊs/
bric-a-brac /'brɪk ə ˌbræk/
car boot sale /ˌkɑː 'buːt seɪl/
checked bag /ˌtʃekt 'bæg/
claim sth /'kleɪm ˌsʌmθɪŋ/
clutter /'klʌtə/
domestic /də'mestɪk/
fashionable /'fæʃənəbəl/
flea market /'fliː ˌmɑːkət/
get hold of /ˌget 'həʊld əv/
lost property /ˌlɒst 'prɒpəti/
market stall /'mɑːkət ˌstɔːl/
old-fashioned /ˌəʊld 'fæʃənd/
online auction /ˌɒnlaɪn 'ɔːkʃən/
ornament /'ɔːnəmənt/
personal belongings /ˌpɜːsənəl bɪ'lɒŋɪŋz/
pre-owned goods /ˌpriː 'əʊnd ˌgʊdz/
reasonably-priced /ˌriːzənəbli 'praɪst/
rotten food /ˌrɒtn 'fuːd/
second-hand clothes /ˌsekənd ˌhænd 'kləʊðz/
stall holder /'stɔːl ˌhəʊldə/
unclaimed /ˌʌn 'kleɪmd/
unwanted /ʌn'wɒntɪd/
used goods trade /ˌjuːzd ˌgʊdz 'treɪd/

4.4 Reading 4.28

afford to do sth /ə'fɔːd tə duː ˌsʌmθɪŋ/
annoying /ə'nɔɪ-ɪŋ/
annual /'ænjuəl/
available /ə'veɪləbəl/
be broke /bi 'brəʊk/
be loaded /bi 'ləʊdəd/
be rolling in money /bi ˌrəʊlɪŋ ɪn 'mʌni/
be short of money /bi ˌʃɔːt əv 'mʌni/
be well-off /bi ˌwel 'ɒf/
bid /bɪd/
bid for sth (in an auction) /'bɪd fə ˌsʌmθɪŋ (ɪn ən 'ɔːkʃən)/
broadcast /'brɔːdkɑːst/
business empire /'bɪznəs ˌempaɪə/
catch the bug /ˌkætʃ ðə 'bʌg/
cause /kɔːz/
come up for auction /ˌkʌm ˌʌp fər 'ɔːkʃən/
consumer behaviour /kənˌsjuːmə bɪ'heɪvjə/
contribute /kən'trɪbjuːt/
cuddly /'kʌdli/
cult following /ˌkʌlt 'fɒləʊɪŋ/
disability /ˌdɪsə'bɪləti/
disabled /dɪs'eɪbəld/
donate /dəʊ'neɪt/
enterprising /'entəpraɪzɪŋ/
entertainer /ˌentə'teɪnə/
fetch /fetʃ/
find it hard to make ends meet /ˌfaɪnd ɪt 'hɑːd tə ˌmeɪk ˌendz 'miːt/
fundraise for charity /'fʌndˌreɪz fə ˌtʃærəti/
have money to burn /hæv 'mʌni tə ˌbɜːn/
hold an auction /ˌhəʊld ən 'ɔːkʃən/
human trafficking /ˌhjuːmən 'træfɪkɪŋ/
hyped /haɪpt/
increase (your) earnings /ɪnˌkriːs (jər) 'ɜːnɪŋz/
in demand /ɪn dɪ'mɑːnd/
jar /dʒɑː/
label /'leɪbəl/
leftover /'leftəʊvə/
limited edition /ˌlɪmɪtɪd ɪ'dɪʃən/
live from hand to mouth /ˌlɪv frəm ˌhænd tə 'maʊθ/
make a fortune /ˌmeɪk ə 'fɔːtʃən/
make a profit /ˌmeɪk ə 'prɒfɪt/
make money /ˌmeɪk 'mʌni/
meaning of life /'miːnɪŋ əv ˌlaɪf/
on trend /ɒn 'trend/
place a bid /pleɪs ə'bɪd/
publicity stunt /pʌ'blɪsəti ˌstʌnt/
put sth up for sale /ˌpʊt ˌsʌmθɪŋ ʌp fə 'seɪl/
raise money /ˌreɪz 'mʌni/
refuse /rɪ'fjuːz/
resell /ˌriː'sel/
reveal /rɪ'viːl/
shredder /'ʃredə/
step in /step ɪn/
streetwear /striːtweə/
sum of money /ˌsʌm əv 'mʌni/
take on a challenge /ˌteɪk ˌɒn ə 'tʃæləndʒ/
winning bid /'wɪnɪŋ ˌbɪd/
wheelchair /'wiːltʃeə/
value /'væljuː/

4.5 Grammar 4.29

bother /'bɒðə/
bracelet /'breɪslət/
exchange /ɪks'tʃeɪndʒ/
in advance /ɪn əd'vɑːns/
it's a pity/it's a shame /ɪts ə 'pɪti/ /ɪts ə 'ʃeɪm/
rash /ræʃ/
receipt /rɪ'siːt/
take sth back /ˌteɪk ˌsʌmθɪŋ 'bæk/

4.6 Speaking 4.30

can't be bothered to do sth /ˌkɑːnt bi ˌbɒðəd tə 'duː ˌsʌmθɪŋ/
choice /tʃɔɪs/
delivery truck /dɪ'lɪvəri ˌtrʌk/
eye-catching /'aɪ ˌkætʃɪŋ/
get the message /ˌget ðə 'mesɪdʒ/

halfway across town /ˌhɑːf'weɪ ə'krɒs ˌtaʊn/
interact with sb /ˌɪntər'ækt wɪð ˌsʌmbədi/
justify /'dʒʌstɪfaɪ/
leaflet /'liːflət/
locally grown /ˌləʊkəli 'grəʊn/
miraculous /mɪ'rækjələs/
on second thoughts /ɒn ˌsekənd 'θɔːts/
order sth online /ˌɔːdə ˌsʌmθɪŋ 'ɒnlaɪn/
poorly /'pɔːli/
take effort /teɪk 'efət/
time-consuming /'taɪm kənˌsjuːmɪŋ/

4.7 Use of English 4.31

a penny saved is a penny earned /ə'peni ˌseɪvd əz ə 'peni ˌɜːnd/
allowance /ə'laʊəns/
attitude /'ætətjuːd/
disadvantaged /ˌdɪsəd'vɑːntɪdʒd/
financial advisor /fə'nænʃəl ədˌvaɪzə/
gain /geɪn/
get a discount /'get ə 'dɪskaʊnt/
guidance /'gaɪdəns/
interest on a loan /ˌɪntrəst ɒn ə 'ləʊn/
luxurious /ləg'ʒʊəriəs/
miss an opportunity /ˌmɪs ən ˌɒpə'tjuːnəti/
money-off voucher/coupon /ˌmʌni ɒf 'vaʊtʃə/'kuːpɒn/
open a bank account /ˌəʊpən ə 'bæŋk əˌkaʊnt/
permit /pə'mɪt/
pocket money /'pɒkət ˌmʌni/
reduction in the price /rɪ'dʌkʃən ɪn ðə ˌpraɪs/
run a seminar /ˌrʌn ə 'semənɑː/
save for a rainy day /ˌseɪv fər ə 'reɪni deɪ/
save up for /ˌseɪv 'ʌp fə/
savings account /'seɪvɪŋz əˌkaʊnt/
stock of /stɒk əv/
succeed in /sək'siːd ɪn/
waste money /ˌweɪst 'mʌni/

4.8 Writing 4.32

accuse sb of /ə'kjuːz ˌsʌmbɒdi əv/
approach /ə'prəʊtʃ/
bowling alley /'bəʊlɪŋ ˌæli/
discriminate against sb /dɪ'skrɪməneɪt əˌgenst ˌsʌmbɒdi/
draw sb's attention to /ˌdrɔː ˌsʌmbədiz ə'tenʃən tə/
embarrassing /ɪm'bærəsɪŋ/
feel offended /fiːl ə'fendəd/
hang out /ˌhæŋ 'aʊt/
humiliated /hjuː'mɪlieɪtɪd/
incident /'ɪnsɪdənt/
kick sb out /ˌkɪk ˌsʌmbɒdi 'aʊt/
make a complaint /meɪk ə kəm'pleɪnt/
on behalf /ɒn bɪ'hɑːf/
overreaction /ˌəʊvəri'ækʃən/
policy /'pɒləsi/
reason with /'riːzən wɪð/
reconsider /ˌriːkən'sɪdə/
security guard /sɪ'kjʊərəti ˌgɑːd/
threaten /'θretn/
treat sb unfairly /ˌtriːt ˌsʌmbədi ˌʌn'feəli/
upset /ˌʌp'set/

MY WORD LIST

SHOPPING	MONEY	OTHER

FOCUS REVIEW 4

VOCABULARY AND GRAMMAR

1 Match the sentence halves.

1 Many consumers are trying to cut ☐
2 New shops are starting to spring ☐
3 Think about the environment before treating yourself ☐
4 It's true that sometimes you have to pay ☐
5 Even if you're a bit short ☐

a out a bit more for ethical products.
b down on the amount of waste they create.
c of money, there are still ways you can cut waste.
d up that offer goods with no plastic packaging.
e to that heavily packaged box of chocolates.

2 Complete the text with the words in the box. There is one extra word.

chain making meet pre-owned
sales support taking

It seems that anywhere you go in the world now, you see the same brand names and the same [1]________ stores selling familiar goods. An increasing number of people, however, are turning to alternatives, such as avoiding the big brands to [2]________ local independent shops or seeking out unique [3]________ goods at auctions or car boot [4]________. Buying and selling second-hand goods is no longer just for those who find it hard to make ends [5]________. For many, selling their unwanted belongings online is a way of reducing waste as well as [6]________ a bit of a profit.

3 Complete the sentences with question tags or reply questions.

1 Nobody has received a refund for their cancelled flight, ____________?
2 That's a nice dress she's wearing tonight, ____________?
3 Let's talk about insuring the house, ____________?
4 Don't forget to call me, ____________?
5 **A:** Tim had to take out a loan to buy a car.
B: ____________?
6 **A:** I'm not going to lend him money ever again!
B: ____________?

4 Choose the correct option.

1 We *should have found / had to find* the receipt before we could take the camera back to the shop.
2 I told you not to order a wedding dress online. You *should listen / ought to have listened* to me then, and we wouldn't have to look for one now!
3 She said she was broke, so she *shouldn't have / ought to have* spent so much on new clothes.
4 I *didn't need to spend / needn't have spent* a fortune on all this fancy food. They didn't come after all.
5 Look at the queue to get into the shop! We *ought to arrive / ought to have arrived* earlier.

USE OF ENGLISH

5 Read the text. Choose the correct answer, A, B, C or D.

BAR CODE

You may have never heard of Joe Woodland or Bernard Silver, but you [1]___ to come across their groundbreaking invention on a daily basis – the bar code.

While studying engineering, Woodland and Silver were approached by a retail food company and asked to find ways to automate checkout operations. They [2]___ design a bar code in the shape of a bull's eye. It meant that employees no longer [3]___ manually input prices for every single product at the checkout, neither were they [4]___ replace price tags whenever an item's cost changed. Even though the idea didn't catch on at first, the food industry didn't give up looking for an easy way to scan products. Finally, an IBM employee, George Laurer, [5]___ designing the bar code we're all familiar with today as a rectangular box with vertical lines and numbers. The first ever item was scanned on 26th June 1974. It was a pack of chewing gum, which is now a museum exhibit, together with the scanner used.

Nowadays, you [6]___ to come across everything from food to furniture branded with a bar code. It has even become a feature in some modern paintings.

1 A are meant B manage C are certain D are required
2 A able to B succeeded C managed to D were allowed to
3 A ought to B must C should D had to
4 A needed to B bound to C had to D obliged to
5 A succeeded in B managed C were able to D supposed to
6 A are able B are likely C are meant D will surely

6 Complete the second sentence using the word in capitals so that it has a similar meaning to the first. Use up to four words in each gap, but do not change the word in capitals.

1 It would have been better if we hadn't given Tony so much money for his birthday. **SHOULD**
We ____________ Tony so much money for his birthday.
2 The offer was so good, they didn't hesitate to accept it. **SUCH**
It was ____________ that they didn't hesitate to accept it.
3 It wasn't necessary for Sarah to pay her university fees because they were covered by her employer. **NEED**
Sarah ____________ her university fees because they were covered by her employer.
4 By law, stores can't sell certain products to under eighteens. **FORBIDDEN**
By law, stores ____________ certain products to under eighteens.
5 We didn't manage to launch a new campaign due to lack of funding. **SUCCEED**
We did ____________ a new campaign due to lack of funding.

LISTENING

7 **2.32 Listen to an interview with Anne, who works as a mystery shopper, and choose the correct answer, A, B, C or D. You will hear the recording twice.**

1 Anne is asked by her clients to
A visit local businesses.
B buy specific products.
C dress in a particular way.
D go to any store she wants.

2 The services of mystery shoppers are in demand mainly because
A shops want to attract wealthier customers.
B they provide information on the online competition.
C there aren't many people who actually do the job.
D online shopping is becoming a danger to regular stores.

3 Which is not true about the stores Anne has visited?
A Some of them are hiring more staff and are cleaner than before.
B Some of them have more customers and longer queues.
C Some of them are becoming more shopper-friendly.
D Some of them are winning awards for customer service.

4 What does Anne say about being a mystery shopper in expensive restaurants?
A It's a task requiring a good memory.
B She has to take notes during the meal.
C It's a good opportunity to speak to the staff.
D She finds it a good way to combine work and spending a nice evening.

5 In the interview, Anne suggests that the mystery shopper job
A cannot bring any satisfaction.
B can sometimes pay very well.
C can be monotonous.
D can be done by anyone.

WRITING

E-mail

8 **Read part of an email you sent to an English friend. Write an email of complaint to the manager of the museum.**

> I really enjoyed our visit to the museum yesterday, but I can't believe that they asked you not to go into the Egyptian room. How can they claim it's in the museum rules and regulations that your wheelchair might damage the delicate exhibits in there! I think their attitude was really wrong and totally unfair. I'm going to write an email to the director of the museum and complain about the behaviour of the museum staff.

SPEAKING

9 **Look at the photos. Your end-of-school ball is taking place soon and you need a suitable formal outfit. Choose the method of getting a new outfit which, in your opinion, is the best, and give reasons for your choice.**

A

B

C

10 **Ask and answer the questions.**

1 Where do you usually buy your clothes?
2 What are the advantages and disadvantages of buying clothes online?
3 In the past, people often had their clothes made or sewed them themselves. Why was it so popular and why did it stop being so common?
4 Do you think it makes sense to spend a lot of money on clothes you will only wear once at a ball or similar occasions?

Off to work

My advice is to never do tomorrow what you can do today. Procrastination is the thief of time.

Charles Dickens

BBC

19 Watch the BBC video.
For the worksheet, go to page 140.

5.1 VOCABULARY

Work • expressions to do with work • phrasal verbs • adjectives from nouns

I can talk about work and employment.

SHOW WHAT YOU KNOW

1 Complete the sentences with the correct form of *work* (noun or verb) or *job* (noun).

1 Brenda has a *part-time/manual/well-paid* _job_ .
2 Tom ______ *from home/long hours/with his hands.*
3 Amy has done a lot of *hard/voluntary/office* ______ over the years.
4 Luca ______ *outdoors/in advertising/abroad.*
5 Hal *applied for/got fired from/resigned from* a ______ in sales.

2 SPEAKING Think about three people with different jobs that you know. Tell your partner about them using the structures in Exercise 1 and your own ideas.

3 SPEAKING Brainstorm ideas for how you can become a more effective worker or student. Then read a summary of some tips from a book called *Eat that Frog!* by Brian Tracy and check your answers.

4 Read the summary again and answer the questions.

1 What is a 'frog' in the summary? What does 'eat that frog' mean?
2 How can making lists help you at work? What two lists does the author suggest?
3 Why should you imitate what other successful people do?
4 Why is developing your skills important?

EAT THAT FROG!

You're almost at the end of school and close to going on to further education or **entering the job market**. In his book, ***Eat that Frog!***, time management expert Brian Tracy outlines some simple tips to help you **reach your full potential** and stop you burning out.

5 SPEAKING **Discuss the questions.**

1 How good are you at time management and getting things done?
2 Which tips describe things you do or would consider doing?
3 Do you think it is always important to 'eat that frog'? Why/Why not?

1 EAT THAT FROG

Imagine the scenario – you've taken up a new job or started a new course, but you're overworked. You've got so many things to do. Your frog is your biggest, most difficult and important task, the one you're most likely to put off until later. Make sure it's the first job you do, and keep at it until it's done.

2 WRITE DOWN YOUR GOALS

Set out your objectives. Make a list of ten goals you'd like to achieve in the next twelve months. If you could only achieve one goal, which one would have the most positive effect on your life? Focus on that objective first and get down to work straight away.

3 WRITE A TO-DO LIST

Get organised. Before you get on with your work, if you take ten minutes to map out exactly how you will spend your time, you can increase your output by 25 percent. Planning can save you time especially when you're working to a deadline.

4 DEVELOP THE RIGHT HABITS

Improve your career prospects by observing what successful people do. Imitate their behaviour: be punctual, think for yourself, speak your mind. Do these things day in, day out until they become second nature. Then you'll be on your way to becoming a successful person, too.

5 GET BETTER AT WHAT YOU DO

Commit to taking on new challenges, picking up new skills and reading about your future profession. The more knowledgeable and skilled you become, the faster you will carry out the tasks at hand. Identify what you're good at and then put your heart into doing those specific things very, very well.

6 MOTIVATE YOURSELF

Always be enthusiastic and purposeful. Try to be conscientious and get the job done – imagine you have to go away for a month and then work towards finishing the job before you leave.

7 REMEMBER – EAT THAT FROG!

Do the hard things first. Focus on the important tasks. Be single-minded. Just do it!

Go to **WORD STORE 5** page 11

WORD STORE 5A Expressions to do with work

6 2.33 **Complete WORD STORE 5A with the verbs in red in the text. Then listen, check and repeat.**

7 **Replace the underlined phrases with the phrases in WORD STORE 5A. Then answer the questions about the text.**

1 How can this book help you to become as good as you can be?
2 Of all the objectives you'd like to fulfil, which one should you do first?
3 How can you make yourself 25 percent more productive?
4 What can help when you have a time limit to do something?
5 How can you make your employment possibilities better?
6 What do you need to do over and over until it becomes second nature?
7 What specific things should you put a lot of effort into?

WORD STORE 5B Phrasal verbs

8 2.34 **Complete WORD STORE 5B with the underlined phrasal verbs in the text. Then listen, check and repeat.**

9 SPEAKING **Complete the sentences with the correct phrasal verb and the pronoun *it*. Discuss which sentence, a or b, is true for you and whether you should change your habits.**

1 When I have English homework, …
 a I ________ till the last minute. (burn out/put off)
 b I ________ as soon as I can. (get down to/keep at)
2 When I have an English essay to do, …
 a I brainstorm ideas and ________ carefully before writing. (carry out/map out)
 b I start writing immediately and ________ until it's finished. (keep at/set out)
3 When I have an English exam coming up, …
 a I make a revision plan and ________ carefully. (carry out/put off)
 b I ________ by doing old exam papers. (burn out/work towards)

WORD STORE 5C Adjectives from nouns

10 2.35 **Complete WORD STORE 5C with the highlighted adjectives in the text. Then listen, check and repeat.**

11 SPEAKING **Complete the statements with an appropriate noun or adjective in WORD STORE 5C. Then discuss whether you agree and give reasons for your answers.**

1 ________ is unhealthy. It causes stress.
2 It is a sign of respect to be ________ and not to waste other people's time.
3 ________ people have the gift of extreme focus. They become successful more often.
4 ________ is power. A good education is important.
5 At work, people with a sense of ________ are motivated and optimistic about the future.

GRAMMAR 5.2

Reported speech

I can use reported speech, making appropriate grammatical changes.

1 2.36 SPEAKING **Listen to some people being interviewed for the jobs shown in photos A–C. Would you employ them? Why?/Why not?**

2 2.36 **Read the reports of the interviews in Exercise 1. Rewrite the underlined parts in Direct Speech. Then listen again and check.**

1 We asked the candidate to tell us about his weaknesses. He told us that he wasn't a morning person. In fact, he said he had struggled to get up that morning. He said he would like to start work after lunch.
A: Tell us ___
B: I ___

2 In the interview we said it was a pity that they hadn't had any experience of restaurant work. They told us not to worry and that they were very good at eating. That was why they thought they should get the job.
A: It's a ___
B: Don't ___
C: That ___

3 In the current interview we've just asked the candidate whether she likes the job she has now. She says she doesn't because she has to answer the phone a lot, and she hates that.
A: Do ___
B: No, ___

3 **Read the GRAMMAR FOCUS. Then look at the way the Direct Speech is reported in Exercise 2 and find examples for each rule.**

GRAMMAR FOCUS

Reported Speech

When you report someone's words, remember these rules:

- You usually move the verbs 'one tense back' when your reporting verb is in a past tense (*She said …*).
- You **don't** change the verb form if your reporting verb is in a present tense (*She says …* or *He has told me …*).
- You **don't** change verbs in the Past Perfect or modal verbs such as *would, should, could, might, must*.
- You change pronouns, possessive adjectives and words for time and place if necessary.
- You change the word order in questions and don't use *do, does* or *did*.
- You use the *to* + infinitive to report orders, suggestions, requests and promises.

4 **Harry is preparing for a job interview. Report his parents' comments. Do not change the tense if it isn't necessary.**

1 'You didn't prepare well enough for your last interview.' They said *(that) he hadn't prepared well enough for his previous interview.*
2 'You'll never get a job if you don't have your hair cut.' They said ___
3 'You forgot to clean your shoes last time and they always look at shoes.' They said ___
4 'You should buy a new suit.' They said ___
5 'You mustn't drink too much coffee beforehand because you'll be nervous.' They said ___
6 'Don't worry if you don't get it. Something better might come up.' They've told him ___

5 SPEAKING **Report these interviewers' comments. Do not change the tense if not necessary. Which comments would you be happy with/worried about? Why?**

1 'Did you write this CV?' They asked me *whether/if I had written that CV.*
2 'Don't call us, we'll call you.' They told me ___
3 'I'll be contacting your references tomorrow.' He says ___
4 'Will you be available to start here next month?' They've asked me ___
5 'You're exactly the person we're looking for.' She says ___
6 'Could we give you some advice?' They asked me ___

6 **Complete the reported statements to make them true for you. Compare with a partner.**

1 The last time my friends gave me good advice, they told me ___
2 My brother/sister/friend annoys me when he/she tells me ___
3 I think I'm pretty good/bad at English. My teacher says ___
4 I heard something interesting recently. Somebody told me ___
5 I don't know what I want to do when I leave school. My parents say ___
6 The last person who spoke to me was ___ . He/She said ___

FOCUS VLOG About job interviews

21 **Watch the Focus Vlog. For the worksheet, go to page 141.**

Grammar page 160

5.3 LISTENING

Matching

I can identify details that support a point of view in an interview about jobs.

1 SPEAKING **Discuss which category A–C each job in the box belongs to. Think of three more jobs for each category.**

actor artist body-part maker dentist factory worker fire fighter lawyer office worker politician robot mechanic shop assistant teacher solar panel engineer space tourist guide wind turbine technician writer

A jobs that will always be needed
B jobs that are at risk
C jobs of the future

2 2.37 **Listen to an interview with a data analyst. Compare his findings with your ideas in Exercise 1.**

3 2.37 **Complete the sentences with the words in the box. Then listen again and check.**

constant decline marked rise sharp

1 There's been **a steady** _________ **in** people working from home.
2 There's been **a** _________ **drop in** the number of people commuting to work.
3 The need for jobs in the medical and teaching professions will **remain** _________ .
4 There will be **a** _________ **increase in** jobs connected with alternative energy.
5 There will be **a gradual** _________ **in** jobs in retail, offices and factories.

WORD STORE 5D Phrases describing change

4 2.38 **Complete WORD STORE 5D with the words in the box to describe change. Then listen, check and repeat.**

5 **Look at the graph and describe what was happening in periods A–E. Use the phrases from WORD STORE 5D.**

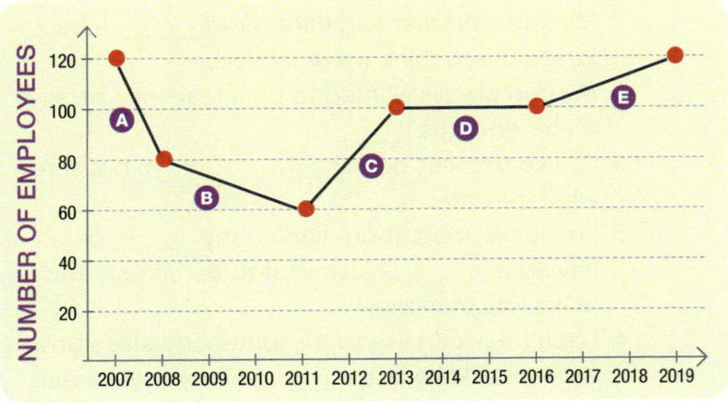

Between 2007 and 2008 there was a sharp decline in the number of employees.

6 SPEAKING **Use the phrases in WORD STORE 5D to describe trends in your country. Think about the ideas in the box.**

cycling to work/school shopping online studying English cost of going out getting married in your twenties living alone using plastic bags

EXAM FOCUS Matching

7 2.39 **Listen to four people talking about their jobs. Match statements A–E with speakers 1–4. There is one extra statement.**

Speaker 1: ☐ Speaker 3: ☐
Speaker 2: ☐ Speaker 4: ☐

The speaker
A is concerned about some elderly people he/she meets at work.
B says that technology has replaced parts of the jobs in his/her industry.
C thinks that it's better to do an apprenticeship than go to university.
D has a hobby that has taught him/her skills that are relevant for his/her job.
E thinks technology allows for more efficiency in his/her job.

8 2.39 **Listen again and answer the questions.**

1 What makes law such a stable profession?
2 Why are law firms now offering apprenticeships?
3 How have dental patients benefited from medical advances?
4 Why is it useful to have good interpersonal skills as a shop assistant?
5 What qualifications and skills do you need to be a wind turbine technician?

9 SPEAKING **Discuss the questions about the future of work.**

1 What other jobs or careers do you think are stable? Which ones are at risk?
2 What are the advantages of working from home compared to commuting to work?
3 What kind of qualifications and skills do you think you'll need for the future?

PRONUNCIATION FOCUS

10 2.40 **Listen and repeat the words said as nouns and as verbs. Mark the stress. Which pairs have different stress patterns?**

~~contract~~ export import increase market recruit review target

a contract/to contract

11 **Take turns to practise the words in Exercise 10. Decide whether your partner is saying a noun or a verb.**

5.4 READING

Multiple choice

I can find specific information in a long text.

1 SPEAKING Discuss the questions.

1 As a child, how did you use to answer this question: *What do you want to be when you grow up?*
2 How would you answer this question now?
3 Is it better to have one or many passions? Why?

2 Look at the title of the blog post. What do you think it is about? Read and check your ideas.

EXAM FOCUS Multiple choice

3 Read the post again. For questions 1–5, choose the correct answer, A, B, C or D.

1 The writer thinks that as we get older we
A tend to lose our imagination.
B find it impossible to make decisions.
C could benefit from career counselling.
D feel pressured to choose a specialisation.

2 In the third paragraph the writer suggests that
A everybody should find a passion and stick to it.
B people refuse to choose a career on purpose.
C people are worried if they don't have one true calling.
D you will never succeed in life unless you find your niche.

3 In the modern workplace, people
A that are curious stay in the same profession.
B can't decide what they want to do.
C are taking responsibility for how they work.
D have fewer opportunities than their parents.

4 In the sixth paragraph the writer's purpose is to show that
A the workplace needs to be modernised.
B the traditional working day is being transformed.
C part-time workers can do several jobs equally well.
D freelancers can choose to be employed or independent.

5 The blog post is about
A the importance of finding your one true calling.
B the negative consequences of being a quitter.
C the best age at which to choose your career.
D people who don't fit neatly into one category.

4 2.42 Match the words and phrases in blue in the blog post with their definitions. Then listen, check and repeat.

1 advice from career experts = career guidance
2 a series of jobs in the same profession = ________
3 a person who gives advice = ________
4 work hours that are not fixed = ________
5 a person who is self-employed = ________
6 one work role carried out by two people = ________
7 a person who doesn't work full-time = ________
8 do well and be successful = ________
9 people who work = ________
10 the place where you work = ________

5 Complete the comments with the words and phrases in Exercise 4 in the correct form.

Sandra, 16

Thanks for this post. I can see now that my problem is that I'm a jack of all trades and master of none! At school I had ¹c______ g______ , but it didn't help me at all. I still don't know what to do at college.

Robert, 18

I agree. The ²c__________ don't really help. It would be more helpful to have counselling once we have some experience and can visualise our future ³c______ p______ more clearly.

Marta, 16

I was really interested in what you're saying about the modern ⁴w__________ being more flexible. I think ⁵j__________ is a great idea – you just have to make sure that communication is really good between both people doing the job.

Paula, 17

Maybe, but I think it's better to work for a big organisation if you want to ⁶t__________ in your career. I don't think you can ever feel like an important part of the workforce if you're a self-employed ⁷f__________ .

James, 17

I don't think I could do the same job day in, day out, even if they had ⁸f__________ in place of rigid nine to five hours. But I can see myself working as a ⁹p__________ in several different jobs.

6 SPEAKING Discuss whether you have similar or different opinions to the people in Exercise 5.

WORD STORE 5E Verb–noun collocations

7 2.43 Complete WORD STORE 5E with the underlined phrases in the blog post. Then listen, check and repeat.

8 SPEAKING Complete the sentences with collocations in WORD STORE 5E. Discuss which sentences are true for you.

1 I wouldn't say I lack ______ . I'm just keeping my options open.
2 My sister/brother and I are wired ______ – it's incredible to think we're related.
3 My dad always wanted to be a teacher – he says it's his one true ______ .
4 I'd like to focus on my ______ , but I'm not sure what they are.
5 I'm not worried about finding my ______ or having a ______ . I just want to be famous and make lots of money!
6 I don't think I'd like to be somebody else's boss, but I would like to be ______ of my own career.

What if you don't have ONE dream job?

2.41

Do you remember being asked what you wanted to be when you grew up? No doubt the more imaginative your answer, the more approval you would get. But once we reach adolescence, there's far less tolerance for answers like, 'I'm going to be a marine biologist, circus clown and journalist!' Now the question translates as *You are allowed one identity in this life, so which is it?*

At school there's pressure to focus on your strengths, and choose a subject to major in at university, which leads to one specific degree, intended for one type of job. The message that you need to specialise is reinforced in many contexts. **Career guidance** books and **counsellors** give you tests to help you find your niche and identify your dream job.

But what happens if you're wired differently? Let's say you're curious about several subjects, and there are many things you'd like to study. If you're unable or unwilling to settle on a single **career path**, you might worry that you don't have one true calling like everybody else and that, therefore, your life lacks purpose. As the saying goes, you're a 'jack of all trades, master of none'.

In reality, few people are just 'one thing'. A rare few have a vocation and stick to it, but for most young people who will make up the **workforce** of the future, 'one thing' is not relevant any more. For our parents' and grandparents' generation, it was normal to work in the same profession and often the same company for thirty or more years. Those days are long gone.

The ambitious young people of today are more interested in moving around and doing different things. In the modern **workplace**, people are working flexibly and the individual is in control of their professional life and in a position to make decisions about how, when and where they work. Rather than finding something and doing it forever, the new challenge is to find a way of working that works for you.

Reflecting the needs of the modern workforce, the workplace is also changing at a rapid rate. Flexible working is becoming the new norm. The standard working day of nine to five has been replaced by **flexitime**. The majority of people no longer believe that attendance in an office is required or necessary on a day-to-day basis. **Job-sharing** is becoming more popular with people who prefer diversity in their working day – work traditionally performed by one person can be split between two **part-timers**. There are also a growing number of **freelancers** choosing self-employment as a way to be in charge of their own professional lives.

This new flexible workplace is one where multipotentialites feel at ease. Multipotentialite is a term invented by Emilie Wapnick, whose TED talk *Why some of us don't have a true calling* has been watched by millions of viewers. She claims to be someone who has a range of interests. She sees herself not as a specialist, but as a generalist, and describes how she used to worry that she wasn't normal because she didn't have a vocation, and so could be dismissed as a quitter, a flake or a jack of all trades, master of none.

She explains how people like herself are suited to the modern workplace in three essential ways. Firstly, they are used to combining two or more fields and it is at the intersection between seemingly unrelated ideas that innovation often happens. Secondly, people who change roles frequently are less afraid of trying new things and stepping out of their comfort zones. They're fast learners. And finally, they are adaptable.

So, if you're a generalist, a polymath, a multipotentialite, or whatever you call yourself, you are the one who will **thrive** in the twenty-first century workplace. The world needs jacks of all trades. And it also needs an updated version of the phrase. How about 'jack of all trades, master of all'?

5.5 GRAMMAR

Reporting verbs

I can use a range of reporting verbs.

1 SPEAKING **Discuss the meaning of the question in the headline. Then read Part 1 of the report and decide what you think the answer is.**

SPOILT BRAT OR NEGLECTED CHILD?

Part 1 US teenager Rachel Canning took her parents to court and tried to sue them for financial support. She accused them of abandoning her when she had turned eighteen and refusing to fund her college education. She claimed that they had thrown her out of her home and explained that she had been living at a friend's house.

Mr Canning refused to accept his daughter's version of events. He denied kicking Rachel out and assured the court that she had left voluntarily after an argument about household rules. He suggested that Rachel's friends had encouraged her to take the matter to court. He insisted that he and his wife loved and missed their child and added that the situation was having a terrible effect on them. He begged his daughter to come home soon.

2 **Look at the six reporting verbs in blue in Exercise 1. Five can be replaced with *said* and one with *told*. Which one and why?**

3 **Read the GRAMMAR FOCUS. Then find five more reporting verbs in the text in Exercise 1. Which verb patterns do they illustrate?**

GRAMMAR FOCUS

Reporting verbs

Verbs without an object

- **verb + *that*:** *add, admit, agree, claim, deny, explain, insist, promise, propose, recommend, suggest*
  She promised that she would come home.
- **verb + *to* + infinitive:** *agree, claim, offer, promise, refuse*
  He offered to help.
- **verb + *-ing*:** *admit, deny, propose, recommend, suggest*
  They suggested talking to the lawyer.
- **verb + preposition + *-ing*:** *apologise for, insist on, object to*
  I insisted on paying for everything.

Verbs with an object

- **verb + object + *that*:** *assure, convince, inform, promise, remind, warn*
  She assured me that she was OK.
- **verb + object + *to* + infinitive:** *advise, beg, convince, encourage, invite, order, persuade, remind, urge, warn (not)*
  He urged them to leave.
- **verb + object + preposition + *-ing*:** *accuse sb of, blame sb for, congratulate sb on, thank sb for*
  He congratulated me on passing the exam.

4 USE OF ENGLISH **Read Part 2 of the report and choose the correct answer, A, B, C or D. Do you agree with the judge's decision?**

Part 2 The judge rejected the teenager's demands, but [1]______ everyone in the court that in future, children may consider suing their parents for a smartphone. The judge [2]______ Rachel and her family to have family counselling. The teenager has [3]______ to return home and the Cannings have [4]______ the media to give the family some privacy while they work things out. The parents have [5]______ to relax the house rules and in return, Rachel has [6]______ them that she won't leave home again.

1	A warned	B explained	C promised	D suggested
2	A denied	B insisted	C advised	D reminded
3	A agreed	B proposed	C reminded	D ordered
4	A refused	B warned	C insisted	D urged
5	A convinced	B offered	C suggested	D told
6	A agreed	B denied	C warned	D promised

5 **Some reporting verbs can have two or more patterns. Report each of these sentences in two different ways.**

1 'I did not kick my daughter out!' Rachel's father denied kicking his daughter out/that he had kicked his daughter out.
2 'We reckon you should take your parents to court.' Rachel's friends suggested ____________.
3 'We have been terribly upset.' Rachel's parents admitted ____________.
4 'You should have some family counselling.' The judge recommended ____________.
5 'OK. We'll relax some of the house rules.' Rachel's parents promised ____________.
6 'All right. I'll move back in.' Rachel agreed ____________.

6 **Complete the sentences with the verbs in the box. Use an appropriate verb pattern and the pronoun *me* as the object if necessary.**

buy have lose not copy owe redecorate

Recently …
1 my friends have persuaded me to have a haircut.
2 my brother has blamed ____________ his camera.
3 a teacher has warned ____________ homework from the Internet.
4 a friend has reminded ____________ him/her some money.
5 my parents have offered ____________ a laptop.
6 Dad has suggested ____________ my bedroom.

7 SPEAKING **Are any of the sentences in Exercise 6 true for you? Use the sentence beginnings to report other things that people have said to you recently.**

Grammar page 161

5.6 SPEAKING

Problem solving

I can discuss problems and solutions, and express annoyance.

1 SPEAKING **Describe what happened last time you experienced one of these problems.**

1 Something was lost or stolen (bag, keys, bike, etc.)
2 Something was broken (computer, car, phone, etc.)
3 Something was forgotten (test, alarm, appointment, etc.)

2 2.44 **Listen to two friends, Hannah and Daniel, discussing a problem and answer the questions.**

1 What was the problem and how did Hannah and Daniel try to solve it?
2 What would be a better solution in your opinion?
3 What do you think might happen next?

3 2.44 **Choose the correct option to complete the SPEAKING FOCUS. Then listen again and check.**

SPEAKING FOCUS

Talking about a problem

What's wrong/the matter?
What's [1]*up / on* (with it)?
I seem/appear to have lost/forgotten/broken …
I haven't (got) a clue./I've no [2]*thought / idea*./I wish I knew.
Every time I try to …, it …
Perhaps there's something wrong/a problem with the …

Talking about a solution

Have you tried … + *-ing*?
It's worth a try/a go, I suppose.
I [3]*doubt / know* it'll/that'll work/help, but let's see.
Problem solved!
No, that doesn't/didn't make any [4]*solution / difference*.

Expressing annoyance

What are we [5]*about / supposed* to do now?
Why on earth did/didn't you …?
How should I [6]*know / think*?
You should have checked/asked first.
You should have thought about that earlier.

4 2.45 **Complete the dialogues with one word in each gap. Sometimes more than one answer is possible. Then listen and check.**

Dialogue 1

Abi and Beth are working in a supermarket during the school holidays.

Abi: What's [1]_________ ?
Beth: Well, unfortunately, I [2]_________ to have broken the bar code scanner.
Abi: Oh no. What happened?
Beth: I put it on the table during the break and spilled my coffee on it – like an idiot!
Abi: Whoops. The manager isn't going to be happy.
Beth: Yeah, tell me about it. [3]_________ time I try to switch it on, it beeps and switches off again.
Abi: Have you [4]_________ drying it under the hand dryer in the toilets?
Beth: Actually no, but it's worth a go, I [5]_________ .

Dialogue 2

Leo is working on his uncle's farm during the summer.

Pete: Hello, Woodtop Farm.
Leo: Uncle Pete, it's me. I'm in the bottom field. The tractor has broken down.
Pete: What? What's the [6]_________ with it?
Leo: Er … I [7]_________ I knew.
Pete: OK. Listen, are the lights working?
Leo: Hang on a second … Yep.
Pete: OK, then it's not the battery. You did remember to put some fuel in it, right?
Leo: Er … oh.
Pete: Leo! I told you it was nearly empty.
Leo: I, er … I forgot. Sorry.
Pete: Well, you'll have to walk back up here and get some, won't you?
Leo: What? It's miles!
Pete: Well, you should have thought about that [8]_________ . Next time, perhaps you'll remember.
Leo: Can't you bring some fuel down in the … hello?

5 SPEAKING **Follow the instructions below to prepare a dialogue. Use the SPEAKING FOCUS to help you.**

As part of a project, you are giving a joint presentation about summer job opportunities in your local area. Together, you prepared a presentation on a laptop.

Student A: You were responsible for bringing a pen drive with all the notes and visuals. The presentation is in twenty minutes, and you have just realised that you left the pen drive at home.

Student B: You worked hard on the presentation and are very annoyed that your partner forgot to bring the pen drive.

There isn't enough time to go home. Together, you need to come up with a solution.

6 **Practise your dialogue and act it out. Take turns to be Student A and Student B.**

ROLE-PLAY Solving problems

23 24 **Watch the video and practise. Then role-play your dialogue.**

5.7 USE OF ENGLISH

Phrasal verbs – advanced points

I can use phrasal verbs with two particles and other advanced phrasal verbs.

1 SPEAKING **List all the social media apps you use. Discuss which are the most popular. How popular is WhatsApp?**

2 **Read the text about WhatsApp. One of the following statements is false. Which one?**

1 Jan Koum, a co-founder of WhatsApp, is from Ukraine.
2 The app is called WhatsApp because it sounds like 'What's up?'
3 Koum was not successful at school or at university in the USA.
4 Koum met Brian Acton, the other co-founder of WhatsApp, at Yahoo.
5 Koum and Acton both got jobs at Facebook in 2007.
6 Koum and Acton sold WhatsApp to Facebook and are now billionaires.

3 **Read and complete the LANGUAGE FOCUS with examples of the three-part phrasal verbs in blue and the underlined nouns and adjectives in the text.**

LANGUAGE FOCUS

Phrasal verbs – advanced points

Three-part phrasal verbs

- Most three-part phrasal verbs are made up of really common verbs like *come, get, put,* etc. plus a variety of adverbial and prepositional particles.
[1]*come up against* (meet or confront), [2]__________ (feel superior to), [3]__________ (compensate for)
- Three-part phrasal verbs are nearly always inseparable.
He came up against bullying. NOT ~~*He came up bullying against.*~~

Word building with phrasal verbs

- **Nouns**
Verb + particle: *clear sth out → a clear-out, let sb down → a* [4]__________ *, warm sth up > a warm-up.* You stress the 'verb' part not the particle.
Particle + verb: *bring sb up → an* [5]__________ *, pour down → a downpour, set out → outset.* You usually stress the 'particle' part not the verb.
- **Adjectives**
Particle + verb -*ing* *put sb off → be off-putting*
Verb (Past Participle) + particle *run sth down → be* [6]__________

4 **Match the remaining three-part phrasal verbs in blue in the text with the definitions. Use a dictionary if necessary.**

1 be the result of = ________
2 think of a new idea = ________
3 leave e.g. a school = ________
4 do sth after = ________
5 develop from sth = ________
6 be very busy with sth = ________

The WhatsApp story

If you use instant messaging services, it's very likely that WhatsApp is one of them. But what do you know about it? Did you know that it was invented by Jan Koum, a Ukrainian-born entrepreneur? After he bought his first iPhone, he got annoyed that he was missing calls when he went to the gym and WhatsApp **grew out of** the simple idea that it's good to let people know if you're available. He **came up with** the name WhatsApp because it sounded like 'What's up?'

There was nothing in Koum's upbringing to suggest that the young Ukrainian would one day change the world of social media. He was brought up in a small village near Kiev. He rarely saw his father who **was** usually **tied up with** work at a government construction company until 10 o'clock at night. But then, when Koum was sixteen, he emigrated to California with his mother and grandmother, while his father stayed behind and never left Ukraine. It was a hard time for the family who lived in very run-down accommodation.

Koum studied computer science and maths, but at school he **came up against** bullying from other boys and often got into trouble. In Ukraine Koum had left behind his close group of friends; now he **looked down on** the casual friendships that people had at high school in America and he eventually **dropped out of** college.

Things changed when he got a job at Yahoo in the early 2000s. First he met Brian Acton, who would **go on to** co-found WhatsApp. When Koum and Acton left Yahoo in 2007, they applied for jobs at Facebook. Both were turned down.

Following rejection from Facebook, the two friends decided to go travelling in South America, and it was when they returned to the USA that they co-founded WhatsApp. The app didn't take off straight away, which was a real letdown for Koum and Acton. However, by 2014 it had more than 400 million users globally. In the end, the huge success of WhatsApp **came down to** the excellent user experience. Facebook paid more than $19 billion to acquire WhatsApp, which more than **made up for** their earlier rejection, turning both Koum and Acton into billionaires.

Jan Koum (right) and Brian Acton (left), co-founders of WhatsApp

5 **Match eight more common three-part phrasal verbs with their definitions.**

1 keep up with sb ☐
2 get on with sb ☐
3 get out of ☐
4 get round to ☐
5 look up to sb ☐
6 put up with sth/sb ☐
7 run out of sth ☐
8 stand up for sth ☐

a admire and respect
b avoid
c use all of sth and have nothing left
d stay at the same level as
e defend
f find time to
g tolerate
h be friends with

6 **Complete the three-part phrasal verbs in the sentences with the correct forms of *come*, *get*, *make* or *put*.**

1 To become rich, you only have to ________ up with one good idea.
2 I ________ on really well with my work colleagues, we are quite a team!
3 Being successful in a job ________ down to hard work – that's all.
4 An interesting job that you love doing can ________ up for a low salary.
5 It's important to keep your social media profile updated, but most people don't ________ round to it.
6 Rich people always try to ________ out of paying their taxes.
7 Wage discrimination isn't a thing of the past; women ________ up against it all the time.
8 You can't choose your work colleagues. If you don't get on, you just have to ________ up with them.

7 SPEAKING **Discuss the statements in Exercise 6. Which ones do you agree with? Give reasons for your answers.**

8 **Complete the second sentence so that it has a similar meaning to the first. Use the noun or adjective form of the underlined phrasal verb.**

1 I was brought up in a similar way to my parents.
I had ________________________
2 Yesterday it poured down on my way home from school.
Yesterday there was ________________________
3 I always warm up before I do any sport.
I like to do ________________________
4 I need to clear out all the junk in my bedroom.
I need to have ________________________
5 Background music puts me off when I am trying to study.
I find background music ________________________
6 If I dropped out of college, my parents would never forgive me.
If I became ________________________

SHOW WHAT YOU'VE LEARNT UNITS 1–5

9 USE OF ENGLISH **Complete the message with one word in each gap.**

Dee
Published 1 hour ago

Dear All,

This is to announce that I've decided to give up social media (no, it's not a joke). I'm just completely fed up with it. Over the last five years I've spent a great 1________ of time and energy on posting, reading, liking and commenting. But now push notifications are driving me mad! I just can't put 2________ with it any longer. I'm also fed up with all my 3________ acquaintances. Over the years, I've 4________ to collect 3,000 friends on social media, but 5________ of them visited me when I was ill – not one! Last, but not least, I'm so busy on social media that I can't 6________ down to any serious school work. It feels like if I don't stop now, I'll 7________ out of school! So, this is my last post.

CU 8________ – in the real world!

Dee

431

10 SPEAKING **Imagine you decided to give up social media. Discuss the questions.**

1 What would be the advantages/disadvantages?
2 What would you miss most/least?
3 How long would you be able to manage without social media?

Use of English page 162

5.8 WRITING

An opinion essay

I can write an opinion essay exploring different aspects of viewpoints.

1 SPEAKING Look at the results of an international student survey about reasons for going to university. Then answer the questions and discuss with a partner.

1 Which three reasons are most important to you?
2 What other reasons to go to university can you think of?
3 Should students choose a degree based on what they are interested in or what is most likely to lead to getting a job? Explain your answer.

Why do you want to go to university?

I want to go to university because:

I want to continue my education and development	58.4%
I am really keen on the subject I want to study	57.9%
this is necessary for my future career	53.7%
I need stimulation and intellectual challenge	52.7%
I want to learn some necessary life skills	50.1%
this will help me find a job (or a better job)	36.1%
I want to experience student life and just have fun	22.8%
my family expects me to continue my education	16.3%

2 Read the task and the essay below. Do you agree with the author's opinion?

Some university degrees are more likely to lead to employment after graduation than others. In your opinion, should young people choose a university subject based on what will help them get a good job rather than what interests them?
Write an opinion essay on this topic analysing the importance of motivation to study and career success.

3 Read the WRITING FOCUS. In the model essay, find:

1 a sentence which states the writer's main opinion.
2 a sentence that says which two aspects will be discussed.
3 a sentence which acknowledges an opposing opinion and states why the writer disagrees with it.
4 a sentence which expands the discussion by giving examples.
5 a sentence which restates the writer's main opinion.
6 a final comment.

Many school-leavers choose a degree based on what is likely to lead to a good job rather than what truly interests them. Personally, I worry this could lead to a negative experience at university and that it may be better to opt for a subject you find stimulating. To explain the reasons for my view, I will examine the issue in terms of motivation and career success.

When it comes to motivation, there is no doubt that four years is a long time to dedicate to a single subject. The high level of commitment required means that enthusiasm for your chosen subject is important. The outcome of struggling through a course you don't enjoy could be low final grades and a negative student experience.

It is also important to consider this issue with regard to career success. It is often the case that those who rise to the very top of their field get there because they are passionate about what they do. Of course, passion does not guarantee career success, but it is undeniably an important factor.

It is true that some subjects appear to offer limited career prospects, however, I am of the opinion that studying for any degree teaches valuable transferable skills. These include the ability to interpret information or communicate complex ideas, for example, and are undoubtedly appreciated by employers.

All in all, I think it is better to choose a university subject that interests you. I would prefer to learn useful skills and work towards high grades in a subject I have enjoyed studying rather than risking low grades in a subject that I do not find motivating.

4 Complete the WRITING FOCUS with the words and phrases in purple in the essay.

WRITING FOCUS

An opinion essay

Introduction

- Introduce the topic and state your main opinion.
- Say which two (or more) points of view or aspects will be discussed.

  To explain the [1]*reasons for my view, I will examine the issue in* [2]______ *of …*

  It is my intention to explore this issue from the viewpoint of …

  This essay will look at this question from the perspective of …

Paragraphs 2 and 3

- Discuss different aspects of the issue and support the main opinion you stated in the introduction.

  When it [3]______ *to …*

  It is also important to consider this issue with [4]______ *to …*

  Another important angle on/aspect of this issue is …

- Expand the discussion by giving examples.

Paragraph 4

- Acknowledge an opposing opinion and say why you disagree with it.

  It is [5]______ *that …, however, I am of the* [6]______ *that …*

  While some people say …, I …

  Some people do not agree and feel that …

Conclusion

- Use a linking phrase to introduce a conclusion.

  In conclusion,/To sum up,/All things considered,/[7]______

- Restate your main opinion.
- Include a final comment.

5 Choose the correct option.

1 It is my *reason / intention* to explore this issue from the viewpoint of both employers and job-seekers.
2 This essay will look at this question from the *perspective / opinion* of an international student.
3 Another important *aspect / angle* on this issue is parental expectations.
4 *While / True* a few lucky people earn a living doing very little, most of us have to work hard to do well.
5 Some people do not *question / agree* and say it's better to study something you think will be easy.
6 All things *concluded / considered*, it is more important to find a good job.

6 Complete the questions with the unerlined words in the essay. Then answer them and compare your ideas with a partner.

1 Which school subjects do you find most ______ ?
2 Which school subjects require the highest ______ ?
3 Which valuable ______ could you learn from studying overseas?
4 Which university subjects offer limited ______ ?
5 Apart from going to university, what other options do ______ have?

7 Read the LANGUAGE FOCUS. Which structures are used in the essay?

LANGUAGE FOCUS

Expressing certainty and describing consequences

Use the following structures to express certainty and describe consequences in a formal way.

- **Expressing certainty**

  Undeniably/Undoubtedly, …

  It's undeniable that/There is no doubt that …

  Without (a) doubt, …

- **Describing consequences**

  The result/consequence/outcome of (such a decision/ choice) could be that …

  As a result/consequence, …

  This could lead to/result in …

8 Rewrite the statements. Use the words in brackets and the LANGUAGE FOCUS. Which of the statements do you agree with?

1 The average secondary student in my country is short of money. (undoubtedly)
2 Employers in my country value work experience as highly as qualifications. (without)
3 Young people can learn some very useful skills by working part time. (doubt)
4 Succeeding at school is more important than earning a bit of extra cash. (undeniable)
5 Having a part-time job teaches you to be more responsible. (undeniably)

9 Complete statements 1–4 with a word from the LANGUAGE FOCUS. Use each word only once.

1 Not gaining experience through a part-time job could ______ in a very bare CV.
2 The ______ of working part-time while you are at school is less time for homework.
3 Focusing on schoolwork only could ______ to better final grades.
4 ______ a result of having a part time job, students gain valuable work experience.

SHOW WHAT YOU'VE LEARNT

10 Do the writing task. Use the ideas in the WRITING FOCUS, the LANGUAGE FOCUS and Exercises 8 and 9 to help you.

More and more young people do weekend or part-time jobs while at secondary school. Is this a good idea or should young people focus exclusively on their school work? Write an essay in which you analyse the consequences of having a part-time job on a person's education and their career prospects.

- Say in the introduction which two aspects will be discussed and state your opinion.
- Support your opinion with examples and acknowledge an opposing opinion.
- Add a conclusion.

5.1 Vocabulary 4.33

achieve a goal /əˌtʃiːv ə ˈgəʊl/
burn out /ˌbɜːn ˈaʊt/
carry out /ˌkæri ˈaʊt/
commit to /kəˈmɪt tə/
conscientious /ˌkɒnʃiˈenʃəs/
conscientiousness /ˌkɒntʃiˈentʃəsnəs/
develop a habit /dɪˌveləp ə ˈhæbɪt/
do sth day in, day out /ˌduː ˌsʌmθɪŋ ˈdeɪ ɪn ˌdeɪ aʊt/
employment possibilities /ɪmˌplɔɪmənt ˌpɒsəˈbɪlɪtiz/
enter the job market /ˌentə ðə ˈdʒɒb ˌmɑːkət/
enthusiasm /ɪnˈθjuːziæzəm/
enthusiastic /ɪnˌθjuːziˈæstɪk/
fulfil an objective /fʊlˈfɪl ən əbˈdʒektɪv/
get down to /get daʊn tə/
goal /gəʊl/
improve your career prospects /ɪmˌpruːv jə kəˈrɪə ˌprɒspekts/
increase your output /ɪnˌkriːs jər ˈaʊtpʊt/
keep at /kiːp ət/
knowledge /ˈnɒlɪdʒ/
knowledgeable /ˈnɒlɪdʒəbəl/
map sth out /mæp ˌsʌmθɪŋ aʊt/
objective /əbˈdʒektɪv/
outline /ˈaʊtlaɪn/
overwork /ˌəʊvəˈwɜːk/
overworked /ˌəʊvəˈwɜːkt/
pick up a new skill /ˌpɪk ˌʌp ə njuː ˈskɪl/
punctual /ˈpʌŋktʃuəl/
punctuality /ˌpʌŋktʃuˈæləti/
purpose /ˈpɜːpəs/
purposeful /ˈpɜːpəsfəl/
put a lot of effort into /ˌpʊt ə lɒt əv ˈefət ˌɪntə/
put sth off /ˌpʊt ˌsʌmθɪŋ ˈɒf/
put your heart into sth /ˌpʊt jə ˈhɑːt ˌɪntə ˌsʌmθɪŋ/
reach your full potential /ˌriːtʃ jə fʊl pəˈtenʃəl/
set sth out /ˌset ˌsʌmθɪŋ ˈaʊt/
single-minded /ˌsɪŋgəl ˈmaɪndɪd/
single-mindedness /ˌsɪŋgəl ˈmaɪndɪdnəs/
skilled /skɪld/
speak your mind /ˌspiːk jə ˈmaɪnd/
take sth up /ˌteɪk ˌsʌmθɪŋ ˈʌp/
think for yourself /ˌθɪŋk fə jɔːˈself/
time management /ˈtaɪm ˌmænɪdʒmənt/
to-do list /tə ˈduː ˌlɪst/
work to a deadline /ˌwɜːk tə ə ˈdedlaɪn/
work towards /ˌwɜːk təˈwɔːdz/

5.2 Grammar 4.34

answer the phone /ˈɑːnsə ðə ˌfəʊn/
interview /ˈɪntəvjuː/
references /ˈrɛfrənsɪz/
struggle to do sth /ˈstrʌgl tə ˌduː ˌsʌmθɪŋ/
weakness /ˈwiːknəs/

5.3 Listening 4.35

alternative energy /ɔːlˌtɜːnətɪv ˈenədʒi/
applied science /əˌplaɪd ˈsaɪəns/
be at risk /bi ət ˈrɪsk/
be constant/unchanged /bi ˈkɒnstənt/ʌnˈtʃeɪndʒd/
benefit /ˈbenəfɪt/
commute to work /kəˌmjuːt tə ˈwɜːk/
concerned about /kənˈsɜːnd əˈbaʊt/
dental patient /ˌdentl ˈpeɪʃənt/
do an apprenticeship /ˌduː ən əˈprentəsʃɪp/
elderly /ˈeldəli/
fulfilling /fʊlˈfɪlɪŋ/
gradual drop/decline in /ˌgrædʒuəl ˈdrɒp/dɪˈklaɪn ɪn/
gradual rise/increase in /ˌgrædʒuəl ˈraɪz/ˈɪnkriːs ɪn/
graduate /ˈgrædʒuət/
growing number /ˌgrəʊɪŋ ˈnʌmbə/
handle sb /ˈhændl ˌsʌmbədi/
high-powered job /ˌhaɪ ˈpaʊəd dʒɒb/
lucrative /ˈluːkrətɪv/
marked rise/increase in /ˌmɑːkt ˈraɪz/ˈɪnkriːs ɪn/
medical advances /ˌmedɪkəl ədˈvɑːnsɪz/
rapid drop/decline in /ˌræpɪd ˈdrɒp/dɪˈklaɪn ɪn/
recruit /rɪˈkruːt/
relevant /ˈreləvənt/
remain constant/unchanged /rɪˌmeɪn ˈkɒnstənt/ʌnˈtʃeɪndʒd/
replace /rɪˈpleɪs/
retail /ˈriːteɪl/
secure /sɪˈkjʊə/
sharp drop/decline in /ˌʃɑːp ˈdrɒp/dɪˈklaɪn ɪn/
sharp rise/increase in /ˌʃɑːp ˈraɪz/ˈɪnkriːs ɪn/
stable /ˈsteɪbəl/
steady drop/decline in /ˌstedi ˈdrɒp/dɪˈklaɪn ɪn/
steady rise/increase in /ˌstedi ˈraɪz/ˈɪnkriːs ɪn/
take sth over /ˌteɪk ˌsʌmθɪŋ ˈəʊvə/
take sth apart /ˌteɪk ˌsʌmθɪŋ əˈpɑːt/
tedious /ˈtiːdiəs/
trainee /ˌtreɪˈniː/
wind turbine /ˈwɪnd ˌtɜːbaɪn/

5.4 Reading 4.36

adaptable /əˈdæptəbəl/
approval /əˈpruːvəl/
at a rapid rate /ət ə ˌræpɪd ˈreɪt/
attendance in the office /əˈtendəns ɪn ði ˌɒfɪs/
be in charge /bi ɪn ˈtʃɑːdʒ/
be suited to /bi ˈsuːtɪd tə/
be wired differently /bi ˈwaɪəd ˌdɪfrəntli/
career guidance /kəˈrɪə ˌgaɪdəns/
career path /kəˈrɪə ˌpɑːθ/
combine /kəmˈbaɪn/
counsellor /ˈkaʊnsələ/
curious about /ˈkjʊəriəs əˌbaʊt/
dismiss sb as /dɪsˈmɪs ˌsʌmbɒdi əz/
diversity /daɪˈvɜːsəti/
essential /ɪˈsenʃəl/
find your niche /ˌfaɪnd jə ˈniːʃ/
flake /fleɪk/
flexitime/flexible working /ˈfleksitaɪm/ ˈfleksəbəl ˌwɜːkɪŋ/
focus on your strengths /ˌfəʊkəs ɒn jə ˈstreŋθs/
freelancer /ˈfriːˌlɑːnsə/
have a vocation /ˌhæv ə vəʊˈkeɪʃən/
have one true calling /ˌhæv wʌn ˌtruː ˈkɔːlɪŋ/
identify /aɪˈdentɪfaɪ/
imaginative /ɪˈmædʒənətɪv/
intersection /ˌɪntəˈsekʃən/
jack of all trades, master of none /ˌdʒæk əv ɔːl ˈtreɪdz ˌmɑːstər əv ˈnʌn/
job-sharing /ˈdʒɒb ˌʃeərɪŋ/
keep your options open /ˌkiːp jɔːr ˌɒpʃənz ˈəʊpən/
lack purpose /ˌlæk ˈpɜːpəs/
multipotentialite / ˈmʌltɪpəˌtenʃɪˈælaɪt/
on a day-to-day basis /ɒn ə ˌdeɪ tə ˌdeɪ ˈbeɪsɪs/
part-timer /ˌpɑːt ˈtaɪmə/
polymath /ˈpɒlɪmæθ/
quitter /ˈkwɪtə/
range of interests /ˌreɪndʒ əv ˈɪntrəsts/
reflect the need /rɪˌflekt ðə ˈniːd/
reinforce /ˌriːənˈfɔːs/
rigid /ˈrɪdʒɪd/
seemingly /ˈsiːmɪŋli/
self-employment /self ɪmˈplɔɪmənt/
settle on /ˈsetl ɒn/
split the work /ˌsplɪt ðə ˈwɜːk/
step out of your comfort zone /ˌstep aʊt əv jə ˈkʌmfət ˌzəʊn/
stick to /stɪk tə/
thrive /θraɪv/
unrelated /ˌʌnrɪˈleɪtɪd/
unwilling /ʌnˈwɪlɪŋ/
work flexibly /ˌwɜːk ˈfleksəbli/
workforce /ˈwɜːkfɔːs/
workplace /ˈwɜːkpleɪs/

5.5 Grammar 4.37

abandon /əˈbændən/
add /æd/
admit /ədˈmɪt/

apologise /ə'pɒlədʒaɪz/
assure /ə'ʃʊə/
beg /beg/
blame /bleɪm/
brat /bræt/
claim /kleɪm/
congratulate /kən'grætʃəleɪt/
convince /kən'vɪns/
demand /dɪ'mɑːnd/
deny /dɪ'naɪ/
encourage /ɪn'kʌrɪdʒ/
explain /ɪk'spleɪn/
family counselling /ˌfæməli 'kaʊnsəlɪŋ/
financial support /ˌfə'nænʃəl sə'pɔːt/
fund /fʌnd/
household rules /ˌhaʊshəʊld 'ruːlz/
insist /ɪn'sɪst/
neglected /nɪ 'glektɪd/
object /əb'dʒekt/
order /'ɔːdə/
persuade /pə'sweɪd/
reckon /'rekən/
remind /rɪ'maɪnd/
relax the rules /rɪˌlæks ðə 'ruːlz/
spoilt /spɔɪlt/
sue sb /'sjuː ˌsʌmbɒdi/
suggest /sə'dʒest/
take sb to court /ˌteɪk ˌsʌmbɒdi tə 'kɔːt/
turn eighteen /ˌtɜːn eɪ'tiːn/
urge /ɜːdʒ/
voluntarily /'vɒləntərəli/
warn /wɔːn/
work things out /ˌwɜːk ˌθɪŋz 'aʊt/

5.6 Speaking 4.38

battery /'bætəri/
break off /ˌbreɪk 'ɒf/
fuel /'fjuːəl/
have no clue /ˌhæv nəʊ 'kluː/
it's worth a try /ɪts ˌwɜːθ ə 'traɪ/
lock /lɒk/
on purpose /ɒn 'pɜːpəs/
solution /sə'luːʃən/
solve a problem /ˌsɒlv ə 'prɒbləm/
spill /spɪl/
switch sth on/off /ˌswɪtʃ ˌsʌmθɪŋ 'ɒn/'ɒf/

5.7 Use of English 4.39

acquire /ə'kwaɪə/
be tied up with /bi ˌtaɪd 'ʌp wɪð/
bring sb up /ˌbrɪŋ ˌsʌmbɒdi 'ʌp/
casual /'kæʒuəl/
clear-out /'klɪəraʊt/
come down to /ˌkʌm 'daʊn tə/
come up against /ˌkʌm ʌp ə'genst/
come up with /ˌkʌm 'ʌp wɪð/
downpour /'daʊnpɔː/
drop out of /ˌdrɒp 'aʊt əv/
dropout /'drɒpaʊt/
entrepreneur /ˌɒntrəprə'nɜː/
get on with /ˌget 'ɒn wɪð/
get out of /ˌget 'aʊt əv/
get round to /ˌget 'raʊnd tə/
grow out of /ˌgrəʊ 'aʊt əv/
keep up with /ˌkiːp 'ʌp wɪð/
leave sb behind /ˌliːv ˌsʌmbɒdi bɪ'haɪnd/
letdown /'letdaʊn/
look down on /ˌlʊk 'daʊn ɒn/
look up to /ˌlʊk 'ʌp tə/
make up for /ˌmeɪk 'ʌp fə/
off-putting /'ɒfˌpʊtɪŋ/
outset /'aʊtset/
put up with /ˌpʊt 'ʌp wɪð/
rejection /rɪ'dʒekʃən/
run out of /ˌrʌn 'aʊt əv/
run-down /ˌrʌn 'daʊn/
stand up for /ˌstænd 'ʌp fə/
take off /ˌteɪk 'ɒf/
upbringing /'ʌpˌbrɪŋɪŋ/
warm-up /'wɔːm ʌp/

5.8 Writing 4.40

acknowledge /ək'nɒlɪdʒ/
appreciated /ə'priːʃɪeɪtɪd/
examine/explore an issue /ɪgˌzæmɪn/ ɪkˌsplɔːr ən 'ɪʃuː/
in terms of /ɪn 'tɜːmz əv/
intention /ɪn'tenʃən/
lead to /'liːd tə/
level of commitment /ˌlevəl əv kə'mɪtmənt/
limited /'lɪmɪtɪd/
outcome /'aʊtkʌm/
question /'kwestʃən/
school-leaver /ˌskuːl 'liːvə/
stimulating /'stɪmjəleɪtɪŋ/
survey /'sɜːveɪ/
transferable skills /trænsˌfɜːrəbəl 'skɪlz/
undeniably /ˌʌndɪ'naɪəbli/
viewpoint /'vjuːpɔɪnt/
with regard to /wɪð rɪ'gɑːd tə/

MY WORD LIST

EMPLOYMENT	DESCRIBING CHANGE	OTHER

FOCUS REVIEW 5

VOCABULARY AND GRAMMAR

1 Complete the sentences with the correct form of the words in the box. There are two extra words.

carry find improve put reach speak thrive

1 I think Chris will need to move to a bigger company if he's going to ___________ his full potential.
2 Robots are being used increasingly to ___________ out simple, repetitive tasks.
3 If you can respond to an email quickly, then do it right away rather than ___________ it off until later.
4 He took a short project management course to try and ___________ his career prospects.
5 Sometimes you have to be diplomatic, but occasionally you need to ___________ your mind.

2 Complete the sentences with the correct form of the words in capitals.

1 We want to see that candidates are ___________ (**ENTHUSIASM**) about the wildlife.
2 She was clearly ___________ (**KNOWLEDGE**) about all aspects of video production.
3 A lot of work is done by ___________ (**FREELANCE**) who work on specific projects.
4 In an interview, you should try and focus on your ___________ (**STRONG**).
5 In recent years, there's been a ___________ (**MARK**) increase in jobs related to social media.

3 Complete the second sentence so that it has a similar meaning to the first. Use Reported Speech.

1 'You should take a few days off,' the manager said.
The manager said that I ___________ a few days off.
2 'I've been working here for ten years,' Olivia told them.
Olivia said ___________ for ten years.
3 'What's your home address?' the man asked.
The man asked him ___________ .
4 'When are you going to look for a permanent post?' my parents keep asking me.
My parents keep asking me ___________ a permanent post.
5 'Send a copy of your CV to head office,' the store manager told me.
The store manager told me ___________ to head office.

4 Complete the sentences with the correct form of the words in brackets. Use up to five words in each gap and make any changes necessary.

1 The other day my mum's boss (refuse/give/she) ___________ a pay rise.
2 Our new interpreter (suggest/make/few/change) ___________ in the speech so that it would sound more natural.
3 The management (thank/team/work) ___________ so hard.
4 My team leader (convince/I/sign up) ___________ for a training course.
5 Last month my dad (offer/show/I/class) ___________ around different departments in his company.

USE OF ENGLISH

5 Read the text. Choose the correct answer, A, B, C or D.

When I left school, I didn't have a(n) [1]___ what I wanted to do as a career. I was quite good at Science, so I decided to study Physics at university. I knew it was the wrong choice though right from the [2]___ . I enjoyed the social side of university and I [3]___ the other students on my course, but I really struggled with the coursework. I tried to be disciplined and work hard, but it didn't make any [4]___ . Physics just wasn't my thing. Soon my tutor noticed that I wasn't [5]___ my classmates and called me in for a chat. She was really understanding. I explained that I was thinking about [6]___ university, but she suggested I look at other options first. She [7]___ the idea that I could sit in on lectures in different subjects to see if any of them might suit me better. I went to some Chemistry and Biology lectures, which didn't really spark my interest, but then I went along to an Engineering class and realised I'd found my [8]___ . I switched courses and I've never looked back!

1 **A** clue **B** idea **C** thought **D** knowledge
2 **A** clear-out **B** downturn **C** letdown **D** outset
3 **A** got out of **B** came up with **C** got on with **D** looked down on
4 **A** change **B** difference **C** solution **D** progress
5 **A** coming up against **B** putting up with **C** keeping up with **D** getting round to
6 **A** standing up for **B** running out of **C** growing out of **D** dropping out of
7 **A** made up for **B** came up with **C** came up against **D** looked up to
8 **A** hole **B** niche **C** corner **D** focus

6 Complete the second sentence using the word in capitals so that it has a similar meaning to the first. Use up to five words in each gap, but do not change the word in capitals.

1 'A scholarship in Brussels?! Fantastic! Well done, Amanda!' Robert said. **CONGRATULATED**
Robert ___________ getting a scholarship in Brussels.
2 'I wouldn't apply for that job', Marion told me. **ADVISED**
Marion ___________ apply for that job.
3 'Did you practise to become a fitness instructor?', she asked. **HAD**
She asked me ___________ become a fitness instructor.
4 Choosing a career is undeniably one of the most challenging decisions you face in life. **DOUBT**
Choosing a career is ___________ one of the most challenging decisions you face in life.

READING

7 Read the text. Choose the correct answer, A, B, C or D.

The Human Scarecrow

Being told to bring a deckchair and a good book for the first day in a new job might not be the kind of advice you'd expect to receive from your new boss, but that's exactly the advice Jamie Fox was given when he took up a post to help out a local farmer.

Fox, aged twenty-two, a recent music graduate from Bangor University, uses a range of musical instruments to scare off partridges that have been destroying crops because ordinary scarecrows don't quite seem up to the job. Despite working from 7:30 a.m. to 4:00 p.m. for a minimum wage, Fox, who is saving up to finance a trip next year to New Zealand, is quite content with his unique position. Indeed, he'd much rather be out in the open air reading and playing instruments, he says, and time passes much quicker than sitting at home doing nothing and claiming unemployment benefit.

Fox can do anything he likes to pass the time. As well as playing musical instruments and reading to relieve the monotony, other perks of the job include doing Sudoku puzzles, observing the wildlife and daydreaming. He does, however, need to get out of the comfort of his chair occasionally to scare the partridges off the fields. And although the work is far from lucrative, some of Jamie's friends, including those with more generously paid jobs, are reportedly envious of his position and the fact that he spends the best part of the day doing largely as he pleases.

His employer, farmer William Youngs, claims that he was forced to take someone on as a human scarecrow after partridges didn't respond to more traditional methods of frightening them away. Since losing thirty acres worth of crops to the birds at a cost of thousands of pounds, Youngs has tried a variety of approaches to protect his livelihood. Now, however, he is happy with the solution and claims that Jamie's presence in the fields is proving very effective and making a real difference.

1 Jamie Fox's plans include
   - **A** joining a band.
   - **B** becoming a farmer.
   - **C** travelling abroad.
   - **D** earning more money.

2 Jamie Fox is happy with his job because
   - **A** he never gets bored.
   - **B** he uses his educational background.
   - **C** he has plenty of free time during the day.
   - **D** he thinks it is better than being out of work.

3 What is true about Jamie's job?
   - **A** He doesn't need to move.
   - **B** He has replaced another person.
   - **C** He gets uncomfortable.
   - **D** He makes a lot of noise.

4 Jamie's friends are envious because of
   - **A** the hours he works.
   - **B** the nature of his work.
   - **C** the money he earns.
   - **D** the variety of his tasks.

5 Mr Youngs decided to employ Jamie because
   - **A** he can pay him a low wage.
   - **B** he has been using human scarecrows for a long time.
   - **C** he had lost lots of crops previously.
   - **D** he wants to help with the problem of unemployment.

SPEAKING

8 Ask and answer the questions.

1. What types of part-time jobs are offered to teens in your area?
2. Would you like to set up your own business? Why?/Why not?
3. What can a young person do to be successful on the job market?
4. Is it better to choose a job that you like doing or one which has a good salary?
5. Some famous people, like footballers, earn very high salaries. Is this a good thing? Why?/Why not?

WRITING

9 Read this announcement on an international students' website and write an article in reply.

Gap year students, we want articles!

- Are you considering taking a year off before university or have you already done this?
- Write an article for our magazine about your plans for a gap year or your experiences. How can a gap year help or hinder your education?
- The best articles will be published in the next edition.

6

A matter of fact

Never let the truth get in the way of a good story.
Mark Twain

BBC

IS SOCIAL MEDIA KILLING CREATIVITY?

25 Watch the BBC video.
For the worksheet, go to page 142.

6.1 VOCABULARY

The media • truth and falsehood • adjective–noun collocations • adverbs

I can talk about the media and fake news.

SHOW WHAT YOU KNOW

1 Complete the sentences with the words in the box. Then write about your media habits. Use the sentences or your own ideas.

clips ~~media~~ podcasts post Twitter

1 I get news from **news apps/social** _*media*_ **posts/local papers**.
2 If I see something interesting, I **'like'/share/** ________ **/retweet** it.
3 I like to read **news blogs/celebrity** ________ **feeds/editorials**.
4 I like to watch **TV drama series/online video** ________ **/reality TV**.
5 I like to listen to ________ **/the radio/music streaming services**.

2 SPEAKING Compare your sentences in Exercise 1. Discuss how similar/different your habits are to your partner's.

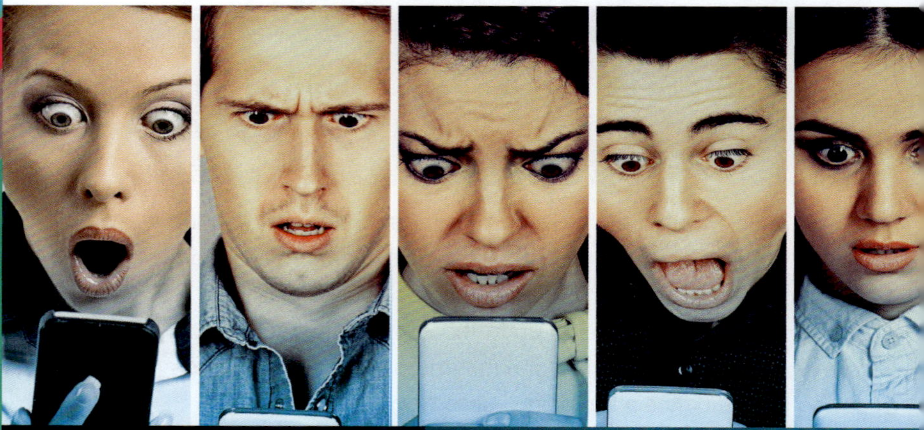

FAKE NEWS

What is it?

Completely made-up stories presented as news and made to go viral, often for politically motivated reasons or commercial gain. Fake news stories are 70 percent more likely to be retweeted because they are usually more eye-catching than the truth. Some people **spread fake news** deliberately while others do it without realising. The Internet is awash with information that cannot be trusted. The smartphone generation are bombarded with such information practically on a daily basis and they're growing up alarmingly misinformed.

How do you know what you're reading is accurate?

Don't **take a story at face value** – step back and ask yourself these questions:

- *Does the story come from a reputable source?* Has this website always shown a clear commitment to newsworthy stories based on fact? Alternatively, is this an article put out knowingly by an organisation that **has an agenda** – an agenda to **manipulate the media** because of a political or commercial motive?
- *Does the photo or video look normal?* If it looks slightly odd, it may have been **tampered with** to **distort the truth** and **mislead people** into believing something that never actually happened.

3 SPEAKING Look at the three news headlines and discuss which one you think is true. Then read the article and check your ideas.

1 **American woman adopts alien baby!**
SPACE BABY SURVIVES UFO CRASH
'I couldn't resist its big sad eyes,' says woman from Ohio.

2 **5 million euros lottery winner leaves winnings on bus**
Joe Smith appeals to public: 'I was going to buy my mum a new house.'

3 **WOMAN BURST INTO FLAMES DURING AN OPERATION!**
Spark ignites cleaning solution and patient becomes ball of fire.

4 Read the article again and answer the questions.

1 Why is fake news usually created?
2 How can we check the reliability of a news source?
3 In what way can images suggest that news is fake?
4 What do your instincts have to do with spotting fake news?

5 SPEAKING Did any information in the article surprise you? What do you do to make sure that what you are reading is true?

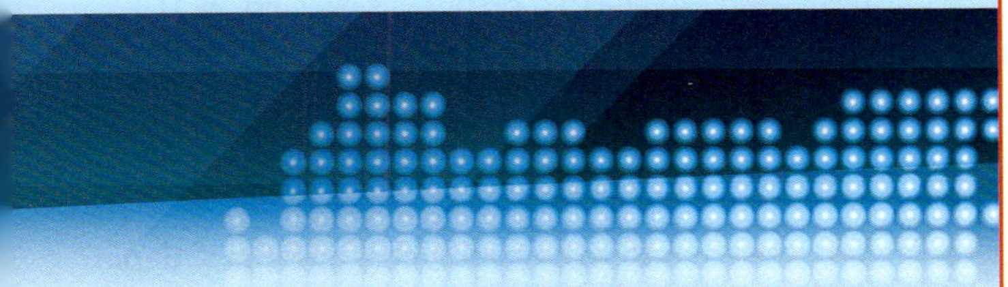

- *Is this story likely to be true?* There are different ways in which a story can be inaccurate or misleading. Start from your gut feeling, **trust your instincts** – does it *sound* believable? American woman adopts alien baby is clearly fake news. But how about the lottery winner? Would he really carry 5 million euros in cash on a bus? Then there's the story of a person bursting into flames. Unbelievable, right? Not exactly – you can **check the accuracy** of this story by searching online where you find out that fires in operating theatres are remarkably common! In fact, the third story is the only true story.

What can you do?

Social media giants have a responsibility to tackle the problem of fake news, but in an era when anyone with an Internet connection can publish stories freely and without any checks, individuals need to learn how to **double-check facts** and **evaluate sources.** In other words, it is essential to read information critically: you should question facts and examine arguments closely, instead of believing everything you read.

Go to WORD STORE 6 page 13

WORD STORE 6A Truth and falsehood

6 3.1 Complete WORD STORE 6A with the verbs in red in the text. Then listen, check and repeat.

7 Complete the questions with one word in each gap. Then answer the questions according to the information in the text.

1 Do people always spread ______ news on purpose?
2 Can you trust your ______ when deciding whether a story is true?
3 What motivates organisations who have an ______ to manipulate the ______ ?
4 What things are sometimes tampered ______ to mislead ______ ?
5 Where can you check the ______ of a story?
6 Who is responsible for identifying people who distort the ______?
7 Why should people learn how to double-check ______ and evaluate ______?

WORD STORE 6B Adjective–noun collocations

8 3.2 Complete WORD STORE 6B with the underlined phrases in the text in the correct form. Then listen, check and repeat.

9 Are the pairs of collocations in WORD STORE 6B similar or different in meaning? Use a dictionary to check your answers.

10 Complete the sentences with an appropriate word in WORD STORE 6B. Are the sentences true for you?

1 I hate being bombarded with so much useless _________ on a daily _________ .
2 I never take anything I read at face value unless it is from a reputable _________ .
3 I have a gut _________ that print-based media will disappear within ten years.
4 I would never make a long-term _________ to any political organisation.
5 Organisations should be heavily fined if they spread fake news for commercial _________ .

WORD STORE 6C Adverbs

11 3.3 Complete WORD STORE 6C with the highlighted adverbs in the text. Then listen, check and repeat.

12 Rewrite each sentence with the correct adverb made from the adjective in brackets.

1 The press and social media are controlled. (close)
2 The number of fake news stories is high. (alarming)
3 News organisations never spread fake news. (deliberate)
4 Students are taught to think about everything they read. (critical)
5 No government minister ever misinforms the public. (knowing)
6 Most people are happy, despite the economic situation. (remarkable)

13 SPEAKING Which of the situations described in Exercise 12 would you like/put up with/not like in a society?

6.2 GRAMMAR

Conditional clauses – alternatives to *if*

I can make conditional sentences using if, unless, imagine, provided, suppose and inversion.

1 SPEAKING **'The dog ate my homework' is a typical excuse used by students. Discuss and list other excuses.**

2 **Read the story. What excuse did the students use for missing their exam? What happened next?**

The Exam Question

Imagine you were taking an important exam on Monday, what would you do the weekend before? You almost certainly wouldn't do what two Chemistry students did in Kansas, Missouri. They went to a different city and partied all weekend. They had a great time, but they knew that unless they got back in time for the exam, they wouldn't be able to take it. So they drove through the night and got back to college in the early hours of Monday morning. Sadly for them, they overslept and missed the exam.

When they found their professor afterwards, they decided to invent a story. They told her that they would have got back for the exam had they not had a flat tyre. The professor thought about this for a moment and then agreed that, provided they arrived before 9 a.m., they could take the exam the next day. She placed them in separate rooms and gave them the exam paper. The first question was simple and worth five points. But they were unprepared for the question on the next page: **(Ninety-five points) Which tyre?**

3 **Read the GRAMMAR FOCUS. Then rewrite the conditional clauses in blue in the story using *if*.**

GRAMMAR FOCUS

Conditional clauses – alternatives to *if*

- You use ***unless*** to mean 'if not' with the sense 'except if'.
  I wouldn't lie to you unless it was necessary.
  (= … if it wasn't necessary.)
- You use ***imagine*** or ***suppose/supposing*** to ask questions.
  Imagine you were getting married, how would you feel?
  (= If you were getting married, …)
- You use ***provided/providing*** to create a condition.
  I'll lend you €10 provided you pay me back tomorrow.
  (= if you pay me back …)
- You can use **inversion** in formal contexts – mostly with the auxiliary verbs *were*, *had* or *should*.
  Had they followed my instructions, they wouldn't have got lost. (= If they had followed …)
  Note: In inversion, you do not contract negative forms.
  Had they not called, we wouldn't have known (…).
  NOT ~~*Hadn't they called …*~~

4 **Rewrite these conditional sentences using *unless*. Which sentences are true for you?**

1 I'll fail all my exams if I don't revise properly.
I'll fail all my exams unless I revise properly.
2 I can't do my homework if I don't have a laptop.
3 I wouldn't study English if I didn't need it to get a job.
4 My parents won't let me go out if I haven't finished my homework.
5 I'd never get to school on time if my mum didn't wake me up every morning.
6 I can't understand American films if I don't watch them with subtitles.

5 USE OF ENGLISH **Complete the second sentence so that it has a similar meaning to the first. Use up to six words including the word in capitals. Are any of the sentences true for you?**

1 I won't go out this evening if I get too much homework. **PROVIDED**
I might go out this evening __________ too much homework.
2 If my mum hadn't reminded me, I would've forgotten her birthday. **NOT**
Had __________ me, I would've forgotten her birthday.
3 I'd never eat fast food unless I was absolutely starving. **WASN'T**
If __________, I'd never eat fast food.
4 I'd have watched *Mr Bean* if I'd known it was on TV last night. **WAS**
Had __________ on TV last night, I'd have watched it.
5 I don't watch football unless my team are playing. **IF**
I don't watch football __________.
6 If I wasn't so tired, I'd go out this evening. **NOT**
Were __________, I'd go out this evening.
7 If I should ever get married, I'd want a huge party. **EVER**
Should __________, I'd want a huge party.

6 **Use ideas 1–6 to write conditional questions. Begin each question with *Imagine …* or *Suppose …* and complete it with your own ideas.**

1 You can't live anywhere in the world.
Imagine/Suppose you could live anywhere in the world, where would you live?
2 You didn't find 100 euros in the street yesterday.
3 You're not able to travel back in time.
4 You don't have to live without technology.
5 You didn't see an old man steal something from a shop last week.
6 You can't have three wishes.

7 SPEAKING **Ask and answer the questions in Exercise 6.**

FOCUS VLOG About time travel

27 **Watch the Focus Vlog. For the worksheet, go to page 143.**

Grammar page 163

6.3

LISTENING

Note completion

I can identify the main points of a discussion about a street artist.

1 SPEAKING **Describe these two murals by controversial British artist Banksy. Also look at *Girl with Balloon* on page 57. Discuss what you think they mean.**

2 3.4 **Listen to a news report about Banksy. Tick the information if it has been confirmed. If not, put a question mark.**

Banksy bio

1 Real name is Robin Gunningham. ☐
2 Was born in Bristol in 1973. ☐
3 Trained to be a butcher. ☐
4 Became famous in the 1990s. ☐
5 Has never been arrested. ☐
6 Authenticates his work on his website. ☐
7 Is a multi-millionaire. ☐

3 **Add *pro-* or *anti-* to the following words to describe whether you think Banksy is for or against these things.**

1 ______ anonymity
2 ______ authority
3 ______ war
4 ______ animal rights
5 ______ peaceful protest
6 ______ fairness
7 ______ animal cruelty
8 ______ equality

4 3.5 **Listen to two people talking about Banksy and check your ideas in Exercise 3.**

EXAM FOCUS Note completion

5 3.5 **Listen again and complete sentences 1–6 with a word or a short phrase.**

1 Robert is doing a school assignment on ________ issues in art.
2 Alice says that Banksy uses graffiti to express his views on ________ .
3 Alice first thought that Banksy was born in ________ .
4 Banksy has remained anonymous thanks to his friends' commitment and ________ .
5 He substituted paintbrushes with stencils and spray cans so that he could paint more ________ .
6 Banksy's artwork on a Welsh garage can be seen as a comment on ________ issues.

WORD STORE 6D Collocations

6 3.6 **Complete WORD STORE 6D with the words in the box. Then listen, check and repeat.**

7 SPEAKING **Complete the statements with the appropriate noun in WORD STORE 6D. Then discuss whether you agree or disagree with them. Give reasons for your answers.**

1 Committing an ________ is always wrong.
2 If you're a street artist, it's a good idea to remain ________ .
3 Teenagers don't do enough to protect their ________ online.
4 Street art can be an effective way of raising ________ and making a ________
5 Only experts can understand the underlying ________ in modern art.
6 Nobody has strong ________ about anything anymore.

PRONUNCIATION FOCUS

8 3.7 **Listen and put these words into the correct column A, B or C depending on the stress.**

~~alteration~~ authority ceremony commentator inauthentic photographer uncomfortable underlying vandalism

A ■ ▪ ▪ ▪	B ▪ ■ ▪ ▪	C ▪ ▪ ■ ▪
________	________	*alteration*
________	________	________
________	________	________

9 3.8 **Listen, check and repeat.**

6.4 READING

Note completion

I can recognise inferred meaning in a structured text.

1 **SPEAKING Discuss the questions.**

1 When was the last time you took a selfie and why did you take it?
2 Which of your friends posts the most interesting selfies?
3 Why do you think selfies are so popular?

2 **Choose the correct option. Then read the text and check your ideas.**

1 The first teenage selfie was taken in *1839 / 1914 / 2006*.
2 One in *three / five / ten* photos taken by eighteen to twenty-four-year-olds is a selfie.
3 The word 'selfie' originated in *Russia / Australia / New York*.
4 Taking selfies occasionally causes *memory / mental health / motivational* problems.

EXAM FOCUS Note completion

3 **Read the article again. Complete the sentences with up to five words from the article in the correct form.**

1 Anybody who ____________ media is also likely to be a selfie-taker, and this doesn't just mean young people.
2 Although Britney Spears and Paris Hilton claim to have taken the first selfie ever, the real pioneer was 19th century photographer Robert Cornelius, whose ____________ was taken in 1839.
3 The first teenager to take a selfie was a young Russian princess who managed to do it by ____________ in a mirror.
4 The selfie as we know it today was first taken by a group of photographers using a ____________ that it required two men to hold it.
5 Since the ____________ in the early 2000s, taking selfies has become much easier and one in three photos taken by a young person has been a selfie.
6 The term 'selfie' comes out of the Australian ____________ adding *-ie* to the end of words.
7 'Selfitis' is a term for people who ____________ and post them on social media in order to feel happier or more accepted.
8 A medical journal has reported that the use of airbrushing apps could make some people see ____________ their appearance, with the result that many seek surgery to look more like their filtered photos.

4 3.10 **Complete the phrases with the verbs in blue in the text. Then listen, check and repeat.**

1 *become* **mainstream** = be ordinary or normal
2 ________ **back to** = begin at a time in the past
3 ________ **popularity** = become more popular
4 ________ **a habit of** = do sth regularly
5 ________ **a claim** = state that sth is true
6 ________ = try to do
7 ________ **sth off** = get rid of
8 ________ = cause sth to happen

5 **Complete the questions with one word in each gap. Then answer the questions according to the information in the text.**

1 When did smartphones become ________ ?
2 Who made the ________ that they had invented the selfie?
3 When does the oldest selfie date back ________ and how was it taken?
4 What do Australians have a habit ________ adding to the end of words?
5 What might some people be ________ by taking a lot of selfies?
6 What can taking lots of selfies help you to shake ________ ?
7 What kind of apps are gaining ________ and why?
8 What does BDD mean and what can ________ it?

WORD STORE 6E Photography

6 3.11 **Complete WORD STORE 6E with the words in the box. Then listen and repeat.**

7 **SPEAKING There is one word missing in each question. Rewrite the questions with an appropriate word in WORD STORE 6E. Then ask and answer the questions.**

1 When was the last time you took a on your smartphone?
When was the last time you took a snap on your smartphone?
2 How do you usually for selfies – is it a smile, duck-face or wink?
3 What is the funniest you have captured on your phone?
4 Do you sometimes put your finger in front of the by mistake?
5 What do you do with photos that are not focus?
6 Have you ever images of yourself to try and improve them?
7 How often do you images to e.g. change their shape?
8 When was the last time you in on something far away when taking a photo?
9 Think of your favourite photo and how it was taken. Was it only one, or many?

A short history of **the selfie**

3.9

They're everywhere – people posing with their phones held out in front of them or on a selfie-stick. And it's not just young people – social media users of all ages take selfies, including space-walking astronauts and the Pope.

So when did this selfie mania begin? Most people would guess that it was around the beginning of this century or perhaps a bit later when smartphones **became mainstream**. But most people would be wrong, just as Britney Spears and Paris Hilton were wrong when they declared on Twitter in 2017 that they had invented the selfie eleven years previously. In fact, they were around 167 years too late to **make that claim**. The oldest existing selfie **dates back to** 1839 when photographer Robert Cornelius took a self-portrait photograph of himself. To achieve this, he had to uncover the lens, run to his place and pose in the same position for up to fifteen minutes and then run back to cover the lens again. Cornelius couldn't take a dozen shots and choose the best one – his selfie had to be just one photo. Half a century later, in 1914, thirteen-year-old Grand Duchess Anastasia Nikolaevna of Russia took a picture of herself in a mirror and became the first teenager to take a selfie.

The first image taken in the same way as today, with the photographer holding the camera at arm's length, was in December 1920. The image shows five photographers standing on the roof of their studio in New York. The men were the main photographers of the Byron Company, a photographic studio founded in Manhattan in 1892 and still in business today. An image taken by another man shows that the camera was so heavy in those days that it took two of the photographers to hold it up. Thanks to innovations and improvements in cameras, a selfie gradually became easier to take, but it was the smartphone coming out in the early 2000s that led to selfie dominance. Surveys have shown that every third photo taken by those aged eighteen to twenty-four is a selfie.

And what about the origin of the word itself? It is thought to come from Australia where people **have a habit of** putting *-ie* on the end of words – barb*ie* for barbecue, post*ie* for postal worker and even Auss*ie* for Australian. In 2002, an Australian man took a photo of an injury to his lip and put it up on a public forum to ask for advice on how to treat it. He referred to the photo as a selfie, and the term was born. Selfie became Oxford Dictionaries' word of the year in 2013.

So, why do we take so many photos of ourselves? A 2017 study into 'selfitis', as the obsessive taking of selfies has been called, found a range of motivations, from **seeking** to feel more part of a group to **shaking off** depressive thoughts and – of course – capturing a memorable moment. Since we live so much of our lives online, there is pressure to present good quality images, and so it is no surprise that airbrushing apps that enable people to retouch images and present an idealised version of themselves are **gaining popularity**.

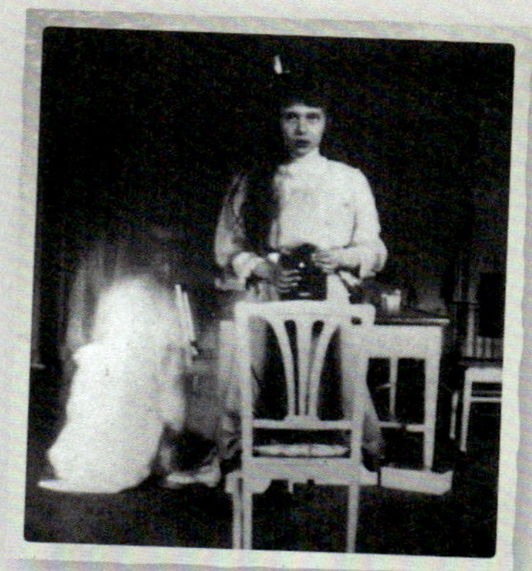

For the most part, this is harmless fun, normal behaviour in the age of social media. But a recent report in a medical journal suggested that filtered images 'blurring the line of reality and fantasy' could be **triggering** body dysmorphic disorder. BDD, as it is known, is a mental health condition where people imagine defects in their appearance. Nowadays it's not unusual for young people to ask for plastic surgery, not to look more like their favourite celebrity, but to look like their own filtered image. In a 2018 report on facial plastic surgery, 55 percent of surgeons said patients' motivation was to look better in selfies, up from just 13 percent in 2016.

Whatever your motivation, once you're in the selfie habit, it's hard to stop. So tousle your hair, extend your arm, check the lighting is right, zoom in, smile/duck-face/wink, and snap a selfie. It's blurred. Take another snap. Once more. Delete the ugly ones and post the cutest shot. Wait for the likes!

6.5 GRAMMAR

Mixed conditionals

I can use mixed conditionals to talk about hypothetical situations in the past or present.

1 Read the text and find out what these two British actors think about their screen characters.

ACTORS LIKE THEIR SCREEN CHARACTERS, OR DO THEY?

Daniel Radcliffe

Daniel Radcliffe doesn't mind being called Harry Potter. If he hadn't played the part of Harry Potter, he wouldn't be one of the richest young stars in cinema today. But there have been times when his fame has been difficult for him to deal with. If he was less famous, he would have gone out dancing with his friends more, but sadly, he's never had that freedom.

Robert Pattinson didn't like the character he played in the *Twilight* series. He says that if Edward Cullen wasn't a fictional character, he would have been a troubled young man. Pattinson understands that he wouldn't be so mega-famous if he hadn't played the role of Edward Cullen, but he says it's really weird being famous for a character he doesn't like.

Robert Pattinson

2 Read the text again and match the real situations with the real results or consequences.

Situations	**Results**
1 Radcliffe played Harry Potter.	a He didn't go out dancing much.
2 Radcliffe is very famous.	b He is very famous.
3 Edward Cullen is fictional.	c He is very rich.
4 Pattinson played Edward Cullen.	d He wasn't a troubled young man.

3 Match the four conditional sentences in blue in the text with the four real situations and results in Exercise 2.

4 Read the GRAMMAR FOCUS and complete the gaps with *past* or *present*.

GRAMMAR FOCUS

Mixed conditionals

You use a **mixed conditional** to describe certain imaginary situations and their imaginary results. There are two main types:

1 imaginary [1]*present* condition → imaginary [2]_________ result

***If* + Past Simple,** ***would/wouldn't have* + Past Participle**

If he was less famous, he would have gone out dancing with his friends more.

2 imaginary [3]_________ condition → imaginary [4]_________ result

***If* + Past Perfect,** ***would/wouldn't* + verb**

If he hadn't played the part of Harry Potter, he wouldn't be one of the richest young stars in cinema today.

Note: As well as *would*, you can also use *could*, *might* and *should* in conditional sentences.

5 For each sentence, tick the explanations (a, b or both) that are correct.

1 If I'd watched the *Twilight* films, I'd know who Edward Cullen was.
 a I didn't watch the *Twilight* films. ☐
 b I know who Edward Cullen is. ☐
2 If I was interested in Harry Potter, I'd have read the books.
 a I'm not interested in Harry Potter. ☐
 b I haven't read any of the books. ☐
3 If Robert Pattinson was ugly, I might not have watched *Twilight*.
 a Robert Pattinson is handsome. ☐
 b I watched *Twilight*. ☐
4 Pattinson and Radcliffe wouldn't be enjoying so much success if they hadn't worked hard on these roles.
 a They aren't enjoying success. ☐
 b They worked hard on these roles. ☐

6 Compare your answers in Exercise 5 and correct the incorrect explanations.

7 Use the words in brackets to write mixed conditional sentences for each situation 1–6. Which sentences are true for you?

1 It's cold today so you came to school by bus. (If …)
 If it wasn't cold today, I wouldn't have come to school by bus.
2 You're reading this book because your friend recommended it. (I …)
3 You don't like football so you didn't watch the game last night. (If …)
4 You passed all your exams because you're a good student. (I …)
5 You didn't have a big breakfast so you're hungry now. (If …)
6 You're learning how to drive because your parents paid for some lessons. (I …)

8 Complete the sentences to make them true for you. Compare with a partner.

1 If I didn't have a smartphone, (*imaginary past result*) _________
2 If antibiotics hadn't been invented, (*imaginary present result*) _________
3 If I had been born in the USA, (*imaginary present result*) _________
4 If I could fly, (*imaginary past result*) _________
5 If I was a better student, (*imaginary past result*) _________
6 If my dad hadn't woken me up this morning, (*imaginary present result*) _________
7 If my parents were famous actors, (*imaginary past result*) _________

Grammar page 164

6.6 SPEAKING

Discussing ethical issues

I can express opinions in discussions on social issues and add comments using adverbials.

1 SPEAKING Discuss which of these ways of highlighting ethical issues you think are the most effective and why.

handing out leaflets   posts on social media   the involvement of public figures   protest marches   petitions

2 SPEAKING Imagine you are organising a 'Say no to fur' campaign at school and need to choose a poster to advertise it. Look at posters 1 and 2 and do the task.

- Choose the poster which you think is more effective and support your choice with reasons.
- Explain why you have rejected the other poster.

3 🔊3.12 Listen to three extracts from an interview with an anti-fur campaigner. For each extract, choose the question the campaigner is answering.

Extract 1

a Do awareness-raising campaigns and protests really make a difference and if so, how?

b Do fashion designers still like using fur and if so, how important is it to stop the fur trade?

Extract 2

c Why do you think fur is still popular with fashion designers and celebrities?

d What are the benefits of getting public figures involved in anti-fur protests?

Extract 3

e Apart from avoiding fur products, what else could members of the public do to help?

f If you could send any message to people who wear fur, what would it be?

4 🔊3.12 Complete the SPEAKING FOCUS with the words in the box. Then listen again and check.

argued   emphasise   ~~firmly~~   obvious   particularly

SPEAKING FOCUS

Beginning your answer

I [1] ___*firmly*___ believe/I'm not convinced they do, because …

One [2] _________ /clear advantage/disadvantage is that …

I think I'd [3] _________ /explain that/how …

It's absolutely vital/quite important I think, because …

As well as (avoiding fur products), other (things that can help) include …

I think the main/one/a significant reason is that …

Expressing opinions

It could be [4] _________ that …

I don't feel [5] _________ strongly about …

I don't have a strong opinion about …

I suppose you could say that …

A

B

5 Match questions a–f in Exercise 3 with appropriate ways to begin answers in the SPEAKING FOCUS.

6 Read the extracts from the interview and complete REMEMBER THIS with the words in orange.

a **Sadly**, fur seems to be fashionable again these days …

b **Obviously**, protesting is a good way to promote awareness …

c **Frankly**, I find some of the pictures extremely difficult to look at.

REMEMBER THIS

You can use comment adverbials to add your opinion to statements you make.

- You use *clearly*/[1]_________ to introduce something that can easily be noticed or understood.
- You use *to be honest*/[2]_________ to show that you are saying what you really think about something.
- You use *regrettably*/[3]_________ to show you wish something was not true.

7 SPEAKING You are going to ask and answer the questions below. Follow the instructions.

- Decide who is Student A and who is Student B.
- In your notebook, make notes on how you will answer the questions.
- Use the SPEAKING FOCUS and REMEMBER THIS to help you.
- Ask and answer the questions.

Student A: Ask Student B the questions below.

1 How important is it to stop the practice of testing cosmetics on animals?

2 If you could send any message to the governments of countries that still test cosmetics on animals, what would it be?

Student B: Ask Student A the questions below.

1 Why do you think hunting animals for sport is still popular with certain groups and individuals?

2 How important is it to stop the practice of hunting animals for sport?

6.7 USE OF ENGLISH

Compound nouns and adjectives

I can understand and use compound words.

A DAY IN THE LIFE OF A NEWS ANCHOR

I'm a **news anchor** on the **morning show** of a local **TV station**. The question I get asked most is what time I get up. 3 a.m.! And I'm in hair and **make-up** at 4:30. I wear block colours – no stripes or frills, and no green. We sometimes use **green screens** so that artificial backgrounds can be superimposed. So if you wear a green top, it doesn't show up against a green **background** and you appear as a floating head and a pair of arms and legs – very **ill-advised** and not a good look!

We go live at 6 a.m., and before that I have to read up on the day's **news stories**. I start by getting an **overview** of the stories I'll be reporting. We're a local **news station**, so we don't report on **foreign affairs**.

You can't rehearse – you have to deal with **breaking news** as it comes in, but I have a lot of **backup**. A **fact-checker** has made sure the details of the story are accurate, a **copy editor** makes sure stories are written in a way that I'd actually say them and when I'm live on air if I become **tongue-tied** or mess up, I have the director in my ear.

On morning TV, we focus on **heartwarming** stories. It's the morning and people are eating breakfast – I don't want to give a **blow-by-blow** account of some hideous crime. Having said that, it's our job to report anything newsworthy.

It's a **four-hour** programme with several **three-minute commercial breaks** – that's when I dash to the **bathroom**, ask about any breaking news and read up on the next interview.

I work nonstop for four hours, but how many jobs finish before midday? It means I can spend time with my **four-year-old** twins. I go to bed at the same time as they do!

1 Decide whether you think the following statements are true (T) or false (F). Then read the article to check your ideas.

1 A news anchor can't wear green. ☐
2 A news anchor can't rehearse the stories. ☐
3 A news anchor can't hear the director while she/he is on-air. ☐
4 A news anchor can't report on crime at breakfast time. ☐
5 A news anchor can't go to the toilet for four hours. ☐

2 SPEAKING Would you like to be a news anchor or work in television? Why/Why not?

3 Match five compound adjectives and nouns in blue in the article with the definitions.

1 likely to have a bad effect = ______
2 a short description including the main ideas = ______
3 unable to speak because of nerves or embarrassment = ______
4 information about a news event that is still happening = ______
5 extremely detailed = ______

4 Check you understand the meaning of all the other compound nouns and adjectives in blue in the article. Use a dictionary if necessary.

5 Read and complete the LANGUAGE FOCUS with the examples in blue from the article.

LANGUAGE FOCUS

Compound nouns and adjectives

Compound nouns

- A compound noun is normally made up of two words. The first word describes or modifies the second word: *a* [1]*morning show* = a show that is on in the morning. Compare: *a company car* (a type of car) and *a car company* (a type of company).
- Compound nouns can consist of:
  noun + noun: [2]______ *anchor, newsreader, health check*
  adjective + noun: [3]______ *affairs*
  verb-*ing* + noun: *breaking* [4]______
  preposition + noun: [5]______*view*
- A significant number of compound nouns are **made from phrasal verbs**: *back sth up > a* [6]______ *, crack down on sth > a crack-down*
- Compound nouns can be written as one word, two words or with a hyphen. Check in a dictionary. The stress is usually on the first syllable.

Compound adjectives

- A compound adjective is usually made from two words and usually written with a hyphen.
- Compound adjectives can consist of:
  number + noun: *three-minute, twenty-four-hour*
  adjective + noun: *high-quality, present-day, deep sea*
  noun + adjective: *user-friendly, waist-high, weatherproof*
  noun/adjective/adverb + *-ed/-ing* participle: [7]*heart*______ *, mouth-watering, short-lived, far-fetched, kind-hearted, weather-beaten, broad-shouldered, flat-footed*
  verb + preposition/adverb: *made-up, unheard-of*
- Some compound adjectives are made from more than two words: *four-year-old, blow-* [8]______ *, state-of-the-art*
- The noun in a compound adjective is usually singular: *a four-* [9]______ programme NOT ~~*a four-hours programme*~~

6 **Match the words from boxes A and B to make common compound colour adjectives. What things can you describe using these colours?**

A	B
~~blood~~ charcoal lemon lime nut sky snow	blue brown green grey ~~red~~ yellow white

a blood-red sky, a blood-red rose, blood-red lips

7 **Rewrite the following descriptions using compound adjectives. Use a dictionary if necessary.**

1 A young woman with rosy cheeks
2 A child with curly hair
3 An old man with thin lips
4 A young sportsman with broad shoulders
5 A high jumper with long legs
6 A teenager with a kind heart

8 **Read the news story and replace the information in brackets with a compound noun or adjective. Do you believe the boy's explanation?**

Real-life teddy bear

A [1]__________ (boy who was three years old) who went missing in woods for two days says a brown bear kept him safe. The boy who survived the [2]__________ (ordeal that lasted two nights) alone in the woods in freezing conditions has told police and family he was helped out by a friendly bear. Rescuers, who had to wade through [3]__________ (water that was high to the waist), found him tangled up in thorny bushes. He was taken to hospital for a [4]__________ (check on his health) and was found to be a little [5]__________ (burned by the sun) but otherwise unhurt. The story of the bear is too far-fetched for some people, but whether a [6]__________ (bear with a kind heart) really took care of him, or whether it was all in his imagination, the important thing is that he is safely home with his family.

9 USE OF ENGLISH **Complete the second sentence so it has a similar meaning to the first. Use up to five words including the word in capitals.**

1 Fifty years ago, nobody had heard of some of the health problems affecting children today. **WERE**
Some of the health problems affecting children today __________ fifty years ago.
2 Local police have announced that they are cracking down on anti-social behaviour. **A**
Local police have announced __________ anti-social behaviour.
3 The Oxford to London bus service, which operates all day and all night, is under review. **TWENTY-FOUR-HOUR**
The __________ from Oxford to London is under review.
4 Phones with voice recognition are easier to use according to a recent survey. **MORE**
Phones with voice recognition are __________ according to a recent survey.
5 I've completely worn myself out playing tennis this afternoon. **AM**
__________ after playing tennis this afternoon.
6 Joe and Becky decided to buy a train pass that would last them seven days. **SEVEN-DAY**
Joe and Becky decided to __________ .

SHOW WHAT YOU'VE LEARNT UNITS 1–6

10 USE OF ENGLISH **Read the text and choose the correct answer A, B, C or D.**

The branch of a well-known pizza company [1]______ up with a [2]______ offer which turned out to be somewhat [3]______ . They promised 100 free pizzas per year for 100 years to [4]______ customer who painted the company's logo on the side of their car and then posted it on social media. The [5]______ response from the general public was loud and [6]______ : the thought of looking [7]______ to a lifetime supply of [8]______-watering pizzas proved irresistible and [9]______ of people [10]______ in posting their photos before the overwhelmed company withdrew their offer early.

1 A put B took C came D made
2 A special B important C significant D particular
3 A short-handed B short-lived C short-range D short-changed
4 A every B all C each of D whole
5 A first B beginning C introductory D initial
6 A obvious B clear C distinct D long
7 A forward B up C out D down
8 A tongue B teeth C mouth D stomach
9 A lot B very many C hundreds D one thousand
10 A were able B managed C succeeded D could

Use of English page 165

6.8 WRITING

A review of a TV series

I can write a review of a television series.

1 SPEAKING Discuss the questions in groups.

1. Which old TV series do you consider to be classics and why?
2. Which of today's TV series do you think are the classics of the future and why?
3. What do you know about the series shown in the picture?

2 Read the notice on the website and answer the questions.

1. What kind of website is Pictureshow? What similar sites do you know?
2. What should readers do to enter the competition?

Pictureshow TV and film reviews by you, for you.

Classic TV

RESULTS

- Classic TV series by genre
- Editor's picks: TV classics
- Fifty classic shows that changed TV forever
- **Tomorrow's Classics Competition**

Tomorrow's Classics Competition

Spotting the classic TV series of tomorrow is no easy task, but that's our challenge for you this month. To enter the competition, send us a review of a recent TV show and explain why you think it will be considered a classic in the future. Our favourite review will appear on the website next month and the winner will receive a €50 cash prize.

3 SPEAKING Read the review. If you have seen *Stranger Things*, do you agree with the writer's opinion of it? If you haven't, does the review make you want to watch the series? Explain your answers.

1 Take a **nostalgic** journey back to small-town America in the 1980s with Netflix's dark mystery *Stranger Things*. This excellent show is heavily influenced by the books and films of Stephen King and Steven Spielberg. Series creators, the Duffer brothers, have combined action, humour and horror to create a **well-reviewed** sci-fi drama. As far as I'm concerned, it's a TV classic.

2 In season one of *Stranger Things*, a schoolboy named Will goes missing. His friends, mother and the rest of the town become part of a series of mysterious events involving an unusual young girl named Eleven. It soon becomes clear that something even stranger is hiding in the woods of their town. In season two, the town and its inhabitants are once again threatened by supernatural forces and we are reminded that the worst villains are not always the monsters. Season three not only presents a continuation of this theme, but also shows how the main characters and their relationships have developed with time.

3 *Stranger Things* is a brilliant show with an **unforgettable** soundtrack. The plot explores friendships, family ties and even romance. The young cast give wonderful performances and the show is beautifully shot. Unlike many modern shows, it doesn't rely too heavily on special effects. While season one is not particularly scary, seasons two and three are more strongly influenced by horror films and are **terrifying** at times.

4 All in all, *Stranger Things* offers viewers a **gripping** story with plenty of twists and turns. From the opening scene, it feels as though you are watching a future TV classic. I can't recommend it enough and have no doubt that people will be talking about it for many years to come.

4 **Read the review again and match points a–d below with paragraphs 1–4.**

a Summarise your opinions and make a recommendation. ☐
b Give your opinion on the story, acting, dialogue, special effects, etc. ☐
c Give key information: the name of the series, where and when it is set etc., and your overall opinion. ☐
d Summarise the story but don't give any spoilers. ☐

5 **Read the WRITING FOCUS and find examples of each point in the review.**

WRITING FOCUS

A review

The goal of a review is to give your personal opinion about something, e.g. a film, a series or a book. The opinion should be supported with examples and recommendations should be given at the end. Reviews are usually written for newspapers, websites or magazines and therefore have a fairly informal style.

Introduction

- Attract the reader's attention with an interesting opening sentence.
- Mention the type of show, the stars/director/writer, the setting, obvious influences, etc.
- State your overall opinion.

Main paragraphs

- Use present tenses to give more details about the plot and the main characters.
- Use present or past tenses to say what you liked/didn't like about the TV series.
- Use a variety of adjectives and modifiers when presenting your opinions.

Conclusion

- Summarise your review.
- Make recommendations.

6 **Complete the sentences from other reviews with one to three words from the review in Exercise 3.**

1 People _________ about how bad this is for many years to come.
2 I can't _________ it enough and look forward to the second season.
3 From the _________ scene, it is clear that the film is going to be slow and predictable.
4 The cast give confident _________ and are a pleasure to watch.
5 The third season is strongly _________ the films of Quentin Tarantino.
6 At times, the show is poorly _________ and relies too heavily on low quality special effects.
7 To sum up, Schumer's new sitcom is hilarious and full of unexpected _________ and turns.
8 The rather far-fetched plot _________ the idea of an alien invasion.

7 **Match the adjectives in purple in the review and Exercise 6 with the definitions in the LANGUAGE FOCUS box. Is each one positive, negative, or a matter of taste?**

LANGUAGE FOCUS

Adjectives for reviews

Use a range of adjectives to make your review interesting.

1 very funny = *hilarious*
2 impossible to forget = _________
3 extremely frightening = _________
4 exciting = _________
5 emotional about the past = _________
6 hard to believe = _________
7 liked by critics = _________
8 easy to guess = _________

8 **Complete the sentences with an appropriate adjective from the LANGUAGE FOCUS. Use each adjective only once.**

1 This comedy is _________ . It will have you laughing out loud.
2 Although the show was _________ on several TV websites, we found it average at best.
3 For me this series is _________ . I haven't stopped thinking about it since I finished watching it.
4 This show takes a _________ look at life in the UK in the 1920s.
5 Don't watch this zombie series alone because it is truly _________ .
6 This _________ sitcom is no different to a thousand others you've seen before.
7 If you don't mind a _________ plot involving aliens and cowboys, you'll probably enjoy this series.
8 Each episode is so _________ , it's almost impossible to stop watching and go to bed.

9 **SPEAKING Discuss what shows, films or actors fit some of the descriptions in Exercises 6 and 8.**

SHOW WHAT YOU'VE LEARNT

10 **Do the writing task. Use the ideas in the WRITING FOCUS and the LANGUAGE FOCUS to help you.**

Imagine you are entering the competition on the website in Exercise 2. Write a review of a TV series that you think will be a future classic.

- Write an interesting opening sentence and state your overall opinion of the series.
- Summarise the plot of the series (but remember to avoid spoilers) and the reasons why you like it/feel it will be a future classic.
- Add a conclusion that includes a recommendation.

6.1 Vocabulary 4.41

accurate /'ækjərət/
alarming /ə'lɑːmɪŋ/
alarmingly /ə'lɑːmɪŋli/
appeal to /ə'piːl tə/
awash with information /əˌwɒʃ wɪð ˌɪnfə'meɪʃən/
believable /bə'liːvəbəl/
bombarded with information /bɒmˌbɑːdɪd wɪð ˌɪnfə'meɪʃən/
burst into flames /ˌbɜːst ˌɪntə 'fleɪmz/
check the accuracy /tʃek ði 'ækjərəsi/
cleaning solution /'kliːnɪŋ səˌluːʃən/
clear commitment /ˌklɪə kə'mɪtmənt/
close /kləʊs/
closely /'kləʊsli/
critical /'krɪtɪkəl/
critically /'krɪtɪkli/
deliberate /dɪ'lɪbərət/
deliberately /dɪ'lɪbərətli/
distinct feeling /dɪˌstɪŋkt 'fiːlɪŋ/
distort the truth /dɪˌstɔːt ðə 'truːθ/
double-check facts /ˌdʌbəl ˌtʃek 'fækts/
evaluate sources /ɪˌvæljueɪt 'sɔːsɪz/
examine sth closely /ɪgˌzæmɪn ˌsʌmθɪŋ 'kləʊsli/
eye-catching story /ˌaɪ ˌkætʃɪŋ 'stɔːri/
fake news /ˌfeɪk 'njuːz/
falsehood /'fɔːlshʊd/
for commercial gain /fə kəˌmɜːʃəl 'geɪn/
for political gain /fə pəˌlɪtɪkəl 'geɪn/
gut feeling /ˌgʌt 'fiːlɪŋ/
have an agenda /ˌhæv ən ə'dʒendə/
ignite /ɪg'naɪt/
inaccurate /ɪn'ækjərət/
knowing /'nəʊɪŋ/
knowingly /'nəʊɪŋli/
long-term commitment /ˌlɒŋ tɜːm kə'mɪtmənt/
made-up /ˌmeɪd 'ʌp/
manipulate the media /məˌnɪpjəleɪt ðə 'miːdiə/
mislead/misinform people /ˌmɪsˌliːd/ mɪsɪnˌfɔːm 'piːpəl/
misleading /mɪs'liːdɪŋ/
newsworthy story /ˌnjuːzˌwɜːði 'stɔːri/
not take a story at face value /nɒt ˌteɪk ə ˌstɔːri ət ˌfeɪs 'væljuː/
on a daily basis /ɒn ə ˌdeɪli 'beɪsɪs/
on a regular basis /ɒn ə ˌregjələ 'beɪsɪs/
operating theatre /'ɒpəreɪtɪŋ ˌθɪətə/
print-based media /ˌprɪnt beɪst 'miːdiə/
question facts /'kwestʃən ˌfækts/
reliable/reputable source /rɪˌaɪəbəl/ˌrepjətəbəl 'sɔːs/
remarkable /rɪ'mɑːkəbəl/
remarkably /rɪ'mɑːkəbli/
spark /spɑːk/
spread fake news /ˌspred ˌfeɪk 'njuːz/
tackle a problem /ˌtækəl ə 'prɒbləm/
tamper with photos /ˌtæmpə wɪð 'fəʊtəʊz/
trust your instincts /ˌtrʌst jər 'ɪnstɪŋkts/
winnings /'wɪnɪŋz/

6.2 Grammar 4.42

flat tyre /'flæt taɪə/
invent a story /ɪnˌvent ə 'stɔːri/
oversleep /ˌəʊvə'sliːp/
starving /'stɑːvɪŋ/
subtitles /'sʌbˌtaɪtlz/

6.3 Listening 4.43

alteration /ˌɔːltə'reɪʃən/
animal cruelty /ˌænəməl 'kruːəlti/
animal rights /ˌænəməl 'raɪts/
anonymity /ˌænə'nɪməti/
authenticate /ɔː'θentɪkeɪt/
authority /ɔː'θɒrəti/
background /'bækgraʊnd/
bar code /'bɑː kəʊd/
butcher /'bʊtʃə/
commit an offence /kəˌmɪt ən ə'fens/
confirm /kən'fɜːm/
equality /ɪ'kwɒləti/
ethical issue /ˌeθɪkəl 'ɪʃuː/
express /ɪk'spres/
fairness /'feənəs/
float away /ˌfləʊt ə'weɪ/
genuine /'dʒenjuɪn/
identity /aɪ'dentəti/
make a statement /ˌmeɪk ə 'steɪtmənt/
out of reach /aʊt əv riːtʃ/
paintbrush /'peɪntbrʌʃ/
peaceful protest /ˌpiːsfəl 'prəʊtest/
protect your identity /prəˌtekt jər aɪ'dentəti/
protestor /prə'testə/
raise awareness /ˌreɪz ə'weənəs/
recognised /'rekəgnaɪzd/
remain anonymous /rɪˌmeɪn ə'nɒnəməs/
stencil /'stensəl/
strong belief /strɒŋ bə'liːf/
substitute /'sʌbstətjuːt/
treatment of animals /ˌtriːtmənt əv 'ænɪməlz/
unconfirmed rumour /ˌʌnkənˌfɜːmd 'ruːmə/
underlying message /ˌʌndəˌlaɪ-ɪŋ 'mesɪdʒ/

6.4 Reading 4.44

airbrush /'eəbrʌʃ/
at arm's length /ət 'ɑːmz ˌleŋθ/
become mainstream /bɪˌkʌm 'meɪnstriːm/
blurred /blɜːd/
body dysmorphic disorder /ˌbɒdi dɪs'mɔːfɪk dɪsˌɔːdə/
capture a memorable moment /ˌkæptʃər ə 'memərəbəl ˌməʊmənt/
crop images /ˌkrɒp 'ɪmɪdʒɪz/
cute /kjuːt/
date back to /'deɪt ˌbæk tə/
declare /dɪ'kleə/
defect /'diːfekt/
duchess /'dʌtʃəs/
duck-face /'dʌkfeɪs/
facial /'feɪʃəl/
gain popularity /ˌgeɪn ˌpɒpjə'lærəti/
harmless /'hɑːmləs/
have a habit of /ˌhæv ə 'hæbɪt əv/
in focus/out of focus /ɪn 'fəʊkəs/aʊt əv 'fəʊkəs/
lens /lenz/
make a claim /ˌmeɪk ə 'kleɪm/
mental health problem/condition /ˌmentl 'helθ ˌprɒbləm/kənˌdɪʃən/
origin /'ɒrɪdʒɪn/
originate /ə'rɪdʒəneɪt/
pose for a photo /ˌpəʊz fər ə 'fəʊtəʊ/
refer to /rɪ'fɜː tə/
retouch images /ˌriːˌtʌtʃ 'ɪmɪdʒɪz/
seek /siːk/
shake sth off /ˌʃeɪk ˌsʌmθɪŋ 'ɒf/
sharp /ʃɑːp/
shot /ʃɒt/
snap /snæp/
snap a selfie /ˌsnæp ə 'selfi/
take a shot/a snap /ˌteɪk ə 'ʃɒt/ ə 'snæp/
tousle /'taʊzəl/
treat /triːt/
trigger /'trɪgə/
wink /wɪŋk/
zoom in/zoom out /ˌzuːm 'ɪn/ˌzuːm 'aʊt/

6.5 Grammar 4.45

fictional character /ˌfɪkʃənəl 'kærəktə/
screen /skriːn/

6.6 Speaking 4.46

awareness-raising campaign /ə'weənəs ˌreɪzɪŋ kæmˌpeɪn/
convinced /kən'vɪnst/

creature /ˈkriːtʃə/
desirable /dɪˈzaɪərəbəl/
do harm /ˌduː ˈhɑːm/
emphasise /ˈemfəsaɪz/
engage with /ɪnˈɡeɪdʒ wɪð/
firmly /ˈfɜːmli/
for the sake of /fə ðə ˈseɪk əv/
frankly /ˈfræŋkli/
fur /fɜː/
fur trade /fɜː treɪd/
general public /ˌdʒenərəl ˈpʌblɪk/
glamorous /ˈɡlæmərəs/
hand out leaflets /ˌhænd ˌaʊt ˈliːflɪts/
involvement /ɪnˈvɒlvmənt/
make a difference /ˌmeɪk ə ˈdɪfərəns/
make your point /ˌmeɪk jə ˈpɔɪnt/
member of the public /ˌmembər əv ðə ˈpʌblɪk/
obviously /ˈɒbviəsli/
peacefully /ˈpiːsfəli/
petition /pəˈtɪʃən/
prevent from /prɪˈvent ˌfrəm/
promote awareness /prəˌməʊt əˈweənəs/
protest march /ˈprəʊtest ˌmɑːtʃ/
public figure /ˌpʌblɪk ˈfɪɡə/
receive criticism /rɪˌsiːv ˈkrɪtəsɪzəm/
regrettably /rɪˈɡretəbli/
take notice of /ˌteɪk ˈnəʊtɪs əv/
vital /ˈvaɪtl/

6.7 Use of English 4.47

background /ˈbækɡraʊnd/
backup /ˈbækʌp/
blood-red /ˈblʌd red/
blow-by-blow /ˌbləʊ baɪ ˈbləʊ/
breaking news /ˌbreɪkɪŋ ˈnjuːz/
broad-shouldered /ˌbrɔːd ˈʃəʊldəd/
bush /bʊʃ/
car company /ˌkɑː ˈkʌmpəni/
charcoal-grey /ˈtʃɑːkəʊl ˌɡreɪ/
commercial break /kəˌmɜːʃəl ˈbreɪk/
company car /ˌkʌmpəni ˈkɑː/
copy editor /ˈkɒpi ˌedɪtə/
crack down on /ˌkræk ˈdaʊn ɒn/
crackdown on /ˈkrækdaʊn ɒn/
curly-haired /ˌkɜːli ˈheəd/
dash /dæʃ/
deep sea /diːp ˈsiː/
fact-checker /ˌfækt ˈtʃekə/
far-fetched /ˌfɑː ˈfetʃt/
flat-footed /ˌflæt ˈfʊtɪd/
float /fləʊt/
foreign affairs /ˌfɒrɪn əˈfeəz/
frill /frɪl/
green screen /ˌɡriːn ˈskriːn/
health check /ˈhelθ ˌtʃek/
heartwarming /ˈhɑːtˌwɔːmɪŋ/
hideous /ˈhɪdiəs/
high-quality /ˌhaɪ ˈkwɒləti/
ill-advised /ˌɪl ədˈvaɪzd/
irresistible /ˌɪrɪˈzɪstəbəl/
kind-hearted /ˌkaɪnd ˈhɑːtɪd/
lemon-yellow /ˌlemən ˈjeləʊ/
lifetime supply /ˌlaɪftaɪm səˈplaɪ/
lime-green /ˌlaɪm ˈɡriːn/
long-legged /ˌlɒŋ ˈleɡəd/
makeup /ˈmeɪkʌp/
mess up /ˌmes ˈʌp/
morning show /ˌmɔːnɪŋ ˈʃəʊ/
mouth-watering /ˈmaʊθ ˌwɔːtərɪŋ/
news anchor /ˌnjuːz ˈæŋkə/
news station /ˌnjuːz ˈsteɪʃən/
news stories /ˌnjuːz ˈstɔːriz/
newsreader /ˈnjuːzˌriːdə/
nonstop /ˌnɒnˈstɒp/
nut-brown /ˌnʌt ˈbraʊn/
on air /ɒn ˈeə/
ordeal /ɔːˈdiːl/
overwhelmed /ˌəʊvəˈwelmd/
overview /ˈəʊvəvjuː/
present-day /ˈprezənt deɪ/
rehearse /rɪˈhɜːs/
report on /rɪˈpɔːt ɒn/
rosy-cheeked /ˌrəʊzi ˈtʃiːkt/
short-lived /ˌʃɔːt ˈlɪvd/
sky-blue /ˌskaɪ ˈbluː/
snow-white /ˌsnəʊ ˈwaɪt/
state-of-the-art /ˌsteɪt əv ði ˈɑːt/
stripe /straɪp/
sunburnt /ˈsʌnbɜːnt/
superimpose /ˌsuːpərɪmˈpəʊz/
tangled up /ˈtæŋɡəld ʌp/
thin-lipped /ˌθɪn ˈlɪpt/
tongue-tied /ˈtʌŋ ˌtaɪd/
thorny /ˈθɔːni/
TV station /ˌtiː ˈviː ˌsteɪʃən/
unheard-of /ʌnˈhɜːd ɒv/
unhurt /ʌnˈhɜːt/
user-friendly /ˌjuːzə ˈfrendli/
waist-high /ˌweɪst ˈhaɪ/
weather-beaten /ˈweðə ˌbiːtn/
weatherproof /ˈweðəpruːf/
withdraw /wɪðˈdrɔː/
worn-out /ˌwɔːn ˈaʊt/
voice recognition /ˈvɔɪs rekəɡˌnɪʃən/

6.8 Writing 4.48

dark /dɑːk/
enter a competition /ˌentər ə ˌkɒmpəˈtɪʃən/
family ties /ˈfæməli taɪz/
genre /ˈʒɒnrə/
go missing /ˌɡəʊ ˈmɪsɪŋ/
gripping /ˈɡrɪpɪŋ/
heavily influenced /ˌhevəli ˈɪnfluənst/
hilarious /hɪˈleəriəs/
nostalgic /nɒˈstældʒɪk/
opening scene /ˌəʊpənɪŋ ˈsiːn/
plot /plɒt/
predictable /prɪˈdɪktəbəl/
soundtrack /ˈsaʊndtræk/
spoiler /ˈspɔɪlə/
spot /spɒt/
terrifying /ˈterəfaɪ-ɪŋ/
threaten /ˈθretn/
twists and turns /ˌtwɪsts ən ˈtɜːnz/
unforgettable /ˌʌnfəˈɡetəbəl/
villain /ˈvɪlən/
well-reviewed /ˌwel rɪˈvjuːd/

MY WORD LIST

EXCHANGING INFORMATION

PHOTOGRAPHY

OTHER

FOCUS REVIEW 6

VOCABULARY AND GRAMMAR

1 Match the words in box A with the words in box B to make collocations, then complete the sentences with the collocations in the correct form.

A commercial daily double-check make raise

B awareness basis the facts gain a statement

1 The company's website is updated on a ___________ with the latest news and events.
2 She set up a campaign to ___________ of the disease amongst the general public.
3 The school have been passing on students' data for ___________, selling lists of names to advertisers.
4 It's vital that, as a journalist, you ___________ in a story before it's published.
5 This morning, the director of the hospital ___________ to the media about the crisis.

2 Complete the sentences with words from the unit. The first letter of each word is given.

1 You shouldn't take stories you read online at **f**________ value, they're often fake news.
2 I just had a **g**________ feeling that something wasn't right about what I'd been told.
3 The name of the witness has been changed to **p**________ her identity.
4 Legally, he hadn't actually **c**________ an offence, but his actions were clearly dishonest.
5 It's really important to check the **a**________ of any statistics you use in your article.
6 I don't believe the files were deleted by accident, they clearly did it **d**________ .

3 Choose the correct option.

1 *Would / Should* you need any further information, please don't hesitate to ask.
2 *Had the government not / Hadn't the government* acted, there would soon have been more riots.
3 I would ask people for their IDs before letting them in *providing / unless* I knew them personally.
4 We wouldn't get involved in your project *weren't we / were we not* enthusiastic about it.
5 *Imagine / Provided* you were offered a job as a foreign affairs correspondent, would you accept it?

4 Complete the sentences with the correct form of the verbs in brackets. Use mixed conditionals.

1 If Karen ___________ (check) her sources before submitting her article last week, she ___________ (not/be) in trouble with the editor today.
2 John ___________ (tell) us the truth about the school incident if he ___________ (be) an honest person.
3 If Jerry generally ___________ (take) his job seriously, his manager ___________ (promote) him a long time ago.
4 If my grandparents ___________ (not/be) such generous people, they ___________ (not/help) me financially at university and I wouldn't be a lawyer.
5 We ___________ (not/have to) take them to court now if they ___________ (pay) the loan back on time.

USE OF ENGLISH

5 Read the text. Choose the correct answer, A, B, C or D.

'Prodigal Summer' by Barbara Kingsolver

This novel is the story of two women whose lives change dramatically over the course of one summer. It doesn't have a(n) [1]___ plot like some of Kingsolver's other books, but neither is it too slow or [2]___ , with one or two surprising twists along the way. First and foremost, it's about the characters. Both women have [3]___ opinions about how they want to live their lives and both [4]___ believe in the importance of respecting the natural world. It's set in the [5]___ USA, in the small farming community of Egg Fork in the Zebulon Mountains, a [6]___ place, but typical of the Appalachian Mountains of North Carolina, and the landscape and its wildlife are ever-present in the [7]___ . The women's stories are also linked up with a third character, an elderly local farmer who is [8]___ for a past way of life and who initially seems angry and bitter, but who turns out to be surprisingly [9]___ .

1 A eye-catching B gripping C newsworthy D remarkable
2 A predictable B unpredictable C reliable D hilarious
3 A hard B tough C strong D heavy
4 A greatly B honestly C completely D firmly
5 A nowadays B real-time C present-day D up-to-date
6 A backup B made-up C far-fetched D fake
7 A foreground B backdrop C background D back-story
8 A nostalgic B memorable C unforgettable D romantic
9 A heartwarming B kind-hearted C hard-hearted D single-minded

6 Complete the sentences with the correct form of the words in brackets. Use up to five words in each gap and make any changes necessary.

1 I ___________ (not/tell) Christie my secret then if she were not a trustworthy person.
2 I'm pretty sure that if you ___________ (listen/advice) which I gave you last time, you wouldn't be in such a terrible situation now.
3 Suppose ___________ (you/miss) your flight last night, what would you have done?
4 If you hadn't forgotten the keys, we ___________ (not/stand) outside our house in the cold right now.
5 I'm sure there will be an investigation ___________(unless/company/release) its financial report.
6 Tim wouldn't be giving you any free lessons ___________ (he/be/not/you) good friend.

READING

7 Read the article. Complete the sentences with up to three words from the article in the correct form.

THE POWER OF IMAGES

It's often said that a picture is worth a thousand words. There's something appealing about images that makes them a powerful tool for communication.

As you scroll through your social media feed or browse a news website, what is it that prompts you to read on? The chances are that it's the images that attract your attention. Online content that is accompanied by an image is more likely to prompt engagement, in the form of clicks, likes and shares, than straightforward text. This phenomenon is especially important to digital marketers. They will tell you that on average people only read around 20 percent of the text on a web page. When it comes to remembering information, it is said that we retain around 80 percent of what we see versus only 20 percent of what we read and just 10 percent of what we hear. Although these figures are criticised by experts as an oversimplification, visuals do play an important role in how we deal with content in an information-rich world. Producing eye-catching visuals to attach to digital content is vital for anyone who wants to get their message across to the maximum number of people.

It's not only in the commercial world that the power of the image is being recognised. Governments and NGOs such as the World Health Organisation are acknowledging the importance of social media in communicating public health messages. Research into social media engagement during one recent disease outbreak, for example, found that it was image-based platforms such as Instagram that were most effective in communicating vital health messages. Whilst there is some concern amongst healthcare professionals that what starts off as helpful messages can easily get distorted as they're shared and reshared, specialists say that social media has huge potential for promoting public health.

Political journalists and campaigners have also long understood the power of an image. In a social media age, though, just posting a striking image that is sure to go viral has been labelled by some as 'slacktivism'. That is the idea that people will like and share an image without really thinking about the ideas behind it or engaging with the political message. The challenge for activists, journalists, marketers and governments is to develop a social media strategy that includes eye-catching visuals but is also more than skin deep.

1 When looking at information online, people are far more likely ___________ with content if it includes an image of some kind.
2 This fact is exploited by those working in ___________ to help make their messages stand out.
3 Apparently, we remember only a tiny percentage of information in the form of text or audio, but a much greater proportion of ideas presented in the form ___________ .
4 Images are also increasingly being used by official bodies to communicate ___________ to the widest possible audience and by journalists and activists to promote political campaigns.
5 The use of eye-catching images that quickly go ___________ has been criticised as an example of 'slacktivism' because it is superficial and doesn't really engage people with the underlying message.

SPEAKING

8 Look at the photos. The local council has decided to close down a community centre in your neighbourhood. Choose the method of protesting against this decision which, in your opinion, is the best, and give reasons for your choice.

A

B

9 Ask and answer the questions.

1 Should young people get involved in campaigns that concern their local areas? Why?/Why not?
2 Is it better to express one's opinion on a controversial issue or to keep quiet? Why?/Why not?
3 What's the most effective way to persuade somebody to change their opinion? What makes you think so?
4 What are the advantages of using social media to organise an event?

WRITING

10 Read the writing task and write a review.

What is your favourite film genre? Comedy, action movie, romantic comedy or something else? Write a review for a film which is the best representation of your favourite genre and could encourage viewers to watch more films of that type.

7

It's not rocket science!

I am among those who think that science has great beauty.

Marie Curie

BLOWING IN THE WIND

29 Watch the BBC video.
For the worksheet, go to page 144.

7.1 VOCABULARY

Science • scientific research • prepositions after verbs and nouns • words in science

I can talk about science and scientific research.

SHOW WHAT YOU KNOW

1 **For each adjective in the box, add a discipline and a person. Add any other science word families that you know.**

archaeological astronomical biological botanical chemical geological mathematical physical

archaeological → archaeology → archaeologist

2 SPEAKING **Look at the subjects in Exercise 1. Which science is the most/least difficult to study?**

3 SPEAKING **Between 1901 and 2019 the Nobel Prize in chemistry and physics was awarded to 386 men and only eight women. Discuss possible reasons for this and say if you think the situation is changing.**

4 **Read the text. What scientists are mentioned and what are their fields of study? What do they have in common?**

FEMALE SCIENTISTS Changing The World

In any web search for the world's famous scientists, Marie Curie always **receives a mention**. Curie, a Polish and naturalised French physicist and chemist, discovered radiation, helped apply it in the field of X-rays and **coined the term** *radioactivity*. She **made a huge contribution** to science, but was one of the very few women who **gained the recognition** they deserved.

Science was a man's world in the nineteenth century. And yet, Mary Anning became an expert in fossils and geology. Coming from a poor family, she collected fossils on the beach and sold them to make a little money. She found fossils of complete marine reptiles that became extinct over 100 million years ago. She gained the respect of scientists, but living in an era when women weren't allowed to vote or attend university, she was not allowed to join the Geological Society of London.

A hundred years later, conditions were still difficult for female scientists. Rosalind Franklin, a chemist born in 1920, was part of a team who discovered the molecular structure of DNA. Tragically, she died aged thirty-seven, four years before her fellow scientists, all men, were **awarded the Nobel Prize** in 1962. They made no reference to Franklin in their acceptance speech.

Rosalind Franklin

5 3.13 **Listen to a podcast about another famous scientist, Ada Lovelace. What was she famous for?**

6 3.13 **Listen again and answer the questions.**

Ada Lovelace QUIZ

1. What did Ada Lovelace collaborate with Charles Babbage on?
2. How do people refer to Charles Babbage?
3. Who is credited with inventing the first computer algorithm?
4. In what way did Lovelace **see the** true **potential** of the computer?
5. How easy was it for women to have access to education in the nineteenth century?
6. When did Ada Lovelace find out that she had an aptitude for calculations?
7. Did many women manage to **win the respect** of their fellow scientists?
8. What did the US Department of Defence name after Lovelace?

A similar injustice happened when British astrophysicist Jocelyn Bell Burnell discovered radio pulsars, described as the greatest astronomical discovery of the twentieth century. Her supervisor and his male colleague were awarded the 1974 Nobel Prize in physics for the discovery, and she was completely left out. Many astronomers criticised the decision, but Bell Burnell finally gained recognition in 2007 when she was made Woman of the Year for her remarkable contributions to science.

In cases where women's **achievements were recognised**, we still find evidence of discrimination in the way these were reported in the press. When the brilliant chemist Dorothy Hodgkin was awarded the Nobel Prize in 1964 for discovering the molecular structure of penicillin and vitamin B_{12}, the paper headline was *Oxford Housewife Wins Nobel*. In fact, this housewife was also a professor at Oxford University.

Today the gender gap in the world of science is slowly closing and there are many female scientists inspiring new generations of girls to study scientific subjects. But there is still some way to go for women to be equally represented in science.

Go to **WORD STORE 7** page 15

WORD STORE 7A Scientific research

7 3.14 **Complete WORD STORE 7A with the words in red in the text and Exercise 6. Then listen, check and repeat.**

8 SPEAKING **Complete the descriptions with the verbs in WORD STORE 7A. Then write short descriptions of the two scientists from the text who are NOT described below. Discuss who you admire the most.**

1 She _________ the true potential of the Analytical Engine and the US Department of Defence _________ her achievements by naming a computer language after her.
2 She _________ the term 'radioactivity' and always _________ a mention as one of the world's most famous scientists.
3 Surprisingly, she was not _________ the Nobel Prize for her discovery of radio pulsars in outer space.
4 She _________ the respect of fellow scientists and found evidence of animals that had become extinct 100 million years ago.

WORD STORE 7B Prepositions after verbs and nouns

9 3.15 **Complete WORD STORE 7B with the underlined prepositions in the text and Exercise 6. Then listen, check and repeat.**

10 SPEAKING **Complete the questions with a verb or a noun in WORD STORE 7B. Then ask and answer the questions. Give reasons for your answers.**

1 What software programmes do you have ______ to at school?
2 What area of science would you like to be an ______ in?
3 If you were doing a science project, who would you ______ with?
4 Which school subjects do you think you have an ______ for?
5 Is there somebody in your family who you were ______ after?

WORD STORE 7C Words in science

11 3.16 **Translate the words in WORD STORE 7C and tick any that appear in the text and Exercise 6. Use a dictionary if necessary. Then listen and repeat. Do you know any other words you could add?**

12 Work together to complete these scientific facts using the words in WORD STORE 7C in the correct form.

1 The periodic table, showing all known ______ , was invented in 1867 by Russian chemist Dmitri Mendeleev.
2 An ______ moves around the ______ of an atom.
3 An ______ is a set of rules to be followed in ______ , especially by a computer.
4 $E = mc^2$ is Einstein's most famous ______ and helps to explain the theory of ______ .
5 Addition (+), subtraction (-), ______ (x) and _________ (÷) are the four basic maths operations.
6 ______ (e.g. lemon juice) have a pH value lower than 7.0.

7.2 GRAMMAR

Advanced passive forms

I can use a variety of advanced passive forms.

1 SPEAKING **Discuss what would happen in your home if all screens were banned for six months. Then read what happened to the Maushart family and compare.**

What happened when mum pulled the plug on technology

Susan Maushart unplugged her teenagers and for six months the family lived without their devices. Family rooms were no longer lit up by the light of screens and no electronic noises **could be heard** through the night.

Maushart decided to unplug the family because nothing was ever properly switched off. She'd constantly told her children to turn their devices off when doing their homework, but even when they **should have been switched off**, they were bleeping away in the background.

So what happened? Once the children **had been made to turn off** their technology, the family rediscovered small pleasures like board games, books and listening to music together. Susan Maushart's son **was given** a saxophone and took up music seriously. If the Internet was needed for homework, her older daughter just went to the library. The youngest daughter **hated being unplugged**, but Susan Maushart believes her children became more focused thanks to being less dependent on technology. She now believes all families **need to be encouraged** to unplug periodically.

2 **Read the GRAMMAR FOCUS. Decide which forms of *be* complete the gaps correctly. Then check your answers in the text.**

GRAMMAR FOCUS

Advanced passive forms

- Passive forms with present or past modal verb structures.
  … no electronic noises ***could*** [1] *be* ***heard*** *through the night.*
  … even when they ***should*** [2] ________ ***switched off****, they were bleeping …*
- Passive forms with verbs that take two objects, i.e. a person – usually the indirect object, and a thing – usually the direct object (*give sb sth*, *send sb sth*, *show sb sth*, etc.)
  Her son [3] ________ ***given*** *a saxophone.* (the 'person' is the topic – more common)
  A saxophone ***was given*** *to her son* (the 'thing' is the topic – less common)
- Passive forms with verbs + *-ing* or verbs + *to* + infinitive.
  The youngest daughter ***hated*** [4] ________ *unplugged.*
  … all families ***need*** [5] ________ *encouraged …*

Note: *make sb* ***do*** *sth* → *be made* ***to do*** *sth*
Once the children ***had been made to turn off*** *their technology …*

3 **Rewrite the sentences in the Passive starting with the underlined object.**

1 You can buy <u>absolutely anything</u> on the Internet these days.
Absolutely anything can be bought on the Internet these days.
2 Nobody could have predicted <u>the importance of the Internet</u> back in the 1970s.
3 You must protect <u>your computer</u> by using anti-virus software.
4 Architects may have designed <u>Bill Gates's house</u> on an Apple computer.
5 You can control <u>the volume of a YouTube video</u> with the up/down arrows on your keyboard.
6 They should have given <u>Albert Einstein</u> a Nobel prize for his theory of relativity.

4 **Underline the indirect object in each sentence. Then rewrite the sentences in the Passive using *by* if necessary. Which sentences are true for you?**

1 Yesterday, people sent <u>me</u> more than fifty messages.
Yesterday, I was sent more than fifty messages.
2 My parents might give me a new laptop for my next birthday.
3 They have promised us some new computers for the school.
4 People owe me lots of money.
5 They should offer my father a new job.
6 Today a temporary teacher is teaching us IT.

5 SPEAKING **Use the ideas below to write sentences using the passive infinitive or *-ing* form. Then discuss the statements.**

Most teenagers …
1 don't enjoy (shout at)
Most teenagers don't enjoy being shouted at.
2 can't stand (ignore)
3 would prefer (not criticise)
4 would like (take seriously)
5 get tired of (judge)
6 just want (love)
7 dislike (tell what to do)
8 aren't interested in (compare to other teenagers)

FOCUS VLOG About science and technology

31 **Watch the Focus Vlog. For the worksheet, go to page 145.**

Grammar page 166

7.3 LISTENING

Multiple choice

I can extract the main points from a news report about problems with technology.

1 SPEAKING **Look at the cartoons and identify what problems they illustrate. Discuss any similar problems you have had with technology.**

2 3.17 **Listen and match cartoons A–D with situations 1–3. There is one extra cartoon.**

1 ☐ 2 ☐ 3 ☐

EXAM FOCUS Multiple choice

3 3.17 **Listen again. For questions 1–3, choose the correct answer A–C.**

1 The shop assistant wants to
- A warn Julie against buying cheap laptops.
- B persuade Julie to increase her planned budget.
- C encourage Julie to store films and music on a laptop.

2 Which sentence best describes the situation?
- A The sat-nav has taken them the wrong way.
- B Luke wants to avoid the motorway.
- C Kate thinks Luke should trust the sat-nav.

3 Choose the most appropriate headline for this news report.
- A MOPED CRIME RISES BY 30 PERCENT IN LONDON
- B MOBILE THEFTS HIGHER ON PUBLIC TRANSPORT
- C MOPED THIEVES TARGET MOBILE PHONE USERS

4 **Complete the sentences about the recordings with the words in the box. There are four extra words.**

drop gaming laptop bag
map memory card mobile phone
rise sat-nav security word processing

RECORDING 1

a The shop assistant says four gigabytes of RAM is not sufficient if Julie wants to **go in for** ________ .

b The shop assistant says he'll **throw in** a ________ if Julie buys the better computer.

RECORDING 2

a Luke wants a ________ to help him **figure out** which way to go.

b Luke was **talked into** using the ________ even though they **wind** him **up**.

RECORDING 3

a Figures have **come out** that show a sharp ________ in moped robberies.

b The police say they are going to **bring in** new ________ measures.

WORD STORE 7D Phrasal verbs

5 3.18 **Complete WORD STORE 7D with the phrasal verbs in the box. Then listen, check and repeat.**

A

B

C

D

6 **Complete the sentences to make them true for you. Then compare with a partner.**

1 I usually listen to the same kind of music. I don't really **go in for** …

2 When I buy my next phone, I'd like the shop to **throw in** …

3 I always find it difficult to **figure out** …

4 I can't **talk** my parents **into** buying me …

5 The person who **winds me up** most is …

6 The government should **bring in** new laws to …

7 The next new book/film/album/game I want to buy is **coming out** …

PRONUNCIATION FOCUS

7 3.19 **Listen and complete the table. Then listen again and repeat.**

NOUN	ADJECTIVE	ADVERB
1 science	*scientific*	scientifically
2 technology	________	________
3 ________	electronic	________
4 ________	electric	electrically

8 3.20 **Mark the stress in the words in Exercise 7. Then listen, check and repeat.**

7.4 READING

Open-ended questions

I can scan a set of related texts to find specific information.

1 **Read the titles of the two texts on page 105. What are they about?**

2 SPEAKING **Discuss the questions. Then read the two texts quickly and check your ideas.**

1 What do you know about bacteria?
2 Do you know what the gut is and what its function is?
3 Do you think of bacteria as a threat to humans? Why?/Why not?

3 SPEAKING **Discuss how you feel about the topic in the texts. Is it something that interests you? Why?/Why not?**

EXAM FOCUS Open-ended questions

4 **Read the texts again and answer the questions.**

TEXT A
1 In which part of the body can we find most microbes?
2 What impact do pathogens have on the body?
3 Why does each person react differently to the same food?
4 What is the connection between the gut microbiome and medication?

TEXT B
1 How are most infections passed between humans?
2 Why could too much washing and cleaning be dangerous?
3 Why should you wash your chopping board immediately after cutting fish or meat?
4 How can having a pet dog influence your health?

5 3.22 **Match the words in blue in the text with their definitions. Then listen, check and repeat.**

1 the response of the body's immune system to some substances = *allergy*
2 a condition that causes breathing difficulties = ______
3 a condition that affects how people communicate and interact with others = ______
4 a condition that causes people to feel unhappy = ______
5 when your blood glucose is too high = ______
6 it protects against infections = ______
7 a disease/condition caused by viruses or bacteria = ______
8 when a person carries excess weight that might affect their health = ______

6 3.23 **Complete the news report with the words in Exercise 5. Then listen and check.**

Cities are taking steps to tackle air pollution following reports into its impact on human health. Children are at the highest risk of being affected because their [1] i________ s________ aren't strong enough to fight off [2] i________ . If they breathe in polluted air over a long period, they may develop [3] a________ or other lung conditions. People who suffer from pollen [4] a________ in the summer get worse symptoms in cities where diesel fumes act as an irritant. [5] O________ and Type 2 [6] d________ are not only due to lifestyle or genetic factors but also to traffic-related air pollution.

WORD STORE 7E Word families

7 3.24 **Complete WORD STORE 7E with the underlined words in the text. Then listen, check and repeat.**

8 SPEAKING **Complete the statements with the correct form of the word in capitals. Then discuss whether you agree with the statements and why/why not.**

1 ________ *is next to godliness.* John Wesley **CLEAN**
2 *Happiness: a good bank account, a good cook and a good* ________ . Jean Jacques Rousseau **DIGEST**
3 *Let your food be your* ________ *and* ________ *be your food.* Hippocrates **MEDICINE**
4 *Happiness is* ________ *for the body but it is grief that develops the powers of the mind.* Marcel Proust **BENEFIT**
5 *Whenever a doctor cannot do good, he must be kept from doing* ________ . Hippocrates **HARM**
6 *Some people are born with a vital and* ________ *energy.* Kate Chopin **RESPONSE**
7 *My honest opinion and my friendly* ________ *is this: do it or do not do it – you will regret both.* Søren Kierkegaard **ADVISE**

I'm not sure I agree with the first statement; it depends on the context. If we're talking about clean hands …

3.21 Text A

THE HUMAN MICROBIOME

Why our microbes could be key to our health

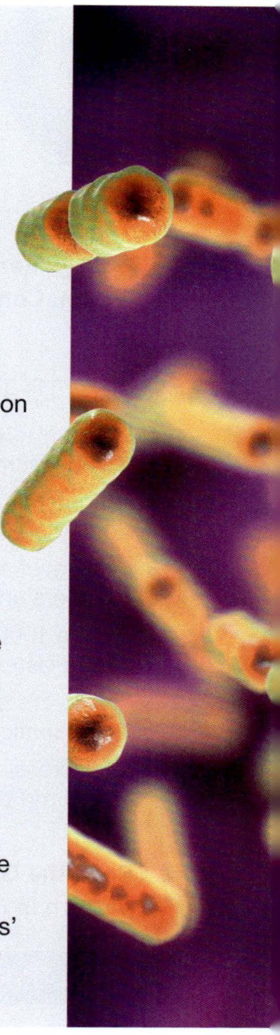

Did you know that more than half of your body is not human? The average adult has just under 40 trillion microbial cells and about 30 trillion human ones. In other words, human cells make up only 43 percent of the body's total cell count. The rest are microbes. No matter how well you wash, nearly every part of your body is covered in microscopic creatures. This includes bacteria, viruses, fungi and archaea, each with their own DNA, and together they are known as the human microbiome. 90 percent of this microscopic life is hidden away in our digestive system. But it would be naive to think that we carry around so much microbial material without it having any effect on our bodies at all.

Microbes and bacteria have a negative reputation and it's true that some microbes are known to cause disease and these are called pathogens. Others only become harmful if they get in the wrong place or grow in number. But the majority of microbes are essential for our health: they regulate the **immune system**, provide nutrients for our cells, help digestion and protect us against disease.

Different parts of the body all have very different communities of microbes. In his book, *I Contain Multitudes*, Ed Yong compares the body's microbiome to the earth's ecosystems. Just as the ecosystems of a rainforest and a desert are very different, he writes, so the microbiome of the skin is completely different from the gut. Microbiomes also differ between two people. In fact, each individual has a unique gut microbiome, as personal as a fingerprint. Rob Knight of the University of California San Diego and an expert on the human microbiome explains that differences in the microbiome of the gut help to explain why people respond differently to the same foods.

It is thought that 90 percent of disease can be linked back in some way to the gut and the health of the microbiome. Over recent years the gut microbiome has been associated with a wide range of conditions such as **diabetes**, **autism**, **depression** and **obesity**. It has also been linked to how individuals respond to certain drugs (and is affected by the drugs we take, such as antibiotics). It has even been suggested that it could be connected with how well we sleep. Microbial medicine is in its early stages, but some researchers think that it will become routine for doctors to keep an eye on the makeup of patients' microbiomes. Microbiome-derived medicine may well be the future of precision medicine.

Text B

ALL YOUR HEALTH QUESTIONS ANSWERED

Being too clean may be bad for your health

I shower every morning, wear clean clothes every day and I carry a hand sanitiser that I use regularly throughout the day to keep my hands clean, especially after touching my pet dog. My house is spotless and you won't see a dirty dish in the kitchen. But now I hear that being too clean may be bad for my health. Is this true?

We need to strike the right balance between keeping obsessively clean and learning to live with the bacteria around us. We know that certain bacteria cause diseases, and in recent times, sanitation and cleanliness have dramatically improved our health. But not all bacteria are bad. In fact, lots of them are extremely useful and beneficial to our health. So the question is, how can we avoid disease from the bad bacteria while nurturing the good bacteria?

First, let me be clear – I'd never suggest skipping the essentials, such as washing your hands. Scientists consider dirty hands as one of the most likely reasons why **infections** are passed between us. Getting your hands clean is not just a question of how long you wash them, but how well. Experts say you have to apply soap and water, rub all surfaces of the hands thoroughly for at least fifteen seconds, then rinse under running water and then dry them. The rubbing with soap detaches the germs from your skin, while the rinsing and drying takes them off the hands. But not all of our body has to be washed so thoroughly. A long shower every day may not be advisable, as it removes the 'good bacteria' from our skin.

Around the house, the solution for fighting the wrong kind of bacteria isn't excessive cleaning, but the right kind of cleaning. For instance, if you chop vegetables on your chopping board, you can wait until after your meal to wash it up. Not so if you've chopped raw fish or meat, when instant action is required, or you may increase the risk of infection.

Sometimes, it's good to get dirty! Research shows that children who grow up on farms are less likely to have problems like **allergies** and **asthma** and this is because they're exposed to a wonderful biodiversity of bacteria in the soil, rich in beneficial microbes. Dogs are also good for helping you to develop healthy bacteria – next time a slobbery dog jumps up at you, don't push it away. Instead, think about how the bacteria in its saliva may be boosting your immune system.

7.5 GRAMMAR

Passive reporting structures

I can use passive reporting structures to talk about general feelings and beliefs.

1 3.25 **Read the *Maths facts* and choose the correct option. Compare with a partner. Then listen and check.**

Maths facts

1 **It is thought that** numbers and counting began with the number *zero / one*.

2 Arithmetic **is considered to have originated** around *20,000 / 6,000* years ago in Sumer.

3 The *Egyptians / Romans* **are known to have invented** the numbers one thousand and one million.

4 Before 1500, the term 'mathematics' **was understood to mean** *'astrology' / 'physics'*.

5 **There are said to be** *limited / unlimited* opportunities for mathematicians.

6 *An increasing / A decreasing* number of students **are expected to be doing** Maths at university in the future.

2 Read the GRAMMAR FOCUS and find examples of each pattern in *Maths facts*.

GRAMMAR FOCUS

Passive reporting structures

You can use the Passive to talk about general feelings or beliefs with reporting verbs like *believe, know, think,* etc. These structures are usually used in more formal contexts.

- ***it* + passive verb** (present or past) **+ *that* clause**
- **subject + passive verb** (present or past) **+ *to* + infinitive** (*to do/to have done/to be doing*, etc.)
- ***there* + passive verb** (present or past) **+ *to be/to have been***

3 3.26 **Read the text. Identify the missing word in each underlined verb structure. Then listen and check.**

1 Pythagoras is understood to have come up with …

4 USE OF ENGLISH Complete the sentences with the correct form of the words in brackets. Make any changes neccessary, but do not change the order of the words.

1 It *is understood that Pythagoras came up with* (understand/Pythagoras/come up) the idea of odd and even numbers.
2 Pythagoras ___________ (say/prepare) the way for many famous Greek mathematicians.
3 It ___________ (think/Archimedes) is one of the greatest mathematicians of all time.
4 Archimedes ___________ (believe/to/make) his most famous discovery in the bath.
5 The Romans ___________ (not/think/be interested) in maths.
6 Several other civilisations ___________ (know/contribute) to the advancement of mathematics.

5 Rewrite each sentence in two ways. Begin with the words in brackets.

1 We know that most mathematical symbols were invented in the 1500s. (It …/Most …)
It is known that most mathematical symbols were invented in the 1500s.
Most mathematical symbols are known to have been invented in the 1500s.
2 Historians consider the seventeenth century to be a high point in the history of mathematics. (The seventeenth …/It …)
3 Many teachers thought that calculators could harm students' maths skills. (It …/Calculators …)
4 They estimate that there are over 10,000 new Maths graduates every year in the UK. (There …/It …)

6 List the school subjects you study by putting them in order from most important to least important. Compare your lists. How important is Maths?

Grammar page 167

WHERE DO OUR NUMBERS COME FROM?

Around 500 BC, the Greek philosopher [1] Pythagoras is understood to come up with the idea of odd and even numbers. [2] It said that Pythagoras prepared the way for many famous Greek mathematicians including Archimedes. [3] Archimedes is considered be one of the greatest mathematicians of all time. He discovered how to measure the volume of an object with an irregular shape. [4] He is believed to been taking a bath when he made the discovery, and leapt out shouting 'Eureka!' ('I have found it!'). Unfortunately, Archimedes was killed by a Roman soldier in 212 BC and mathematics entered a dark age. [5] It thought that the Romans just weren't interested in mathematics.

Brahmi numerals around 300 AD

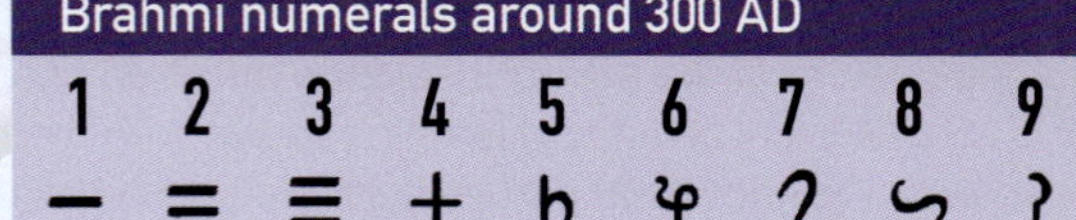

[6] There are known to been several other civilizations, including the Maya people in Mexico and scholars in ancient China, who contributed to the advancement of mathematics. However, the next big breakthrough was probably in 500 AD when the Indians invented 'zero'. They had already created symbols for the numbers one to nine. In fact, [7] it could argued that our 'Arabic numerals' should rather be known as 'Indian numerals'. After all, it was actually the Indians who invented them.

7.6 SPEAKING

Clarification

I can ask for and give clarification.

1 SPEAKING **Discuss which of these machines you would trust in place of a human and which you would not.**

1 A self-driving car
2 A robotic surgeon
3 A computer-generated online friend
4 A virtual teacher
5 A robot police officer

2 SPEAKING **Imagine you are going to a science and technology exhibition. Look at the posters and discuss which you would rather visit and why.**

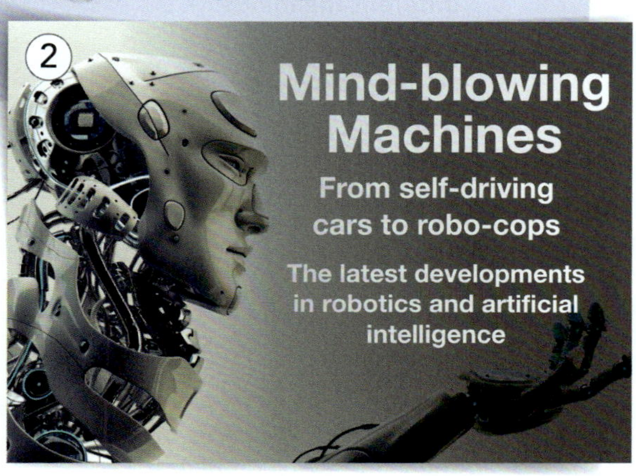

3 3.27 **Listen to a conversation at the 'Mind-blowing Machines' Exhibition. What type of machine is Sam describing?**

4 3.27 **Listen again. Which phrases from the SPEAKING FOCUS do you hear?**

SPEAKING FOCUS

Signalling confusion

Sorry, I'm not with you.
I'm not sure I follow (you).
I'm afraid you've lost me there.
I don't know what you mean by …

Checking your understanding

So, in other words, …
Are you saying …?
If I understand correctly, you mean …, right?

Giving clarification

Yes, precisely/exactly.
Yes, (that's) pretty much (it).
No, that's not (quite) what I meant.
What I meant was …

5 3.28 **Complete the conversations with words from the SPEAKING FOCUS. Then listen and check.**

Dialogue 1

A: Not many people agree with me, but I think computer games are a bit of a waste of time. I'd rather kick back with my friends than stare at a screen for hours on end.
B: Er … sorry, but I don't know what you mean [1]_________ 'kick back'.
A: What I [2]_________ was spend time together, you know, hang out, chat, relax.

Dialogue 2

A: I think I'd die without my phone.
B: And this year's Oscar for best actress goes to …
A: Ha ha, very funny. Are you [3]_________ I'm being dramatic?
B: Yes, [4]_________ . I think you'd survive without it.

Dialogue 3

A: Dan, I have to answer this question for homework. Can you help, please?
B: Sure, what's the question?
A: 'In what ways might socially intelligent robots benefit human society?'
B: Hmm. Well, I suppose the ability to have conversations with our machines will make a big difference.
A: I'm not sure I [5]_________ you.
B: Well, we interact with today's machines mostly by typing or pushing buttons, but some phones and tablets already understand voice commands, right? Imagine they and other machines could react to what you say and talk back to you properly.
A: Hmm. OK. If I understand [6]_________ , you mean we'll be able to have a conversation with our television or our fridge, right?
B: Yes, that's [7]_________ much it.
A: I'm not sure I'd want to have a conversation with a fridge.
B: Why not?
A: Well, they have a reputation for being rather cold.
B: Oh, very funny.

6 SPEAKING **Discuss the questions. Use the SPEAKING FOCUS to help you.**

1 In what ways are computer games good or bad for the people who play them?
2 What do you think has been the most important technological development during your lifetime?
3 Have social media made us more or less sociable? Explain your opinion.
4 In what ways might socially intelligent machines benefit human society?

ROLE-PLAY Clarification

33 34 **Watch the video and practise. Then role-play your dialogue.**

7.7 USE OF ENGLISH

Easily confused words

I can understand and use words that are easily confused.

1 SPEAKING What do you know about GPS? Discuss the questions.

1 What does GPS stand for?
2 How does GPS work?
3 When do *you* use GPS?
4 What other uses do you think it has?

2 Read the text. Match headings a–d with paragraphs 1–4. Check your ideas in Exercise 1.

a GPS takes Einstein's theory into account
b GPS is owned and operated by the US government
c GPS isn't just for determining location
d GPS isn't the only navigation system

Four things you didn't know about GPS

1 ______

Originally the system was built by the US Navy to locate submarines, and consisted of six satellites which **eventually** grew to ten. This model **preceded** the Global Positioning System or GPS as we know it today. At first, GPS was reserved for military use, but in 1983 US President Reagan made a **historic** decision to let all civilian commercial aircraft use it.

2 ______

GPS is just one of several space-based radio navigation systems. **Currently**, there are four global navigation systems: GPS (US), GLONASS (RUSSIA), Galileo (EU) and BeiDou (China). These navigation systems are essential for military operations, so some countries prefer not to be **dependent** on another country in case problems **arise**.

3 ______

Twenty-four satellites **ensure** that at least four satellites are in **sight** of any location on Earth at all times. Four satellites are needed to provide **data** to calculate an exact position. The GPS receiver measures the distance to three satellites by the amount of time it takes to receive a transmitted signal. A fourth satellite is used to account for Albert Einstein's general theory of relativity, that time moves faster for those satellites that are further from sources of gravity. Without correction, this would **affect** the exact location by about six miles. That, in a nutshell, is the **principle** on which the GPS is based.

4 ______

Most people associate GPS with giving directions when driving. But there are other important uses for this powerful tool. GPS helps farmers by gathering data about soil, weather patterns and expected rainfall. It is also used to find evidence of the speed at which the ice caps are melting, or the **deserts** are advancing, and this information contributes to environmental **advice** and warnings. GPS can even predict **whether** a natural disaster is likely and help to manage the consequences.

3 Choose the correct option, then answer the questions.

1 What was the purpose of the original US system that *proceeded / preceded* GPS?
2 What *historic / historical* decision did US President Reagan make in 1983?
3 *Actually / Currently* how many systems are there and who do they belong to?
4 How would your location be *affected / effected* if only three satellites were in *sight / site*?
5 How can GPS contribute to environmental *advice / advise*?

4 Read and complete the LANGUAGE FOCUS with the words in blue in the text.

LANGUAGE FOCUS

Easily confused words

Lots of English words cause problems because they are easily confused. If in doubt, it is always best to check in a dictionary.

- **Words that look or sound similar, but have different meanings**

cite/site/[1] sight
conscious/conscientious
dessert/[2] ______
late/lately
lose/loose
principal/[3] ______
proceeded/[4] ______
sensible/sensitive
weather/[5] ______

- **Words that look or sound similar and have similar meanings (this often includes words from the same word family)**

alike/likely
advise/[6] ______
alone/lone/lonely
assure/insure/[7] ______
breathe/breath
dependant/[8] ______
economic/economical
effect/[9] ______
historical/[10] ______
lay/lie
migrate/immigrate/emigrate
raise/rise/[11] ______

- **Words that look or sound different, but have similar meanings**

after all/finally/lastly/[12] ______
comprise/consist of/include
occasion/opportunity

- **False friends are words that look or sound similar to words in your language, but have different meanings**

realise (know or understand) ≠ *perform or carry out*
actually (in fact) ≠ [13] ______
[14] ______ (information) ≠ *date*

5 **Choose the correct option. Which statements do you agree with?**

1 It's so easy to *lose* / *loose* track of time when you're on your phone.
2 Technology is useful, but it makes you *lone* / *lonely* / *alone*.
3 Going to bed *late* / *lately* every night is not good for your health.
4 The *arise* / *raise* / *rise* in antisocial behaviour is due to too much screen time.
5 So it seems, *after all* / *finally* / *lastly*, that money doesn't buy you happiness.
6 If *present* / *actual* trends continue, cybercrime will *affect* / *effect* all of us.

6 **Complete the sentences with different parts of speech by changing one letter in the words in bold.**

1 You can *advise* someone or give someone **advice.**
2 You can **practise** the guitar or do some guitar _________ .
3 You can **breathe** in deeply or take a deep _________ .
4 You can be_________ on someone or be someone's **dependant**.
5 A situation can **affect** you badly or have a bad _________ on you.

7 USE OF ENGLISH **Complete the text with the correct form of the words in the box. There are two extra words.**

affect depend economy interest
like migration sense sure

Many species of bird ¹_________ twice a year often travelling long distances, especially if their natural habitat suffers harsh winters. Scientists are ²_________ in finding out how they navigate on these journeys. They know that birds are ³_________ to light and use the sun and stars to ⁴_________ that they know where north is located. Some researchers think they may also recognise landmarks, but it's doubtful that they are completely ⁵_________ on this method, because they can still navigate on cloudy days and fly across the oceans where there are no landmarks. The latest thinking is that they're ⁶_________ to use more than one method, including detecting the Earth's magnetic field.

8 SPEAKING **Choose the correct option. Then ask and answer.**

1 Are you *economic* / *economical*? Do you hate waste?
2 Do you *lay* / *lie* on your front when you're sleeping?
3 Are there any *historic* / *historical* buildings near your school?
4 Will you ever get an *occasion* / *opportunity* to go to Australia?
5 Would you say you were a person of strong *principles* / *principals*?
6 Are you a *conscious* / *conscientious* student?

9 **Replace the underlined phrases with words with a similar meaning in the box.**

actually complement compliment currently
eventually fantastic genial possibly sight site

1 I always say I've got lots of Facebook friends, but …
  a in fact I've only got 100. b at the moment I've only got 100.
2 'Are you going to buy a new laptop?'
  a 'In the end, yes.' b 'Maybe, yes.'
3 My grandma and grandpa always …
  a work well with each other. b say nice things to each other.
4 We love our family doctor. He's a …
  a great guy. b friendly guy.
5 Our local festival takes place in the grounds of a historic castle. It's a …
  a wonderful place. b wonderful spectacle.

10 SPEAKING **Discuss whether the words in the box in Exercise 9 have any false friends in your language. Are any of the sentences true for you?**

SHOW WHAT YOU'VE LEARNT UNITS 1–7

11 USE OF ENGLISH **Choose the word or phrase, A, B or C, that has a similar meaning to the underlined words in each sentence.**

1 If you're late for the bus home, you will be banned from coming on the next trip.
  A not be allowed to come
  B be permitted to come
  C be able to come
2 Some of the exhibits are on loan from private collections, while others belong to the museum.
  A when B where C whereas
3 The robot demonstration is very popular and people have to tolerate crowds at the venue.
  A put down to B put up with C put off to
4 If you like, you can join a half-hour tour of the exhibition. The tour is free.
  A thirty-minute B thirty minutes C thirty-minutes
5 You're welcome to discuss the exhibition, but you have to remain silent during the demonstration.
  A are made to B are able to C are required to
6 The exhibition booklet consists of fifty pages and contains all the data about the exhibits as well as some photos.
  A comprises B includes C is

Use of English page 168

7.8 WRITING

A narrative

I can write an entertaining narrative using a variety of verbs to describe ways of speaking.

1 SPEAKING Work in groups. Discuss the questions about Artificial Intelligence (AI).

1 What is AI? Write a short definition.
2 How do you feel about the idea of living in a world where AI is more advanced than human intelligence?
3 What problems might there be if it was impossible to tell the difference between a human and a robot?

2 SPEAKING The image on this page is from the story you are about to read. Say what might be happening in it. Now read the story and find out.

3 SPEAKING What did Robert discover about himself in his parents' office? What exactly do you think his parents' job is?

4 Study the WRITING FOCUS and find examples of each point in the story in Exercise 2.

WRITING FOCUS

Structure of a narrative

Short stories are usually written from a first-person point of view (the main character tells the story) or a third-person point of view (the writer tells the story but is not a character in it).

Beginning

- Get the reader's attention with a dramatic or mysterious opening, a statement by one of the main characters, or a detail concerning an important place or person from the story.
- Set the scene. Say where and when the story takes place and introduce the main characters.

Middle

- Use narrative tenses to describe the action.
- Add drama and interest with shorter sentences.
- Use language that appeals to the senses to describe what the characters see, hear and feel.
- Report speech using a variety of verbs.
- Give characters a voice using direct speech.

End

- Conclude the story with a twist, a lesson learned, a decision taken (as a result of what happened), or a later event linked to the story.

ROBERT WEAVER discovered he was not in fact Robert Weaver on Independence Day, 2092. His parents were celebrating at their company headquarters on Earth-Station One and had left the seventeen-year-old home alone for the weekend. They worked in advanced computing, though exactly what they did, their son wasn't sure. Their office, in the basement of the house, remained locked at all times and Robert was strictly forbidden from entering. 'Top secret and extremely dangerous,' his parents had warned him many times.

With his mother and father away, Robert had decided to throw a party. It was going well, just a few friends hanging out and having fun. But word had spread, and soon the house was full. A small group had gone downstairs and seen a strange blue glow coming from under one of the doors. 'Something's in there,' **whispered** one of the girls and insisted they find out what it was. Just as they were breaking in, Robert appeared at the bottom of the stairs. 'What are you … No!' he **yelled**, terrified of what his parents would say. But it was too late.

The room was more of a high-tech laboratory than an office, and in its centre they all saw what appeared to be a glowing blue holographic model of a human body. Robert raised his hands to his mouth in shock, and the hologram made precisely the same movement. As he turned to the others, the hologram mirrored him once again. 'What is this?' **gasped** Robert.

One of the girls in the doorway **screamed,** and another said in a shocked voice 'You're not human, Robert! You're … You must be an android. And that is your 3D image … because ONLY androids have holographic models!'

5 Look at the beginnings of six stories (1–6). Which beginnings ...

a use a dramatic or mysterious opening?
b use a direct quote to get the reader's attention?
c describe a detail or a place important for the story?

1 The morning after the brain implant, Zara Jones stretched, **sighed** and got out of bed. When she pulled back the curtains, she realised nothing was the same as it had been yesterday.

2 'Stand against the wall!' **snapped** the home-help droid at the frightened family. The revolution had begun at exactly four minutes past six.

3 Neither of the suns had risen that day and the only light in Milo Haver's apartment came from the communications screen. The extra hours of darkness presented tech-thieves like Milo with a rare opportunity.

4 'Please let me out!' **sobbed** seventeen-year-old Kevin Saunders, but the Saunders' smart-house refused once again.

5 They had been hunting for Robot AI71 for almost a week when they finally found her. She was missing a finger and her battery was critically low.

6 The sensors showed that the child was asleep. His mother remembered switching off his AI toys. So why could she hear **giggling** coming from the bedroom?

6 Match the base forms of the speech verbs in purple in the story and in Exercise 5 with the definitions in the LANGUAGE FOCUS.

LANGUAGE FOCUS

Speech verbs

You can make your writing more descriptive and dramatic by using alternatives to *say*. Use them to describe the way in which the characters speak, or the noises they make to express their emotions.

1 breathe in suddenly because you are surprised or in pain = *gasp*
2 say something quietly using your breath rather than your voice = ________
3 shout something loudly, to get someone's attention or because you are angry = ________
4 speak suddenly in an angry way because you have lost your temper = ________
5 laugh quickly in a high voice = ________
6 let out a long loud breath because you are sad, relieved, or frustrated = ________
7 cry noisily while taking short breaths = ________
8 make a high, long, loud noise because you are hurt or afraid = ________

REMEMBER THIS

When you use direct speech in a narrative, the words that are actually spoken should be written inside inverted commas. There should always be a comma, full-stop, question mark or exclamation mark at the end of what is said, and inside the inverted commas.
e.g. *'Something's in there,' whispered one of the girls.*
'What is this?' gasped Robert.

7 Read REMEMBER THIS, then choose an appropriate verb from the LANGUAGE FOCUS to complete each sentence. Add inverted commas where necessary.

1 Keep still! she ________ as quietly as possible, afraid that the hunter-drone might hear us.
2 How long was this going to take? wondered Leila as she ________ with frustration and told the system to reboot for the third time.
3 Tom ________ in terror when he opened the curtains and saw two sets of piercing red eyes staring out of the darkness at him.
4 The child's furry AI friend was always making jokes and they would often spend the whole evening ________ together in his room.
5 As Marlon ________ , pale blue tears ran down his cheeks and into both of his mouths.
6 Put the vacuum cleaner on the floor! ________ the security guard at the cleaner-bot, and this time it did as it was told.
7 Keila ________ with surprise as her feet left the ground and she rose gently to the ceiling.
8 Will you just be quiet! ________ the pilot at Dee-dee as the light-bike flew towards the clouds.

SHOW WHAT YOU'VE LEARNT

8 Do the writing task. Use one of the beginnings in Exercise 5 or your own ideas. Use the WRITING FOCUS and the LANGUAGE FOCUS to help you.

Write a narrative which features a character with artificial intelligence.

- Write when and where the story takes place, and who the main characters are.
- Decide what happens and how the story ends.

7.1 Vocabulary 4.49

acceptance speech /ək'septəns ˌspiːtʃ/
acid /'æsɪd/
addition /ə'dɪʃən/
algorithm /'ælgərɪðəm/
apply /ə'plaɪ/
atom /'ætəm/
award a prize /əˌwɔːd ə 'praɪz/
base /beɪs/
become an expert in /bɪˌkʌm ən 'ekspɜːt ɪn/
calculation /ˌkælkjə'leɪʃən/
capable of doing sth /'keɪpəbəl əv ˌduːɪŋ ˌsʌmθɪŋ/
coin a term /kɔɪn ə tɜːm/
collaborate with /kə'læbəreɪt wɪð/
collect /kə'lekt/
contribution /ˌkɒntrə'bjuːʃən/
credit sb with /'kredɪt ˌsʌmbɒdi wɪð/
discriminate against sb /dɪ'skrɪməneɪt əˌgenst ˌsʌmbɒdi/
division /də'vɪʒən/
electron /ɪ'lektrɒn/
element /'eləmənt/
equation /ɪ'kweɪʒən/
extinct /ɪk'stɪŋkt/
fellow scientists /ˌfeləʊ 'saɪəntɪsts/
fossil /'fɒsəl/
fraction /'frækʃən/
gain recognition /ˌgeɪn ˌrekəg'nɪʃən/
gender gap /'dʒendə gæp/
have access to /ˌhæv 'ækses tə/
have an aptitude for /ˌhæv ən 'æptɪtjuːd fə/
injustice /ɪn'dʒʌstəs/
make a contribution /ˌmeɪk ə ˌkɒntrə'bjuːʃən/
make reference to/refer to /ˌmeɪk 'refərəns tə/rɪ'fɜː tə/
marine reptile /mə'riːn ˌreptaɪl/
molecular structure /mə'lekjələ ˌstrʌktʃə/
multiplication /ˌmʌltəplə'keɪʃən/
name sth after sb /'neɪm ˌsʌmθɪŋ ˌɑːftə ˌsʌmbɒdi/
nucleus /'njuːkliəs/
outer space /'aʊtə speɪs/
periodic table /ˌpɪəri'ɒdɪk 'teɪbəl/
provided (that) /prə'vaɪdəd (ðæt)/
radioactivity /ˌreɪdiəʊæk'tɪvəti/
radiation /ˌreɪdi'eɪʃən/
receive a mention /rɪˌsiːv ə 'menʃən/
recognise an achievement /ˌrekəgnaɪz ən ə'tʃiːvmənt/
relativity /ˌrelə'tɪvəti/
remarkable /rɪ'mɑːkəbəl/
see the potential /ˌsiː ðə pə'tenʃəl/
subtraction /səb'trækʃən/
supervisor /'suːpəvaɪzə/
theory of relativity /ˌθɪəri əv ˌrelə'tɪvəti/
value /'væljuː/
velocity /və'lɒsəti/
win the respect /ˌwɪn ðə rɪ'spekt/

7.2 Grammar 4.50

ban /bæn/
bleep /bliːp/
periodically /ˌpɪəri'ɒdɪkli/
plug /'plʌg/
unplug /ʌn'plʌg/

7.3 Listening 4.51

(be) on the rise /ˌ(bi) ɒn ðə 'raɪz/
bring in /ˌbrɪŋ 'ɪn/
come out /ˌkʌm 'aʊt/
commuter /kə'mjuːtə/
distracted /dɪ'stræktɪd/
exit /'egzɪt/
figure /'fɪgə/
figure sth out /ˌfɪgə ˌsʌmθɪŋ 'aʊt/
go in for /ˌgəʊ 'ɪn fə/
look up directions /ˌlʊk ˌʌp daɪ'rekʃənz/
moped /'məʊped/
motorway /'məʊtəweɪ/
offence /ə'fens/
offender /ə'fendə/
price range /'praɪs ˌreɪndʒ/
reveal /rɪ'viːl/
robbery /'rɒbəri/
route /ruːt/
sat-nav /'sæt næv/
security measures /sɪ'kjʊərəti ˌmɛʒəz/
stick to /'stɪk tə/
storage /'stɔːrɪdʒ/
store /stɔː/
sufficient /sə'fɪʃənt/
take advantage of /ˌteɪk əd'vɑːntɪdʒ əv/
talk sb into /ˌtɔːk ˌsʌmbədi 'ɪntə/
target /'tɑːgət/
theft /θeft/
throw sth in /ˌθrəʊ ˌsʌmθɪŋ 'ɪn/
top-of-the-range /ˌtɒp əv ðə 'reɪndʒ/
turn around /ˌtɜːn ə'raʊnd/
urge sb to do sth /'ɜːdʒ ˌsʌmbədi tə 'duː ˌsʌmθɪŋ/
wind sb up /ˌwaɪnd ˌsʌmbədi 'ʌp/
word processing /'wɜːd ˌprəʊsesɪŋ/

7.4 Reading 4.52

advice /əd'vaɪs/
advisable /əd'vaɪzəbəl/
advise /əd'vaɪz/
allergy /'ælədʒi/
apply /ə'plaɪ/
archaea /ɑː'kiːə/
asthma /'æsmə/
autism /'ɔːtɪzəm/
beneficial /ˌbenə'fɪʃəl/
benefit /'benəfɪt/
biodiversity /ˌbaɪəʊdaɪ'vɜːsəti/
boost /buːst/
cell /sel/
chopping board /'tʃɒpɪŋ ˌbɔːd/
cleanliness /'klenlinəs/
community /kə'mjuːnəti/
condition /kən'dɪʃən/
depression /dɪ'preʃən/
derived /dɪ'raɪvd/
detach /dɪ'tætʃ/
diabetes /ˌdaɪə'biːtiːz/
digest /daɪ'dʒest/
digestion /daɪ'dʒestʃən/
digestive system /daɪ'dʒestɪv ˌsɪstəm/
essentials /ɪ'sentʃəlz/
excessive /ɪk'sesɪv/
exposed /ɪk'spəʊzd/
fight off /ˌfaɪt 'ɒf/
fingerprint /'fɪŋgəˌprɪnt/
fumes /fjuːmz/
fungi /'fʌŋgiː/
genetic factor /dʒəˌnetɪk 'fæktə/
germ /dʒɜːm/
grow in number /ˌgrəʊ ɪn 'nʌmbə/
gut /gʌt/
harm /hɑːm/
harmful /'hɑːmfəl/
hidden away /ˌhɪdn ə'weɪ/
immune system /ɪ'mjuːn ˌsɪstəm/
infection /ɪn'fekʃən/
impact /'ɪmpækt/
instant /'ɪnstənt/
irritant /'ɪrətənt/
linked back to /'lɪŋkt bæk tə/
lung condition /'lʌŋ kənˌdɪʃən/
medicate /'medɪkeɪt/
medicinal /mə'dɪsənəl/
medicine /'medsən/
microbe /'maɪkrəʊb/
microbiome /ˌmaɪkrəʊ'baɪəʊm/
nervous system /'nɜːvəs ˌsɪstəm/
nurture /'nɜːtʃə/
nutrients /'njuːtriənts/
obesity /əʊ'biːsəti/
pathogen /'pæθədʒən/
pollen allergy /'pɒlən ˌælədʒi/
provide /prə'vaɪd/
raw /rɔː/
regulate /'regjəleɪt/
regulation /ˌregjə'leɪʃən/
regulatory /ˌregjə'leɪtəri/
respiratory system /rɪ'spɪrətəri ˌsɪstəm/
respond /rɪ'spɒnd/

response /rɪˈspɒns/
responsive /rɪˈspɒnsɪv/
rinse /rɪns/
risk of infection /ˌrɪsk əv ɪnˈfekʃən/
rub /rʌb/
saliva /səˈlaɪvə/
sanitation /ˌsænəˈteɪʃən/
sanitiser /ˈsænətaɪzə/
skip /skɪp/
slobbery /ˈslɒbəri/
soil /sɔɪl/
spotless /ˈspɒtləs/
strike a balance /straɪk ə ˈbæləns/
surface /ˈsɜːfəs/
thoroughly /ˈθʌrəli/

7.5 Grammar 4.53

advancement /ədˈvɑːnsmənt/
breakthrough /ˈbreɪkθruː/
decreasing /diːˈkriːsɪŋ/
even number /ˌiːvən ˈnʌmbə/
increasing /ɪnˈkriːsɪŋ/
invent /ɪnˈvent/
leap out /ˌliːp ˈaʊt/
measure /ˈmeʒə/
numeral /ˈnjuːmərəl/
odd number /ˌɒd ˈnʌmbə/
scholar /ˈskɒlə/
unlimited /ʌnˈlɪmətəd/
volume /ˈvɒljuːm/

7.6 Speaking 4.54

artificial intelligence /ˌɑːtɪˈfɪʃəl ɪnˈtelədʒəns/
clarification /ˌklærəfəˈkeɪʃən/
exhibition /ˌeksəˈbɪʃən/
fully-automated /ˌfʊli ˈɔːtəmeɪtəd/
kick back /kɪk bæk/
mind-blowing /ˈmaɪnd ˌbləʊɪŋ/
perform an operation /pəˌfɔːm ən ˌɒpəˈreɪʃən/
range of movement /ˌreɪndʒ əv ˈmuːvmənt/
remote /rɪˈməʊt/
robotic surgeon /rəʊˌbɒtɪk ˈsɜːdʒən/
scary /ˈskeəri/
steady /ˈstedi/
surgical unit /ˈsɜːdʒɪkəl ˌjuːnət/
voice command /ˈvɔɪs kəˌmɑːnd/

7.7 Use of English 4.55

account for /əˈkaʊnt fə/
actually /ˈæktʃuəli/
advance /ədˈvɑːns/
affect /əˈfekt/
after all /ˈɑːftər ɔːl/
alike /əˈlaɪk/
alone /əˈləʊn/
arise /əˈraɪz/
assure /əˈʃʊə/
breath /breθ/
breathe /briːð/
cite /saɪt/
civilian /səˈvɪljən/
commercial aircraft /kəˌmɜːʃəl ˈeəkrɑːft/
comprise /kəmˈpraɪz/
conscious /ˈkɒnʃəs/
consist of /kənˈsɪst əv/
currently /ˈkʌrəntli/
data /ˈdeɪtə/
date /deɪt/
dependant /dɪˈpendənt/
dependent /dɪˈpendənt/
desert /ˈdezət/
dessert /dɪˈzɜːt/
determine /dɪˈtɜːmɪn/
economic /ˌekəˈnɒmɪk/
economical /ˌekəˈnɒmɪkəl/
effect /ɪˈfekt/
emigrate /ˈeməgreɪt/
ensure /ɪnˈʃʊə/
eventually /ɪˈventʃuəli/
exact /ɪgˈzækt/
finally /ˈfaɪnəl-i/
gather /ˈgæðə/
genial /ˈdʒiːniəl/
historic /hɪˈstɒrɪk/
historical /hɪˈstɒrɪkəl/
ice cap /ˈaɪs kæp/
immigrate /ˈɪmɪgreɪt/
in a nutshell /ɪn ə ˈnʌtʃel/
include /ɪnˈkluːd/
insure /ɪnˈʃʊə/
lastly /ˈlɑːstli/
lately /ˈleɪtli/
lay /leɪ/
lie /laɪ/
likely /ˈlaɪkli/
locate /ləʊˈkeɪt/
lone /ləʊn/
lonely /ˈləʊnli/
loose /luːs/
lose /luːz/
migrate /maɪˈgreɪt/
occasion /əˈkeɪʒən/
opportunity /ˌɒpəˈtjuːnəti/
practice /ˈpræktɪs/
practise /ˈpræktɪs/
precede /prɪˈsiːd/
principal /ˈprɪnsəpəl/
principle /ˈprɪnsəpəl/
proceed /prəˈsiːd/
rainfall /ˈreɪnfɔːl/
raise /reɪz/
receiver /rɪˈsiːvə/
rise /raɪz/
sensible /ˈsensəbəl/
sensitive /ˈsensətɪv/
sight /saɪt/
site /saɪt/
source of gravity /ˌsɔːs əv ˈgrævəti/
submarine /ˈsʌbməriːn/
take sth into account /ˌteɪk ˌsʌmθɪŋ ˌɪntʊ əˈkaʊnt/
weather /ˈweðə/
whether /ˈweðə/

7.8 Writing 4.56

basement /ˈbeɪsmənt/
gasp /gɑːsp/
giggle /ˈgɪgəl/
glow /gləʊ/
headquarters /ˈhedˌkwɔːtəz/
piercing /ˈpɪəsɪŋ/
scream /skriːm/
sigh /saɪ/
snap /snæp/
sob /sɒb/
whisper /ˈwɪspə/
yell /jel/

MY WORD LIST

SCIENCE

DOING RESEARCH

OTHER

VOCABULARY AND GRAMMAR

1 Complete the sentences with the correct form of the words in the box.

award coin digest figure wind

1 In 2018, Donna Strickland and Gerard Mourou were ___________ the Nobel Prize in physics.
2 It took the team months of trial and error to ___________ out the solution to the problem.
3 It really ___________ me up how people presume Engineering is a 'boys' subject'.
4 Grace Hopper was a computer scientist who ___________ the term 'debugging'.
5 Patients may have trouble ___________ certain types of foods.

2 Complete the sentences with the correct form of the words in capitals.

1 Well-balanced meals at school might help to solve the problem of ___________ among pupils. **OBESE**
2 A simple ___________ gives us the average number of pupils per class. **CALCULATE**
3 This new technology will be extremely ___________ for teaching blind students. **BENEFIT**
4 Her innovative designs are gaining ___________ internationally. **RECOGNISE**
5 It is always ___________ to wear safety glasses when handling chemicals. **ADVICE**

3 Complete the sentences with the correct passive form of the verbs in brackets.

1 I'm sure you ___________ (show) the results soon.
2 Your invention needs ___________(describe) in detail before you submit it to the Patent Office.
3 I don't mind ___________ (not pay) much for testing video games because I love playing them.
4 The spare parts should ___________ (deliver) a week ago.
5 Mr Jenkins ___________ (make/undergo) a stomach operation by his surgeon.

4 Complete the second sentence so that it has a similar meaning to the first. Use passive forms.

1 One report argued that the archaeologists had damaged some artefacts during the excavations.
It ___________ the archaeologists had damaged some artefacts during the excavations.
2 Some writers believe that the lost city of Atlantis existed until the ninth century BC.
The lost city of Atlantis ___________ until the ninth century BC.
3 It's not clear why the lights went out. They say there was a short circuit.
It's not clear why the lights went out. There ___________ a short circuit.
4 The police think that a dangerous hacker has been stealing sensitive data for over a year.
A dangerous hacker ___________ sensitive data for over a year.

USE OF ENGLISH

5 Complete the text with the correct form of the words in the box. There are two extra words.

breath depend digest economy history respond

No one likes walking through a busy city during rush hour. There's the noise and the traffic and perhaps worst of all, the pollution. When air pollution levels are high, we all [1]___________ in tiny particles of substances that are harmful to our health. As an asthma sufferer, for me the effects of air pollution are not just unpleasant, but potentially life-threatening. So, I really welcomed the [2]___________ decision by my home city to ban cars from the city centre altogether. It's just one of a growing number of cities taking bold action to reduce air pollution. Of course, politicians are cautious about the [3]___________ impact of banning vehicles from their cities. As a society, we've become [4]___________ on road vehicles not just to get around but to transport goods. The health problems associated with pollution, however, also bring huge costs.

6 Complete the sentences with the correct form of the words in brackets. Use up to five words in each gap and make any changes necessary.

1 Psychologists (think/establish) ___________ a connection between genes and specific types of behaviour, but there isn't enough information available yet.
2 When I saw Julia last week, she looked much better, so I guess the treatment she received (must/do/trick) ___________ .
3 My younger brother (not/enjoy/tell) ___________ to switch his computer off every evening at 8 p.m.
4 A place at the research station (offer/Tiago) ___________ after he had become a laureate in a national competition in physics.
5 Even primary school pupils (expect/do) ___________ many experiments nowadays.
6 Ada Lovelace (believe/study) ___________ the art of flying when she was twelve.

LISTENING

7 **3.29** **Listen to three recordings and choose the correct answer, A, B or C. You will hear the recordings twice.**

1 What's the most appropriate headline for this news report?
  A INTERNET PIRACY ON THE INCREASE AGAIN
  B NEW LAWS SET TO PUNISH ILLEGAL DOWNLOADERS MORE HARSHLY
  C ILLEGAL DOWNLOADERS TO RECEIVE NEW KIND OF WARNING

2 Which sentence is NOT true in this situation?
  A The woman is sure the man will fail his exam.
  B The woman is concerned about the man's health.
  C The woman believes the game is affecting the man's moods.

3 Which of the following is stated in the text as a fact, not an opinion?
  A To connect to the Internet, you should go to settings.
  B The phone has got some pre-installed applications.
  C The Wi-Fi option isn't on.

SPEAKING

8 **Do the task in pairs.**

Student A

Together with Student B, you are preparing a school exhibition about important inventions. Start the conversation and mention:

- Inventions included in the exhibition
- Display options
- Extra attractions
- Invitation to the exhibition

Student B

Use some or all of the following sentences after Student A starts the conversation:

- So, tell me, which inventions should we choose?
- I'm afraid you've lost me there.
- How about making some posters with basic information about them?
- Are you saying that we should just publish the invitation online?

9 **Look at the diagram. It shows different places where robots might change our lives in the future. In pairs, follow these steps.**

- Talk to each other about the changes robots might make in these places.
- Decide in which place robots would help us the most.

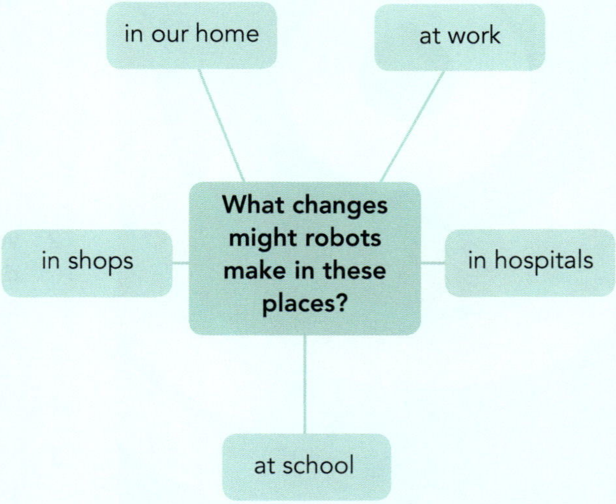

10 **Ask and answer the questions.**

1 Do you think robots will ever be able to think like human beings?
2 What other kinds of technological changes will change our lives in the future?
3 Do you think we rely on computers too much? Why?/Why not?
4 Some people think Science lessons are boring. How can teachers make them more interesting?
5 Some people believe the computer is the most important invention ever. Do you agree?

WRITING

11 **Read the writing task and write a story.**

Write a story featuring modern technology used to solve a problem.

8

Costing the earth

We do not inherit the Earth from our ancestors, we borrow it from our children.

Native American quote

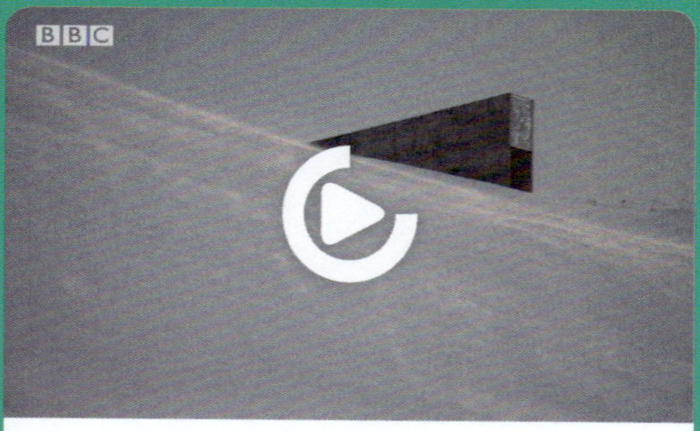

THE GLOBAL SEED VAULT

35 Watch the BBC video.
For the worksheet, go to page 146.

8.1 VOCABULARY

Nature • environmental issues • landscapes • animals

I can talk about the environment and animals.

SHOW WHAT YOU KNOW

1 Match the words from boxes A and B to make collocations.

A climate economic endangered global recycling renewable solar water

B bins change energy growth panels shortages species warming

2 Which collocations in Exercise 1 describe problems and which describe solutions? Complete the table.

PROBLEMS	SOLUTIONS
climate change	

3 SPEAKING Discuss the questions.

1 Are you optimistic or pessimistic about the future of our planet? Why?
2 Which environmental problems are the most serious? Which ones have you personally noticed?
3 Do you or your family use any of the solutions in Exercise 2? Why/Why not? Are they effective?

The Life Journey of a PLASTIC BOTTLE

Go to WORD STORE 8 page 17

4 Read the infographic. Which statistic is most shocking?

5 3.30 Listen to a commentary on the life journey of a plastic bottle. Why does it use humour and irony?

6 3.30 Match stages of the bottle's journey A–F with places 1–6 on the infographic. Then listen again and check.

A It remains on the loose and blows across open countryside through **orchards**, **meadows** and **ploughed fields** avoiding farmers and **ditches** if it can. ☐
B Somebody drinks the liquid and throws the bottle away – it is released into the wild and it begins its migration, avoiding eco-warriors who could lead to their extinction. ☐
C Eventually it reaches the open sea and joins the thriving population of plastic waste in the Pacific Ocean. ☐
D A plastics factory is the breeding ground for our plastic bottle. It hatches here and then moves to its natural habitat, the supermarket. ☐
E In **built-up areas** nowhere is safe – not even parks. Children want to kick it and park wardens want to catch it and put it in captivity. ☐
F It drops into a **stream** which takes it out of the **foothills** and onto the **plain**. ☐

7 SPEAKING Discuss how much plastic you and your family throw away in a typical week and how you could cut down on plastic waste.

WORD STORE 8A Environmental issues

8 3.31 Complete WORD STORE 8A with the words in the box. Then listen and repeat.

9 SPEAKING Complete the statements with an appropriate word or phrase in WORD STORE 8A.

1 The Great Pacific Garbage Patch is one of five such 'patches' in the oceans and they are doing ________ .
2 40 percent of all plastic produced is ________ used in packaging. Most of it is not recycled.
3 1 million plastic drinks bottles are sold every minute. None of them are ________ .
4 Plastic trash causes serious ________ of the________ . By 2050, oceans will contain more plastic than fish.
5 ________ such as Greenpeace use spectacular methods to protest against climate change.

WORD STORE 8B Landscapes

10 3.32 Label the pictures in WORD STORE 8B with the words in red in Exercise 6. Then listen, check and repeat.

11 SPEAKING Take it in turns to explain the difference in meaning between the following words.

1 a built-up area/open countryside
2 a foothill/a mountain
3 a stream/a river
4 an orchard/a forest
5 a meadow/a ploughed field
6 a desert/a plain
7 a ditch/a canal

WORD STORE 8C Animals

12 3.33 Complete WORD STORE 8C with the underlined words and phrases in Exercise 6. Then listen, check and repeat.

13 Complete the animal fact file with the words or phrases in WORD STORE 8C.

Did you know ...?

- There are only about 3,900 tigers living in the wild now and facing [1]________ . About 10,000 are kept in [2]________ .
- The Arctic tern makes the longest [3]________ of any bird. Every year it flies nearly 71,000 km from its [4]________ grounds in the Arctic to the Antarctic and back.
- In the 1980s only a few giant pandas remained in the wild. The Chinese government took action to protect their natural [5]________ and there is now a [6]________ population of over 2,000.
- The emperor penguin lays one egg which takes more than two months to [7]________ . During that time it lives through Antarctic temperatures of minus 40 degrees Celsius and wind speeds of over 200 km/h.

8.2 GRAMMAR

Unreal past and regrets – *wish*, *if only*, *it's time* and *would rather*

I can talk about present or future wishes and past regrets and use phrases with it's time and 'd rather.

1 SPEAKING **Discuss your vision of an ideal holiday and a nightmare holiday.**

2 3.34 **Listen to the Moss family discussing what to do for their next holiday. Answer the questions.**

1 What suggestions do they make?
2 What do you think they will probably do?

3 3.34 **Who said what? Write B for Ben, E for Ellie, M for Mum and D for Dad. Then listen again and check.**

1 '<u>If only</u> we could go somewhere exciting for a change.' ☐
2 'I think <u>it's time</u> we did something cultural.' ☐
3 'I <u>wish</u> you all realised how much I look forward to doing nothing for two weeks.' ☐
4 'I'<u>d rather</u> we went to the same campsite we went to last year.' ☐

4 **Read GRAMMAR FOCUS I and answer the questions about the sentences in Exercise 3.**

1 Which sentences refer to the present and which to the future?
2 Which tense is used after the underlined structures?

GRAMMAR FOCUS I

Unreal past

- You use ***wish/if only*** **+ sb + Past Simple** to say that somebody really wants a present or future situation to be different.
- You use ***it's (high) time*** **+ sb + Past Simple** to say that somebody should do something (now or in the future).
- You use ***would rather*** **+ sb + Past Simple** to say what somebody would prefer somebody else to do (now or in the future).

5 **Complete the second sentence so it has a similar meaning to the first. Which sentences are true for you?**

1 It isn't summer. I wish it *was summer* .
2 We always go to the mountains, but I prefer the sea. I'd rather we ____________ .
3 I ought to learn how to ski. It's time I ____________ .
4 I can't drive. I wish I ____________ .
5 I really need to plan my next holiday. It's high time I ____________ .
6 It's raining. If only it ____________ .

6 3.35 **Listen to the Moss family talking after their holiday. Choose the correct option to explain the meaning of these extracts.**

1 'If only I'd worn more sunscreen.' = Ellie *wore / didn't wear* enough sunscreen.
2 'I wish I hadn't forgotten my camera.' = Ben *had / didn't have* his camera with him.
3 'I wish you'd fallen in, too, Ben.' = Ben *fell out / didn't fall out* of the raft with Ellie.
4 'I just wish I'd known about the mosquitoes.' = Mum *knew / didn't know* that there were mosquitoes.

7 **Look at the example phrases in Exercise 6 and choose the correct tense in the rule in GRAMMAR FOCUS II.**

GRAMMAR FOCUS II

Past regrets

You use ***wish/if only*** **+ sb +** ***Past Simple / Past Perfect*** to talk about past regrets.

If only I'd worn more sunscreen.

I wish I hadn't forgotten my camera.

Note: ***If only*** is much stronger than ***wish***.

8 **Complete the sentences with the correct form of the verbs in brackets. Do you have any of these regrets?**

1 I wish I *had gone* (go) on holiday with my friends last summer.
2 If only I ____________ (revise) more for my last English test.
3 I wish my parents ____________ (be born) in another country.
4 I wish I ____________ (not give up) piano lessons a few years ago.
5 If only I ____________ (go) to bed earlier last night.

9 **Complete the sentences to make them true for you. Then compare with a partner.**

1 I wish I could …
2 It's high time I …
3 I'd rather people didn't …
4 If only I hadn't …
5 I wish my parents …

FOCUS VLOG About regrets

37 **Watch the Focus Vlog. For the worksheet, go to page 147.**

Grammar page 169

8.3 LISTENING

Note completion

I can identify the main points in a lecture about intelligent animals.

1 SPEAKING **Discuss which adjectives in the box you would use to describe the animals in the pictures.**

affectionate agile aggressive competitive friendly gentle harmless independent intelligent loyal playful social stupid wise

2 3.36 **Decide whether you think the statements below are true (T) or false (F). Then listen to a wildlife expert and check your ideas.**

1 Chimpanzees share half of the same genes as humans. ☐
2 Dolphins sometimes attack each other. ☐
3 Cats have more developed brains than dogs. ☐

EXAM FOCUS Note completion

3 3.36 **Listen to the lecture again and complete sentences 1–7 with a word or a short phrase.**

1 Dr Mathews is talking about the ________ animal species on Earth.
2 The reason why chimpanzees attack and often kill some of their own kind is the need ________ .
3 Dolphins are capable of fighting aggressively when they compete to win over ________ .
4 Not only are sheep intelligent, but they also have great memory and highly developed ________ .
5 Dr Mathews says ________ can be misleading, and owls are a good example.
6 Cats' unsociability is often associated with the fact that, unlike dogs', their ________ have not developed for centuries.
7 According to the speaker, cats' indifference to pleasing their owners results from the fact that they simply don't care for human ________ .

WORD STORE 8D Word building

4 3.37 **Complete WORD STORE 8D. Use the prompts below to help you. Then listen, check and repeat.**

1 a period of time in teenagers' lives when they are developing into adults
2 showing very strong desire to be more successful than others
3 an idea that is wrong, but people believe it because they don't understand the issue properly
4 appearing to be one thing, but being in fact very different
5 almost certainly
6 an opinion people have of something or someone based on what happened in the past
7 to look like or be like something or someone else
8 considered to be less important than it really is

5 **Complete the text with the words in WORD STORE 8D.**

Bird-brained or highly intelligent?

We know it's a common [1]________ to think that owls are wise. In fact, they're rather stupid. But what about other birds, do they deserve the same [2]________ ? Many scientists are convinced that the intelligence of some birds has been seriously [3]________ . Take the crow family. Crows are [4]________ top of the list when it comes to brain power. They perform even better than chimpanzees in some research tests. It just shows that appearances can be [5]________ . Not all birds are bird-brained – in the same way that not all humans are intelligent!

6 SPEAKING **Discuss the questions.**

1 Which domesticated animal do you think is most/least useful to society? Why?
2 How could wild animals be better protected? Is it ever OK to keep them in captivity?
3 Do you know any organisations, international or local, which help to protect animals and nature? Can you give examples of their activities?

PRONUNCIATION FOCUS

7 3.38 **Listen and repeat these word pairs.**

1 sheep /ʃiːp/ ship /ʃɪp/
2 keys /kiːz/ kiss /kɪs/
3 cats /kæts/ cuts /kʌts/
4 prove /pruːv/ proof /pruːf/
5 bag /bæg/ back /bæk/

8 3.39 **Listen and write down the five words in Exercise 7 that you hear.**

9 **Choose five words from Exercise 7 and take turns to dictate them to your partner. Check the words. Has your partner written the correct words?**

8.4 READING

Matching

I can scan a set of texts to find specific information.

1 SPEAKING Think about the most extreme weather conditions you have ever experienced. Tell your partner where you were, what you were doing and how extreme the weather was.

2 3.40 Look at the words and phrases below. Translate them using a dictionary if necessary. Then listen and repeat.

1 avalanche = ________
2 blizzard = ________
3 drought = ________
4 earthquake = ________
5 gale-force winds = ________
6 hurricane = ________
7 tsunami = ________
8 wildfire = ________

3 Complete the gaps with the words in Exercise 2 and then finish each piece of news in an appropriate way.

1 The ________ , measuring 7.4 on the Richter scale, lasted for seven seconds, but …
2 Roofs were blown off and cars overturned in the latest ________ to hit the coast of …
3 It has already been fifteen weeks since the ________ began. All the water holes have dried up and …
4 Fishing villages were destroyed by the latest ________ , as a thirty-metre wall of water …
5 Fire fighters are trying to prevent the ________ from spreading any further by …
6 Heavy snowfall has led to a high risk of ________ and skiers have been warned …
7 Not only drivers had problems during yesterday's ________ . A group of young hikers from the local college lost their way in the snow due to poor visibility and …

4 SPEAKING Discuss when and where the natural disasters in Exercise 2 might occur:

a in your region
b in your country
c on your continent
d elsewhere in the world.

5 SPEAKING Look at the photos in the film blog and discuss the questions.

1 Which of these films, if any, have you seen?
2 What is each film about and what do they have in common?
3 Which words in Exercise 2 would you associate with each film?

3.41

FILM BLOG

THIS WEEK'S THEME:
DISASTER MOVIES BASED ON TRUE STORIES

The subject of this week's Film Blog is natural disasters. Here are four films, all based on true stories, that will have you sitting on the edge of your seat! NB: The summaries contain SPOILERS!

A EVEREST

Everest tells the story of an attempt to reach the summit of Mount Everest in 1996. Several teams of climbers encounter a severe blizzard and eight climbers die, including two expedition leaders.

Once the climbers depart the base camp and **begin the ascent**, the film becomes **a gripping tale** of survival, life and death. When they **begin their descent** the blizzard hits. Climbers are blinded in the snowstorm and can see no more than thirty centimetres in front of them. It is best not to move in a whiteout, but if you stay still on Everest, you'll freeze to death. With gale-force winds of 160 kilometres per hour, and a lack of oxygen, the climbers fight for their lives. The **severe weather conditions** make rescue impossible.

The special effects make you feel as though you are right there with the climbers. During filming on Everest, an avalanche struck, killing sixteen Sherpa guides – a harsh reminder that Everest is one of the most dangerous places on Earth.

In films like *Everest*, it's difficult to feel sorry for the characters. If they want to take risks by climbing mountains, it's up to them. Not my problem. ***Ada***

B ADRIFT

There are few forces on Earth more deadly than a Category 4 hurricane. At its centre, a Category 4 generates winds of over 200 km/h and waves up to thirty metres in height. *Adrift* begins with Californian Tami Oldham waking up on her yacht after being unconscious for some time. She searches the boat for her British fiancé Richard Sharp, and soon realises he must have been **swept overboard** during the hurricane.

The film then goes back to five months before the hurricane when Tami and Richard are hired to deliver a luxury yacht from Tahiti to San Diego, 6,500 kilometres away. Two weeks into the voyage, they hear on the radio that a huge **storm is brewing** on their route, so they change course. Meanwhile, Hurricane Raymond changes direction unexpectedly, and they end up sailing straight into the eye of the storm.

The yacht is battered by twelve-metre waves and Tami wakes up alone. Then she spots Richard in the water.

When she manages to save him, she realises that he has **life-threatening injuries**. So she has to repair the boat and reach Hawaii. The unexpected twist is when Tami realises that Richard is actually a hallucination. At the end of the film, she is eventually rescued by a Japanese boat after being all alone aboard the yacht for forty-one days.

When I saw *Adrift*, I couldn't help wondering whether I'd be able to survive on my own, lost at sea. I'm not sure. 41 days is a long time. ***Fred***

6 SPEAKING **Read the reviews on the blog and check your ideas in Exercise 5. Which film would you like to see the most/least and why?**

EXAM FOCUS Matching

7 **Read the reviews again. Match texts A–D with statements 1–6. Two texts have two matching statements.**

In this film

1 the special effects led to difficult filming conditions for the actors. ☐
2 the director gave the characters their own voice. ☐
3 the main characters take action to try and avoid the disaster. ☐
4 the actors witnessed another disaster while making the film. ☐
5 the characters are not expecting the disaster. ☐
6 the characters are starving due to man-made problems. ☐

WORD STORE 8E Collocations

8 3.42 **Complete WORD STORE 8E with the words in blue in the reviews. Then listen, check and repeat.**

9 **Answer the questions about the blog reviews using the collocations in WORD STORE 8E.**

A
1 What phrase does the reviewer use to describe the type of story told by the film?
2 When did the climbers' problems start?
3 Why are rescuers unable to help the climbers?

B
1 What do Tami and Richard hear on the radio to make them change course?
2 What does Tami assume happened to her boyfriend during the hurricane?
3 In Tami's hallucination, where does she see Richard and what is wrong with him?

C
1 What does a large part of the film focus on?
2 How does the reviewer describe the conditions in which the actors had to perform?

D
1 What problems confronting William's village does the film investigate?
2 Despite the problems, how does the film end and why?

10 SPEAKING **Read the four comments under the reviews and discuss whether you agree with the views. Give reasons for your answers.**

C THE IMPOSSIBLE

The film is based on the story of a Spanish family who went on a Christmas holiday to Khao Lak in Thailand in 2004 and were caught up in the tsunami that hit Southeast Asia, killing 230,000 people in fourteen countries.

The filming of the tsunami itself is spectacular and uses a mixture of digital effects and real waves filmed in slow motion in a water tank.

Most of the film deals with the aftermath of the tsunami and the **agony suffered** by the family when they are split up and have no idea whether the others have survived.

In the film, the family are British, with Naomi Watts and Ewan McGregor giving honest and compassionate performances as the parents of three young boys. The director, Juan Antonio Bayona, wanted the film to be as realistic as possible, so the actors had to spend five weeks of **physically demanding** filming in a massive water tank.

The Impossible tells a captivating true story in which survival, society, family ties and human kindness all shine through.

The Impossible is an amazing film, but it made me question how sensible it is to develop tourism in areas that are likely to suffer natural disasters. Isn't it too risky? ***Boris***

D THE BOY WHO HARNESSED THE WIND

Set in Africa, the film tells the story of Malawian inventor William Kamkwamba. When he was just fourteen years old, he saved his family and village from famine by building an electricity-generating windmill from spare parts, working from rough plans he found in a library book. The film explores a community facing **extreme poverty and hunger**. Although the Kamkwamba family is struggling to survive, the parents do their best to focus on their children's education, but William is forced to leave school when the family can no longer afford the school fees.

The film is directed by and stars Chiwetel Ejiofor who spent a decade getting to know the Malawi people and learning their language. He uses subtitles so that the characters in the film mostly speak Chichewa, the Malawian language, and this is one of the reasons why the characters are so believable.

Drought and the underlying issues of deforestation, colonialism and climate change are dealt with in detail. But the movie ends **on a positive note**, with science-obsessed William Kamkwamba saving his village, bringing them electricity and more importantly, water.

The Boy Who Harnessed the Wind shows yet again how unfair life is and how important it is for rich countries to help people in poor countries to survive. ***Jessica***

8.5 GRAMMAR

Emphasis – cleft sentences and inversion

I can use a variety of sentence structures to change the emphasis.

1 3.43 **Read and listen to a conversation between two friends. Why does Will get angry?**

Will: I've been watching a programme about extreme weather events – interesting but very scary! **What they did was show** the effects of some recent floods where people had lost absolutely everything. **Rarely have I seen** such devastating scenes. **What I find shocking is that** some people still believe that humans have nothing to do with climate change.

Emma: I don't think you can blame humans.

Will: What? **It's those kind of comments that** really annoy me. How can you say that?

Emma: **All I'm saying is that** there's no link between carbon emissions and climate change. **What's happened is that** scientists have invented global warming so they can get more funding.

Will: Are you serious?! **Not only are you** making ridiculous accusations, **but** you don't even know the basic facts. Of course it's carbon emissions that are to blame for global warming.

2 Read and complete the GRAMMAR FOCUS with the words in blue in Exercise 1.

GRAMMAR FOCUS

Emphasis – cleft sentences and inversion

There are a variety of ways in which you can change the emphasis in a sentence.

- **Cleft sentences:** 'divide' a sentence by adding a clause to emphasise key information.
  What's [1]happened is (that) scientists have invented …
  (= Scientists have invented …)
  What they [2]_________ was (to) show the effects of …
  (= They showed the effects of …)
  [3]_________ *I find shocking is (that)* … (= I find it shocking (that) …)
  [4]_________ *those kind of comments that* … (= Those kind of comments …)
  [5]_________ *I'm saying is (that)* … (= I'm just saying (that) …)
- **Inversion: negative expression (*never, rarely, not only* etc.) + auxiliary verb + subject (formal).**
  [6]_________ *have I seen* … (= I have rarely seen …)
  [7]_________ *are you making ridiculous accusations, but you don't even know the basic facts.* (= You are making … and you don't even know …)

3 Rewrite the sentences using the structures from the GRAMMAR FOCUS and the words in capitals.

1 Will and Emma had an argument. **HAPPENED**
What happened was (that) Will and Emma had an argument.
2 Will (not Emma) started talking about climate change. **IT**
3 Will told Emma how strongly he felt. **DID**
4 Emma only suggested that you couldn't blame humans. **ALL**
5 Will couldn't believe Emma's views on scientists. **WHAT**
6 Will hadn't ever heard such ridiculous accusations. **NEVER**

4 Complete the sentences with the words in the box. There are two extra words.

all are do does has is ~~it's~~ what

1 ___*It's*___ the gases from industrialisation that have caused the greenhouse effect.
2 What scientists _________ is analyse air that's 800,000 years old, trapped under the ice in Antarctica.
3 Never _________ there been more carbon dioxide in the atmosphere than there is now.
4 _________ happened was that average temperatures rose by one degree Celsius last century.
5 Not only_________ we observing a rise in sea levels, but also many more extreme weather events.
6 If we don't act now, _________ we're doing is creating problems for future generations.

5 Make sentences from the prompts. Begin with the underlined words.

1 worry about most / I / is / global warming / What
2 I / money / my next birthday / All / for / want / is
3 it gets dark so early / What / winter / I / about / that / hate / is
4 most / the food / What / I / my country / about / love / is
5 who / in our house / the cooking / my father / does / It's
6 to do / What / buy a laptop / is / want / I
7 my clothes / to any of my friends / Under no circumstances / lend / would I

6 SPEAKING Discuss which sentences in Exercise 5 are true for you. Give reasons for your answers. Make more true sentences with the same sentence beginnings.

What I worry about most is …

Grammar page 170

8.6 SPEAKING

Giving a presentation

I can introduce new information during a presentation.

1 SPEAKING **Follow the instructions below.**

1 Make a list of well-known natural wonders.
2 Compare your list with another pair of students.
3 In groups of four, discuss which of the places you have visited or would like to visit.

2 **Look at the photo. Then describe it using the words in the box.**

cave/cavern crystal geologists minerals underground

3 3.44 **You are going to listen to a presentation about the Giant Crystal Cave. How does the information below relate to the topic? Listen and check.**

1 the year 2000
2 half a million years
3 fifty-five tons
4 58 degrees Celsius
5 ten minutes

4 3.44 **Complete the SPEAKING FOCUS with the words in the box. Then listen again and check.**

aware during familiar free realise ~~wondered~~

SPEAKING FOCUS

Introducing the topic

Have you ever thought about/considered/ [1]*wondered* how/why/what, etc. …?

[2]_________ my/this presentation, I plan to tell you about …

You may be wondering why I've chosen to talk about … today. Well, let me explain …

Introducing familiar information

We are (probably) all [3]_________ with …

You may be [4]_________ that …

You may already know that …

Perhaps you have heard of/about …

Introducing surprising information

Most people aren't aware/don't [5]_________ that …

… but, did you know that …?

You might not know that …

Finishing your presentation

OK, that's all from me.

Thank you for listening.

I hope you found the presentation interesting.

If anyone has any questions, please feel [6]_________ to ask now.

Giant Crystal Cave

5 **Complete the extracts from presentations with words and phrases from the SPEAKING FOCUS.**

1 You may be _________ why I've chosen to talk about Ha Long Bay in Vietnam today. Well, let me explain.
2 You may already _________ that Wolin, an island in Poland, is home to around 200 bird species.
3 Perhaps you have _________ of Table Mountain in South Africa. It rises high above the city of Cape Town.
4 We are probably all familiar with the Dolomite Mountains in northeastern Italy, but most people aren't _________ that this mountain range was added to the UNESCO World Heritage list in 2009.
5 Thanks for listening. If _________ has any questions, please feel free to ask now.

6 **Choose which is the correct piece of advice for each pair of tips on giving presentations.**

1 a Speak with a clear voice at a natural speed.
  b Speak more loudly and a little more slowly than normal.
2 a Look at a point just above the audience.
  b Make eye contact with members of the audience.
3 a Ask the audience questions to keep them involved.
  b Don't ask the audience questions.
4 a Write a script and read out every word when you present.
  b Have some notes with you when you present, but don't read them out.
5 a If you forget something, keep going. Nobody knows what you were planning to say anyway!
  b If you forget something, say sorry and finish the presentation.
6 a When you finish, thank the audience and sit down.
  b When you finish, thank the audience and invite questions.

7 **Prepare a presentation on a natural wonder. Follow the steps below.**

- Select a natural wonder that interests you.
- Do some research and plan your presentation.
- Find some interesting photographs to illustrate the presentation, if possible.
- Select useful language from the SPEAKING FOCUS.
- Learn and practise your presentation.
- Give your presentation to the class. Follow the advice in Exercise 6.

8.7 USE OF ENGLISH

Prefixes

I can recognise and form a wide range of words using prefixes.

1 Think about how the weather affects human behaviour. Choose the option you think is correct.

1 *Rainy / Sunny* weather makes you sleepy.
2 *Rainy / Sunny* weather makes you hungry.
3 *Rainy / Sunny* weather makes you more violent.
4 *Calm / Stormy* weather makes children hyperactive.
5 *Dull / Sunny* weather makes your memory better.
6 *Rainy / Sunny* weather makes you feel comforted.

2 Read the blog and check your ideas in Exercise 1.

HOW WEATHER AFFECTS HUMAN BEHAVIOUR

Are you **incapable** of getting up in the morning? That may be because it's raining, and the absence of sunlight causes the sleep hormone melatonin to be **overactive**. Heavy rain can also make you hungry. When it's cloudy, the hormone serotonin decreases, and you need more carbohydrates.

The effect of rain on crime rates cannot be **underestimated**. A *New York Times* investigation found that crimes committed on dry days far **outnumber** those committed in bad weather because people (including criminals) are **unwilling** to go out in the rain. Perhaps we should **reconsider** our negative opinion of British weather in the light of these statistics!

High temperatures on the other hand have long been linked with an **upturn** in violence. Raised temperatures cause an increase in heart rates and people are less able to control their temper.

Another study concluded that the behaviour of children can predict when a storm is brewing. When the barometer hits **pre-storm** lows, children become **hyperactive** and start **misbehaving**. One theory is that the positive electrical forces in the atmosphere increase blood pressure and cause **antisocial** behaviour.

An Australian study shows that sunshine can affect our mental sharpness: it may seem **illogical**, but it has been proven that people think better on days when the sky is grey. A selection of shoppers saw ten **unusual** objects in the checkout area of a shop and were asked to recall the objects later. Shoppers on cloudy days could remember them better than shoppers on sunny days.

Ending on a positive note, it's not all bad news for rain. If your emotions are **off-balance** or you're feeling **off-colour**, the sound of raindrops can be comforting. So if it's raining where you are, the best thing is to curl up and have a nap.

3 Read and complete the LANGUAGE FOCUS with the examples in blue in the blog.

LANGUAGE FOCUS

Prefixes

Prefixes can be added to the same root word to create different words. For example from the root word *use* you can form ***re****use* and ***mis****use*.

Prefix	Meaning	Examples
un- in- dis- il- im- ir-	not (mainly adjectives)	1 *incapable*, 2 ________, 3 ________, 4 ________
un- dis-	opposite (mainly verbs)	*undo, disallow*
re-	do again	*remarry*, 5 ________
hyper-	extremely	6 ________, *hypersensitive*
mis-	bad(ly), wrong(ly)	7 ________, *misinformation*
multi-	many or several	*multicultural*
off-/on-	not the case/ a place where …	8 ________, 9 ________ / *onstage*
out-	more than or better	10 ________, *outdo*
over-/ under-	too much/ not enough	11 ________ / 12 ________
anti-/ pro-	against/in favour	13 ________ / *pro-democracy*
pre-/ post-	before/after	14 ________ / *post-match*
self-	done to/by yourself	*self-esteem, self-obsessed*
sub-	inferior or lower	*substandard*
up-/ down-	increase or improve/become worse	15 ________ /*downturn*

4 Look the example words in the table. Does your language have similar prefixes?

5 Work out the meaning of the words in the box. Then choose three words and write example sentences for them.

antinuclear misjudge multipurpose overpaid pre-election self-awareness uncontrollable understaffed

I believe self-awareness can be learned.

6 **Match the words in the box with the correct prefixes to make twelve new words. What spelling rules can you work out for *il-*, *im-* and *ir-*?**

adequate approve aware believe capable legal literate mature probable relevant responsible safe

1 dis-______ , ______
2 il-______ , ______
3 im-______ , ______
4 in-______ , ______
5 ir-______ , ______
6 un-______ , ______

7 **Rewrite the sentences so they have the opposite meaning by changing the underlined word. Which statements do you agree with?**

1 It's probable that people will live on Mars one day.
2 The money I get from my parents is adequate.
3 It ought to be legal to cycle without a helmet.
4 Most people would describe me as responsible.
5 The roads in my country are really safe.
6 Doctors are underpaid for the job they do.
7 People who are pro-nuclear don't understand the dangers.
8 Pre-match interviews with footballers are boring.

8 **USE OF ENGLISH Complete the two comments about the blog with the correct form of the words in brackets.**

I don't like winter. I suffer from low **(ESTEEM)** 1 ________ and I fall out with friends because I'm very **(SOCIAL)** 2 ________ . I'm **(CAPABLE)** 3 ________ of getting up in the morning and I know that my work is **(STANDARD)** 4 ________ because I lack concentration. I need sunshine to feel alive.

Jonny

All this weather stuff is **(RELEVANT)** 5 ________ for people like me. I work all day in a shop, I travel to work and back by bus and I go to the gym in the evening. I'm totally **(AWARE)** 6 ________ of the weather most of the time!

Julie

9 **USE OF ENGLISH Complete another two comments about the blog with the correct forms of the words in the box.**

balance comfortable controllable able obsessed sensitive

Personally, I'm 1 ________ to changes in the weather. I find the transition from one season to another particularly 2 ________ . For a couple of weeks I don't feel like myself – I feel 3 ________ and 4 ________ to concentrate. Then I go back to normal again.

Emma

It really annoys me when people say the weather affects them. These people think it's all about them! They're 5 ________ and I get an 6 ________ desire to shout 'It's not the weather – it's just another excuse to talk about yourself!'.

Tim

10 **SPEAKING Read the comments in Exercises 8 and 9 again. Which do you agree or disagree with? Discuss how the weather affects your behaviour or how you feel.**

11 **SPEAKING Complete the sentences with the correct forms of the words in capitals. Then discuss whether you share any of these worries.**

I worry about …

1 jobs. Youth ________ is a big problem in my country. **EMPLOY**
2 the environment. People should use more ________ energy. **NEW**
3 the media. There is too much ________: you can't trust anybody. **INFORM**
4 health. There aren't enough doctors. Our hospitals are ________ . **STAFF**
5 politics. There has been a ________ in the numbers of people who vote in elections. If you can vote, you should. **TURN**
6 our society. I think it should be more diverse and more ________ . **CULTURE**

SHOW WHAT YOU'VE LEARNT UNITS 1–8

12 **USE OF ENGLISH Complete the second sentence so that it has a similar meaning to the first. Use between two and five words including the word in capitals.**

1 Could you tell me when the conference starts? **WONDERING**
I ________ you could tell me when the conference starts.
2 My parents are both extremely clever and I can't overestimate how much they've taught me. **HIGHLY**
Both of my ________ and I can't overestimate how much they've taught me.
3 I'm not allowed to use my electronic devices after 10 p.m. **BANNED**
I'm ________ my electronic devices after 10 p.m.
4 In my class, all the students turn off their phones in school time. **WHOLE**
The ________ turn off their phones in school time.
5 My last birthday wasn't as good as I expected and I was disappointed. **LETDOWN**
My last birthday was a bit ________ and I was disappointed.
6 I get very short of breath when I run for more than five minutes. **BREATHE**
I ________ when I run for more than five minutes.
7 My brother is so broad-shouldered that it's difficult to find tops to fit him. **SUCH**
My brother ________ that it's difficult to find tops to fit him.
8 I think football players earn too much for what they do. **ARE**
I think football players ________ for what they do.

Use of English page 171

8.8 WRITING

A letter to an editor

I can write a formal letter using a variety of linking devices.

1 SPEAKING Discuss the questions. Use the collocations in the box.

1 Why are some areas made into national parks?
2 Describe a well-known national park you know.

cultural heritage	diverse landscapes	environmental impact
natural beauty	sustainable tourism	wildlife protection

2 SPEAKING Read Alice's comment in *Young Traveller* magazine. Do you agree with her point of view? Why?/Why not?

3 Read Nick's letter to the magazine in response to Alice's comments. Why does he choose to write about Zakynthos? Would you like to visit the island? Why?/Why not?

HAVE YOUR SAY ...

Last month we asked you: Is enough being done to protect the natural environment in popular tourist destinations?

ALICE, 17, WROTE:

I'm a nature lover and it seems to me that governments and tour operators care mainly about the money that tourism generates and not about the negative impact that visitors have on natural environments. Development of facilities for tourists often takes priority over protection of areas of natural beauty and local wildlife, and not enough is done to establish national parks or develop tourism responsibly.

NICK, 18, WROTE:

Dear Editor,

1 I am contacting you after reading Alice's comments in January's *Young Traveller* magazine. Although I understand Alice's concerns, I would like to point out that there are tourist resorts where a great deal is being done to promote wildlife protection and preserve natural beauty.

2 Having just returned from a holiday to beautiful Zakynthos, I have personally seen sustainable tourism in action. Zakynthos is a picturesque Greek island surrounded by turquoise waters. In the southern part of the island lies the Bay of Laganas, a major nesting area for the Loggerhead Sea Turtle. The island's natural environment is vital to its success as a tourist destination, yet it is only relatively recently that the authorities have begun to protect it.

3 Under pressure from environmental groups, the Greek government made parts of the coastline into a marine national park in 1999. As a result, strict rules for tourists have been introduced on and near the beach. Walking on the beach is allowed only very close to the sea. Vehicles and artificial lights (e.g. torches) are banned on the beach. Similarly, speedboats are so disruptive that they are not permitted close to the beach. Despite the importance of tourism to Zakynthos, it is not actually possible to visit the beaches after sunset. While tourists can visit some of the nesting beaches during the day, they cannot get close to or touch the cages protecting the nests, leave rubbish or light fires. Having said this, the turtles continue to be a major tourist attraction.

4 The situation in Zakynthos is not perfect; nevertheless, it is undeniable that the negative impacts of tourism have been reduced and the turtles continue to lay their eggs there. To my mind, the island proves that some tourist destinations are concerned about more than just money. Perhaps the positive example set by Zakynthos could trigger other resorts to care more for their natural environments.

Yours faithfully,

Nick Mason

4 Answer the questions. Then study the WRITING FOCUS and check your ideas.

1 In which section(s) does Nick:
  a support his opinion with examples?
  b summarise his opinion then make a final comment?
  c give a reason for writing and opinion on the topic?
2 Why doesn't Nick use contracted forms (*it's, there's, can't*, etc.), abbreviations or informal language in his letter?

WRITING FOCUS

A letter to an editor

A letter to an editor is written in response to an article you have read or a film or programme you have watched. It should be formal in style and contain the following elements:

Introduction
- Your reason for writing and your point of view on the topic.

Body paragraphs
- Support for your point of view, further opinions and examples.

Conclusion
- A summary of your opinion and a recommendation or final comment.

5 **Complete the headings in LANGUAGE FOCUS I with the words in the box.**

cause and result ~~concession~~
certainty consequences reason

LANGUAGE FOCUS I

Formal language – review

- **Express** [1]concession

Although/Even though I understand Alice's concerns, I would like to point out that … .

Despite/In spite of the importance to tourism of Zakynthos, it is not actually possible to visit the beaches after sunset … .

- **Express** [2]________ **formally using participle clauses**

  Having just returned from a holiday to beautiful Zakynthos, I have personally seen … .

  Being a responsible tourist, I am happy to follow the rules.

- **Express** [3]________

  Speed boats are so disruptive that they are not permitted.

  Litter became such a problem that the area was closed.

- **Express** [4]________

  It is undeniable that/There is no doubt that the negative impacts of tourism have been reduced.

  Undeniably/Undoubtedly, there is still work to be done.

  Without (a) doubt, the situation is improving.

- **Describe** [5]________

  As a result/consequence, strict rules for tourists have been introduced.

  The result/consequence/outcome of (such a decision/choice) is that the turtles are left in peace.

  This could trigger other resorts to care more about their natural environments.

  This could lead to/result in other destinations introducing similar schemes.

6 **Which words from Nick's letter complete LANGUAGE FOCUS II correctly?**

LANGUAGE FOCUS II

Expressing comparison and contrast

***While/Whereas** many parts of the forest are protected, others are not.*

*Some tourists behave responsibly **while/whereas** others do not.*

***That said/**[1]________ **said this**, the turtles remain a major tourist attraction.*

The situation is not perfect; [2]________**/even so** *it is undeniable that the negative impacts of tourism have been reduced.*

Introducing unexpected or surprising contrasts

The island's natural environment is vital to its success as a tourist destination, [3]________ *it is only relatively recently that the authorities have begun to protect it.*

Despite the importance of tourism to Zakynthos, it is not [4]________ *possible to visit the beaches after sunset.*

7 **Read LANGUAGE FOCUS II, then rewrite extracts 1–7 using the words in brackets.**

1 Some beaches are protected while others are not. (whereas)
Whereas ____________________________

2 Whereas Zakynthos protects its wildlife, many other destinations fail to. (while)
Zakynthos ____________________________

3 Closing the beaches at night wasn't easy. That said, it was necessary for the sake of the turtles. (Having)
Closing ____________________________

4 Things are improving; nevertheless it will take years for the bay to recover completely. (even so)
Things ____________________________

5 Even though bins are provided, visitors continue to leave litter in the sand. (yet)
Bins ____________________________

6 In fact, the seabird population has begun to recover. (actually)
The seabird population ____________________________

7 Some of the forest is private while other parts are open to the public. (whereas)
Whereas ____________________________

8 **Read the message which was printed after Nick's letter in *Young Traveller* magazine. Then plan your letter to an editor.**

Thank you for your interesting contribution, Nick. We would like to hear from other readers who have visited, or know of places where similar efforts are being made. Write a letter describing a place in which negative impacts of tourism on the natural environment are being controlled.

YOUNG TRAVELLER

1 Do some research. Use your own ideas or try one of the following:
- Masai Mara National Reserve, Kenya
- Fraser Island, Great Sandy National Park, Australia
- Punta Tombo Penguin Rookery, Argentina
- Ao Phang Nga National Park, Thailand

(*Hint*: *search for 'visitor rules' or 'visitors' guide'.*)

2 Take some notes about the place:
- Where is it located?
- Why is it interesting?
- How are negative impacts of tourism controlled?

SHOW WHAT YOU'VE LEARNT

9 **Do the writing task. Use the ideas in Exercise 8, the WRITING FOCUS and LANGUAGE FOCUS I and II to help you.**

Write a letter to an editor in response to the message in Exercise 8.

8.1 Vocabulary 4.57

biodegradable /ˌbaɪəʊdɪˈɡreɪdəbəl/
breeding ground /ˈbriːdɪŋ ɡraʊnd/
built-up area /ˌbɪltˌʌp ˈeəriə/
contamination /kənˌtæməˈneɪʃər/
countryside /ˈkʌntrisaɪd/
current /ˈkʌrənt/
discard /dɪsˈkɑːd/
ditch /dɪtʃ/
eco-warrior /ˈiːkəʊˌwɒriə/
extinction /ɪkˈstɪŋkʃən/
food chain /ˈfuːd ˌtʃeɪn/
foothill /ˈfʊtˌhɪl/
gust of wind /ˌɡʌst əv ˈwɪnd/
hatch /hætʃ/
(have a) narrow escape /(hæv ə) ˌnærəʊ ɪˈskeɪp/
in captivity /ɪn kæpˈtɪvəti/
irreparable damage /ɪˌrepərəbəl ˈdæmɪdʒ/
leafy /ˈliːfi/
litter /ˈlɪtə/
meadow /ˈmedəʊ/
migration /maɪˈɡreɪʃən/
natural habitat /ˌnætʃərəl ˈhæbɪtæt/
on the loose /ɒn ðə ˈluːs/
orchard /ˈɔːtʃəd/
park warden /ˌpɑːk ˈwɔːdn/
patch /pætʃ/
plain /pleɪn/
plastic waste /ˌplæstɪk ˈweɪst/
ploughed field /ˌplaʊd ˈfiːld/
predator /ˈpredətə/
prey /preɪ/
release into the wild /rɪˌliːs ˌɪntə ðə ˈwaɪld/
reunite /ˌriːjuːˈnaɪt/
roam /rəʊm/
set free /set friː/
single-use plastics /ˌsɪŋɡəl juːs ˈplæstɪks/
stream /striːm/
tern /tɜːn/
thriving population /ˌθraɪvɪŋ ˌpɒpjəˈleɪʃən/
trapped /træpt/
trash /træʃ/

8.2 Grammar 4.58

campsite /ˈkæmpsaɪt/
for a change /fər ə ˈtʃeɪndʒ/
lounge /laʊndʒ/
raft /rɑːft/
sunbed /ˈsʌnbed/
sunscreen /ˈsʌnskriːn/
white water rafting /ˌwaɪt ˌwɔːtə ˈrɑːftɪŋ/

8.3 Listening 4.59

adolescence /ˌædəˈlesəns/
adolescent /ˌædəˈlesənt/
affectionate /əˈfekʃənət/
agile /ˈædʒaɪl/
bird-brained /ˈbɜːd ˌbreɪnd/
bond /bɒnd/
competition /ˌkɒmpəˈtɪʃən/
competitive /kəmˈpetətɪv/
conceive /kənˈsiːv/
deception /dɪˈsepʃən/
deceptive /dɪˈseptɪv/
developed /dɪˈveləpt/
domesticate /dəˈmestəkeɪt/
doubt /daʊt/
embrace /ɪmˈbreɪs/
establish a community /ɪˌstæblɪʃ ə kəˈmjuːnəti/
extend a territory /ɪkˌstend ə ˈterətəri/
gentle /ˈdʒentl/
hug /hʌɡ/
loner /ˈləʊnə/
mindlessly /ˈmaɪndləsli/
misconception /ˌmɪskənˈsepʃən/
notion /ˈnəʊʃən/
playful /ˈpleɪfəl/
please /pliːz/
recognition skills /ˌrekəɡˈnɪʃən ˌskɪlz/
reputable /ˈrepjətəbəl/
reputation /ˌrepjəˈteɪʃən/
resemblance /rɪˈzembləns/
resemble /rɪˈzembəl/
undervalued /ˌʌndəˈvæljuːd/
undoubtedly /ʌnˈdaʊtɪdli/
wise /waɪz/

8.4 Reading 4.60

a storm is brewing /ə stɔːm əz ˈbruːwɪŋ/
adrift /əˈdrɪft/
aftermath /ˈɑːftəmæθ/
avalanche /ˈævəlɑːntʃ/
battered /ˈbætəd/
begin the ascent/descent /bɪˈɡɪn ðə əˈsent/dɪˈsent/
believable /bəˈliːvəbəl/
blind /blaɪnd/
blizzard /ˈblɪzəd/
captivating /ˈkæptəveɪtɪŋ/
deforestation /diːˌfɒrəˈsteɪʃən/
disaster movie /dɪˈzɑːstə ˌmuːvi/
drought /draʊt/
earthquake /ˈɜːθkweɪk/
electricity-generating /ɪˌlekˈtrɪsəti ˌdʒenəreɪtɪŋ/
extreme hunger /ɪkˌstriːm ˈhʌŋɡə/
extreme poverty /ɪkˌstriːm ˈpɒvəti/
famine /ˈfæmɪn/
fee /fiː/
gale-force winds /ˌɡeɪl fɔːs ˈwɪndz/
gripping tale /ˌɡrɪpɪŋ ˈteɪl/
harness /ˈhɑːnəs/
harsh reminder /ˌhɑːʃ rɪˈmaɪndə/
hurricane /ˈhʌrɪkən/
life-threatening injuries /ˌlaɪf ˌθretənɪŋ ˈɪndʒəriz/
on a positive note /ɒn ə ˈpɒzətɪv ˌnəʊt/
on the edge of your seat /ɒn ði ˈedʒ əv jə ˌsiːt/
overturn /ˌəʊvəˈtɜːn/
physically demanding /ˌfɪzɪkli dɪˈmɑːndɪŋ/
rough /rʌf/
severe weather conditions /səˌvɪə ˈweðə kənˌdɪʃənz/
snowfall /ˈsnəʊfɔːl/
spare parts /ˌspeə ˈpɑːts/
split up /ˌsplɪt ˈʌp/
(be) swept overboard /(bi) ˌswept ˈəʊvəbɔːd/
suffer agony /ˌsʌfər ˈæɡəni/
summit /ˈsʌmɪt/
tsunami /tsʊˈnɑːmi/
twist /twɪst/
water tank /ˈwɔːtə ˌtæŋk/
whiteout /ˈwaɪtaʊt/
wildfire /ˈwaɪldfaɪə/
windmill /ˈwɪndˌmɪl/

8.5 Grammar 4.61

accusation /ˌækjəˈzeɪʃən/
carbon dioxide /ˌkɑːbən daɪˈɒksaɪd/
devastating scene /ˈdevəsteɪtɪŋ ˌsiːn/
flood /flʌd/
funding /ˈfʌndɪŋ/
greenhouse effect /ˈɡriːnhaʊs ɪˌfekt/
industrialisation /ɪnˌdʌstriəlaɪˈzeɪʃən/
ridiculous /rɪˈdɪkjələs/

8.6 Speaking 4.62

astonishingly /əsˈtɒnɪʃɪŋli/
astounding /əˈstaʊndɪŋ/
audience /ˈɔːdiəns/
awe-inspiring /ˈɔːr ɪnˌspaɪərɪŋ/
cave/cavern /keɪv/ˈkævən/
demolish /dɪˈmɒlɪʃ/
diameter /daɪˈæmɪtə/
drain /dreɪn/
miner /ˈmaɪnə/
natural wonder /ˌnætʃərəl ˈwʌndə/
wonder /ˈwʌndə/

8.7 Use of English 4.63

anti-nuclear /ˌænti ˈnjuːkliə/
anti-social /ˌænti ˈsəʊʃəl/
carbohydrates /ˌkɑːbəʊˈhaɪdreɪts/
comforting /ˈkʌmfətɪŋ/

curl up /ˌkɜːl ˈʌp/
disallow /ˌdɪsəˈlaʊ/
disapprove /ˌdɪsəˈpruːv/
disbelieve /ˌdɪsbəˈliːv/
downturn /ˈdaʊntɜːn/
hyperactive /ˌhaɪpərˈæktɪv/
hypersensitive /ˌhaɪpəˈsensətɪv/
illegal /ɪˈliːgəl/
illiterate /ɪˈlɪtərət/
illogical /ɪˈlɒdʒɪkəl/
immature /ˌɪməˈtʃʊə/
improbable /ɪmˈprɒbəbəl/
inadequate /ɪnˈædəkwət/
incapable /ɪnˈkeɪpəbəl/
irrelevant /ɪˈreləvənt/
irresponsible /ˌɪrɪˈspɒnsəbəl/
misbehave /ˌmɪsbɪˈheɪv/
misinformation /ˌmɪsɪnfəˈmeɪʃən/
misjudge /ˌmɪsˈdʒʌdʒ/
multicultural /ˌmʌltiˈkʌltʃərəl/
multipurpose /ˌmʌltiˈpɜːpəs/
nap /næp/
off-balance /ˌɒf ˈbæləns/
off-colour /ˌɒf ˈkʌlə/
onstage /ˌɒnˈsteɪdʒ/
outdo /aʊtˈduː/
outnumber /aʊtˈnʌmbə/
overactive /ˌəʊvərˈæktɪv/
overestimate /ˌəʊvərˈestəmeɪt/
overpaid /ˌəʊvəˈpeɪd/
post-match /ˌpəʊst mætʃ/
pre-election /ˌpriː ɪˈlekʃən/
pre-storm /ˌpriː stɔːm/
pro-democracy /ˌprəʊ dɪˈmɒkrəsi/
raindrop /ˈreɪndrɒp/
recall /rɪˈkɔːl/
reconsider /ˌriːkənˈsɪdə/
remarry /ˌriːˈmæri/
renewable /rɪˈnjuːəbəl/
self-awareness /ˌself əˈweənəs/
self-esteem /ˌself ɪˈstiːm/
self-obsessed /ˌself əbˈsest/
sharpness /ˈʃɑːpnəs/
substandard /ˌsʌbˈstændəd/
unable /ʌnˈeɪbəl/
unaware /ˌʌnəˈweə/
uncomfortable /ʌnˈkʌmftəbəl/
uncontrollable /ˌʌnkənˈtrəʊləbəl/
underestimate /ˌʌndərˈestɪmeɪt/
understaffed /ˌʌndəˈstɑːft/
undo /ʌnˈduː/
unemployment /ˌʌnɪmˈplɔɪmənt/
unsafe /ˌʌnˈseɪf/
unusual /ʌnˈjuːʒuəl/
unwilling /ʌnˈwɪlɪŋ/
upturn /ˈʌptɜːn/
violent /ˈvaɪələnt/

8.8 Writing 4.64

coastline /ˈkəʊstlaɪn/
concession /kənˈseʃən/
cultural heritage /ˌkʌltʃərəl ˈherətɪdʒ/
diverse landscape /daɪˌvɜːs ˈlændskeɪp/
facilities /fəˈsɪlɪtiz/
lay eggs /ˌleɪ ˈegz/
natural beauty /ˌnætʃərəl ˈbjuːti/
nesting beach /ˈnestɪŋ ˌbiːtʃ/
speedboat /ˈspiːdbəʊt/
sustainable tourism /səˌsteɪnəbəl ˈtʊərɪzəm/
take priority /ˌteɪk praɪˈɒrəti/
tourist resort /ˈtʊərɪst rɪˌzɔːt/
wildlife protection /ˈwaɪldlaɪf prəˌtekʃən/

MY WORD LIST

NATURE

ECOLOGY

OTHER

FOCUS REVIEW 8

VOCABULARY AND GRAMMAR

1 Complete the sentences with the words in the box. There are two extra words.

ditch drought habitat meadow orchard severe strong thriving

1 There was a small ____________ at the back of our house where we'd pick apples in the autumn.
2 The car skidded on an icy road and ended up in a ____________ but thankfully no one was hurt.
3 It was amazing to see tigers in their natural ____________ in India.
4 The village is in a remote mountain area and experiences some ____________ weather conditions.
5 The region is facing its worst ____________ in decades with no rain in months now.
6 Thanks to conservation efforts, there's now a ____________ population of wildcats.

2 Complete the sentences with the correct words to replace the words in brackets. The first letter is given.

1 The clearance of hundreds of trees has caused **i**____________ (*impossible to repair*) damage to the forest.
2 There are less than a hundred animals in the wild and just a handful in **c**____________ (*not in the wild*).
3 Despite its **r**____________ (*being similar*) to a bat, this creature is actually a type of squirrel.
4 The packaging is **b**____________ (*capable of being decomposed*).
5 Many of the villagers live in extreme **p**____________ (*being poor*) getting by on less than a dollar a day.
6 Raccoons are extremely **c**____________ (*that like to compete and win*) animals.

3 Complete the sentences with the correct form of the verbs in brackets.

1 If only you ____________ (sort out) the recycling properly, I wouldn't have to waste time doing it!
2 It's high time you ____________ (start) cycling to school. It's not too far.
3 If only the motorway ____________ (not build) near the nature reserve, it wouldn't have affected the local wildlife so much.
4 I'd rather you ____________ (use) reusable bags while shopping instead of those plastic ones.
5 I wish my parents ____________ (ask) me what breed of dog I wanted to get before buying me a poodle.

4 Complete the second sentence so that it has a similar meaning to the first.

1 Tim not only saw a school of dolphins, but he also spotted a whale.
Not ____________ a school of dolphins, but he also spotted a whale.
2 Claudia needs to mow the lawn before she goes on holiday.
What ____________ the lawn before she goes on holiday.
3 We have never experienced such cold weather while skiing.
Never ____________ such cold weather while skiing.
4 Josh only recommended you should buy more organic food.
All ____________ should buy more organic food.

USE OF ENGLISH

5 Choose the correct answer, A, B or C.

1 Don't you agree that it is ____________ time you started training your dog?
A best B high C right
2 Never before ____________ so many robins in our garden.
A do we see B we saw C have we seen
3 Pollution might be tightly controlled in one country, whereas ____________ country regulations may be less strict.
A in another B in other C others
4 Under ____________ are you to leave home now. There is a tornado approaching so we need to stay inside.
A no circumstances
B no way
C no conditions
5 I wish ____________ to my brother when he told me not to swim in the river with such a strong current.
A I had listened
B I listened
C I have listened
6 If only ____________ a presentation about endangered species! I'm struggling with the topic of acid rain.
A I have chosen
B I had chosen
C I chose

6 Complete the sentences with the correct form of the words in capitals.

1 The country is struggling to deal with the outbreak of malaria due to ____________ healthcare facilities. **ADEQUATE**
2 Max was facing the other direction and was completely ____________ of what was happening behind him. **AWARE**
3 Where a person comes from should be ____________ ; what's important is whether they have the skills for the job. **RELEVANT**
4 We don't want to lose Sophia and have asked her to ____________ her decision to resign. **CONSIDER**
5 The company has been forced to close some shops due to a sharp ____________ in sales. **TURN**
6 There have been complaints about vandalism and other ____________ behaviour. **SOCIAL**
7 He's a strict vegetarian and ____________ of keeping animals for meat. **APPROVE**
8 The clinic is severely ____________ with often only one or two nurses on duty. **STAFF**
9 The idea that space exploration has led to the loss of the ozone layer is a common ____________ . **CONCEIVE**
10 The bird's north–south ____________ route is 3,000 miles from Canada to Southern Mexico. **MIGRATE**

READING

7 Read texts A–D and match them with questions 1–6. Two texts match two of the questions.

Which text mentions an environment where ...

1 young creatures are protected from potential harm? ☐
2 temperatures can change dramatically during a single day? ☐
3 water levels change several times a day? ☐
4 a very wide range of species thrive? ☐
5 there are no distinct seasons? ☐
6 few plants and animals can live? ☐

A

DESERTS

Contrary to popular perception, temperature alone does not directly define whether an area of land is described as a desert. The key factor instead is rainfall, with desert areas averaging less than 254 millimetres of rain a year. There are, in fact, what are known as 'cold deserts', such as in the Antarctic, where temperatures can be below freezing. Even the hot, dry deserts we most typically think of, such as the Sahara, can experience very dramatic temperature drops at night. This is because the lack of cloud cover allows hot air to escape very quickly once the sun has set.

B

RAINFORESTS

As their name suggests, rainforests are found in areas with consistently high levels of rainfall, typically in tropical regions of the world around the equator. They may receive more than 2,000 millimetres of rain a year and with an average daily temperature of around 28 degrees Celsius, they are hot and humid. This climate is consistent all year round which creates the perfect habitat for an incredibly diverse range of plants and animals and makes them some of the most biodiverse environments on the planet.

C

TUNDRAS

One of the world's harshest environments are tundras, treeless ecosystems found in the Arctic and on the tops of mountains. These areas are very cold and windy with little rainfall, making it difficult for both plants and animals to survive. Most of the plants found on the tundra are very low-lying, growing in gaps in the rocks where they have some protection from the wind. The Arctic tundra is covered in snow for much of the year, with the soil below the surface permanently frozen. Tundra plants have a very short growing season of just fifty to sixty days during the short Arctic summer.

D

MANGROVE FORESTS

Mangrove forests are found in coastal areas around the world where trees and shrubs grow with their roots submerged in water that is a mix of freshwater and seawater. Mangrove forests are typically tidal, so water levels rise and fall twice a day. They play a vital role in preventing coastal erosion as well as providing a home to numerous species of fish, which use them as nurseries because the mass of roots creates a safe space for young fish away from the reach of larger predators.

SPEAKING

8 Look at the photos. You and your friend would like to spend some time helping the environment during the summer holidays. Choose the option which, in your opinion, is the best, and give reasons for your choice.

A

B

C

9 Ask and answer the questions.

1 What could be done to persuade people to recycle more?
2 How can you use social media to promote an environmentally-friendly lifestyle?
3 Is the work of environmental organisations effective? What makes you think so?
4 What are the advantages of living next to large green areas?

WRITING

10 Read the writing task and write a letter to an editor.

Read the question asked in a newspaper and Brian's reply. Write to the editor of the newspaper expressing your critical opinion to Brian's comment.

Have your say ...
As air travel contributes almost 10 percent of the world's carbon emissions, should we be travelling in ways that have less of an impact on the environment?

While I agree that we need to cut air travel, in an era of cheap flights other forms of transport, such as rail travel, are disproportionately more expensive and also significantly slower. Until there's an affordable alternative, I'm afraid people are still going to fly away on holiday. *Brian, 17*

BBC Learning a new skill

BEFORE YOU WATCH

1 SPEAKING In what order do children typically learn these life skills? Discuss how old you were when you learnt how to do them.

Learning how to …

read ride a bike speak swim
tie your shoelaces type walk write

2 SPEAKING Discuss the questions.

1 What new skills have you learnt since you became a teenager?
2 Is it easier to learn a new skill as a child, a teenager or an adult? Why?
3 Have you ever learnt how to juggle? Would you like to? Why/Why not?

WHILE YOU WATCH

3 1 Watch Chris (38) and Tahoe (8) learning how to juggle. Who is learning faster and why?

4 1 Choose the correct option and decide whether the statements are true (T) or false (F). Then watch the video again and check your answers.

1 Chris decides to up the ante by pitting himself *against / with* Tahoe. ☐
2 The *catch / trick* is that Tahoe is three decades younger than Chris. ☐
3 Scarves help to *find / form* a juggling network because they speed the process up. ☐
4 The practice stage is enjoyable. One step *onward / forward*, two steps back. ☐
5 Chris claims that he's not a *big / large* one for excuses, but he hasn't done enough practice. ☐
6 Chris is not impressed when he says to Tahoe: 'Give it your best *shot / throw*'. ☐
7 White matter fixes new brain pathways creating a sense of everything clicking into *point / place*. ☐

5 Replace the underlined phrases with the correct form of an appropriate phrase in Exercise 4.

1 If something seems too good to be true, it's because there is a hidden problem.
2 Learning a language is often a case of getting better and then getting worse.
3 I don't like reading about things. I prefer listening to podcasts.
4 When you are faced with a difficult challenge, always try your best. Never walk away.
5 Learning a new skill is so satisfying – that moment when everything starts to work perfectly.
6 In some sports – e.g. motor-racing – women should compete with men in an equal contest.
7 Whenever you meet interesting people, it's worth collecting their phone numbers so that you can create a group of useful contacts.

6 SPEAKING Discuss the statements in Exercise 5. Do you agree with them?

7 1 Watch the video again. What is happening during stages 1–3?

1 The cognitive stage
2 The practice stage
3 The automatic stage

AFTER YOU WATCH

8 SPEAKING Think about your experience of learning English and discuss the questions.

1 What is the best age to start learning a language? Why?
2 Which learning stage do you think you are at now?
3 How does learning English compare with other learning experiences such as learning how to dance, to drive, to play the piano, to ski, etc.?

Focus Vlog About daily routines

What was your daily routine when you were younger and how does it compare to now?

What did you use to do when you were a teenager that you miss doing now?

1 **Name a person you know well who is in their twenties or older. Think about their daily routine when they were teenagers. Which statements could describe what they used to do?**

1 He/she used to have a structured routine. ______
2 He/she used to make their own breakfast. ______
3 He/she used to play football with friends. ______
4 He/she used to belong to an athletics club. ______
5 He/she used to go to dance classes. ______
6 He/she used to chill at home in the evenings. ______
7 He/she used to do stretches in the morning. ______
8 He/she used to drive around listening to music. ______

2 **Does the person you know do any of the things in Exercise 1 now?**

3 3 **Watch the video and match the statements in Exercise 1 with the teenage daily routine of the speakers in the box.**

Aaron Hannah Harriet Natasha Nobuse

4 SPEAKING **Compare your daily routine now with the one your parents had. Discuss how similar or different they are.**

5 3 **Put the words in the correct order to make questions. Then watch the first part of the video (up to 3:18) again and answer the questions.**

1 Hannah / with / Who / to / would / school / walk ? ______
2 school / would / to / Aaron / How / get ? ______
3 use / Why / 'quite intense' / be / routine / Natasha's / to / daily / did ? ______
4 eat / school / home / to / way / use / the / What / Nobuse / did / from / on ? ______
5 routine / structure / to / What / some / Harriet's / used / daily / give ? ______

6 3 **Discuss the questions. Then watch the rest of the video (3:19–4:26) and check your answers.**

1 What would Hannah like to get back into?
2 Why did Aaron use to drive around a lot?
3 Why did Natasha use to see her friends much more?
4 What does Nobuse miss doing?
5 Why did Harriet use to get more things done?

7 SPEAKING **Are you a person who likes to have structure or variety in your day-to-day life? Why?**

FOCUS ON LIFE SKILLS

Communication • Critical thinking

8 SPEAKING **Discuss these sayings about youth. What do they mean and how much do you agree with them?**

- School days are the best days of your life.
- Youth is wasted on the young.
- Youth is the best time to be rich and the best time to be poor.

9 **Think about how life as a teenager was different for your grandparents. Write notes under the headings. Think about daily routines, free time, friends, school and your own ideas.**

Ways life is easier for teenagers now	Ways life was easier for teenagers in the past

10 SPEAKING **Discuss your notes. What is your conclusion?**

BBC Nature or nurture?

BEFORE YOU WATCH

1 **SPEAKING** **Look at the photo and the title of the video you're going to watch. Discuss what you think the video is about. Use some of the key words and phrases in the box to help you.**

| genes | growing up apart | identical twins | nature | nurture | upbringing |

WHILE YOU WATCH

2 (5) **Watch the video and check your ideas in Exercise 1.**

3 (5) **Complete the commentary with the words in the box. There are two extra words. Then watch the first part of the video (up to 0:55) and check your answers.**

| between | born | collection | environment | experienced | gathering | nurture | rare |

We're in London at St Thomas' hospital for a very special [1] ____________ of twins. Scientists love identical twins because they're perfect for examining how nature and [2] ____________ affect our lives. By studying both the similarities and differences [3] ____________ identical twins, scientists can begin to answer the big question – are we [4] ____________ , or are we made the way we are? If twins have grown up in the same [5] ____________ , it's difficult to know whether it's genes or experiences that have made them similar. It would be easier to check if they'd had different lives. Cases of twins growing up apart are [6] ____________ , but they do exist.

4 (5) **Watch the second part of the video (0:56–2:17) and complete the information about the girls.**

	MIA	ALEXANDRA
Nationality at birth	1 ____________	2 ____________
Age	3 ____________	4 ____________
Lives in	5 ____________	6 ____________
Parents	7 Angela and Andy	8 Wenche and Sigmund
Goes to school?	9 ____________	10 ____________

5 **SPEAKING** **Whose upbringing, Mia's or Alexandra's, is the most similar to your own up to the age of six? Discuss with your partner.**

6 (5) **Watch the third part of the video (2:18–4:10) with no sound. It shows the moment when Alexandra and Mia meet each other for the first time. Make notes about the following:**

- The feelings that Mia has just before Alexandra arrives.
- Their very first reaction to one another outside the house.
- The first thing they do when they get inside the house.

7 (5) **Compare your notes. Then watch the video again with sound and check your ideas.**

8 (5) **Watch the rest of the video (4:11–5:30) and notice Mia's mother's reflections about the following:**

- genetics
- parental control
- her own role as a parent

9 **SPEAKING** **Discuss whether you agree with Mia's mother's reflections in Exercise 8.**

AFTER YOU WATCH

10 **SPEAKING** **Are the following human attributes determined more by nature or nurture?**

| health | intelligence | life expectancy | looks | musicality | personality | size | sporting ability |

Focus Vlog About important people

Could you tell me about a family member or friend you look up to?

What have you learned from a friend or family member that has helped you later in life?

1 SPEAKING **Discuss who has influenced you most in your life. Refer to people in the box or your own ideas.**

aunt brother cousin famous person father friend (great-) grandmother (great-) grandfather mother roommate sister teacher uncle

2 **8 Watch the first part of the video (up to 2:17) in which the speakers say who has influenced their lives most. Match a person from the box in Exercise 1 with each speaker.**

1 Lilee – ____________
2 Hassan – ____________
3 Hannah – ____________
4 Aaron – ____________
5 Shaelyn – ____________

3 **8 Match the reasons why each speaker in Exercise 2 looks up to their family member with the names of the people. Then watch the first part of the video (up to 2:17) again and check your answers.**

1 She was the first woman pilot in West Virginia. *Aaron's great-grandmother*
2 She's kind-hearted and honest. ____________
3 He's following his dreams. ____________
4 He encourages me to keep going. ____________
5 She inspired me to be mature and responsible and make good decisions. ____________

4 **8 Watch the rest of the video (2:18–3:41). Which two speakers mention a friend rather than a family member?**

5 **8 Complete the quotes with appropriate verb forms. Then watch the whole video again and check your answers.**

1 **Lilee:** She ____________ out of home and she ____________ everything really well and she ____________ me up on her own.
2 **Hassan:** He's ____________ his dreams and that ____________ me to follow mine as well.
3 **Shaelyn:** I'm ____________ acting in the UK and I can always phone him back home and he's always able to ____________ me to keep going.
4 **Lilee:** She always told me to ____________ up for what I believe in and be who I ____________ to be.
5 **Aaron:** Small leaks ____________ big ships… And the same can be ____________ to finances as well. Buying small things here and there ____________ up very quick.
6 **Shaelyn:** My grandfather taught me how to ____________ independent, which has helped me since ____________ to the UK from Canada to feel like I can ____________ on my own two feet.

6 SPEAKING **Lilee and Aaron both mention women who were ahead of their times. Do you have any family members who were or are ahead of their times?**

FOCUS ON LIFE SKILLS

Critical thinking • Collaboration • Digital skills

7 SPEAKING **Work together to put the qualities of a good role model in order from 1 to 7 (1 being the most important). Add ideas of your own.**

A good role model is someone who …

- is independent ☐
- is a good communicator ☐
- is educated and hard-working ☐
- believes in themselves ☐
- prioritises the important things in life ☐
- is brave and takes risks ☐
- is kind-hearted and honest ☐

8 **Present your ideas in Exercise 7 to the class and give reasons for the order you have chosen.**

9 **Prepare a multimedia presentation introducing a person you admire the most and explaining what makes this person your role model. Share the presentation with the class.**

BBC Smog-free Mexico City

BEFORE YOU WATCH

1 **SPEAKING Imagine living in the metropolis of Mexico City, home to 22 million people. Discuss the questions.**

1 How different would your life be?
2 What kind of problems would you encounter?
3 What kind of things could the city authorities do to tackle traffic pollution?

2 **SPEAKING Compare the streets in Mexico City on Monday and Sunday. What difference do you notice? Why do you think that is?**

Monday

Sunday

WHILE YOU WATCH

3 **9 Watch the video and check your ideas in Exercise 2.**

4 **9 Match 1–8 with a–h to make phrases and collocations used in the commentary. Then watch the video again and check your answers.**

1 close	☐	a of a city
2 cycling	☐	b down
3 the heart	☐	c enthusiast
4 one-off	☐	d levels
5 smog	☐	e of life
6 tackle	☐	f measures
7 take	☐	g a problem
8 walks	☐	h event

5 **Complete the newspaper article about what Mexico City is doing about pollution. Use the phrases and collocations in Exercise 4.**

In an attempt to 1 ____________ its traffic problems and reduce 2 ____________ levels, the Mexican authorities have 3 ____________ measures to 4 ____________ down several main streets in the 5 ____________ of Mexico City on Sundays so that cyclists can have the streets to themselves. Mexico City now has a bike mayor, the campaigner and 6 ____________ enthusiast Areli Carreón. This is not a 7 ____________ event. Every Sunday, 50,000 people enjoy the car-free centre. Areli Carreón says that one of the things she likes best is that it doesn't matter who you are, people from all 8 ____________ of life come together and enjoy car-free Sundays.

6 **9 Make a list of all the non-polluting means of transport you can use in a city. Then watch the video again and tick the ones you see.**

7 **SPEAKING Discuss the questions.**

1 What does Anita Rani mean by 'progressive civic planning'?
2 What are the pros and cons of banning cars from main streets for one day a week?
3 What do you think of the idea of a 'traffic-free Sunday'?

AFTER YOU WATCH

8 **SPEAKING Imagine your local city authorities want to have a 'traffic-free Sunday'. First, they want to conduct a survey to measure public opinion. Complete the task.**

- Write a questionnaire with at least six questions.
- Interview other students in the class and record their responses.
- Write a summary of the results and make a recommendation.

Focus Vlog About dreams

Where do you think you'll be living five years from now?

What life goals will you have achieved by the time you turn fifty?

1 **Complete the three sentences and make one of them false. Can your partner guess which one is false?**

1 My dream is to one day …
2 In five years' time, I'll be living in …
3 By the time I'm fifty, I'll have …

2 **11 Watch the video. Does anyone mention the things you wrote in Exercise 1? Who do you think has the most ambitious plans?**

3 **11 Read the future predictions and complete them with the names of the speakers in the box. Then watch the first part of the video (up to 2:07) and check your answers.**

Hannah Kat Lilee Lucy Natasha Nick Nobuse

In five years' time …

1 ___________ will still be working freelance.
2 ___________ hopes to be living in a house with a music studio.
3 ___________ doesn't know what he/she'll be doing.
4 ___________ will be enjoying the outdoor life of Australia.
5 ___________ would like to be living in a hot country.
6 ___________ hopes to be living in a different part of London.
7 ___________ will be living in his/her mum's house.

4 **11 Match verbs 1–8 with noun phrases a–h to make collocations. Watch the rest of the video (2:08–3:26) and check your answers.**

1 play	☐	a a family
2 be in a	☐	b a book
3 travel round	☐	c the world
4 raise	☐	d TV series
5 publish	☐	e yoga teacher training
6 go further	☐	f top ten album
7 achieve a	☐	g a leading lady
8 complete my	☐	h in my career

5 **SPEAKING What will you have achieved by the time you turn fifty? Use the collocations in Exercise 4 or your own ideas.**

FOCUS ON LIFE SKILLS

Communication • Critical thinking

6 **SPEAKING Think about ten years from now. Answer the questions and compare with a partner.**

1 What would you like to be doing?
2 Where would you like to be living?
3 What would you like to have achieved?

7 **How important are these life goals for you? Write the list of your goals in the diagram and add at least one goal to each circle. Then compare your ideas with a partner.**

- be true to yourself
- make a lot of money
- have a big family
- make a difference
- travel the world
- do something I love
- make my parents proud
- be happy
- be famous

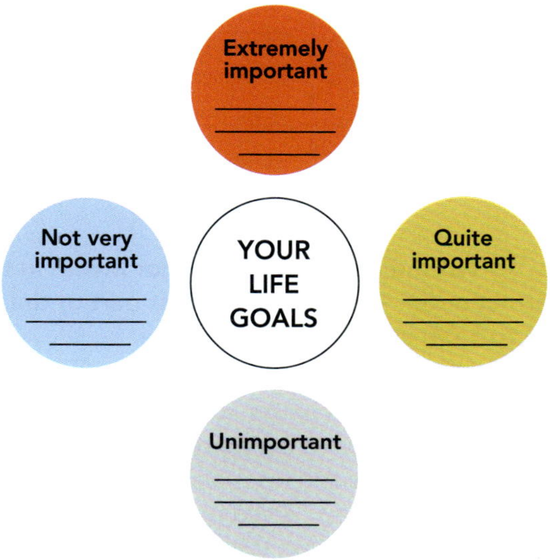

BBC Young entrepreneurs

BEFORE YOU WATCH

1 **SPEAKING You are going to watch a video about two young entrepreneurs. Discuss the questions.**

1 What sort of person do you think of when you read 'young entrepreneur'? Describe them.
2 What sort of industries do you think a young entrepreneur is most likely to go into?
3 Do you know any young entrepreneurs? Tell your partner about them.

2 **SPEAKING Imagine you have launched an exciting new business. How would you go about marketing your product?**

WHILE YOU WATCH

3 **14 Watch the video. Are any of the ideas you discussed in Exercises 1 and 2 included in the clip?**

4 **14 Complete the fact file about the two young entrepreneurs. Then watch the video again and check your answers.**

FACT FILE

Name	1 ______	6 ______
Age when she launched	2 ______	7 ______
Job	3 ______	8 ______
Marketing strategy	4 ______	9 ______
Help and inspiration	5 ______	10 Cara Delevingne

5 **14 Put the description of Minor Mynas in the correct order. Then watch the first part of the video (up to 1:04) and check your answer.**

a language. Minor Mynas provides a safe ☐
b Minor Mynas is an online educational platform 1
c and make friends across borders. ☐
d in conversations and learn one another's ☐
e place for children to communicate, chat ☐
f that connects children so they can engage ☐

6 **14 Replace the underlined words and phrases in the questions with words and phrases in the box. Then answer the questions and watch the second part of the video (1:04–2:54) to check your answers.**

entrepreneurs get along network profound think big

1 Why does Hillary think it's easier for kids to be friendly than adults?
2 What makes it easy to make connections in Hong Kong?
3 What makes Hong Kong such a good place for people who start their own business?
4 Who encouraged Hillary to have huge ambitions?
5 What did Nelson Mandela say that Hillary thinks is deep?

7 **Put the phrases into the correct order to explain how Georgia first launched and now runs her business. What is her recipe for success?**

- get orders ☐
- bake cakes ☐
- big boost ☐
- Cara Delevingne ☐
- upload more photos ☐
- Instagram tag ☐
- bake more cakes ☐
- upload photos ☐

8 **14 Watch the rest of the video (2:55–4:20) and check your ideas in Exercise 7.**

AFTER YOU WATCH

9 **SPEAKING Look at some businesses young people make money on and add your own ideas. Discuss what you think each business does and whether or not it would be suitable for you. Explain why.**

e-sport player meme creator online reviewer social media influencer vlogger YouTuber

Focus Vlog About money

Do you usually pay with cash or card? What sort of things are you likely to pay for with cash?

What ways of paying are likely to become popular in the future?

1 SPEAKING **Which of the following do people usually pay for by card/in cash in your country? Discuss, then answer the questions.**

clothes coffee groceries hairdressers public transport taxi tips

1 What are the advantages and disadvantages of paying by card or with cash?
2 What other ways of paying can you think of?
3 Which way of paying do you use most?

2 18 **Watch the first part of the video (up to 1:58) and complete the sentences with the names of the speakers in the box. Which speakers prefer cash to all other ways of paying?**

Kat Lilee Lucy Sam Shaelyn

1 ___________ thinks it's too easy to overspend with a card.
2 ___________ uses cash for everyday necessities.
3 ___________ only uses cash for tips.
4 ___________ uses a card except for paying her nail lady.
5 ___________ prefers cash, but can't always find an ATM.

3 18 **Watch the rest of the video (1:59–3:18). Match the ways of paying the people think will be popular in the future with the explanations. Then watch the video again and check your answers.**

Sam: contactless ☐
Kat: a digital currency ☐
Lilee: phone-pay ☐
Shaelyn: e-wallets ☐
Lucy: contactless ☐

1 because it will be easy for people to leave the house and not have to take a bag or wallet.
2 because it saves people the hassle of having to go for currency exchange and carry loads of cash.
3 and maybe if they input that in other devices as well, that might become more popular too.
4 using a cellular device and a back-up – maybe a contactless card – if your phone dies.
5 but he/she personally hopes that people will stick to cash.

4 SPEAKING **Discuss which predictions in Exercise 3 you agree with. Can you imagine a world without any cash at all?**

FOCUS ON LIFE SKILLS

Communication • Critical thinking

5 SPEAKING **Read the travel advice and discuss questions 1–3 with your partner.**

Travel Advice
How much to tip in the USA

Meal in a restaurant	15–20% of the bill
Home delivery	10% of the order
Toilet attendant	50c–$3
Hotel cleaner	$2–5 a day
Taxi	15–20% of the fare
Hair, nails, etc.	15–20% of the price

1 Is it common to leave a tip in your country in the places listed above?
2 How much do people usually tip?
3 Do you think tipping should be banned? Why/ Why not?

BBC Feeling like a leader

BEFORE YOU WATCH

1 SPEAKING You are going to watch an animation video about leadership. Discuss the questions.

1 Which leaders in your school, community, country or the world do you admire? Why?
2 What qualities do you think natural leaders have in common?
3 Are there things you can do to 'fake' leadership qualities?

2 Complete the summary in the screenshot from the video about four ways to appear more like a leader.

WHILE YOU WATCH

3 ▶19 Watch the video and check your answers in Exercise 2.

4 Match 1–8 with a–h to make phrases or expressions from the video. Use a dictionary if necessary.

1 use expansive hand ☐
2 give ☐
3 look as ☐
4 have a profound ☐
5 project ☐
6 social ☐
7 take up more ☐
8 make ☐

a assumptions
b leadership qualities
c effect
d animals
e gestures
f if you own the place
g the impression
h room

5 Complete the extracts from the commentary with the phrases and expressions in Exercise 4.

1 … the bigger you are, the easier it is to ____________ .
2 As ____________ , we can ____________ about a person from the way they look, and the way they behave.
3 If ____________ , people will think you do!
4 The way you present yourself has a really ____________ on the way you think about yourself.
5 If you use big gestures, you ____________ , and people get the idea that you're more powerful.
6 Politicians or religious preachers use huge ____________ and this ____________ that these people are bigger than they actually are.

6 ▶19 Watch the video again and check your answers in Exercise 5.

7 SPEAKING Discuss how much you agree with the statements in Exercise 5.

AFTER YOU WATCH

8 SPEAKING Complete the sentence to best sum up the conclusion in the video. Then discuss whether you think it's possible to 'fake it till you make it'.

If you act like a leader, …

Focus Vlog About job interviews

Have you ever been to a job interview?
What sort of questions did they ask you?
What did you reply?

1 SPEAKING **Look at the interview questions in Exercise 2 and discuss the following:**

1 Which questions are easy/difficult?
2 Which questions are predictable/unexpected?
3 Which questions would you most/least like to answer?

2 21 **Watch the video and match the people with the questions they were asked. What sort of jobs do you think they were being interviewed for?**

1 Hannah ☐
2 Sam ☐
3 Kat ☐
4 Shaelyn ☐
5 Harriet ☐
6 Lilee ☐

A What do you know about the store?
What can you bring to the table?

B Will you be able to help customers?
Why are you fit for the job?
Why do you want to work for our company?

C What experience do you have with kids?
Do you have a car?

D Why do you want the job?
What are your strengths and weaknesses?

E What is your previous experience working in foods?

F Are you willing to move for the job?
Are you willing to work overtime?
What is your favourite food?
Are you willing to walk up the stairs?

3 **Answer the questions with the names of the speakers in Exercise 2.**

1 Who said he/she would always be there with a smile? ___________
2 Who told the interviewer that he/she was a good team player? ___________
3 Who said he/she was willing to work as hard as he/she possibly could? ___________
4 Who said he/she was used to kids because he/she was from a big family? ___________
5 Who described how he/she had served foods in his/her previous job? ___________
6 Who said he/she had been asked some strange questions? ___________
7 Who told the company that he/she thought they were ecologically-friendly? ___________

4 21 **Watch the video again and check your answers in Exercise 3.**

5 SPEAKING **Have you ever had a job interview? What questions were you asked and how did you reply?**

FOCUS ON LIFE SKILLS

Communication • Collaboration • Digital skills

6 SPEAKING **What would be important to you in a job? Discuss the list and add any other ideas you may have. Decide on your top three.**

- a good salary and benefits
- opportunities for advancement
- interesting, varied work
- competent, approachable managers
- a positive company culture and mission
- an informal, 'fun' working environment
- flexible hours and conditions

7 **Poll other students in your class on their top three. Make notes and count which aspects of work are most important for students. Calculate the percentage. Then use online tools to prepare a bar graph or pie chart to present the poll results.**

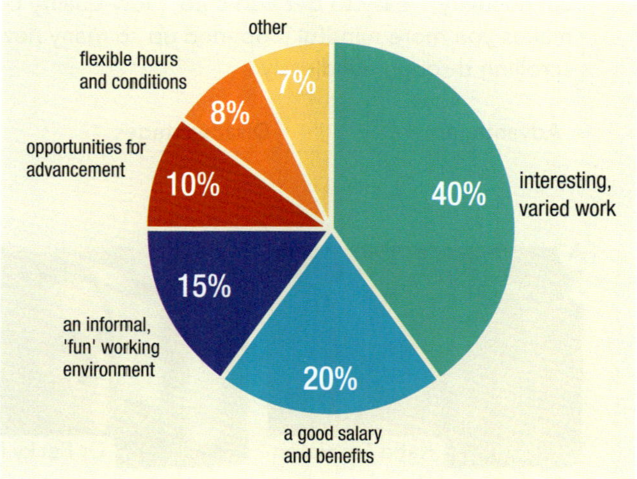

BBC Is social media killing creativity?

BEFORE YOU WATCH

1 Complete the sentences to make them true for you. Then compare with a partner.

1 I carry my phone in … (e.g. my pocket, my bag)
2 I check my phone … (e.g. every five minutes, once a day)
3 My favourite social media app is … (e.g. Instagram, WhatsApp)

2 SPEAKING Discuss some of the questions asked in the video you are going to watch.

1 Is the amount of time we spend on social media a problem?
2 What are some of the ways that you and I can use social media in a better way?
3 Is it true that creativity can actually be good for our health?
4 Do you think that social media can be good for your creativity?

WHILE YOU WATCH

3 25 Watch the video and compare your ideas in Exercise 2 with the answers given in the video.

4 Complete the table with some of the comments describing the use of phones in the video. What's the most important advantage/disadvantage of mobile phones for you?

be very careful with your privacy · being creative · connectivity · easy to get addicted · low-quality content · makes you more mindful · opened up so many new activities · scrolling through mindlessly

Advantages	Disadvantages

5 Look at the photos A–D of the four people in the video. Who …

1 warns that you should educate yourself because you're the publisher of your own data? ____________
2 doesn't have to plan ahead to bring her phone with her, it's always with her? ____________
3 can't even count the number of times a day she's on social media? ____________
4 says creative activities can provide really targeted support for people with mental health conditions? ____________
5 admits that by nature she's sort of a lazy person? ____________
6 thinks social media has been fascinating with what it's done to creativity? ____________
7 is surprised to hear that art on prescription is available on the NHS (National Health Service) already? ____________

6 25 Watch the video again and check your answers in Exercise 5.

AFTER YOU WATCH

7 SPEAKING Based on the video and your own ideas, discuss the question which is the title of this lesson: *Is social media killing creativity?* Use ideas and phrases from Exercise 4 and your own ideas.

A

Katie Thistleton

B

Dr Becky Inkster

C

Ty

D

Dr Daisy Fancourt

Focus Vlog About time travel

Imagine you could travel back in time. Which decade, century or era would you visit?

Suppose you could meet any famous person dead or alive. Who would you like to meet?

1 SPEAKING **Put the periods in the box on the time line. Discuss why people might want to visit those periods.**

A Dickensian period (mid nineteenth century)
B The 1980s
C Ancient Egypt
D The late 1930s/early 1940s
E The Middle Ages
F The early 1960s

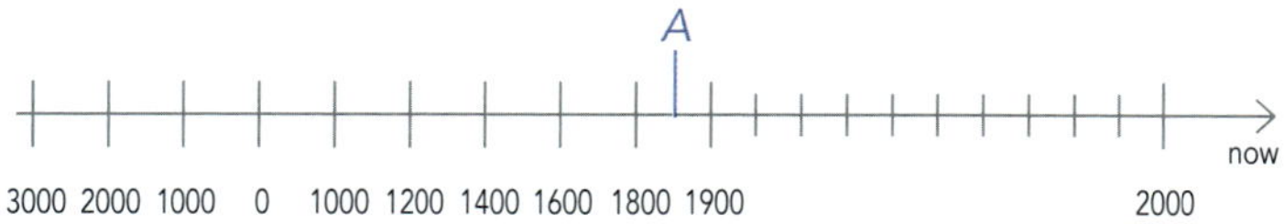

2 27 **Watch the first part of the video (up to 2:30) and complete the table. Which periods would the people like to visit and why? Did the answers match any of your ideas in Exercise 1?**

	When – which decade, century or era?	Why?
Nick		
Kat		
Sam		
Hassan		
Luke		
Ellie		

3 SPEAKING **Discuss how much you know about the people in the photos. Who would you like to meet?**

A

Winston Churchill
1874–1965

B

Duke Ellington
1899–1974

C

Salvador Dali
1904–1989

D

Frank Sinatra
1915–1998

E

Mark Tremonti
1974–

F

Rafael 'Rafa' Nadal
1986–

4 27 **Watch the rest of the video (2:31–4:21). Match each speaker with the person they would like to meet.**

1 Nick ☐ 2 Kat ☐ 3 Sam ☐ 4 Hassan ☐
5 Luke ☐ 6 Ellie ☐

5 **Answer the questions.**

1 What would Nick like to ask Mark Tremonti?
2 How does Kat think Salvador Dali influenced modern art?
3 Why would Sam like to meet Frank Sinatra?
4 What does Hassan think of Rafael Nadal?
5 Which period does Luke want to ask Winston Churchill about?
6 What would Ellie like to know more about Duke Ellington?

6 27 **Watch the second part of the video (2:31–4:21) again and check your answers in Exercise 5.**

FOCUS ON LIFE SKILLS

Communication • Collaboration

7 SPEAKING **Think about the history of your own country or the world. Discuss which period you would most like to visit and which person you would most like to meet.**

8 **Prepare a short presentation about the period and the person you chose in Exercise 7.**

- Describe the period and say why you would like to visit it.
- Describe the person and say why you would like to meet them.
- Give as much detail as possible and include at least three phrases in the box.

Had I … If I … Imagine I … Provided that …
Suppose I … Were I to …

BBC Blowing in the wind

BEFORE YOU WATCH

1 SPEAKING **Discuss what kind of renewable sources of energy are most common where you live (wind power, solar panels, hydropower, etc.)**

2 **Do the quiz and compare your answers with a partner.**

TODAY'S QUICK QUIZ
Wind Power Points

1 The largest offshore wind farm in the world is in **Britain / Denmark / China**.

2 The wind farm is built **1 / 10 / 20** miles from the coast (1.6km / 16km / 32km).

3 It takes **12 / 24 / 48** hours to construct one turbine in the sea.

4 A wind turbine is **50 / 100 / 120** metres wide.

5 A single wind turbine can power **30 / 300 / 3,000** houses.

WHILE YOU WATCH

3 29 **Watch the video and check your answers in Exercise 2.**

4 **Complete the extracts from the commentary with the words in the box. There are two extra words.**

constant engineering nightmare offshore platform skilled turbine wind

1 If you want to harness enough ____________ energy to power a town or city you need to go where the wind is at its strongest.
2 The largest ____________ wind farm in the world is here in Britain.
3 Getting these monsters out here presents a whole host of ____________ challenges.
4 The unpredictable weather conditions and ____________ threat of stormy weather makes this an extremely difficult construction site.
5 It's an incredibly ____________ operation, but they make it look so easy.
6 It's just quite awe-inspiring seeing how enormous these ____________ blades are.

5 **Put the description of the ship in the correct order.**

a stilts to make a stable ☐
b With everything constantly moving, the wind 1
c solid to work from a solid ☐
d platform standing on the ☐
e turbines are on board. ☐
f base, and this is the solution. A huge ☐
g going and the waves going, you need somewhere ☐
h parts necessary to build the giant ☐
i of the water and stand on giant ☐
j ship called Discovery. It can lift completely out ☐
k seabed. All of the different ☐

6 29 **Watch the video again and check your answers to Exercises 4 and 5.**

AFTER YOU WATCH

7 SPEAKING **What are the advantages and disadvantages of being a wind turbine engineer or a TV presenter like Dallas Campbell? What special qualities would you need for each job?**

Focus Vlog About science and technology

What kind of technology would you like to be developed in the future?

What technology should be provided free for everyone?

1 SPEAKING **Discuss the questions.**

1 Would you call yourself technology-dependent, not into technology at all or something in between?
2 What technology makes your life better?
3 What technology would you like to be developed in the future?

2 31 **Watch the first part of the video (up to 1:54). Does anyone mention your ideas from Exercise 1?**

3 31 **Complete as much of the table as you can from memory. Then watch the first part of the video (up to 1:54) again and check your answers.**

	Technology	Reason
Lilee	electric cars	
Luke	teleportation	
Sam	solar batteries	
Nick	digital musical instruments	
Nobuse	virtual learning	

4 31 **Watch the rest of the video (1:55–2:27). What technology do the speakers think should be free for everyone?**

Lilee: ____________ Nick: ____________
Luke: ____________ Nobuse: ____________
Sam: ____________

5 **Put the answers in Exercise 4 in order of importance for society from 1 to 5 (1 being the most important). Compare with a partner.**

FOCUS ON LIFE SKILLS

Communication • Critical thinking

6 **Read a list of tips to pass on to young people when using the Internet. Discuss what you think each tip means. Then read the explanations below.**

1 Sharing isn't always caring
2 A lasting impression
3 Remember the human
4 True or False?
5 Don't believe the hype

THE FIVE GOLDEN RULES OF NETIQUETTE

Sharing isn't always caring
Ask your friends for permission before you post photos of them on social media. They may not like the way they look or come across.

A lasting impression
If you're sending a message or email to someone, think about how you come across. CAPITAL LETTERS or **bold** can look aggressive. Too many emojis and exclamation marks can look childish or silly. Check spelling and punctuation if it's a formal email.

Remember the human
Think before you post. Never post unkind comments on other people's photos and posts, including celebrities and other famous people. They're human too.

True or False?
Be careful not to share fake news. Check that something is factually correct and from a reputable source before you share it.

Don't believe the hype
If social media makes you feel that everyone's having more fun and a better lifestyle than you, remember that it's easy to give the impression that life is perfect by choosing photos cleverly. But it's not real life.

7 SPEAKING **Discuss whether you agree with the rules of netiquette. Is there anything you'd add or change?**

BBC The Global Seed Vault

BEFORE YOU WATCH

1 SPEAKING **Look at the screenshots from the video and discuss the questions.**

1 What is the Global Seed Vault?
2 Where is it located and why?
3 Why do we need it? What is it for?

WHILE YOU WATCH

2 35 **Watch the video and check your ideas in Exercise 1.**

3 35 **Complete the sentences with the numbers in the box. Then watch the video again and check your answers.**

4,000 12 130 –20 800,000 250 800

1 The average temperature inside the vault is ___________ degrees Celsius.
2 Some seeds will survive for ___________ years.
3 Most food comes from just ___________ varieties of plants.
4 The Seed Vault is only ___________ miles from the North Pole.
5 There are more than ___________ plastic packets stored in the vault.
6 The Seed Vault is cut ___________ metres deep into the permafrost.
7 The vault is ___________ metres above sea level.

4 SPEAKING **Discuss the questions about the video.**

1 Why was the vault built in this **remote, isolated and hostile terrain**?
2 Why was the construction of the vault **a major achievement** for Norway?
3 Why is the box of seeds carried by the scientists referred to as **precious**?
4 Why would the vault survive if global warming melted all the **ice caps**?
5 Why does the employee refer to the pharaohs and their pyramids?
6 Why does the video show images of **drought, flooding** and **industrial-scale farming**?
7 Why is the **Seed Vault** considered to be a 'global insurance policy'?

5 **Complete the gaps with the words in bold in Exercise 4. Then complete the sentences to make them true for you.**

1 My most ___________ possession is …
2 A ___________ achievement in my life is …
3 The most remote, hostile ___________ I've ever experienced is …
4 The worst ___________ or flooding in my country was …
5 If all the ice ___________ melted, my country would …
6 I think the Global ___________ Vault is …

6 SPEAKING **Compare and discuss your sentences in Exercise 5.**

AFTER YOU WATCH

7 SPEAKING **The Global Seed Vault is a project to store and preserve seeds 'just in case'. Discuss what else you think the world should store and preserve 'just in case'.**

Focus Vlog About regrets

Is there anything you wish you had or hadn't done when you were younger?

How would you like your life to be different from what it is now?

1 **Complete the two sentences and compare with a partner. Do you share similar wishes and regrets?**

When I was younger, I wish I had …

When I was younger, I wish I hadn't …

2 37 **Watch the first part of the video (up to 1:51) and complete the first column of the table.**

	As a child …	Wishes he/she …
Lilee		
Hannah		
Nick		
Shaelyn		
Kat		
Harriet		

3 37 **Complete as much of the second column of the table as you can from memory. Then watch the first part of the video again and check your answers. Did the answers match any of your ideas in Exercise 1?**

4 37 **Watch the rest of the video (1:52–3:09). Who do you think is the happiest with their life? Who would like to change where they live?**

5 37 **Complete the quotes with appropriate prepositions. Then watch the rest of the video (1:52–3:09) again and check your answers.**

Lilee: I've got some great friends that I've made ____________ the way with my travels.
Hannah: I would like to have my friends ____________ England living in Sydney so everyone is together.
Nick: I'm very happy with what I have and the people that I have ____________ my life.
Shaelyn: I wish I lived ____________ , say, Mexico, because it has the sea and the surf.
Kat: I think that all my mistakes and choices I made, I made ____________ a reason.
Harriet: I'm actually really happy ____________ the way my life is now.

6 **Whose answer do you agree with most? Compare with a partner.**

FOCUS ON LIFE SKILLS

Communication • Collaboration

7 **Take five minutes to do the 'gratitude exercise' below.**

- Write down the name of someone in your life who you are grateful to, and why.
- Write down the name of someone in your past who changed your life for the better and explain how.
- Write down three things that have gone well today and explain why.

8 SPEAKING **Compare your answers and discuss the benefits of feeling grateful. Use the phrases below or your own ideas.**

I'm grateful to … because …

If it wasn't/hadn't been for him/her …

What he/she did was …

Not only was he/she …

What I really admire …

It's … that really makes me feel …

1.2 Present and past habits

To talk about someone's habits and typical behaviour, we can use:

- the Present Simple or the Past Simple to talk about repeated present or past actions or states:
  When I ***get*** *home, I* ***do*** *my homework and* ***practise*** *the violin.*
  My grandfather ***picked*** *me* ***up*** *from school every day.*
- *used to* + infinitive to talk about states (e.g. with the verbs *be, have, believe, like*) or actions that happened regularly in the past but are no longer happening in the present. We do not use this structure to talk about single past actions:
  When I was at primary school, I ***used to be*** *very eager to learn.*
  I ***didn't use to fall behind*** *with my schoolwork.*
  Did *you* ***use to like*** *Chemistry?*
- *would* + infinitive to talk about past actions or behaviour typical for someone (but not states):
  Our Maths teacher ***would give*** *us loads of homework.*
- *will* + infinitive to talk about repeated present actions or typical behaviour (but not states):
  *She****'ll watch*** *TV or* ***play*** *games all day instead of studying for her exams.*

Note: We do not use the verbs *will/would* in this meaning in questions.

- the Present Continuous or Past Continuous with the adverb *always* to complain about someone's behaviour:
  *She****'s always putting*** *things off.*
  My neighbours ***were always complaining*** *about the noise.*

1 Choose the correct option.

1 When Marco and I shared a room in a hall of residence, he *was always borrowing* / *will always borrow* my things without asking.
2 When I was a kid, I *would* / *used to* believe that my dad was a spy.
3 Did you ever *use to* / *used to* cheat in exams?
4 It's so annoying. She *will always lose* / *is always losing* her notebook.
5 Martha *would ask* / *was asking* the teacher plenty of questions after every lesson. She was very curious.
6 I always *forget* / *will forget* to bring a pen. Can I borrow one of yours?

2 Complete the sentences with one word in each gap.

1 I didn't ________ to worry about exams, but now I do because I need to get the best grades possible.
2 When Jim gets home, he ________ start doing his homework until he has something to eat.
3 Our Science teacher ________ always tell us to be careful when we do experiments using chemicals.
4 Cathy isn't committed to her studies. She ________ always chatting to her friends online for hours instead of doing her homework.
5 '________ you use to study a lot when you were at school, Grandpa?' 'Of course! I was an excellent student.'
6 When she was a teacher, she ________ correct homework every day after school and at the weekend.

3 Complete the sentences with the correct form of the words in brackets. Add extra words where necessary.

1 I had a kindergarten teacher who ________ (use/wear) a flower in her hair.
2 Have you noticed our History teacher ________ (always/tap) his pen on the desk?
3 Our Maths teacher is really forgetful. Sometimes, she ________ (will/set) us homework but forget to collect it.
4 Years ago, teachers ________ (not/use/have) the equipment they do now. There was just a blackboard.
5 At my secondary school we used to watch videos on an old TV that ________ (always/break down).
6 When you were at school, ________ (use/have) a favourite teacher?

4 Choose the correct option, A, B or C to complete the text.

In every class, you get a mix of different personalities. There's generally one kid who's [1]___ the centre of attention. They [2]___ something completely inappropriate in the middle of a lesson so everyone laughs. Then there's the shy kid who [3]___ at the back of the class and [4]___ at their desk when the teacher asks a question. When I was at primary school, I found reading and writing quite difficult and I struggled to keep up with my classmates. I [5]___ much self-confidence. I [6]___ questions because I was convinced I'd get them wrong and look stupid. It seemed like the other kids [7]___ awards for something and I never did. That was until we started studying IT and I suddenly found the thing I was good at. Now I'm regularly top of the class ... at least in one subject anyway.

1 **A** used to be **B** always trying to be **C** always being
2 **A** 'll say **B** 're saying **C** said
3 **A** 's sitting **B** is used to sitting **C** sits
4 **A** would always look down **B** is always looking down **C** won't look down
5 **A** didn't use to have **B** wouldn't have **C** wasn't always having
6 **A** wouldn't answer **B** wasn't answering **C** 'm not used to answering
7 **A** used to always winning **B** were always winning **C** will win

1.5 Verb patterns

Verb patterns

Verbs preceded by other verbs or verb phrases may follow these patterns:

- verb + *to* + infinitive, e.g. *agree, arrange, can't afford, decide, intend, learn, manage, offer, prefer, refuse, remember, seem, tend:*
  *I **decided to leave** school and find a job.*
  *My sister **agreed to help** me with my homework.*
- verb + object + *to* + infinitive, e.g. *advise, allow, cause, enable, encourage, expect, force, remind, urge, warn:*
  *Robert's mother **encouraged him to study** Law.*
  *The teacher **reminded us not to use** our mobile phones during lessons.*
- verb + object + infinitive without *to*, e.g. *make, let:*
  *Do his parents **let him hang out** with his friends? My parents used to **make me do** a lot of house chores.*
- verb + gerund (*-ing* form), e.g. *admit, avoid, can't help, can't stand, enjoy, fancy, imagine, keep, miss, practise, spend/waste time, stop:*
  *I **can't stand wearing** a school uniform.*
  *She recently **stopped eating** fast food, and she feels better already.*
- verb + gerund (*-ing* form)/*to* + infinitive:
  After the verbs *begin, continue, hate, intend, like, love, prefer* and *start* we can use both the *-ing* form and the *to* infinitive. The meaning stays the same or changes very slightly.
  *I **started playing** chess. I **started to play** chess.*
  *He **intends using** the school website. He **intends to use** the school website.*

Change in meaning

- After the verbs *remember, forget, stop* and *try* we can use both the *-ing* form and the *to* infinitive form, however the meaning of the sentence changes:
  *Jenny **remembers locking** the door.* (She remembers that she locked the door.)
  *Jenny **remembers to lock** the door.* (She always remembers to lock the door.)
  *Dad**'ll forget giving** me the money.* (He will forget that he gave me the money.)
  *Dad**'ll forget to give** me the money.* (He hasn't given me the money and he'll forget to do it.)
  *Liz **stopped drinking** coffee.* (Liz doesn't drink coffee anymore.)
  *Liz **stopped to drink** some coffee.* (Liz stopped doing something in order to drink coffee.)
  *I **tried turning** the computer **off** and **on** again, but it didn't help.* (I tried this as an experiment to see if it would work).
  *I **tried to turn** the computer **off**, but the shutdown command didn't work.* (I made an effort to turn the computer off).
- We use *feel, hear, see, watch* + infinitive without *to* in order to say we saw the whole action from beginning to end:
  *I **saw** Mary **paint** a picture.* (I saw Mary start on the painting, paint it and finish painting).
  We use *feel, hear, see, watch* + *-ing* form when we witness only a part of the action.
  *I **saw** Mary **painting** a picture.* (Mary was painting a picture when I saw her).

1 Complete the second sentence so that it has a similar meaning to the first. Use up to five words including the word in capitals.

1 Are you looking for volunteers? You could put a poster up in the school. **TRIED**
Have you _________ a poster in the school?
2 It's really important that you hand in your assignment on Friday. **FORGET**
You must _________ your assignment on Friday.
3 I told him that dropping Spanish was a bad idea. **ENCOURAGED**
I _________ Spanish.
4 Those boots are much too expensive for me to buy. **AFFORD**
I _________ those boots.
5 Janice doesn't go to dance classes any more. She quit two years ago. **STOPPED**
Janice _________ two years ago.
6 We watched the gardener when he planted some flowers in front of the building. They look great. **WATCHED**
We _________ some flowers in front of the building. They look great.
7 Would John like to come to the concert on Sunday? **FANCY**
Does John _________ the concert on Sunday?
8 Jorge has been forbidden from using his dad's computer. **ALLOWED**
Jorge _________ his dad's computer.

2 Complete the sentences with the correct form of the verbs in the box.

add admire bring do drive eat fix learn splash wear

1 Thankfully, my sister's really practical and she managed _________ my bike for me.
2 When we arrived at the cabin, it was really dark, but luckily Sam had remembered _________ a torch.
3 When we're at the farm, my uncle sometimes lets me _________ his old van around the fields.
4 I saw some people _________ to kayak on the river and it looked really fun.
5 Of course you can use the bikes, but can you just remind everyone _________ helmets?
6 Everyone needs to wear plastic gloves to avoid _________ the cleaning liquid on their skin.
7 When we reach the top of the hill, we'll stop for a while by that wooden gate _________ the view.
8 Obviously, if you keep _________ white paint to the mix, the colour will get lighter and lighter.
9 My mum makes me _________ lots of fish because it's considered to be brain food.
10 Harry tends _________ his homework at the last minute, which is why he isn't doing well at school.

1.7 Register – formal and informal language

Formal language is used in official documents, letters and emails to people who we do not know very well, and in official invitations. In speech it usually appears in notifications, presentations and speeches.

Informal language is used in private conversations, letters or emails to friends, notes and postcards.

Formal and informal language is expressed through the relevant grammatical structures and suitable vocabulary.

Grammar

- In formal language we use full verb forms, in informal language – contractions, e.g.:
  ***I am** contacting you .../**I'm** contacting you ...*
- We do not use abbreviations in formal language, but they are used in informal language:
  *Could you do it **as soon as possible**?/Could you do it **ASAP**?*
- Formal language features more passive voice and indirect speech, while in informal language active forms and direct speech are more often used:
  *The dissertation **must be submitted** today./You **must submit** the dissertation today.*
  ***It is said/They say** that spinach is healthy.*
- Formal language also features more indirect questions, beginning with expressions such as:
  I was wondering .../Could you tell me ...?/Do you happen to know ...?
  We use direct questions in informal language:
  ***I was wondering if there are** enough volunteers./**Are there** enough volunteers?*

Vocabulary

- We use more complex expressions and abstract nouns in formal language, while in informal language the expressions or adjectives are simpler:
  employment opportunities/a chance to get a job
  Is it possible to be happy?/Is happiness possible?
- Many of the words used in formal language are derived from Latin, e.g. ***to depart, to cease***. Informal language features more vocabulary of Anglo-Saxon origin, e.g. ***to go, to stop***.
- Formal language features more common verbs, e.g. ***appear***. Informal language uses more phrasal verbs, e.g. ***turn up***.
- We also use more complex prepositional phrases in formal language, e.g. ***in favour of***, and simpler ones in informal language, e.g. ***for***.
- Examples of formal linkers are ***furthermore/however.*** In informal language ***and/but*** are commonly used.

1 Complete the second sentence in each pair by replacing the words in bold with the correct form of the phrasal verbs in the box.

come along   go into   leave out   put off   take away

1 Tomorrow's meeting has been **postponed** due to the adverse weather conditions.
We've ____________ tomorrow's meeting because of the bad weather.

2 Do not **enter** the recording studio when the 'on-air' light is illuminated.
You can't ____________ the recording studio if the 'on-air' light's on.

3 Kindly inform the centre in advance if you are unable **to attend** the workshop.
Can you please let us know if you can't ____________ to the workshop?

4 Applicants under the age of eighteen should **omit** section 4.
If you're under eighteen, you can ____________ section 4.

5 Bottled water may be **confiscated** by airport security.
If you try to take bottled water through security, they might ____________ from you.

2 Choose the best option for the context.

1 **An email to a friend**: *Who's coming to / Who is attending* the party?

2 **An official document**: *More info's / More information is* available via the school website.

3 **A job application**: *I'm really into / I especially enjoy* outdoor activities.

4 **A social media comment**: The whole thing just *isn't OK / is unacceptable* to me.

5 **A conversation**: Sorry, *I've got to go / I must leave* now, I'll call you later.

6 **An announcement at an event**: *There are toilets / Toilet facilities are located* near each exit gate.

3 Read the advertisement and use the information to complete the social media post. Use up to two words in each gap.

Wildlife photography workshop

A one-day photography workshop is being held at the zoo on 28 June with wildlife photographer, Mark Ellis. The event will consist of an introductory session during which Mark will introduce some of the key concepts in wildlife photography and demonstrate a number of techniques.

Then, participants will have the opportunity to photograph some of the zoo's animals. The workshop will conclude with a session during which Mark will critique participants' work.

This event is open to all those interested in wildlife photography. Special equipment is not required, but participants should bring their own camera or mobile device.

I've just spotted some info about a wildlife photography workshop. Fancy going? It's on 28th June at the zoo with a top photographer. 1____ an intro session in the morning where the guy will chat a bit about wildlife photography and 2____ some tips. Then you get to go round the zoo and 3____ of the animals. And at the end, he'll take a 4____ your shots. Anyone can go and you don't 5____ any fancy gear, just take your 6____ or camera.

2.2 Past Perfect Simple and Past Perfect Continuous

Past Perfect Simple

We use the Past Perfect Simple:

- to talk about actions that happened before a particular time or event in the past (for which we usually use the Past Simple):
  *When I arrived at the wedding reception, the bride's father **had** already **made** his speech.*
  *By the age of sixteen, he **had learnt** to speak three foreign languages.*
- to talk about states that were true or happening before a particular time in the past:
  *When my parents got married, they **had known** each other for fifteen years.*

Past Perfect Continuous

We use the Past Perfect Continuous to talk about actions that were in progress up to a particular time in the past (or finished shortly before it):

*The guests **had been waiting** for forty minutes before the bus picked them up.*
*We **hadn't been thinking** about selling the house, but then we got this great offer.*
*How long **had** you **been sitting** there before I woke up?*

Affirmative			Negative		
I/You/ He/ She/ It/We/ They	had been	sleeping.	I/You/ He/ She/It/ We/ They	hadn't been (had not been)	sleeping.
Yes/No questions			**(Short answers)**		
Had	I/you/he/ she/it/ we/they	been sleeping?	Yes, I/you/he/she/it/we/they had. No, I/you/he/she/it/we/they hadn't.		

Wh- questions				Subject questions		
How long	had	I/you/he/ she/it/ we/they	been sleeping?	Who	had	been sleeping?

Past Perfect Simple vs Past Perfect Continuous

- We use the Past Perfect Simple:
  - to talk about finished actions:
    *My father **had visited** his Scottish relatives twice before he finally went to live with them.*
  - to talk about states using stative verbs, e.g. *be, have, know, see, believe*:
    *I went to see the castle. I **had** never **seen** such a magnificent building.*
- We use the Past Perfect Continuous to talk about actions, but not states. We stress the duration of the action rather than the result:
  *When the head teacher finally arrived, we**'d been discussing** the problem for two hours.*
- When we use time expressions such as *before* or *after*, we do not need to use the Past Perfect Simple or Past Perfect Continuous, because the order of events is clear:
  *The children **went** to sleep **before** we came.*

1 Choose the correct option.

1 By the time our guests arrived, we *had tidied / had been tidying* the living room.
2 My neighbours *had played / had been playing* music quite loudly all night and I was unable to sleep.
3 How long *had you looked / had you been looking* for a new apartment before you came across this place?
4 My flatmates were annoyed with me because I *hadn't done / hadn't been doing* the dishes last night.
5 Emma *hadn't saved / hadn't been saving* money for long before she bought a second-hand car.
6 *Had they bought / Had they been buying* their new furniture before they moved into their new home?

2 Complete the sentences with the correct form of the verbs in brackets. Use the Past Perfect Simple or the Past Perfect Continuous.

1 Robert watches a lot of French cinema but fortunately he ________ (not see) that film before. He loved it!
2 I didn't speak to Janet at the reception. By the time I arrived she ________ (already/leave).
3 It was such a shame. She ________ (decorate) the tree for about an hour before it fell over.
4 I was really tired. I ________ (drive) all the way there without stopping.
5 Gina locked the cat in the wardrobe by mistake. The poor thing ________ (cry) for ages before she finally let him out.
6 Barbara ________ (not know) that Alex was going to be at the party.
7 On the way to the airport I realised that I ________ (leave) my passport at home.
8 The streets were all wet because it ________(rain) heavily since the morning.

3 Complete the text with the correct form of the verbs and verb phrases in the box.

get on get to know move out share stay work

Last year, I moved to a new city to start a job with a big insurance company. I [1] ________ there for a couple of weeks when I met Natalie in the coffee shop one lunchtime. Up to that point, I [2] ________ okay with my job, but I [3] ________ many people. We immediately hit it off. We had lots of things in common and we were soon chatting away. I told her that I [4] ________ in a hostel since I'd arrived and that I was looking for a place to live. Coincidentally, her previous flatmate [5] ________ just a few days before, so she was looking for someone else to share with. I went to see the flat that evening and I moved in a few days later. I was a bit unsure at first because I [6] ________ a flat with anyone before, but we got on really well and we soon became best friends.

2.5 Relative clauses

Defining relative clauses

- They provide information integral to the sentence (without which the sentence makes no sense):
  *A stepfather is a man **who** is married to your mother but isn't your father.*
- We do not use commas to separate a defining relative clause from the rest of the sentence:
  *The girl **who** is sitting next to the bride is her sister Kerry.*
- Defining relative clauses can start with:
  – *who* or *that*, when talking about people:
  *Mrs Wilkes is the person **who/that** moved in last week.*
  – *which* or *that*, when talking about things:
  *Would you like to see the house **which/that** is for sale?*
  – *whose*, when talking about possession or ownership:
  *I know a girl **whose** parents own a yacht.*
  *You shouldn't drive a car **whose** bumper is about to fall off.*
  – *where*, when talking about places:
  *This is the place **where** my parents first met.*
- We can leave out the relative pronouns *who*, *which* and *that* when they are followed by a noun or a pronoun:
  *He is the man (**who/that**) I want to marry.*
  BUT: *This is the man **who/that** wants to marry me.*

Non-defining relative clauses

- They always include a relative pronoun:
  *Hector, **who** is a brilliant actor, took the main role.*
- They give additional information, without which the sentence still makes sense:
  *Jill, **who** used to be my neighbour, is going to marry my nephew.*
- They are separated by commas from the rest of the sentence:
  *The new film, **which** stars Leonardo DiCaprio, will be a huge success.*
- They begin with the same relative pronouns as defining relative clauses, with the exception of *that*:
  *My father, **who** lives in Montreal, couldn't come to the funeral.*
  *Joyce's new Lexus, **which** she bought last month, cost a fortune.*
  *The college building, **where** the event is going to be held, was built in 1645.*
  *Yesterday I bumped into Angus, **whose** brother is studying Medicine.*
- Non-defining relative clauses can also comment on the rest of the sentence and are then begun with the pronoun *which*:
  *Tom was late for dinner again, **which** made his mother furious.*
  *The waiter continued to stare at me, **which** I found extremely annoying.*

Reduced relative clauses

- We use the Present Participle (in the active voice) or the Past Participle (in the passive voice) instead of the relative pronoun and the verb:
  *Elderly people **living** alone (= who live alone) should have friends or family to care for them.*
  *Children **raised** (= who were raised) in a bilingual environment may begin to speak a little later.*
- They can be both defining and non-defining:
  *Do you know the man **talking** (= who is talking) to Mr Schwartz?* (defining)
  *Rich people, **accustomed** (= who are accustomed) to luxurious living, will never understand poor people.* (non-defining)

1 Choose the correct option, A, B or C to complete the sentences.

1 Kim's the one _____ likes to be the centre of attention the whole time. That's her in the red dress.
A who **B** whom **C** which

2 There's a new magazine on the market _____ you how to play guitar.
A what teaches **B** teaches **C** teaching

3 Barbara is an only child, _____ a lot about her behaviour at times.
A explaining **B** which explains **C** that explains

4 Isn't this the same place _____ we saw on the way here?
A what **B** – **C** where

5 The wedding I went to, _____ was in Porto, was actually very nice. And the bride was beautiful.
A where **B** that **C** which

6 According to some, children _____ to break rules become more independent thinkers.
A taught **B** teaching **C** that taught

7 That's the man _____ conducted the ceremony last night. Doesn't he look different in casual clothes?
A – **B** that **C** which

2 Complete the second sentence so that it has a similar meaning to the first. Use the number of words shown in brackets.

1 My older brother, who is studying in Australia, doesn't get home very often.
My older brother, ____________ , doesn't get home very often. (3)

2 Children who grow up with two languages at home find it easy to switch between them.
Children ____________ two languages at home find it easy to switch between them. (3)

3 Spanish and French are the languages which were spoken by my family as I was growing up.
Spanish and French are the languages ____________ as I was growing up. (4)

4 My mother, who was sent away to school at a young age, didn't have a close relationship with her parents.
My mother, ____________ at a young age, didn't have a close relationship with her parents. (4)

5 My sister, who was diagnosed with dyslexia at school, went on to get a PhD in Physics.
My sister, ____________ at school, went on to get a PhD in Physics. (3)

2.7 Collocations

Collocations are formed when two or more words are used together to form a logical expression. Unlike in idioms, the meaning of a collocation is derived from the meaning of its parts. Collocations may be divided into two categories: weak, where one word can form many collocations with other lexical items, e.g. ***take a photo/notes/a break*** and strong ones, where the separate words do not form many other collocations, e.g. ***common sense.*** Often collocations are made from more than two words, e.g.:

healthy lifestyle

lead a healthy lifestyle

When we use collocations correctly, the language we speak or write seems more natural.

Types of collocations:

- **adjective + noun:**
  *My brother has a **vivid imagination**.*
  *I only wear these earrings on **social occasions**.*
- **verb + noun:**
  *Try not to **lose touch** with your friends after high school.*
  *Make sure you **keep an eye** on Maggie.*
- **noun + verb:**
  *Be careful when the **doors open** so that you don't get hit.*
  ***Snow has been falling** heavily recently.*
- **noun (of/and/for) + noun:**
  *Tim's **desire for knowledge** is impressive.*
  *What's your **home town** like?*
- **verb + adjective/numeral:**
  *Who **came first**?*
  *You **looked beautiful** at the ball.*
- **adjective + adjective:**
  *The rooms looked **neat and tidy**.*
  *We were told **loud and clear** what to do in an emergency.*
- **verb + adverb:**
  ***Hold tightly** onto me when you're going down those stairs.*
  *She **smiled politely**.*
- **adverb + adjective:**
  *We want to rent a **fully furnished** flat.*
  *It's **perfectly normal** that you're afraid of the operation.*

1 Choose the correct option.

1 Max has a *mean / nasty* habit of coughing without covering his mouth.
2 Her incredible *sense / feeling* of humour has made her popular among her colleagues.
3 Yesterday's flooding of several neighbourhoods was the result of *hard / heavy* rainfall.
4 He had raised his voice and I could hear him loud and *clearly / clear* from the other room.
5 Sam *shook / shrugged* her shoulders in reply when I asked her if she wanted to go out.

2 Choose the correct option, A, B or C to complete the sentences.

1 When I finally heard the news I just _____ into tears. It was such a relief.
A fell B broke C burst
2 Diana is _____ shy and she absolutely hates speaking in public.
A bitterly B painfully C perfectly
3 When the lights suddenly _____ , several people in the hall screamed.
A went out B switched off C closed down
4 Make sure you hold the fabric _____ in place while you stitch around the edges.
A clearly B tightly C strongly
5 If everyone's prepared to compromise, I'm sure we can _____ an agreement.
A reach B find C make
6 If they start talking about the competition, just _____ quiet and pretend you don't know anything.
A come B keep C hold
7 The company expects _____ standards of all its staff, especially those dealing directly with customers.
A high B full C good
8 Joanna's always had a _____ imagination. It's no surprise she became a novelist.
A strong B creative C vivid

3 Complete the text with the words in the box. There are two extra words.

attention come interest leave neat normal quiet smart spare strong

Empty Nest Syndrome

When children [1]_________ home to go off to university, many parents are looking forward to a [2]_________ life without all the noise and disruption of a houseful of teens. They dream about how easy it'll be to keep the house [3]_________ and tidy at last. They plan to turn the kids' bedrooms into [4]_________ rooms so that friends can come and visit. They can't wait to do things as a couple again without the kids being the centre of [5]_________ .

But when the time comes and the house is suddenly quiet, it can [6]_________ as a bit of a shock. Many parents experience [7]_________ feelings of loss. Others suffer anxiety about how their offspring are coping without them. All these emotions are perfectly [8]_________ though and just part of adjusting to a new stage of life. There's even a name for it: Empty Nest Syndrome.

3.2 Future forms including the Future Perfect Continuous

Future Continuous

We use the Future Continuous:

- to talk about actions which will be in progress at a particular time in the future:
  *This time tomorrow we**'ll be flying** to the Maldives.*
- to talk about planned or routine future events, actions or situations:
  ***I'll be going** to the supermarket after work.*
- to form polite questions or requests:
  ***Will** you **be doing** the first aid course this month?*
  ***Will** you **be using** your car tomorrow?* (because I'd like to borrow it)

Affirmative			Negative		
I/You/ He/She/ It/We/ They	'll (will)	be sleeping.	I/You/ He/ She/ It/We/ They	won't (will not)	be sleeping.

Yes/No questions			Short answers
Will	I/you/ he/she/ it/we/ they	be sleeping?	Yes, I/you/he/she/it/we/they will. No, I/you/he/she/it/we/they won't.

Wh- questions				Subject questions		
How long	will	I/you/he/ she/it/ we/they	be sleeping?	Who	will	be sleeping?

Future Perfect Simple

We use the Future Perfect Simple to talk about actions or situations which will be completed before a certain time in the future:

*They **will have left** by 6 o'clock.*

Affirmative			Negative		
I/You/ He/She/ It/We/ They	'll (will)	have finished by 10.	I/You/ He/She/ It/We/ They	won't (will not)	have finished by 10.

Yes/No questions			Short answers
Will	I/you/ he/she/ it/we/ they	have finished by 10?	Yes, I/you/he/she/it/we/they will. No, I/you/he/she/it/we/they won't.

Wh- questions				Subject questions		
How long	will	I/you/he/ she/it/ we/they	have finished?	Who	will	have finished by 10?

Future Perfect Continuous

We use the Future Perfect Continuous to talk about actions or states which will have been in progress for some time by a certain time in the future:

*By the end of the year, we **will have been living** in Toronto for eight years.*

Affirmative			Negative		
I/You/ He/She/ It/We/ They	'll (will)	have been working for twelve hours.	I/You/ He/ She/ It/We/ They	won't (will not)	have been working for twelve hours.

Yes/No questions			Short answers
Will	I/you/ he/she/ it/we/ they	have been working for twelve hours?	Yes, I/you/he/she/it/we/ they will. No, I/you/he/she/it/we/ they won't.

Wh- questions				Subject questions		
How long	will	I/you/ he/she/ it/we/ they	have been working?	Who	will	have been working for twelve hours?

Typical time expressions used with the Future Perfect Simple and Future Perfect Continuous are:

- ***by 2030/next month/next year***
- ***by then***
- ***by the time***
- ***in two days'/three weeks'/one month's/ten years' time***

1 Complete the sentences with the correct form of the verbs in brackets. Use the Future Continuous, the Future Perfect Simple or the Future Perfect Continuous.

1 This time next week I ____________ (work) here for three years. Doesn't time fly?
2 Robert can't meet us at 6 p.m. He ____________ (not finish) his homework by then.
3 ____________ (you/read) that book by Friday? I promised to lend it to Ana.
4 Sasha ____________ (visit) her grandfather tomorrow, so we can't meet for coffee like we usually do.
5 I ____________ (volunteer) as a lifeguard for three years in a row after this summer.
6 This article says we ____________ (not live) in space for at least another 200 years.
7 ____________ (you/collect) Pietro from the train station tomorrow or do I need to go?
8 By June next year, we ____________ (come) to France for our annual holiday for ten years.

3.5 Quantifiers

Quantifier	Countable nouns	Uncountable nouns
each/every	each/every ***Each/Every** book costs 10 pounds.*	
all	all ***All the** books were quite cheap.* ***All the** furniture was quite cheap.*	
most	most ***Most** books were quite cheap.* ***Most of the** furniture was quite cheap.*	
whole	whole *I've read the **whole** book.*	
many/much/ a great deal of	many **Questions/negative:** *Have you got **many** books?* *I haven't got **many** books.*	much/a great deal of **Questions/negative:** *Have you got **much/a great deal of** furniture?* *I haven't got **much/a great deal of** furniture.*
a lot of/ lots of/ loads of/ plenty of	a lot of/lots of/loads of/plenty of *I've got **a lot of/lots of/loads of/plenty of** books.* *I've got **a lot of/lots of/loads of/plenty of** furniture.*	
a number of/several/ a few/ a couple of/a little	a number of/several/ a few/a couple of *I've got **a number of/ several/a few/ a couple of** books.*	a little *I've got **a little** furniture.*
some	some *I've got **some** books/furniture.*	
few/little	few *I've got very **few** books.*	little *I've got **little** furniture.*
both	both ***Both** these books are mine.*	
either	either **(for two people/things)** *You can buy **either** book.*	
neither	neither **(for two people/things)** ***Neither** book was expensive.*	
no/none of	no *I've got **no** books/furniture.* none of ***None of** the books/furniture belongs to me.*	

- The following quantifiers are always used with the preposition *of*: *a number of, a couple of, a great deal of, a lot of, lots of, loads of, plenty of, none of.*
- All other quantifiers (except *no* and *every*) can be used with the preposition *of*, if it is followed by: a personal pronoun, a pronoun (possessive or demonstrative) + noun or the article *the*:
  ***Most** shops/**Most of the** shops were open.*
  *John spent **most of his** life on a farm.*
  ***A few of us** took a taxi home.*

1 Choose the correct option, A, B or C to complete the sentences.

1. I'm afraid only _____ people decided to come, so we won't be putting on the show.
   A a few B little C few
2. I hear that _____ people are still unaware of the plans to build a multi-storey car park in the city centre.
   A most of B most C none of
3. The head teacher said that _____ of the students that caused the fire will be allowed to go on the trip next week.
   A none B no C very little
4. This flat has a slightly bigger living room than the other one, but I'm afraid _____ of them have cable TV.
   A either B both C neither
5. Why is there only _____ water left? Barbara bought three bottles for the trip.
   A any B a few C a little
6. Jenny can come in our car too – there's _____ of space.
   A plenty B some C a couple
7. There's a great _____ of traffic on the roads today, so I'm going to take the underground to work.
   A number B lot C deal
8. There are _____ vacant shops on the high street, which is a bad sign for the local economy.
   A plenty B several C few

2 Complete the sentences with the quantifiers in the box. There are three extra words.

a couple all each either few little many much neither no none plenty some whole

1. There are two single beds in the spare room, but ____________ of them have sheets on them at the moment, I'm afraid.
2. You'll find ____________ of cups and mugs in the cupboard above the kettle. There should be enough for everyone.
3. There isn't ____________ space left in the wardrobe, but you could put a box of stuff under the bed.
4. We have a separate heating control in ____________ room, so you can keep the rooms you use warm without wasting energy.
5. Modern kitchen appliances are pretty energy efficient and use very ____________ electricity.
6. Annoyingly, there's ____________ mobile signal inside the flat, so you have to go out on the balcony if you want to make a call.
7. When we got home, ____________ of the lights were working. It turned out there was a power cut, so we had to find ____________ candles.
8. We've only got ____________ of chairs in the kitchen, so Maggie and Jan took those and I brought in a stool from the other room.
9. How greedy of Tom to eat a ____________ family-sized pizza by himself!
10. There are two ways to get to the capital from the village and we can take ____________ route.

3.7 Determiners

Both

Both is used to refer to two people or things. It may be used with countable nouns or pronouns:

***Both (of the) cities** are interesting.*

*I've visited **both of them**.*

Each, every and all

- The determiners **each** and **every** are used with singular nouns. *Each* is used when we separately refer to two or more things/people in a group, while *every* is used to talk about the whole group of three or more people or things together (similarly to *all*):
  ***Each tourist** learnt to say a few words in the tribe's native language.*
  *The tourists listened attentively to **every word** the guide said.*
- ***Every*** and ***all*** (but not *each*) may be modified by the adverbs *almost, nearly, practically*:
  *Kate has seen **nearly every** art gallery.*
- ***All*** is used with plural nouns or pronouns and refers to three or more items/people:
  ***All (of) the guidebooks** were interesting.*
  ***All of them** were interesting.*
- *Both, each (one), every one* and *all* may be followed by **of** when they precede either a personal pronoun, or a pronoun (possessive or demonstrative) + plural noun, or a definite article + plural noun:
  ***Both maps** were useful.*
  ***Both of my maps** were useful.*
  ***Both of the maps** were useful.*
  ***Both of them** were useful.*

All and whole

- ***Whole*** is used with countable singular nouns:
  *I spent **a whole day** on the beach.*
- ***All*** is usually used with uncountable nouns. When used with countable nouns, it refers to a period of time:
  ***All the accommodation** is booked.*
  *He stayed there **all winter**.*

Another, other, the other(s), the other ones

- ***Another*** is used with singular nouns or the pronoun *one*:
  *Let's think about **another place** to meet.*
  *I've already had a sandwich, so I don't want **another one**.*
- ***Other*** is used with plural countable nouns, uncountable nouns or the pronoun *ones*:
  *We need **other people** to help us.*
  *I think you should pick **other furniture** – it should be easy to clean.*
  *These curtains are ugly. We need **other ones**.*
- ***The other*** is used with countable nouns or the pronoun one/ones. It also refers to one item out of two:
  *I booked this hotel because **the other ones** are full.*
  *Can you show me **the other side** of your hand?*
- ***The others*** is not followed by any nouns or pronouns:
  *I can see some tourists from our group. Where are **the others**?*

Each other/one another

We use *each other* and *one another* to describe a relation or an activity performed by two or more persons, and when the subject and object are different:

*The tourists helped **each other/one another** with their bags.*

1 Complete the second sentence so that it has a similar meaning to the first. Use the words in capitals.

1 The biscuits are delicious. Do you mind if I have one more? **ANOTHER**
The biscuits are delicious. Do you mind if I ____________?

2 The cottage isn't suitable for wheelchair users because the two bedrooms are located on the first floor. **BOTH**
The cottage isn't suitable for wheelchair users because ____________.

3 There's enough room at the dining table for all the family to eat together. **WHOLE**
There's enough room at the dining table ____________

4 All the rooms in the hotel are unique and decorated in a different style. **EACH**
____________ unique and decorated in a different style.

5 The buses from the city centre to the castle leave at twenty-minute intervals. **EVERY**
The buses from the city centre to the castle ____________.

6 Some of our friends are here, but where is everybody else? **OTHERS**
Some of our friends are here, but where are ____________?

7 The plans for the bridge were approved by every person on the committee. **ALL**
____________ on the committee approved the plans for the bridge.

2 Complete the text with the words and phrases from the box. There are two extra options.

all of | another | both of | each | each of | every | other | others

Unique stays

Have you ever dreamed of staying in a treehouse in the middle of the Black Forest? Or perhaps you'd like to fall asleep looking up at the stars high in the Arctic Circle from the comfort of a warm bed? Now you can. We offer the chance for you to stay in [1]__________ these unique locations plus [2]__________ equally special places across Europe and beyond.

We have more than twenty unique holiday rentals; [3]__________ them has their own special charms. There are cosy cabins hidden deep in the woods, glass cubes with 360° wilderness views and even a hut that rotates to follow the sun. We have properties in almost [4]__________ type of landscape imaginable; forest, mountains, coast, Arctic wilderness, even desert. [5]__________ property sleeps two to six people and [6]__________ them offer luxury accommodation.

Visit our website to start your adventure now.

4.2 Question tags and reply questions

Question tags

- Question tags are short questions added at the end of the sentence to ask for confirmation (falling intonation) or ask a question (rising intonation):
  She's gorgeous, ***isn't she****?*
- We form question tags using auxiliary verbs *be, have, do, will* or modal verbs, e.g. *can, should*, and the pronoun corresponding to the subject, e.g. *I, you, she, they*.
- Question tags for affirmative sentences usually take the negative form:
  *You****'ve*** *already been to this café,* ***haven't you?***
  They ***made*** *a formal complaint,* ***didn't they?***
- Question tags for negative sentences usually take the affirmative form:
  Olivia ***can't*** *swim,* ***can she?***
  You ***aren't*** *going to reduce the price,* ***are you?***

Other forms of question tags

- In sentences with *I'm* we use the question tag ***aren't I?***:
  I'm *late,* ***aren't I?***
- In sentences with *Let's* we use the question tag ***shall we?***:
  Let's *meet for a coffee later,* ***shall we?***
- In sentences with negative adverbs, such as *never, rarely, seldom, hardly* or *barely*, or the words *no* or *nobody*, we use an affirmative question tag:
  I ***hardly*** *know you,* ***do I?***
  They ***never*** *listen to you,* ***do they?***
- In affirmative imperative sentences we use *will, would, can/can't* or *could*, depending on the context. In negative imperative questions we always use the question tag ***will you?***:
  Wait *for me here,* ***will you/could you?***
  Don't spend *too much,* ***will you?***
- In sentences where the pronoun *something* or *nothing* is the subject, we use a question tag with the pronoun *it*. If the subject is *nothing*, we always use an affirmative question tag:
  Something *is wrong,* ***isn't it?***
  Nothing *can be done,* ***can it?***
- In sentences with *everybody, everyone, no one* or *nobody* as the subject, we use a question tag with the pronoun **they** and the plural form of the verb. If the subject is *no one* or *nobody*, we always use an affirmative question tag:
  Everybody/Everyone *will ask questions,* ***won't they?***
  Nobody/No one *signed up for the dressmaking course,* ***did they?***
- In sentences with the pronoun *that* as the subject, we use a question tag with the pronoun ***it***:
  That*'s your new car over there,* ***isn't it?***
- In sentences with *there is/there are* (in all tenses), we repeat the pronoun *there* in the question tag:
  There *was a security alarm in the store,* ***wasn't there?***
  There *won't be any problems with the complaint,* ***will there?***

Reply questions

We use reply questions to show interest in what somebody is saying and to signal that we want more details.

Affirmative sentence + affirmative reply question:
'I ***went*** *to the new shop in Green Street yesterday.'* ***'Did you?'***
'Your dad ***lent*** *me some money.'* ***'Did he?'***

Negative sentence + negative reply question:
'Chris and Lisa ***aren't flying*** *to Japan after all.'* ***'Aren't they?'***
'I ***never buy*** *shoes online.'* ***'Don't you?'***

1 Choose the correct option.

1 She hates being criticised, *isn't / doesn't* she?
2 Don't buy the first coat you see, *will / could* you?
3 I'm the last to arrive, *don't / aren't* I?
4 Nobody in the complaints department helped you, *did / didn't* they?
5 There wasn't anything affordable in that shop, was *it / there*?
6 He's just placed his order, *hasn't / didn't* he?

2 Complete the sentences with the correct question tag.

1 You've forgotten to post my letters, __________ ?
2 I think I'm going to have to start again from the beginning, __________ ?
3 No matter what we do, nothing will change, __________ ?
4 Don't get lost, __________ ?
5 I guess there'll be no buses going to Woodside on New Year's Day, __________ ?
6 Everybody loves chocolate cake, __________ ?
7 Nobody's in the changing room at the moment, __________ ?
8 Let's get something to eat first, __________ ?

3 Write the correct reply questions to complete the dialogues.

1 **A:** I'm not going to the theatre tomorrow.
B: ______________________________ ?
2 **A:** My brother never buys anything online.
B: ______________________________ ?
3 **A:** I think the shop on the corner sells bus tickets.
B: ______________________________ ?
4 **A:** I don't think you can book a table in advance.
B: ______________________________ ?
5 **A:** They don't allow you to take your own drinks into the stadium.
B: ______________________________ ?
6 **A:** Don't worry, most foreign films have subtitles.
B: ______________________________ ?

4.5 Present and past modal structures

The present

To give advice, express necessity or lack of necessity, we use:

- modal verbs ***should/shouldn't*** and ***ought to/oughtn't to***:
  *You **should/ought to eat** more fruit and vegetables.*
  *You **shouldn't/oughtn't to spend** so much money on clothes.*
- modal verb ***must/mustn't***:
  *You **must try** that spa – it's really wonderful!*
  *You **mustn't spoil** her.*
- verb ***need to/needn't***:
  *You **need to have** the receipt if you want to return the dress.*
  *I can hear you, you **needn't shout**.*
- the structure ***had better/had better not***:
  *You**'d better check** the price online before you buy a phone here.*
  *You**'d better not be** late this time.*

The past

- To say that something was or wasn't necessary, we use ***had to/didn't have to***:
  *Ella's car broke down, so she **had to** take a taxi.*
  *There was nobody at the desk, but luckily I **didn't have to** wait long.*
- To express regret or criticism about something that happened or didn't happen, or to give advice, we use **ought (not) to/should (not) + have + Past Participle**:
  *We **should have booked/ought to have booked** a different hotel. This one is terrible.*
  *My parents **shouldn't have sold/oughtn't to have sold** their camper van.*
- To say that an action was not necessary, we can also use ***didn't need to* + infinitive** or ***needn't have* + Past Participle**. There is a difference in meaning:
  *I **didn't need to cook** dinner for the children yesterday because they were away. (So I didn't cook it.)*
  *I **needn't have cooked** dinner for the children yesterday because they weren't hungry and didn't touch anything. (I cooked it but didn't have to.)*
- The modal verb *must* and the structure *had better* are not used in the past.

1 Match the sentence halves.

1 We really ought ☐
2 You'd better ☐
3 We should have ☐
4 You mustn't ☐
5 She needn't ☐

a not wait too long before you book your flight.
b have made a cake as I'd bought one earlier.
c to reduce our spending and try to save.
d taken the train instead of driving; just look at the traffic!
e speed when you drive; it's quite dangerous.

2 Choose the correct option, A, B or C to complete the sentences.

1 We got a travel card when we arrived in the city so that we _____ tickets every time we went on the metro.
A didn't have to buy B needn't have bought
C shouldn't have bought

2 Of course, we _____ in the city centre. The car parks are ridiculously expensive.
A didn't have to park B needn't have parked
C shouldn't have parked

3 We booked a table in advance, but when we arrived, the restaurant was fairly empty, so we _____ .
A didn't need to bother B mustn't have bothered
C needn't have bothered

4 If you're going to be queuing for a long time, _____ some water with you. It's going to be a really hot day.
A you'd better take B you had to take
C you needn't take

5 Legally, if the customers were under sixteen, the venue ought _____ sold them tickets without permission from an adult.
A to have not B not have
C not to have

6 I bought a ticket for the bus, but I _____ it to anyone when I got on or during the journey.
A needn't have shown B didn't need to show
C shouldn't have shown

3 Complete the second sentence so that it has a similar meaning to the first. Use up to five words including the word in capitals.

1 It was wrong that you told her that I was leaving. I thought I could trust you. **OUGHT**
You really ____________ her that I was leaving. I thought I could trust you.

2 It's not very wise to write your PIN number on your credit card. **BETTER**
You ____________ your PIN number on your credit card.

3 My train was cancelled but fortunately another one came quite quickly. **HAVE**
My train was cancelled, but fortunately I ____________ long for another.

4 It was a mistake to buy the tickets for the auction in advance. There were still plenty on sale on the door. **NEEDN'T**
It wasn't until they got to the auction that they realised they ____________ the tickets in advance.

5 Patty returned the shoes because the sole came off. **HAD**
Patty ____________ the shoes because the sole came off.

6 The car isn't here. I'm sure Jake took it. **MUST**
The car isn't here. Jake ____________ it.

4.7 Modality – alternative structures

We can also use alternative structures to express modality in situations when modal verbs are not usually used (e.g. in past or future tenses, or infinitive clauses):

*I **must** help him.*

*I **had to/was obliged to** help him.*

Probability

Modal verbs: ***can, can't, could, may, might, must*** and:

- ***be likely unlikely to do that:***
  *Tim **is likely to sell** the house.*
  *It **was unlikely that** Jenny's offer would win.*
- ***be bound to do:***
  *You**'re bound to feel nervous** before the auction.*
- ***be sure to do:***
  *She **is sure to pay** a lot if she wants to buy that flat.*
- ***be certain to do:***
  *The manager **is certain to ask** difficult questions.*

Ability

Modal verbs: ***can, can't, could*** and:

- ***be able/unable to do:***
  *Zoe **was unable to open** a bank account.*
- ***manage to do:***
  *Will you **manage to help** her?*
- ***succeed in doing:***
  *I **succeeded in exchanging** the trousers with no receipt.*

Permission

Modal verbs: ***can, could, may*** and:

- ***be allowed to do:***
  ***Will** I **be allowed to join** the club?*
- ***be permitted to do:***
  *Students **were permitted to open** a charity shop.*

Prohibition

Modal verbs: ***can't, couldn't, may not, shouldn't, mustn't*** and:

- ***not be allowed to do:***
  *The school shop **isn't allowed to sell** any sweets.*
- ***be forbidden to do/from doing:***
  *Guests **are forbidden to use** the pool after 11 p.m.*
- ***be banned from doing:***
  *Students **were banned from taking** food into the room.*

Obligation

Modal verbs: ***must, should*** and:

- ***have to do:***
  *You **have to pay** for extra luggage.*
- ***need to do:***
  *We **need to borrow** money to go on a holiday.*
- ***ought to do:***
  *Producers **ought to choose** names for their products carefully.*

Ought to is a 'semi-modal' verb. Although unlike modal verbs, it is used with the *to* + infinitive and it shares the other features of modal verbs.

- ***be obliged to do:***
  ***Is** he **obliged to pay** for the damage?*
- ***be required to do:***
  *They **are required to be** punctual.*
- ***be supposed to do:***
  *You**'re supposed to sign** both copies.*
- ***be meant to do:***
  *I **meant to text** you but I forgot.*

1 Complete the second sentence so that it has a similar meaning to the first. Use between three and five words including the words in capitals.

1 Unfortunately, they didn't manage to meet their crowdfunding target. **SUCCEED**
Unfortunately, they ____________ their crowdfunding target.

2 The band's very popular, so the tickets will probably sell out quickly. **LIKELY**
The band's very popular, so the tickets ____________ quickly.

3 You can't go into the backstage area without a security pass. **ALLOWED**
You ____________ into the backstage area without a security pass.

4 We couldn't get the book you wanted because it was out of stock. **MANAGE**
We ____________ the book you wanted because it was out of stock.

5 The phone should come with a charger, but it wasn't in the box. **MEANT**
The phone ____________ a charger, but it wasn't in the box.

6 Alex can't train with the team because he insulted one of the instructors. **BANNED**
Alex ____________ with the team because he insulted one of the instructors.

7 It's highly likely he'll withdraw from the tournament due to his injury. **BOUND**
He ____________ from the tournament due to his injury.

8 Karl couldn't answer the professor's tricky questions. **ABLE**
Karl ____________ the professor's tricky questions.

9 Students can't leave the school without parental permission. **FORBIDDEN**
Students ____________ the school without parental permission.

5.2 Reported speech

- In Reported Speech we change the following:
  - time expressions and words referring to places (depending on the context)
  - demonstrative pronouns, personal pronouns, object pronouns and possessive adjectives (depending on the context)
  - most tenses in affirmative sentences and in questions, but only when the reporting verb is in the past tense (e.g. *he said, she told me, he asked*).
- If the reporting verb is in the present tense (e.g. Present Simple or Present Perfect), we do not change the tense in the reported statement:

  *'**I'm not satisfied** with your performance.' → The teacher **has said** she **is not satisfied** with my performance.*

  *'**How** do you handle stress?' → She **wants to know** how I **handle** stress.*
- Even when the reporting verb is in the past tense, we do not change the following in the reported statement:
  - verbs in the Past Perfect Simple and Past Perfect Continuous:

    *'Before my resignation I **had been working** on an environmental project.' → The candidate said that before his resignation he **had been working** on an environmental project.*

    *'**Had** you ever **been** to a job interview before that last one?' → I asked my neighbour if she **had** ever **been** to a job interview before that last one.*
  - modal verbs *would, should, could, might, must*:

    *'During the interview you **should** try to make eye contact.' → The advisor told me that during the interview I **should** try to make eye contact.*

    *'We **must** all try harder.' → The manager said that we **must** all try harder.*

1 Report the statements. Tick the statements which DON'T move back one tense when reported.

1 'You need to fill out an application form.'
She says ______________ . ☐
2 'Candidates must speak good English.'
The job advert said ______________ . ☐
3 'I really want to improve my career prospects.'
Ben's told me ______________ . ☐
4 'I'd like to express my interest in this vacant post.'
He said ______________ . ☐
5 'Magda hasn't really achieved her goals.'
Rob told me ______________ . ☐
6 'I had never had a job interview before.'
Paula said ______________ . ☐
7 'We're struggling to meet our deadline.'
Matt said ______________ . ☐
8 'They have found the perfect candidate for the job.'
She said ______________ . ☐

2 Report the questions and requests.

1 'Can you wait here for a few minutes?'
She wants to know ______________ .
2 'Please, sign in at reception when you arrive.'
They told me ______________ .
3 'Have you already sent us a copy of your qualifications?'
She asked ______________ .
4 'Log on to our website to update your contact details.'
The job agency has asked us ______________ .
5 'Could you give me the report by noon today?'
John asked ______________ .
6 'Will I need to wear a uniform?'
I asked the interviewer ______________ .

3 Choose the correct option, A, B or C to complete the dialogue.

Max: How did your interview go?
Nina: I think it was okay, but I struggled with some of the questions.
Max: Like what?
Nina: Well, she asked me what [1]_____ .
Max: Oh, that's difficult. What did you say?
Nina: I said that I [2]_____ at speaking in public. I told her that I [3]_____ in front of a big group of people.
Max: That sounds okay. But do you need to speak in public for the job?
Nina: Not really. I asked her [4]_____ in front of people and she told me [5]_____ . She said that I might [6]_____ presentations in meetings occasionally, but she said that it [7]_____ in front of a lot of people.
Max: It was a good answer to the question, then. You were honest, but you didn't say [8]_____ a weakness that's going to affect your ability to do the job.

1 **A** my biggest weakness was **B** was my biggest weakness **C** is my biggest weakness
2 **A** haven't been very good **B** hadn't been very good **C** wasn't very good
3 **A** 've got nervous **B** 'd got nervous **C** got nervous
4 **A** if I need to speak **B** will I need to speak **C** whether I'd need to speak
5 **A** to not worry **B** not to worry **C** don't worry
6 **A** have needed to give **B** need to give **C** need to have given
7 **A** won't be **B** wouldn't have been **C** wouldn't be
8 **A** you've had **B** you had **C** you'd had

4 Now write the conversation between Nina and the interviewer in Exercise 3.

Interviewer: What's ______________ ?
Nina: I ______________ . ______________ .
______________ ?
Interviewer: ______________ . ______________

5.5 Reporting verbs

Although we usually use the verbs *say* or *tell* to report statements, there are also many other reporting verbs that may be used in different forms.

Verbs without a direct object

- verb + (*that*) (e.g.: *add, admit, agree, claim, complain, deny, explain, insist, promise, propose, recommend, regret, suggest*):
  'I wasted a lot of money.' → *Sue* ***complained (that)*** *she had wasted a lot of money.*
- verb + (*not*) *to* + infinitive (e.g.: *agree, claim, decide, offer, promise, refuse, threaten*):
  'I'll hire two new employees.' → *The manager* ***decided to*** *hire two new employees.*
- verb + (*not*) *-ing* (e.g.: *admit, deny, propose, recommend, regret, suggest*):
  'I didn't take the money.' → *The cashier* ***denied taking*** *the money.*
- verb + preposition + (*not*) *-ing* (e.g.: *apologise for, insist on, object to*):
  'I'm sorry I was rude.' → *I* ***apologised for being*** *rude.*

Verbs with a direct object

- verb + object + (*that*) (e.g.: *advise, assure, convince, inform, persuade, promise, remind, tell, warn*):
  'The meeting will start in an hour.' → *The secretary* ***reminded them (that)*** *the meeting would start in an hour.*
- verb + object + (*not*) *to* + infinitive (e.g.: *advise, ask, beg, convince, encourage, invite, order, persuade, recommend, remind, tell, warn, urge*):
  'You really should apply for this job.' → *Everybody* ***encouraged me to apply*** *for that job.*
- verb + object + preposition + (*not*) *-ing* (e.g.: *accuse sb of, blame sb for, criticise sb for, congratulate sb on, praise sb for, suspect sb of, thank sb for*):
  'It's your fault that the car was damaged.' → *Joe's boss* ***blames him for damaging*** *the car.*

1 Complete the sentences with the correct form of the verbs in brackets. Use a preposition if necessary.

1 She reminded me ______________ (fulfil) my duties.
2 Jonathan suggested ______________ (hire) an interior designer.
3 She persuaded me ______________ (not/step down).
4 I was blamed ______________ (cause) unnecessary problems.
5 He threatened ______________ (tell) the boss about my lack of experience.
6 She congratulated me ______________ (win) first prize.
7 Would you advise me ______________ (do) a course in accountancy?
8 He is suspected ______________ (sell) top-secret information.

2 Complete the text with the correct form of the reporting verbs in the box. There are two extra verbs.

agree congratulate explain invite persuade promise suggest thank warn

Recently, my cousin asked me to help him sell his homemade cookies at a music festival. I wasn't very keen at first, but he [1]__________ me to do it, saying it would probably only take a couple of hours. He [2]__________ that he only had a few boxes of cookies to sell and that they'd sell really quickly. He also [3]__________ to split the profits fifty-fifty. I [4]__________ to help out, but I [5]__________ him that I wouldn't stay longer than two or three hours. To my surprise, the cookies proved to be really popular and they sold out in just over an hour! My cousin was delighted and [6]__________ me for making his new business such a success. He's also [7]__________ me to work with him again at the next festival.

3 Complete the sentences with the correct prepositions or write Ø if no preposition is needed.

1 The company later apologised ______ misleading its customers.
2 Some people object ______ receiving marketing emails from companies.
3 The store denied ______ selling fake goods.
4 The manager thanked everyone ______ their hard work.
5 At least one person has admitted ______ using a fake ID to get into the venue.
6 He blamed problems with the IT system ______ missing the deadline.
7 Several experts have proposed ______ cutting the working day to just five hours.

4 Complete the second sentence so that it has the same meaning as the first. Use the reporting verbs in brackets.

1 'The service here is terrible!'
  She ______ . (complain)
2 'You really must invest in the company,' he said to me.
  He ______ . (convince)
3 'Put your wallet away; we're going to pay for dinner.'
  They ______ . (insist)
4 'Take your umbrella,' she said to him.
  She ______ . (remind)
5 'I bought shares in that company; what a stupid thing to do!'
  He ______ . (regret)
6 'You committed fraud,' they said to her.
  They ______ . (accuse)

5.7 Phrasal verbs – advanced points

Three-part phrasal verbs

Three-part phrasal verbs are usually formed with a common verb and a variety of adverbial and prepositional particles:

*Tom **dropped out of** school after failing his exams.*

*You should **stand up for** what you believe in.*

*Kate couldn't **keep up with** other students.*

Three-part phrasal verbs are inseparable; the object (a noun or pronoun) follows the whole phrasal verb:

*We are sure to **come up against** a lot of opposition.*

~~*We are sure to **come up** a lot of opposition **against**.*~~

Word building with phrasal verbs

- **Nouns**
  - **verb + adverbial/prepositional particle**: *clear out – a clear-out, let sb down – a letdown, warm sth up – a warm-up, burn out – burnout*

    *I had a **clear-out** because I needed more space for some new equipment.*

    *A friend of mine took a year out to avoid **burnout**.*

    In such words, the stress falls on the 'verb' part.
  - **adverbial and prepositional particle + verb**: *bring up → upbringing, pour down → downpour, set out → outset, put in → input*

    *Please, allow me to say a few words at the **outset**.*

    *They had the greatest **input** into our company*

    In such words, the stress falls on the 'particle' part.
- **Adjectives**
  - **adverbial/prepositional particle + verb + *-ing***: *put off → off-putting, lift up → uplifting, stand out → outstanding*

    *Our teacher told us an **uplifting** story.*

    *For such **outstanding** work, you deserve a pay rise.*
  - **verb (Past Participle) + adverbial/prepositional particle:** *run down → run-down, build up → built-up, wear out → worn-out*

    *You are driving through a **built-up** area.*

    *The boys grew up in this **run-down** building you see.*

Note: remember to check the spelling of such nouns and adjectives in a dictionary before you use them.

1 Rewrite the sentences replacing the underlined verb with the correct form of a phrasal verb from the box. There is one extra verb.

come up against	come up with	drop out of
get on with	get out of	look up to	put up with

1 You should not <u>tolerate</u> such working conditions.
2 I try to <u>avoid</u> early shifts if I can.
3 Two students <u>quit</u> the course.
4 Of course we <u>encountered</u> problems, but we found ways to deal with them.
5 We <u>found</u> an efficient way of dealing with applications.
6 He's aware that young athletes <u>admire</u> him as a role model.

2 Choose the correct option, A, B or C to complete the sentences.

1 To prevent injury, make sure you _____ before you do any physical exercise.
   A heat up **B** warm up **C** keep up
2 The position looked quite interesting, but the low salary _____ .
   A wore me out **B** looked me up **C** put me off
3 He doesn't know when he'll _____ completing the annual report as he has so much other work.
   A get round to **B** get out of **C** get over
4 We've _____ printing paper. Could you order some more?
   A come up against **B** made up for **C** run out of
5 I dislike dealing with difficult customers, but I can't _____ it as it's one of my duties.
   A drop out of **B** get out of **C** get on with

3 Complete the text with one word in each gap.

Hanna did well at school, but she decided not to [1]_________ on to further education. Instead, she got a job in a local restaurant working in the kitchen. She got [2]_________ really well with her colleagues and loved working as part of a team. Although she didn't have any formal qualifications, she [3]_________ up for that with her enthusiasm and willingness to learn. Over the next few years, she first worked her way up to become a chef and eventually went on to run her own restaurant. She now goes into schools to talk about her career path. She explains that people looked [4]_________ on her because of her lack of education. She talks about how she had to stand up [5]_________ herself and prove her abilities.

4 Complete the sentences using a noun or adjective form of the phrasal verb in brackets.

1 The film was a bit of a ___________ – not as good as I'd expected. (let down)
2 We got caught in a complete ___________ without an umbrella. (pour down)
3 It's important that everyone knows what's involved from the ___________. (set out)
4 The smell is a bit ___________ but it actually tastes really good. (put off)
5 The cupboard in my office is full of old paperwork, it needs a ___________. (clear out)
6 He grew up in a rather ___________ neighbourhood. (run down)
7 She had a fairly traditional ___________ and education. (bring up)
8 Messi pulled a muscle during the ___________ and couldn't play. (warm up)

6.2 Conditional clauses – alternatives to *if*

To form Zero, First, Second and Third Conditionals, we can use the following words and structures, apart from ***if***:

- conjunction ***unless***:
  *I won't tell you what happened **if** you **don't** promise to keep it secret.* → *I won't tell you what happened **unless** you promise to keep it secret.*
- conjunction ***provided (that)/providing (that)***:
  *You can go with us **if** you pay for your own meals.* → *You can go with us, **provided that** you pay for your own meals.*
- expressions ***Imagine*** … or ***Suppose/Supposing*** … used in questions:
  If someone published a private email from you on Facebook, would you be angry? → ***Imagine/Suppose/ Supposing** someone published a private email from you on Facebook, would you be angry?*

Inversion

- We use inversion in formal language (mostly in writing) to emphasise the rhetorical effect of the sentence.
- We can use inversion in sentences with the auxiliary verbs *were* and *had*, and the verb form *were* is also used with the first and third person singular. In order to transform a conditional clause using inversion, we do not use *if*, but start the sentence with the auxiliary verb:
  *If it **were** my photograph, I wouldn't let anyone publish it.* → ***Were** it my photograph, I would not let anyone publish it.*
  *If I **had considered** all the aspects more carefully, I would probably have made the right decision.* → ***Had** I **considered** all the aspects more carefully, I would probably have made the right decision.*
- We can also use inversion with *should* if we want to say that the condition is rather improbable. In such cases the conditional clause must first be transformed into a more formal sentence using *should* + infinitive, which replaces the verb in the Present Simple. At the next step we use inversion, starting the sentence with *should* and omitting *if*:
  ***If** you **are dissatisfied** with the product, you are entitled to a refund.* (the least formal) → ***If** you **should be** dissatisfied with the product, you are entitled to a refund.* (more formal) → ***Should** you **be** dissatisfied with the product, you are entitled to a refund.* (the most formal)
- When using inversion, we do not use contractions with negatives in the dependent clauses:
  *If I **hadn't told** the police the truth, an innocent person would have been arrested* → ***Had** I **not told** the police the truth, an innocent person would have been arrested.*

1 Choose the correct option.

1 I won't help you *if / unless* you stop misleading me.
2 I'll lend you the book *providing / supposing* you give it back to me on Friday.
3 You would never have read the news story *unless / if* I hadn't sent you the link.
4 *Providing / Supposing* I refused to tamper with the picture, what would you do then?
5 *Imagine / Provided* you had your own TV show, what would it be about?
6 *Had I not / Hadn't I* distorted the truth, there would have been even more trouble.
7 *Should / If* you be unhappy with the portrait, you can always get a photo taken.

2 Complete the second sentence so that it has a similar meaning to the first. Use up to four words including the word in capitals.

1 I don't generally believe a news story online if it isn't from a reputable source. **UNLESS**
I don't generally believe a news story online ____________ a reputable source.
2 You can only use statistics in your essay if you state where they're from. **PROVIDED**
You can include statistics in your essay ____________ where they're from.
3 If a company used your image in an advert, what would you do? **SUPPOSE**
____________ your image in an advert, what would you do?
4 We won't publish someone's photo unless we get their permission first. **IF**
We will only publish someone's photo ____________ their permission first.
5 If someone posted lies about you on social media, how would you feel? **IMAGINE**
____________ about you on social media, how would you feel?
6 Everything should be okay unless it rains. **PROVIDING**
Everything should be okay ____________ rain.

3 Put the words in brackets in the correct order to complete the sentences.

1 I'm sure that, ____________ (here / she / today / were), she'd be shocked by this behaviour.
2 ____________ (had / used / you) a stronger password, your account might not have been hacked.
3 ____________ (customers / need / should) further help, there's a customer service desk in store.
4 ____________ (contacted / had / not / someone) the media, the story wouldn't have become public.
5 ____________ (we / to / use / were) his real name in the story, he might be put in danger.
6 Don't hesitate to call me, ____________ (arise / ever / problem / should / the same) again.

6.5 Mixed conditionals

We can mix Second and Third Conditional forms, creating mixed conditional sentences of Type I or Type II.

Mixed conditionals Type I

If + Past Simple, *would/wouldn't have* + Past Participle

We use Type I mixed conditionals to speculate about permanent states or situations which had a result in the past, and the verb form *were* can be also used with the first and third person singular:

*If Sergio **didn't speak** English with an Italian accent, he **wouldn't have been recognised** and arrested last month.* (But because he speaks with an accent, he was arrested.)

*If I **was/were taller**, I **would have got** the main role in the school play a year ago.* (But I didn't get the role because I'm not taller.)

Mixed conditionals Type II

If + Past Perfect, *would/wouldn't* + infinitive

We use Type II mixed conditionals to speculate about past situations which didn't happen, and this has certain effects or consequences in the present:

*If she **hadn't changed her job** two years ago, Gina **wouldn't be** so unhappy now.* (But she did and now she is unhappy.)

*He **would be** a free man now if the police **had stopped** looking for him then.* (But the police didn't stop looking and he isn't free.)

As with all types of conditionals, we can use *could, might* or *should* instead of *would* in mixed conditional sentences.

1 Match the sentence halves.

1 If someone had proofread the article, ☐
2 She probably wouldn't have got it wrong ☐
3 If he wrote a bit more slowly, ☐
4 The text would be more natural ☐
5 If they checked their facts, ☐
6 They could reach a wider audience ☐

a if they'd paid for a proper translator.
b if she was more willing to ask for advice.
c if they'd created an English version of their website.
d he might have made fewer spelling mistakes.
e it wouldn't contain so many errors.
f they'd have known the figures were out of date.

2 Complete the sentences with the correct form of the verbs in brackets. Use mixed conditionals.

1 If you ____________ (not move), the photo ____________ (not be) so blurred.
2 Jared ____________ (be) a much better actor today if he ____________ (take) lessons when he was younger.
3 The paper ____________ (not report) the story if it ____________ (not involve) a celebrity.
4 If you ____________ (not eat) so much for dinner, you ____________ (feel) sick now.
5 She ____________ (not be) angry with you now if you ____________ (tell) her the truth this morning.
6 If Gina ____________ (be) a better liar, they ____________ (might/believe) the story she told them.

3 Choose the correct option, A, B or C to complete the text.

Scrolling through your social media feed, it's easy to think that everyone's holidays are perfect. However, if those same people [1]_________ so selective about what they shared, the impression would be very different. For example, you see a shot of your friend sitting on a beach in the sun, but if they'd taken a picture a few hours earlier, it [2]_________ grey clouds. Or you see them alone looking out at a stunning view, but if they had turned the camera round just a few degrees, it [3]_________ crowds of other tourists. Personally, I like to have a more realistic record of my travels. If I had only captured the 'picture perfect' moments of my recent trip to Asia, I [4]_________ laugh at some of the disasters now. If I [5]_________ photographic evidence of me walking through water up to my knees when the monsoon rain arrived early, my friends just wouldn't believe my story.

1 A hadn't been B haven't been C wouldn't be
2 A will show B would show C will have shown
3 A would reveal B had revealed C reveals
4 A didn't B wouldn't be able to C wouldn't have been able to
5 A hadn't got B didn't get C haven't got

4 Rewrite the two sentences as a single sentence using a mixed conditional.

1 My dad threw away the receipt. I can't take the T-shirt back to the shop. **If my dad ...**
2 Maria's not very tall. She couldn't become a professional basketball player. **If Maria ...**
3 The editor didn't give me his contact details. I can't send him copies of the photos. **If the editor ...**
4 The venue doesn't have good public transport links. Lots of people drove to the concert. **Fewer people ...**
5 The signs at the airport aren't very clear. We got lost and missed our flight. **If the signs ...**
6 The organiser didn't book tickets in advance. We're standing in this long queue. **We ...**
7 We didn't take your advice. We're in trouble. **If we ...**
8 Lucy is very shy. She didn't ask for a promotion. **She ...**
9 He doesn't get good roles. He didn't go to drama school. **If he ...**
10 I didn't see the film because I don't like the leading actor. **I ...**

6.7 Compound nouns and adjectives

Compound nouns

Compound nouns are usually made up of two words. The first word describes or modifies the second word, e.g. *time travel* (= travel in time) and *travel time* (= travel duration).

Compound nouns structures include:

- **noun + noun:**
  We always watch a ***news bulletin*** *first thing in the morning.*
- **adjective + noun:**
  Everybody should be interested at least a little bit in ***foreign affairs****.*
- **verb -*ing* + noun:**
  Have you seen my ***reading glasses****?*
- **preposition + noun:**
  Our local radio station is located ***on the outskirts*** *of town.*
- nouns derived from phrasal verbs:
  Don't forget to ring me if you need any ***backup****.*

Compound nouns are written as one word, two separate words or two words with a hyphen.

Compound adjectives

Compound adjective structures include:

- **numeral + noun:**
  We were extremely tired after the ***twenty-hour flight*** *to Australia.*
- **adjective + noun:**
  The setting of the film is ***present-day London****.*
- **noun + adjective:**
  The evening ***blood-red sun*** *promises good weather the next day.*
- **noun/adjective/adverb + -ed/-ing participle:**
  It was such a ***heart-warming message****.*
  I ***got tongue-tied*** *when I saw that so many people came to hear me speak.*
- **verb + preposition/adverb:**
  Nowadays, there are a lot of ***made-up stories*** *on social media.*

Compound adjectives are usually hyphenated.

Some compound adjectives are made from more than two words, e.g. *fifteen-year-old, state-of-the-art.*

Note: the noun in a compound adjective is usually singular:
two-minute conversation NOT ~~*two-minutes conversation*~~
flat-footed NOT ~~*flat-feeted*~~

1 Complete the sentences with the words in the box. There are two extra words.

actual affairs art breaking commercial present science stop

1 People now learn about the latest ____________ news via social media.
2 Our journalists cover both domestic news and foreign ____________ .
3 People are fed up with the non____________ coverage of the elections.
4 They use state-of-the-____________ camera technology to capture the action.
5 After the ____________ break, we'll hear from our reporter on the scene.
6 This ancient tradition is still practised in ____________-day Turkey.

2 Replace the underlined phrase in the first sentence with an appropriate compound adjective in the second one.

1 They've produced a video that lasts for five minutes.
They've produced a ____________ video.
2 We're using a name we made up to protect the woman's identity.
We're using a ____________ name to protect the woman's identity.
3 People had to walk through water that was as high as their waist to get to safety.
People had to walk through ____________ water to get to safety.
4 The hospital has an emergency department that is open for twenty-four hours a day.
The hospital has a ____________ emergency department.
5 We've created a new online booking system that's very easy for people to use.
We've created a new ____________ online booking system.

3 Choose the correct option.

1 Ford, the US *car company / company car*, is planning to open a factory in the town.
2 The job also comes with a *car company / company car* and private health insurance.
3 There's a jug of *tap water / water tap* on the table or you can order mineral water.
4 There's an outside *tap water / water tap* we use to water the garden.
5 If *time travel / travel time* were possible, I'd go back to Ancient Egypt.
6 The new high-speed rail link cuts *time travel / travel time* to two hours.
7 You turn off the main road and go down a small *roadside / side road*.
8 A group of schoolchildren were standing by the *roadside / side road* waiting for a bus.

7.2 Advanced passive forms

Passive forms with modal structures

We can use the Passive:

- with modal verbs in the present (**modal verb + be + Past Participle**):
  *The project **must be completed** by tomorrow.*
  *Mobile phones **may be used** as directed by the staff.*
- with modal verbs in the past (**modal verb + have been + Past Participle**):
  *The competition **should have been cancelled** after the accident.* (But it wasn't, and the competition continued).
  *The server **couldn't have been repaired** properly yesterday.* (And it still isn't working properly).
  *Her Facebook profile **must have been removed** because I can't find it.*

Passive forms with verbs that take two objects

- Some verbs, e.g. *ask, bring, buy, give, hand, offer, pay, promise, sell, send, show, teach, tell*, etc. can take a direct and an indirect object.
  *They promised **a bonus and a pay rise*** (indirect object) *to **John*** (direct object).
  *The pupils gave **the teacher*** (direct object) ***a bunch of flowers***. (indirect object)
- Depending on what we want to emphasise, we can form passive statements by beginning with either the direct or the indirect object:
  *A bonus and a pay rise **were promised** to John.* (indirect object becomes the subject with emphasis on 'a bonus and a pay rise'):
  *John **was promised** a bonus and a pay rise.* (direct object becomes the subject with emphasis on 'John')
  ***A bunch of flowers** was given to the teacher by the pupils.* (indirect object becomes the subject with emphasis on 'a bunch of flowers')
  ***The teacher** was given a bunch of flowers by the pupils.* (direct object becomes the subject with emphasis on 'the teacher').

Passive forms with verbs + *-ing* and verbs + *to* infinitive

- To form the Passive of verbs and phrases followed by a gerund, e.g. *be interested in, can't stand, don't mind, enjoy, get tired of, hate, like/dislike, love, miss*, etc., we use **verb/phrase + *being* + Past Participle**:
  *My IT teacher **doesn't mind being asked** millions of questions.*
  *I **got tired of being** constantly **criticised**.*
- To form the Passive of verbs and phrases followed by *to* + infinitive, e.g. *can't afford, choose, decide, hope, need, prefer, pretend, refuse, want, would like*, etc., we use **verb/phrase + *to be* + Past Participle**:
  *Millions of people **hope to be cured** of the disease.*
  *At some point your son will **need to be told** the truth.*
- To form the Passive of the phrase *make sb do sth* we use **form of *be* + *made* + *to* infinitive**:
  *My mother **made me clean** the bathroom and the kitchen.* (active sentence)
  *I **was made to clean** the bathroom and the kitchen (by my mother).* (passive sentence)

1 **Complete the sentences with the correct forms of the verb *be* and the verbs in brackets.**

1 Your phone might __________ (set) to silent mode. Have a look in the settings.
2 These samples can't __________ (checked) properly. There are far too many errors.
3 The laptop must __________ (leave) on overnight. The battery's completely dead.
4 The volume can __________ (adjust) using the button on the side of the tablet.
5 All mobile devices should __________ (switch) to flight mode during the flight.
6 When the drug was originally developed, these side-effects couldn't __________ (predict).

2 **Put the words in brackets in the correct order to complete the sentences.**

1 Hopefully, __________ (an email / been / everyone / has / sent) with a link to the video.
2 They claim __________ (made / they / to / sign / were) the contract without reading it first.
3 Customers said __________ (any / been / explanation / had / not / offered / they) for the delay.
4 Remember that __________ (be / from / laptops / need / removed / to / your bag) at security check.
5 __________ (already / been / had / more money / promised / the school) for science equipment.
6 __________ (been / have / I / kept / should) more up-to-date with what was going on.
7 The package __________ (customer / to / been / must / the / sent / have) by now.
8 Honestly, __________ (stand / I / interrupted / can't / being) when I'm concentrating on my work.

3 **Complete the second sentence so that it has a similar meaning to the first. Use up to four words including the word in capitals.**

1 It is a bad idea not to address all of the issues. **OUGHT**
All of the issues __________ addressed.
2 Everybody could hear the music despite my closing the windows. **COULD**
The music __________ despite my closing the windows.
3 She had shown me the password for the site the previous afternoon. **HAD**
I __________ the password for the site the previous afternoon.
4 They said that I mustn't surf the Internet. **TOLD**
I __________ surf the Internet.
5 I don't like it when someone orders me around. **BEING**
I dislike __________ around.
6 The babysitter made the kids go to bed early. **MADE**
The children __________ to bed early.

7.5 Passive reporting structures

To talk about general opinions and views, we use verbs such as *agree, believe, claim, consider, expect, feel, hope, know, report, say, think, understand*, etc. and the following structures:

- ***it* + passive verb (present or past) + *that*:**
  People claim that optimists live longer. → ***It is claimed that*** *optimists live longer.*
  People believed that mathematics was the link between the supernatural and the world of men. → *It* ***was believed that*** *mathematics was the link between the supernatural and the world of men.*
- **subject + passive verb (present or past) + to infinitive:**
  Computer scientists consider wearable technology to be the future of computing. → ***Wearable technology is considered to be*** *the future of computing.*
  Doctors knew that almonds protected against diabetes. → ***Almonds were known to protect*** *against diabetes.*
  The infinitive may also be replaced by ***be*** **+ Present/Past Participle**:
  They expect that over three million smartphones will be sold. → *Over three million smartphones* ***are expected to be sold***.
  People thought that the Ministry of Health was preparing new regulations. → *The Ministry of Health* ***was thought to be preparing*** *new regulations.*
- **subject + passive verb (present or past) + *to have* + Past Participle**
  Experts estimate that the earthquake has killed more than 1,000 people. → ***The earthquake is estimated to have killed*** *more than 1,000 people.*
  The press previously reported that the company's profit had reached £100 million. → ***The company's profit was*** *previously* ***reported to have reached*** *£100 million.*
- ***there* + passive verb (present or past) + *to be*:**
  Analysts expect that there will be a rise in the number of jobs offered across the UK. → ***There is expected to be*** *a rise in the number of jobs offered across the UK.*
- ***there* + passive verb (present or past) + *to have been*:**
  Historians think that there were over twenty inventors before Edison who invented various light sources. → ***There are thought to have been*** *over twenty inventors before Edison who invented various light sources.*

1 Choose the correct option.

1 Some years ago, the university's Physics department *was considered that / was considered to be* the best in the country.
2 The ancient treasure *was thought to lose / was thought to have been lost*, until it was unexpectedly discovered.
3 Our government *is said to look / is said to be looking* into ways to lower carbon emissions.
4 Chemicals from factory waste *are estimated to have caused / are estimating to cause* the death of thousands of river fish.
5 A 5G network for faster communication *is expected to be established / is expected to establish* within months.

2 Rewrite the sentences using passive reporting structures.

1 Many people consider Bob Dylan to be the most influential musician of the 20th century.
Bob Dylan ____________ .
2 In February, newspapers reported that crime levels were falling faster in Poland than in other EU countries.
It ____________ .
3 Linguists expect that by 2050 another 7,000 languages will disappear.
It ____________ .
4 Nutritionists say that salmon is one of the most nutrient-dense foods there is.
Salmon ____________ .
5 Palaeontologists think there were over 500 different species of dinosaur.
There ____________ .
6 Experts believe that 1.24 million people were killed in road traffic accidents in 2010.
Road traffic accidents ____________ .
7 We now know that cats are able to produce about ninety different sounds more than dogs.
Cats ____________ .

3 Choose the correct option, A, B or C to complete the text.

How safe are your passwords? In a recent study, 123456 [1]_________ the most commonly used password. In the study data, there [2]_________ more than 23 million rather unimaginative people using it. The equally easy-to-guess 'password' [3]_________ in the top five. Names of people, football teams and bands were popular because [4]_________ they're easy to remember. However, people who use well-known words or names as passwords [5]_________ themselves at high risk of being hacked. A string of three random words together [6]_________ a strong password that will best protect you from fraud.

1 **A** was found that it was
B is found to have been
C was found to be
2 **A** showed to have been
B was shown to be
C were shown to be
3 **A** was reported that it appeared
B was reported to appear
C is reported to be appearing
4 **A** it is thought that
B there were thought
C were thought that
5 **A** are said to be putting
B are said that they put
C are said to have been put
6 **A** it is considered that it makes
B is considered to be made
C is considered to make

7.7 Easily confused words

- Words that look or sound similar but have different meanings, e.g.:
  cite (quote), ***site*** (place), ***sight*** (view)
  conscious (aware/awake), ***conscientious*** (dutiful)
  dessert (something sweet), ***desert*** (dry land with no vegetation)
  late (unpunctual), ***lately*** (recently)
  principal (main/head teacher), ***principle*** (rule)
  proceed (go ahead), ***precede*** (come first)
  sensible (reasonable), ***sensitive*** (delicate)
  weather (atmospheric conditions), ***whether*** (if)
  *The **principal** talked to the parents.*
  *The **principle** of being a vegetarian is not eating meat.*
- Words that look or sound similar and have similar meanings (and often belong to the same word family), e.g.:
  alike (similar), ***likely*** (probable),
  advise (give advice), ***advice*** (noun)
  alone (on your own), ***lone*** (one), ***lonely*** (alone and unhappy)
  assure (promise that sth will happen), ***ensure*** (make certain), ***insure*** (provide insurance)
  breathe (draw breath), ***breath*** (noun)
  dependant (sb dependent on sth/sb else), ***dependent*** (needing sth to exist)
  economic (related to the economy), ***economical*** (cost-effective)
  effect (result), ***affect*** (influence sth/sb)
  historical (relating to the past), ***historic*** (important as part of the past)
  lay (put sth down, e.g. on a bed), ***lie*** (be placed flat, e.g. on a bed)
  migrate (move), ***immigrate*** (move to another country), ***emigrate*** (move out of a country)
  raise (lift/move sth higher), ***rise*** (increase), ***arise*** (happen)
  *Please, **lay** your phones on the desks.*
  *My grandfather likes to **lie** on the couch after lunch.*
- Words that look or sound different but have similar meanings, e.g.:
  after all, finally, lastly
  eventually, comprise, consist of, include
  occasion, opportunity
  ***After all**, it's simple.*
  ***Finally/Eventually**, he started the car.*
  ***Finally/Lastly**, add some salt.*
  *The course **comprises/consists of** a coursebook and a CD.*
  *The course **includes** a CD.*
  *It was the only **opportunity**.*
  *I bought it for a special **occasion**.*
- False friends are words that look or sound similar to words in your language, but have different meanings, e.g.:
  data (information):
  *I lost all the **data**.*
  date (a point in time):
  *I'd like to fix the **date**.*
  realise (know/understand):
  *Do you **realise** how dangerous it is?*
  carry out (do/perform):
  *We used to **carry out** a lot of experiments.*
  actually (in fact):
  *This flat looks smaller, but **actually** is bigger.*
  currently (now):
  *The company **currently** employs 1,000 people.*

1 Complete the sentences with the words in capitals.

1 Maria works ____________ studying wildlife in Alaska. She admits to feeling ____________ occasionally, but she loves her job. **ALONE / LONELY**
2 Of course, trains sometimes arrive a few minutes ____________ , but on some routes ____________ , the delays have become extreme. **LATELY/ LATE**
3 We ____________ people to bring warm clothes, but there are people who don't listen to ____________ and turn up in shorts. **ADVISE / ADVICE**
4 At first ____________ it looks just like an empty field, but it's actually the ____________ of one of Europe's most significant battles. **SITE / SIGHT**
5 If any significant issues ____________ , you should ____________ them with your manager later. **RAISE / ARISE**
6 Today our teacher is absent, so we're having a class with the ____________ , who's a physicist. We're going to discuss the most important ____________ of quantum physics. **PRINCIPAL / PRINCIPLE**
7 Unfortunately, the ____________ being what it is today, we won't be able to go hiking. We'll see tomorrow ____________ it will be safer to hike. **WHETHER / WEATHER**
8 We need to ____________ that all equipment is cleaned and put away after use. The lab director wants us to ____________ him that we'll leave the lab tidy. Otherwise, he won't let us in again. **ASSURE / ENSURE**

2 Complete the words in the text with the correct endings.

VOLUNTEER RESEARCHERS NEEDED

We can't live without water, but for those living in [1]des______ regions with little or no rainfall, water is a constant challenge. What's more, these areas are typically more [2]sens______ to the effects of climate change. Communities here often have very limited access to clean water. Our project is looking to recruit hardworking, [3]consc______ volunteers to help design water filtering systems that are both effective and [4]econ______ to run. This would be ideal work experience for engineering students. Our research is entirely [5]depen______ on charitable donations, so we aren't able to offer payment, but you'll gain valuable experience putting the engineering [6]prin_________ you've studied into practice, as well as making a really valuable contribution to this vital area of development.

8.2 Unreal past and regrets – *wish, if only, it's time* and *would rather*

Present and future

- To express regret about a present situation which seems to be impossible to change, we use **wish/if only + subject + Past Simple**:

*I **wish I knew** more about ecology.*
*I **wish oceans** weren't used as rubbish tips.*
***If only we could** save sea animals from starvation.*
***If only I didn't have** to work so much.*

- To say that we believe somebody should do something in the present or in the near future, we use **it's (high) time + subject + Past Simple**:

***It's high time people stopped** driving cars in cities.*
***It's high time you started** recycling your rubbish.*

- To talk what we would prefer somebody to do in the present or in the future, we use **would rather + subject + Past Simple**:

***I'd rather we switched** to organic fruit and vegetables.*
*My mum **would rather I studied** more.*

Past

- To express regret about a past situation, we use **wish/if only + subject + Past Perfect**:

*I **wish we had done** more to prevent this tragedy.*
*My sister **wishes we hadn't moved** to this area, but I'm happy about it.*
***If only the city council hadn't reduced** the funds for environmental protection.*
***If only I had listened** to you when you advised me not to go on that expedition!*

1 Choose the correct option.

1 If only I *lost / hadn't lost / didn't lose* my camera on the beach.
2 It's high time we *stop / stopped / had stopped* dumping waste in the seas.
3 My back's all red. I wish I *had / did / would* put more sun cream on.
4 I'd rather she *couldn't / didn't / won't* go alone, to be honest.
5 If only I *hadn't to / had to / didn't have to* go camping. I hate sleeping in tents.
6 I wish you all *knew / had known / know* just how much effort I put into this trip.
7 If only I *had seen / saw / did see* her earlier. I'd have asked her to join us.
8 I'd rather we *use / used / had used* less plastic than we currently do.
9 If only the fire *doesn't destroy / didn't destroy / hadn't destroyed* the forest.
10 I wish I *could / did / will* do more to protect endangered species.

2 Complete the sentences with the correct form of the verbs in brackets.

1 If only more people ______ (leave) a patch of their garden to grow wild, it would help wildlife.
2 So many products damage the environment. It's time consumers ______ (take) more interest in how the things they buy are made.
3 It's difficult to know what products contain. I'd rather companies ______ (label) them more clearly.
4 Some species are now at risk of extinction. I wish we ______ (do) more to protect them earlier.
5 I wish supermarkets ______ (not/sell) fruit and vegetables wrapped in plastic.
6 The new road blocks a migration route for animals. If only they ______ (consult) wildlife experts, it could have been avoided.
7 We all contribute to pollution. It's high time we ______ (recognise) that fact.
8 The heat is terrible! If only it ______ (not/be) so hot today!
9 It sounds like the lecture you attended was fascinating. I wish I ______ (know) about it.
10 I'd rather we ______ (not/discuss) the issue right now if you don't mind.

3 Complete the text with the correct form of the verbs in the box.

do know not assume not fly switch warn

I love travelling, but lately I've become more conscious of my environmental footprint. When I look back on the amazing places I've visited, I have fond memories, but I also wish I [1]______ quite so many air miles. It's time more of us [2]______ to less polluting forms of transport. I've been trying to cut my air travel, but it's not always that easy. I wish big travel companies [3]______ that everyone wants to fly. Of course, they don't offer other transport options, because they'd rather everyone [4]______ the same to keep things simple. Researching different routes yourself can be fun, but it doesn't always work out. When I planned to take a ferry from Spain to Morocco last year, for example, I wish I [5]______ that it sometimes gets cancelled in bad weather. I got stuck in Cádiz for two days and missed the train I'd booked from Tangier to Marrakesh. If only someone [6]______ me about possible delays, I'd have waited to buy my train ticket when I arrived.

8.5 Emphasis – cleft sentences and inversion

In order to add emphasis to a sentence, we may use cleft sentences or inversion.

Cleft sentences

- Cleft sentences are formed from two parts, and usually start with the pronouns *what*, *it* or *all*. Although the meaning they convey could be expressed in a simpler way, cleft sentences are used to give emphasis to the person performing an action or to the place, time or reason of the action:

  I love helping other people. → ***What I really love** is helping other people.*

  The company covered up the scandal. → ***What the company did was (to) cover up** the scandal.*

  I raised the subject of sewage being dumped into the river. → ***It was me who raised** the subject of sewage being dumped into the river.*

  We helped the flood victims clean up the debris. → ***All we did was (to) help** the flood victims clean up the debris.*

  You need love. → ***All you need is** love.*

Inversion

- We use inversion in sentences which start with negative adverbs, e.g. *never, rarely, seldom, hardly, barely, scarcely, no sooner* or phrases with *no* or *not*, e.g. *under no circumstances, on no condition, on no account, at no time, in no way, not until, not only*, etc. In these sentences an affirmative sentence takes on the order and verb form of a question, i.e.

  negative adverb/phrase with *no* or *not* + auxiliary verb + subject + main verb:

  He had never been so devastated. → ***Never had he been** so devastated.*

  We rarely hear about such powerful mother and child bonds in animals. → ***Rarely do we hear** about such powerful mother and child bonds in animals.*

  He had entered the house and the phone rang. → ***No sooner had he entered** the house than the phone rang.*

  She had not only survived the disaster, but she saved two other people as well. → ***Not only had she survived** the disaster, but she saved two other people as well.*

  You are not permitted to leave the building under any circumstances. → ***Under no circumstances are you permitted** to leave the building.*

1 Match the sentence halves.

1 The figure that surprised me ☐
2 What's happened in some countries ☐
3 Never have our rivers ☐
4 It's people in the hottest parts of the world ☐
5 Not only ☐
6 What many of us see as a basic necessity ☐

a is the population has migrated to cities putting pressure on resources.
b who are already experiencing water shortages.
c is becoming a luxury in some regions.
d was the amount of water wasted through leaking pipes.
e been under such pressure from human water use.
f is water scarce in these areas, but it's frequently contaminated.

2 Choose the correct option.

1 *All / It's / What's* meat production that accounts for most of the world's agricultural land use, representing around 80 percent of farmland worldwide.
2 Not only *are / did / do* cattle take up land themselves, but farmland is also used to grow animal feed.
3 *It's / What / What's* many people find shocking is that huge areas of forest are being cleared just to grow grain to feed to cows.
4 In some parts of the world, what farmers *are doing / are doing is / do are* cutting down previously wildlife rich forests just to keep up with our demand for meat.
5 *It's / What's / What* this loss of habitat that especially concerns environmentalists.
6 With a growing population and changing eating habits, never before *has demand for meat been / has been demand for meat / is demand for meat* so high.
7 To protect natural habitats, *all / it's / what's* we need to do is declare them areas for conservation.
8 What this teen eco-warrior *is doing is / is doing / does* raising awareness about a problem that adults should be dealing with.
9 *What / It's / What's* increased industrialisation that has greatly contributed to the problem of global warming.

3 Rewrite the sentences changing the emphasis.

1 Tess promised to help tidy up the garden.
It was ______________________ .
2 We are only handing out leaflets in protest.
All ______________________ .
3 She has never been so disappointed by the results.
Never ______________________ .
4 You are not going out in that raging storm under any circumstances.
Under ______________________ .
5 The protestors started the violence.
What ______________________ .
6 We rarely see such extreme temperatures at this time of year.
Rarely ______________________ .
7 They had only just got back to the flat when they heard the news.
Hardly ______________________ .
8 I don't believe in telling lies.
What ______________________ .
9 He asked the question and answered it too.
Not ______________________ .
10 I can't stand your ignorance of the issue.
It's ______________________ .

8.7 Word families – prefixes

Prefixes

Prefixes may be added to the same root word to create new words, e.g. **take, retake** and **overtake.**

Common prefixes:

- ***un-***, ***in-***, ***dis-***, ***il-***, ***im-***, ***ir-*** are usually added to adjectives, to create a negative adjective.
  The prefix ***il-*** precedes adjectives beginning with *l-*, ***ir-*** precedes adjectives beginning *r-*, while ***im-*** goes with adjectives beginning with *m-* or *p-*.: ***unwilling, incurable, disobedient, illegible, immoral, impatient, irrelevant***
- ***un-***, ***dis-*** are used with verbs to create opposites: ***unlock, discontinue***
- ***re-*** means to do something again: ***reapply, rebuild***
- ***hyper-*** means something extreme: ***hypertension, hypersensitive***
- ***mis-*** means something bad or wrong: ***misunderstand, misbehave, mismanagement***
- ***on-/off-*** denote either a specific place, or 'not the case': ***onshore, offshore, on-site, off-site***
- ***out-*** often precedes verbs and means 'more than or better': ***outlive, outnumber***
- ***over-/under-*** mean either 'too much' or 'not enough': ***overdeveloped, underdeveloped, overweight, underweight***
- ***anti-/pro-*** are used for 'against' or 'in favour': ***anti-social, anti-ageing, pro-family, pro-ecological***
- ***pre-/post-*** are used to describe that something happened before or after something else: ***preschool, pre-tax, post-tax, post-match***
- ***self-*** describes actions done to or by yourself: ***self-control, self-portrait***
- ***sub-*** means something inferior or lower: ***sub-standard, sub-zero***
- ***up-/down-*** denotes an increase, improvement or fall: ***upturn, downturn***

1 Complete the words in the sentences with appropriate prefixes.

1 We can cut waste by ____using plastic bags and bottles rather than throwing them away.
2 The number of kids cycling to school has grown and they now ____number those being dropped off by car.
3 It's hard to persuade people to leave their cars at home because they're ____willing to give up the convenience of driving.
4 There's been an ____turn in demand for organic products as people become more eco-conscious.
5 In the winter, the area experiences heavy snow and ____-zero temperatures.
6 People are naturally ____patient and they don't like having to wait for things.
7 We ____estimated the number of people who might come and we soon ran out of chairs.
8 All the students took a ____-course test to decide which class they should join.

2 Choose the correct option.

1 The builders painted the room the wrong colour and they had to *undo / redo* the work.
2 Workers are asking for more money, complaining they're *overpaid / underpaid*.
3 We have strict security to prevent the *misuse / reuse* of confidential information.
4 People get frustrated by politicians' *inability / disability* to give a direct answer.
5 The hall is a *multi-purpose / repurpose* space that can be used for all kinds of events.
6 The books are aimed at *preschool / postschool* children aged between three and five.
7 In private, she's quite shy; the complete opposite of her *offstage / onstage* personality.
8 A group of *anti-nuclear / pro-nuclear* activists were protesting against plans for a new power station.

3 Complete the sentences with the correct form of the word in capitals.

1 Inspectors found the company had ____________ safety training for staff. **ADEQUATE**
2 It's a very ____________ community, with students from all over the world. **CULTURE**
3 The wildfires spread and quickly became ____________ . **CONTROL**
4 It seems ____________ now that we'll get finished by the deadline. **PROBABLE**
5 His arguments are completely ____________ and don't make any sense. **LOGICAL**
6 They were living in ____________ conditions with no electricity or clean water. **STANDARD**
7 Such high levels of air pollution are clearly ____________ and need to be tackled urgently. **SAFE**
8 All kinds of wildlife is now treating this ____________ factory as a home. **USED**

4 Complete the text using the correct forms of the words in brackets.

The Earth is in grave danger from decades of [1]_________ (development) that has resulted in the destruction of forests and other habitats. Such [2]_________ (manage) of our planet cannot be tolerated any longer. If governments continue to act so [3]_________ (responsible), not only will all animal life face extinction, but humans will as well. Politicians who are [4]_________ (willing) to put the survival of the planet above short-term profits should be ashamed of themselves. In order to [5]_________ (build) confidence in our governments, they should make greater efforts to fight global warming and pollution.

PERSONAL PRONOUNS AND POSSESSIVE PRONOUNS

Personal pronoun as a subject	Personal pronoun as an object	Possessive pronoun (+noun)	Possessive pronoun (no noun)
I'm a student.	Come with **me**.	It's **my** house.	It's **mine**.
Have **you** got a cat?	I like **you**.	It's **your** bike.	It's **yours**.
He works at home.	Can you help **him**?	It's **his** book.	It's **his**.
She's been to Prague.	Listen to **her**.	It's **her** room.	It's **hers**.
Is **it** a famous city?	I can't find **it**.	Oxford (= it) is famous for **its** university.	—
We live in Poland.	Wait for **us**.	It's **our** tablet.	It's **ours**.
You can't sit here.	Can I talk to **you**?	It's **your** car.	It's **yours**.
Are **they** working?	Do you know **them**?	It's **their** money.	It's **theirs**.

DEMONSTRATIVE PRONOUNS, INTERROGATIVE PRONOUNS, RELATIVE PRONOUNS

Demonstrative		Interrogative	Relative
Singular	Plural		
this that	these those	What? Who? Whose? Which? Where? When? Why? How? (How often? How long? How far? How much? How many?)	who which that whose when where

NUMERALS

Numbers: 1 – 100

Cardinal numbers	Ordinal numbers	Cardinal numbers	Ordinal numbers
1 – one	first (1st)	20 – twenty	twentieth (20th)
2 – two	second (2nd)	21 – twenty-one	twenty-first (21st)
3 – three	third (3rd)	22 – twenty-two	twenty-second (22nd)
4 – four	fourth (4th)	23 – twenty-three	twenty-third (23rd)
5 – five	fifth (5th)	24 – twenty-four	twenty-fourth (24th)
6 – six	sixth (6th)	25 – twenty-five	twenty-fifth (25th)
7 – seven	seventh (7th)	26 – twenty-six	twenty-sixth (26th)
8 – eight	eighth (8th)	27 – twenty-seven	twenty-seventh (27th)
9 – nine	ninth (9th)	28 – twenty-eight	twenty-eighth (28th)
10 – ten	tenth (10th)	29 – twenty-nine	twenty-ninth (29th)
11 – eleven	eleventh (11th)	30 – thirty	thirtieth (30th)
12 – twelve	twelfth (12th)	40 – forty	fortieth (40th)
13 – thirteen	thirteenth (13th)	50 – fifty	fiftieth (50th)
14 – fourteen	fourteenth (14th)	60 – sixty	sixtieth (60th)
15 – fifteen	fifteenth (15th)	70 – seventy	seventieth (70th)
16 – sixteen	sixteenth (16th)	80 – eighty	eightieth (80th)
17 – seventeen	seventeenth (17th)	90 – ninety	ninetieth (90th)
18 – eighteen	eighteenth (18th)	100 – one/a hundred	hundredth (100th)
19 – nineteen	nineteenth (19th)	101 – one/a hundred and one	hundred and first (101st)

Numbers over 100

Numbers over 100
1,000 – one/a thousand
3,555 – three thousand, five hundred **and** fifty-five
56,223 – fifty-six thousand, two hundred **and** twenty-three
725,000 – seven hundred **and** twenty-five thousand
1,000,000 – one/a million
1,000,000,000 – one/a billion

IRREGULAR VERBS

Infinitive	Past Simple	Past Participle
be [biː]	**was/were** [wɒz/wɜː]	**been** [biːn]
beat [biːt]	**beat** [biːt]	**beaten** ['biːtn]
become [bɪ'kʌm]	**became** [bɪ'keɪm]	**become** [bɪ'kʌm]
begin [bɪ'gɪn]	**began** [bɪ'gæn]	**begun** [bɪ'gʌn]
bite [baɪt]	**bit** [bɪt]	**bitten** ['bɪtn]
bleed [bliːd]	**bled** [bled]	**bled** [bled]
blow [bləʊ]	**blew** [bluː]	**blown** [bləʊn]
break [breɪk]	**broke** [brəʊk]	**broken** ['brəʊkən]
bring [brɪŋ]	**brought** [brɔːt]	**brought** [brɔːt]
broadcast ['brɔːdkɑːst]	**broadcast** ['brɔːdkɑːst]	**broadcast** ['brɔːdkɑːst]
build [bɪld]	**built** [bɪlt]	**built** [bɪlt]
burn [bɜːn]	**burned** [bɜːnd]/**burnt** [bɜːnt]	**burned** [bɜːnd]/**burnt** [bɜːnt]
burst [bɜːst]	**burst** [bɜːst]	**burst** [bɜːst]
buy [baɪ]	**bought** [bɔːt]	**bought** [bɔːt]
can [kæn]	**could** [kʊd]	**been able to** [biːn 'eɪbl tə]
catch [kætʃ]	**caught** [kɔːt]	**caught** [kɔːt]
choose [tʃuːz]	**chose** [tʃəʊz]	**chosen** ['tʃəʊzn]
come [kʌm]	**came** [keɪm]	**come** [kʌm]
cost [kɒst]	**cost** [kɒst]	**cost** [kɒst]
cut [kʌt]	**cut** [kʌt]	**cut** [kʌt]
deal [diːl]	**dealt** [delt]	**dealt** [delt]
dig [dɪg]	**dug** [dʌg]	**dug** [dʌg]
do [duː]	**did** [dɪd]	**done** [dʌn]
draw [drɔː]	**drew** [druː]	**drawn** [drɔːn]
dream [driːm]	**dreamed** [driːmd]/**dreamt** [dremt]	**dreamed** [driːmd]/**dreamt** [dremt]
drink [drɪnk]	**drank** [drænk]	**drunk** [drʌnk]
drive [draɪv]	**drove** [drəʊv]	**driven** ['drɪvn]
eat [iːt]	**ate** [et]	**eaten** ['iːtn]
fall [fɔːl]	**fell** [fel]	**fallen** ['fɔːlən]
feed [fiːd]	**fed** [fed]	**fed** [fed]
feel [fiːl]	**felt** [felt]	**felt** [felt]
fight [faɪt]	**fought** [fɔːt]	**fought** [fɔːt]
find [faɪnd]	**found** [faʊnd]	**found** [faʊnd]
fit [fɪt]	**fit** [fɪt]	**fit** [fɪt]
fly [flaɪ]	**flew** [fluː]	**flown** [fləʊn]
forget [fə'get]	**forgot** [fə'gɒt]	**forgotten** [fə'gɒtn]
forgive [fə'gɪv]	**forgave** [fə'geɪv]	**forgiven** [fə'gɪvən]
freeze [friːz]	**froze** [frəʊz]	**frozen** ['frəʊzən]
get [get]	**got** [gɒt]	**got** [gɒt]
give [gɪv]	**gave** [geɪv]	**given** ['gɪvən]
go [gəʊ]	**went** [went]	**gone** [gɒn]/**been** [biːn]
grow [grəʊ]	**grew** [gruː]	**grown** [grəʊn]
hang [hæŋ]	**hung** [hʌŋ]	**hung** [hʌŋ]
have [hæv]	**had** [hæd]	**had** [hæd]
hear [hɪə]	**heard** [hɜːd]	**heard** [hɜːd]
hide [haɪd]	**hid** [hɪd]	**hidden** ['hɪdn]
hit [hɪt]	**hit** [hɪt]	**hit** [hɪt]
hold [həʊld]	**held** [held]	**held** [held]
hurt [hɜːt]	**hurt** [hɜːt]	**hurt** [hɜːt]
keep [kiːp]	**kept** [kept]	**kept** [kept]
know [nəʊ]	**knew** [njuː]	**known** [nəʊn]
lead [liːd]	**led** [led]	**led** [led]
learn [lɜːn]	**learned** [lɜːnd]/**learnt** [lɜːnt]	**learned** [lɜːnd]/**learnt** [lɜːnt]
leave [liːv]	**left** [left]	**left** [left]
lend [lend]	**lent** [lent]	**lent** [lent]
let [let]	**let** [let]	**let** [let]
lie [laɪ]	**lay** [leɪ]	**lain** [leɪn]
light [laɪt]	**lit** [lɪt]	**lit** [lɪt]
lose [luːz]	**lost** [lɒst]	**lost** [lɒst]
make [meɪk]	**made** [meɪd]	**made** [meɪd]
mean [miːn]	**meant** [ment]	**meant** [ment]
meet [miːt]	**met** [met]	**met** [met]
overtake [ˌəʊvə'teɪk]	**overtook** [ˌəʊvə'tʊk]	**overtaken** [ˌəʊvə'teɪkən]
pay [peɪ]	**paid** [peɪd]	**paid** [peɪd]
put [pʊt]	**put** [pʊt]	**put** [pʊt]
read [riːd]	**read** [red]	**read** [red]
ride [raɪd]	**rode** [rəʊd]	**ridden** ['rɪdn]
ring [rɪŋ]	**rang** [ræŋ]	**rung** [rʌŋ]
rise [raɪz]	**rose** [rəʊz]	**risen** [rɪzən]
run [rʌn]	**ran** [ræn]	**run** [rʌn]
say [seɪ]	**said** [sed]	**said** [sed]
see [siː]	**saw** [sɔː]	**seen** [siːn]
seek [siːk]	**sought** [sɔːt]	**sought** [sɔːt]
sell [sel]	**sold** [səʊld]	**sold** [səʊld]
send [send]	**sent** [sent]	**sent** [sent]
set [set]	**set** [set]	**set** [set]
shake [ʃeɪk]	**shook** [ʃʊk]	**shaken** [ʃeɪkən]
shine [ʃaɪn]	**shone** [ʃɒn]	**shone** [ʃɒn]
show [ʃəʊ]	**showed** [ʃəʊd]	**shown** [ʃəʊn]
shut [ʃʌt]	**shut** [ʃʌt]	**shut** [ʃʌt]
sing [sɪŋ]	**sang** [sæŋ]	**sung** [sʌŋ]
sit [sɪt]	**sat** [sæt]	**sat** [sæt]
sleep [sliːp]	**slept** [slept]	**slept** [slept]
slide [slaɪd]	**slid** [slɪd]	**slid** [slɪd]
smell [smel]	**smelled** [smeld]/**smelt** [smelt]	**smelled** [smeld]/**smelt** [smelt]
speak [spiːk]	**spoke** [spəʊk]	**spoken** ['spəʊkən]
spend [spend]	**spent** [spent]	**spent** [spent]
spill [spɪl]	**spilled** [spɪld]/**spilt** [spɪlt]	**spilled** [spɪld]/**spilt** [spɪlt]
split [splɪt]	**split** [splɪt]	**split** [splɪt]
spread [spred]	**spread** [spred]	**spread** [spred]
spring [sprɪŋ]	**sprang** [spræŋ]	**sprung** [sprʌŋ]
stand [stænd]	**stood** [stʊd]	**stood** [stʊd]
steal [stiːl]	**stole** [stəʊl]	**stolen** ['stəʊlən]
stick [stɪk]	**stuck** [stʌk]	**stuck** [stʌk]
sting [stɪŋ]	**stung** [stʌŋ]	**stung** [stʌŋ]
strike [straɪk]	**struck** [strʌk]	**struck** [strʌk]
swell [swel]	**swelled** [sweld]	**swollen** ['swəʊlən]
swim [swɪm]	**swam** [swæm]	**swum** [swʌm]
take [teɪk]	**took** [tʊk]	**taken** ['teɪkən]
teach [tiːtʃ]	**taught** [tɔːt]	**taught** [tɔːt]
tear [teə]	**tore** [tɔː]	**torn** [tɔːn]
tell [tel]	**told** [təʊld]	**told** [təʊld]
think [θɪŋk]	**thought** [θɔːt]	**thought** [θɔːt]
throw [θrəʊ]	**threw** [θruː]	**thrown** [θrəʊn]
understand [ˌʌndə'stænd]	**understood** [ˌʌndə'stʊd]	**understood** [ˌʌndə'stʊd]
upset [ʌp'set]	**upset** [ʌp'set]	**upset** [ʌp'set]
wake [weɪk]	**woke** [wəʊk]	**woken** ['wəʊkən]
wear [weə]	**wore** [wɔː]	**worn** [wɔːn]
win [wɪn]	**won** [wʌn]	**won** [wʌn]
write [raɪt]	**wrote** [rəʊt]	**written** ['rɪtn]

KEY TO PHONETIC SYMBOLS

CONSONANTS

p **p**en, co**p**y, ha**pp**en
b **b**ack, bu**bb**le, jo**b**
t **t**ea, ci**t**y, bu**tt**on
d **d**ay, la**dd**er, o**dd**
k **k**ey, s**ch**ool, du**ck**, **c**ool
g **g**et, **g**i**gg**le, **gh**ost

tʃ **ch**ur**ch**, ma**tch**, na**t**ure
dʒ **j**u**dge**, a**ge**, sol**di**er

f **f**at, co**ff**ee, tou**gh**, **ph**ys cs
v **v**iew, hea**v**y, mo**v**e
θ **th**ing, au**th**or, pa**th**
ð **th**is, o**th**er, smoo**th**
s **s**oon, **c**ea**s**e, **s**i**s**ter
z **z**ero, **z**one, ro**s**e, bu**zz**
ʃ **sh**ip, **s**ure, sta**ti**on
ʒ plea**s**ure, vi**si**on
h **h**ot, **wh**ole, be**h**ind

m **m**ore, ha**mm**er, su**m**
n **n**ice, **kn**ow, fu**nn**y, su**n**
ŋ ri**ng,** lo**ng**, tha**n**ks, su**ng**
l **l**ight, va**ll**ey fee**l**
r **r**ight, so**rr**y, a**rr**ange

j **y**et, **u**se, b**e**auty
w **w**et, **o**ne, **wh**en, q**u**een

VOWELS

ɪ k**i**t, b**i**d, h**y**mn
e dr**e**ss, b**e**d
æ b**a**d, c**a**t, tr**a**p
ɒ l**o**t, **o**dd, w**a**sh
ʌ l**o**ve, b**u**t, d**u**ck
ʊ f**oo**t, g**oo**d, p**u**t

iː s**ea**, f**ee**l, mach**i**ne
eɪ f**a**ce, d**ay**, st**ea**k
aɪ pr**i**ce, h**igh**, tr**y**
ɔɪ b**oy**, ch**oi**ce

uː tw**o**, bl**ue**, g**oo**se
əʊ g**oa**t, sh**ow**, n**o**
aʊ m**ou**th, n**ow**
ɪə n**ear**, h**ere**, ser**i**ous
eə f**air**, var**i**ous, squ**are**
ɑː st**ar**t, f**a**ther
ɔː th**ough**t, l**aw**, n**or**th
ʊə c**ure**, p**oor**
ɜː n**ur**se, st**ir**
i happ**y**, rad**i**ation, glor**i**ous
ə **a**bout, comm**o**n
u sit**u**ation, ann**u**al, infl**u**ence

Pearson Education Limited
KAO Two
KAO Park
Hockham Way
Harlow, Essex
CM17 9SR
England
and Associated Companies throughout the world.

english.com/focus

Focus 4 Second Edition Student's Book

The right of Sue Kay, Vaughan Jones, Daniel Brayshaw, Bartosz Michałowski, Beata Trapnell and Dean Russell to be identified as authors of this Work has been asserted by them in accordance with the Copyright, Designs and Patents Act 1988.

First published 2020
Second impression 2021

ISBN: 978-1-292-39056-7

Set in Avenir LT Pro
Printed by Neografia, Slovakia

Acknowledgements
The publishers and authors would like to thank the following people and institutions for their feedback and comments during the development of the material:

Humberto Santos Duran
Ewa Goldnik-Ciok
Anna Maria Grochowska
Beata Gruszczyńska
Inga Lande
Magdalena Loska
Barbara Madej
Rosa Maria Maldonado
Juliana Queiroz Pereira
Tomasz Siuta
Elżbieta Śliwa
Katarzyna Ślusarczyk
Katarzyna Tobolska
Renata Tomaka-Pasternak
Beata Trapnell
Aleksandra Zakrzewska
Beata Zygadlewicz-Kocuś

Sue Kay and Vaughan Jones's acknowledgements
We would like to thank all the students and teachers we have met and observed during the development of Focus Second Edition. We are also especially grateful to our wonderful editorial team for their expertise, encouragement and dedication.
Finally, a big thank you to our families without whose support and understanding none of this would have been possible.

Texts
Page 6 Excerpt(s) from The Element: How Finding Your Passion Changes Everything by Ken Robinson with Lou Aronica, copyright © 2009 by Ken Robinson. Used by permission of Viking Books, an imprint of Penguin Publishing Group, a division of Penguin Random House LLC. All rights reserved; Page 22 Experience: I found my friend after 40 years, and married her by Emily Cunningham, Joo Crisstomo, The Guardian, 26/10/2013, © 2013 The Guardian. Used with permission; Page 22 How long-lost love letter led to couple marrying after 16 years apart Daily Mail, by Daily Mail reporter, Daily Mail. July 20, 2009. © 2009 Daily Mail. Used with permission; Page 25 Excerpt(s) from Me Before You: A Novel by Jojo Moyes, copyright © 2012 by Jojo Moyes. Used by permission of Viking Books, an imprint of Penguin Publishing Group, a division of Penguin Random House LLC. All rights reserved; Page 36 Quotes by Desmond Morris, 2019; Page 40 Experience: I am 16 and live alone in the wilderness by Joan McFadden, Zeki Basan, The Guardian, 29 April 2016, © 2019 The Guardian. Used with permission

Images
123RF.com: ammentorp 19, bluebay 7, borisblik 73, bowie15 56, foxterrier2005 73, gajus 105, Igor Zakharevich 73, Irina Ukrainets 73, Lightwave Stock Media 73, Maksym Topchii 38, mklrnt 127, NejroN 63, rawpixel 99, Sattapapan Tratong 119, serezniy 73, Tatiana Zherebtsova 83, Volodymyr Krasyuk 73; **Alamy Stock Photo:** Adam Asar 109, age fotostock 51, Alistair Heap 39, ART Collection 101, Barry Lewis 87, Claire Doherty 57, Everett Collection Inc 143, Granger Historical Picture Archive 143, H Lansdown 91, Hero Images Inc. 131, History and Art Collection 89, Idealink Photography 90, Jon Arnold Images Ltd 36–37, Keystone Press 143, Lebrecht Music & Arts 143, LJSphotography 73, Mark Reinstein 10, MARKA 143, MBI 86, Nick Star 57, OJO Images Ltd 27, ONOKY – Photononstop 14, Panagiotis Michalopoulos 45, Paris Market 55, Pixhall 87, Prasit Rodphan 39, Radius Images 56, Realimage 46, Rehman Asad 122, Storms Media Group 90, Tetra Images, LLC 131, UPI 143, World History Archive 89, 100; **Barcroft Media:** Matt Writtle 60; **BBC Worldwide Learning:** 4, 20, 36, 52, 68, 84, 100, 116, 132, 134, 136, 136, 136, 136, 136, 138, 138, 140, 142, 142, 142, 142, 142, 144, 146, 146, 146, 146, 146, 146, Avpics 57; **Corbis:** Reuters / Carlo Allegri 74, 74; **Fotolia.com:** fmarsicano 131, Francois Poirier 66, magcom 12, 46, 55, Monkey Business 11, 99, vasosh 123; **Getty Images:** BlackJack3D 100–101, Brad Barket / Stringer 8, David LeFranc 39, David M. Benett 25, Jose Luis Pelaez Inc 35, Martin Deja 22, Mirrorpix 6, Museum of the City of New York 89, National Geographic / Speleoresearch & Films / Carsten Peter 123, Robert Gallagher / The Forbes Collection / Contour by Getty Images 76–77, rubberball 91; **Murdo Macleod:** 40–41; **Pearson Education Ltd:** Silversun Media Group 133, 135, 137, 139, 141, 143, 145, 147; **Courtesy of Pest Control Office:** Banksy, Love Is In The Air, 2005 57; **Shutterstock.com:** 2p2play 114, Africa Studio 70, Alekcey 23, Alex Bailey/Mgm/New Line Cinema/Kobal 25, 25, 25, Andis Rea 106, Andrea Izzotti 119, Andrey Arkusha 26, Andrey Popov 53, Andrii Zastrozhnov 23, Antonio Guillem 67, Arina P Habich 59, Artem Podporin 67, Blanscape 119, Bobex-73 75, Boryana Manzurova 23, ChameleonsEye 73, Claudia Paulussen 19, Damir Khabirov 58, dencg 22, dotshock 29, Dragon Images 70, 104, Dusan Petkovic 78, El Nariz 35, Eldar Nurkovic 92, elenavolf 119, Erika Cross 56, Fedyaeva Maria 13, foxie 52–53, Gabriel Guzman 126, GaudiLab 43, Giancarlo Liguori 118, Gudkov Andrey 119, Halfpoint 63, Ilze Kitshoff/Netflix/Kobal 121, Jacob Lund 30, Jasin Boland/Universal/Kobal 120, Kateryna Kon 105, Khomulo Anna 89, kuzmaphoto 28, Kzenon 70, Loris De Lillo 27, Madcat Madlove 23, MilanMarkovic78 42, mimagephotography 29, Monkey Business Images 28, Netflix/Kobal 94, New Line/Kobal 44, NinaMalyna 52–53, Ociacia 107, Olena Yakobchuk 124, Olesia Bilkei 14, one photo 59, Oscarporras 37, pathdoc 84, Peter Hermes Furian 41, Pressmaster 11, Riccardo Piccinini 12, Rudmer Zwerver 119, s.sermram 56, Sabphoto 30, Sergey Uryadnikov 93, Snap Stills 121, Spasiblo 107, SpeedKingz 30, Stx Entertainment/Moviestore 120, Tony Stock 119, Top Photo Engineer 119, Tyler Olson 34, UfaBizPhoto 67, vasosh 60, Victoria Chudinova 59, wavebreakmedia 54, Wayhome Studio 4, Zally23 9; **Superstock:** Blend Images 46; **Telegraph Media Group:** Adam Nadel 102

Illustrations
Stephen Collins (Central Illustration) 68–69
Tim Marrs 73
Ewa Olejnik WS2, WS4, WS5, WS8
Ben Swift (NB Illustration) 103
Jamie (KJA Artists) 110–111

Videos
BBC video footage supplied by BBC Studios Distribution Limited
FOCUS VLOGS and Interactive Speaking Videos supplied by A Silversun Media Group production for Pearson

Every effort has been made to trace the copyright holders and we apologise in advance for any unintentional omissions. We would be pleased to insert the appropriate acknowledgement in any subsequent edition of this publication.

Open cloze

1 Complete the text with one word in each gap.

Why do we yawn?

Yawning is natural. Newly born babies, teenagers and adults – we all [0] ___*do*___ it. Even animals yawn! But yawning [1] ________ be a problem at school. Teachers sometimes [2] ________ their temper when faced with yawning students since they think their students are bored.

In the past, scientists [3] ________ to think that people yawned because of boredom or tiredness. They believed that yawning helped bring more oxygen into your lungs and brain, and thus woke you up. However, scientists have recently [4] ________ some research on yawning and they have come to different conclusions. It is believed now that we do it to allow our brain [5] ________ cool so that it can function better.

So why do we tend to yawn late in [6] ________ evening or when we are tired? Mainly because tiredness raises brain temperature. We also yawn more frequently in summer than in winter!

In many situations, you will be incapable [7] ________ stopping yourself from yawning. So, why [8] ________ you try to do it in such a way so that no one sees you?

Key word transformation

2 Complete the second sentence so that it has a similar meaning to the first. Use between two and five words including the word in capitals. Do not change the word given.

0 'You can go to Mike's party,' my dad said. **LET**
My dad ___*let me go to*___ Mike's party.

1 I haven't used this computer for a week. **STOPPED**
I ________________ a week ago.

2 Would you like to go out for a pizza later? **FANCY**
Do ________________ out for a pizza later?

3 Our town has got much bigger in recent years. **USED**
Our town is much bigger ________________ .

4 Sam never stops complaining about the amount of homework he has. **IS**
Sam ________________ about the amount of homework he has.

5 I'm sure I met you at Richard's party. **REMEMBER**
I ________________ at Richard's party.

6 My mum's routine was to have a bath just before going to bed. **WOULD**
My mum ________________ just before going to bed.

WORD STORE 1A | Phrasal verbs

1 *fall behind* – make less progress than others
2 ____________ – quit doing sth; stop hoping sb will change
3 ____________ – start working in a type of job
4 ____________ – do sth after finishing another thing
5 ____________ – study sth as your main subject
6 ____________ – only just succeed in doing sth
7 ____________ – become calm or confident

WORD STORE 1B | Describing teachers and students

1 having problems reading/spelling
2 relaxed, permissive
3 demanding
4 someone who studies too hard (negative)
5 someone who uses his/her strength to hurt others
6 causing trouble
7 talented
8 able to work well alone

Mystery word: ____________

WORD STORE 1C | Collocations

1 *attend/give* a lecture
2 ____________ of interest to sb
3 ____________ your knowledge
4 ____________ on a course
5 ____________ a degree/a scholarship
6 ____________ expelled
7 ____________ a passion for sth
8 ____________ an exam
9 ____________ in the field of sth
10 ____________ a dissertation

WORD STORE 1D | Memory

jog memory sieve vague ~~vivid~~

1 have a clear/ *vivid* memory of sth
2 have a ____________/distant memory of sth
3 have a good/terrible memory for sth
4 have a photographic ____________
5 have a memory like a ____________
6 ____________ your memory
7 lose your memory
8 sb's earliest memory

WORD STORE 1E | Collocations

1 *acquire* / sharpen – **a skill**
2 ____________ / be found – **unconscious**
3 ____________ / be hit by – **lightning**
4 ____________ / come out of – **a coma**
5 ____________ / get – **an urge**
6 ____________ / regain – **consciousness**
7 ____________ / solve – **a mystery**
8 ____________ / recover from – **an injury**

WORD IN FOCUS | *do*

do = perform (an action or activity)
I'd like to do a master's degree in Business Studies.

do + noun
You don't have to be a savant to do amazing things.

do in idioms
It has to do with the strength of the neuron networks in your brain.

Multiple-choice cloze

1 Read the text and choose the correct answer A, B, C or D.

Best man

When my older brother Josh told us he was [0]_____ married, we weren't surprised. He [1]_____ with Angie for years. What I didn't expect, though, was that he would ask me, an eighteen-year-old who had never been [2]_____ a wedding before, to be his best man. I was painfully shy, but I knew I needed to pluck up the [3]_____ to deliver a speech in front of all the guests. After all, it was my brother [4]_____ was getting married. If I were getting married, I would only invite my closest family – no [5]_____ acquaintances. But Josh and Angie sent wedding invitations to each and every person they had ever been friends with. And there were plenty of them. So on the wedding day, more than 250 people [6]_____ up. I was absolutely terrified when it was my turn to [7]_____ a speech. But afterwards, when I could relax, it was brilliant and I had the [8]_____ of my life.

0	A going	B getting	C being	D becoming
1	A is going out	B went out	C had gone out	D had been going out
2	A to	B for	C by	D on
3	A pride	B courage	C strength	D personality
4	A where	B whose	C that	D which
5	A informal	B loose	C everyday	D casual
6	A came	B made	C took	D turned
7	A propose	B do	C give	D tell
8	A moment	B event	C time	D hour

Word building

2 Complete the text with the correct form of the words in capitals.

Friend for life

I first met my friend Eva when we started primary school together.

That day was [0] *unforgettable* and I can still picture every single moment.	FORGET
I remember meeting Eva. That first [1]__________ was terrible! She was	IMPRESS
everything that I wasn't. She was [2]__________ and she was pretty.	BRAIN
She loved sport and she had an amazing [3]__________ of fashion, pop stars and animals! I was extremely envious of her. However, in a short	KNOW
time, somewhat [4]__________ , we became good friends and this	SURPRISE
[5]__________ has lasted for years.	RELATION
In our [6]__________ we have supported each other through various	ADOLESCENT
problems. We were at each other's [7]__________ parties and then	ENGAGE
at each other's weddings. It's amazing but the [8]__________ of our friendship has grown from year to year.	STRONG

WORD STORE 2A | Personality adjectives

1 *affectionate* = showing affection
2 ____________ = brave
3 ____________ = modest
4 ____________ = not confident
5 ____________ = well-educated, serious
6 ____________ = changing moods often
7 ____________ = noticing things quickly
8 ____________ = doing things without planning
9 ____________ = considerate of others
10 ____________ = careful, paying attention to detail
11 ____________ = full of trust
12 ____________ = clever and entertaining

WORD STORE 2B | Compound adjectives

1 *fair* -minded
2 ______-natured
3 ______-hearted
4 ______-back
5 ______-headed
6 ______-centred
7 ______-conscious
8 ______-critical
9 ______-tempered
10 ______-willed

WORD STORE 2C | Describing personality

1 (be) full *of* oneself
2 (be) larger ______ life
3 (be) the life and soul ______ the party
4 (have) a love ______ learning
5 (make sb) feel ______ ease
6 think ______ the box

WORD STORE 2D | Relationship phrases

attracted fall madly obsessed out split

1 be *attracted* to sb
2 be ____________ in love with sb
3 be ____________ with sb
4 ____________ for sb
5 go ____________ with sb
6 ____________ up with sb

WORD STORE 2E | Ways of looking

Look at sth for a LONG time …

1 with interest, wonder or delight = ____________
2 carefully and with difficulty = peer
3 in surprise, anger or boredom = ____________

Look at sth for a SHORT time …

4 and then look away = ____________
5 too quickly to see it clearly = glimpse
6 secretly – i.e. through a keyhole = peep

WORD IN FOCUS | *take*

take* = *accept
You will take enormous risks to win this person.

take* = *do or have
She's taking her driving test.

***take* + time expression**
I live on the outskirts of the city and it takes me ages to get to the centre.

***take* in phrases**
Take turns to be Student A and Student B.

***take* in phrasal verbs**
The teacher was so taken aback she had to get the teacher from next door and tell her what had happened.

Word building

1 Complete the text with the correct form of the words in capitals.

Olite, Spain

Many [0] *visitors* to Spain head to Madrid or Barcelona, the country's	**VISIT**
biggest cities, which offer excellent museums, sites of cultural [1] ______	**IMPORTANT**
and vibrant nightlife. But there's more to Spain than those popular	
destinations. Consider Spain's smaller towns. They have [2] ______	**WONDER**
architecture, exceptional food and warm people.	
One such place is Olite, a [3] ______ town of approximately 4,000	**PICTURE**
residents in the north-west of the country. The town became famous when	
a palace was built there for the Kings of Navarre. No one lives in the palace	
now and it's open to the public. Beyond the palace lies the [4] ______	**RESIDE**
area of the town. Its [5] ______ is quite charming with their pretty,	**NEIGHBOUR**
traditional houses and [6] ______ streets. Getting there is easy with the	**COBBLE**
[7] ______ network of buses from the nearby city of Pamplona, and there	**RELY**
are [8] ______ services from other towns too.	**DAY**

Key word transformation

2 Complete the second sentence so that it has a similar meaning to the first. Use between two and five words including the word in capitals. Do not change the word given.

0 There are several parking spaces in front of my house. **NUMBER**
There *is a number of* parking spaces in front of my house.

1 When we went on holiday, we always started our journey early to avoid the traffic. **SET**
When we went on holiday, we used ______ early to avoid the traffic.

2 James, do you think you'll travel to Mexico before you're twenty? **BEEN**
James, will ______ to Mexico by the time you're twenty?

3 Both Paul and Tina were unaware of the situation. **NEITHER**
______ were aware of the situation.

4 The hotel is a short walk from the convention centre. **WITHIN**
The hotel ______ the convention centre.

5 Olga likes spending her Sundays by herself. **COMPANY**
Olga enjoys ______ on Sundays.

6 Our dinner will be over by 8:30. **FINISHED**
We ______ our dinner by 8:30.

WORD STORE 3A | Prepositions describing location

at in ~~on~~ within

1 *on* — the coast / the outskirts / the border

2 ______ — walking distance / easy reach / 500 metres

3 ______ — the traffic lights / the roundabout / the town hall

4 ______ — the city centre / the suburbs / the park

WORD STORE 3B | Describing places

1 *bustling* — square / market / streets

2 ______ — centre / architecture / castle

3 ______ — old town / village / scenery

4 ______ — backstreet / town / neighbourhood

5 ______ — city centre / building / house

6 ______ — development / area / space

7 ______ — atmosphere / nightlife / colours

WORD STORE 3C | In the city

1 cobbled *streets*
2 cycle ______
3 daily ______
4 home ______
5 noise ______
6 on-street ______
7 pedestrian ______
8 reliable ______
9 rolling ______
10 underground ______

WORD STORE 3D | Collocations and compound nouns

1 domestic ch*o*r*e*
2 household _ppl_ _nc_
3 housing d_v_l_pm_nt
4 m_lt_-st_r_y car-park
5 r_s_d_nt_ _l area
6 s_c_nd home
7 s_lf-c_nt_ _n_d flat
8 t_w_r block

WORD STORE 3E | Idiomatic expressions

1 be/become second *nature* to sb
2 enjoy your own ______
3 have a hairy ______
4 keep a cool ______
5 keep your ______ about you
6 not be everyone's cup of ______
7 practise what you ______
8 run ______

WORD IN FOCUS | *at*

at + a place or an event
at the traffic lights, at the roundabout, at home

at with verbs
Look at the expressions.

at with adjectives
You're very good at making people feel at ease.

at in phrases
at the end, at the moment, at the right price

at + a time, a price, an age, a speed or a temperature
He was knocked out in a baseball game at the age of ten.
At 11 a.m. tomorrow, I'll be doing an exam.

Open cloze

1 Complete the text with one word in each gap.

Ziferblat – a café with a twist

Can you imagine a café [0] *where* the coffee is free? In fact, at Ziferblat all drinks and snacks are complimentary! You might be thinking, 'It can't be true, [1] ________ it?' Well, it is! At [2] ________ unusual Manchester outlet, you only pay for the time you spend there – three pence per minute.

Are there any other differences [3] ________ Ziferblat and any chain café? At Ziferblat you are given more freedom. You can ask a [4] ________ of staff to serve you a cappuccino or you can learn to prepare it on your own. Some people even wash [5] ________ own dishes. However, you don't [6] ________ to do it. It's optional.

The opening of the first café of this type in Russia in 2011 drew the [7] ________ of the media and attracted a crowd of trendsetters. And while now such pay per minute cafés are very common, it was, [8] ________ a doubt, one of the most innovative business ideas at the time.

Key word transformation

2 Complete the second sentence so that it has a similar meaning to the first. Use between two and five words including the word in capitals. Do not change the word given.

0 Are we going? **WE**
Let's go, *shall we* ?

1 The security guard said the boys had stolen the bag. **OF**
The security guard ________ the bag.

2 Anna will be angry if I'm late. **BETTER**
I ________ or Anna will be angry.

3 We went to the cinema and then to a night club. **BEEN**
After we ________ , we went to a night club.

4 It wasn't necessary for me to buy all those crisps because Jim got some too. **NEEDN'T**
I ________ all those crisps because Jim got some too.

5 It wasn't a good idea for Jacky to buy that expensive pair of shoes. **HAVE**
Jacky ________ that expensive pair of shoes.

6 We spent a lot of money on a really nice dinner at a restaurant. **OUT**
We ________ a really nice dinner at a restaurant.

WORD STORE 4A | Phrasal verbs

1 check *up* on = find information about
2 cut ______ on = reduce
3 look ______ for = look carefully for sth
4 pay ______ for = spend (a lot of money)
5 put sth ______ = reserve
6 send sth ______ = return
7 shop ______ = look in many different shops
8 spring ______ = appear

WORD STORE 4B | Shopping collocations

1 *bargain* price
2 ______ store
3 ______ value
4 ______ purchase
5 ______ brand
6 ______ product
7 ______ shopping
8 ______ attitude
9 ______ fabric
10 ______ society

WORD STORE 4C | Verb phrases

1

be on a limited budget

2

______

3

______

4

______

5

______

6

______

WORD STORE 4D | Noun phrases

belongings boot flea ~~house~~ pre-owned property

1 auction *house*
2 car ______ sale
3 checked bags
4 ______ market
5 lost ______
6 market stall
7 personal ______
8 ______ goods

WORD STORE 4E | Being rich and poor

rich

1 be loaded
2 *with money to burn*
3 ______
4 ______

poor

5 be broke
6 ______
7 ______
8 ______

WORD IN FOCUS | *of*

of to describe a part/feature/quality, etc. of sth
organic versions of natural materials, a piece of paper

of after a numeral
hundreds of years, thousands of bags

of to show possession
the recipient of the email

of in phrasal verbs
How does Martin get hold of the second-hand goods?

of as a dependent preposition
The manager accused us of being too noisy.

Multiple-choice cloze

1 Read the text and choose the correct answer A, B, C or D.

First job interview

I remember all too well my first [0]_____ interview. I was eighteen and I was hoping to [1]_____ an apprenticeship with a local business. I thought the interview was going to be an informal chat with the owner of the company, but in [2]_____ , I had a formal interview with the HR department. When they asked me why I [3]_____ to apply for a position with the company, I didn't know [4]_____ to say. In the end, they accepted me as an apprentice, but the interviewer [5]_____ me to prepare better for any future interview.

A [6]_____ years later, I had an important interview, but this time I was really well-prepared. The job I got turned out to be more [7]_____ than I had expected. Apart from a great salary, the company offered me a company car and gym membership. I've never been short [8]_____ money since.

	A	B	C	D
0	A working	B career	C job (circled)	D profession
1	A do	B have	C take	D make
2	A true	B fact	C actual	D reality
3	A decide	B were deciding	C have decided	D had decided
4	A what	B how	C if	D which
5	A suggested	B insisted	C advised	D assured
6	A several	B lots of	C some	D few
7	A wealthy	B lucrative	C well-off	D loaded
8	A with	B of	C at	D on

Key word transformation

2 Complete the second sentence so that it has a similar meaning to the first. Use between two and five words including the word in capitals. Do not change the word given.

0 'Have you seen Alice?' Stuart asked. **WHETHER**
Stuart asked _*whether I had seen*_ Alice.

1 Dan said he would help me with my work. **TO**
Dan __________________ with my work.

2 I'm responsible for the research team. **CHARGE**
I'm __________________ the research team.

3 They gave him a job as a school caretaker. **GIVEN**
He __________________ as a school caretaker.

4 He decided to sue the company after all. **COURT**
He decided to __________________ after all.

5 Suddenly there are fewer people working from home. **SHARP**
There has __________________ the number of people working from home.

6 My friends said I shouldn't pay more than £20 for a ticket. **ADVISED**
My friends __________________ more than £20 for a ticket.

WORD STORE 5A | Expressions to do with work

1 *achieve* a goal
2 ________ sth day in, day out
3 ________ the job market
4 ________ your career prospects
5 ________ your output
6 ________ your heart into sth
7 ________ your full potential
8 ________ your mind
9 ________ for yourself
10 ________ to a deadline

WORD STORE 5B | Phrasal verbs

1 *burn out* = become ill because of hard work
2 ________ = do/complete a task
3 ________ = start doing sth
4 ________ = continue doing sth
5 ________ = plan sth in detail
6 ________ = not do sth till later
7 ________ = arrange or describe sth
8 ________ = do things to make progress

WORD STORE 5C | Adjectives from nouns

NOUN	ADJECTIVE
1 conscientiousness	*conscientious*
2 enthusiasm	________
3 knowledge	________
4 overwork	________
5 punctuality	________
6 purpose	________
7 single-mindedness	________

WORD STORE 5D | Phrases describing change

decline (in) **gradual** **increase (in)** **number of** **rapid** ~~**sharp**~~ **unchanged**

QUICK/BIG CHANGE

Up
1 a *sharp*
2 a marked
→ **rise (in)** / ________

Down
3 a ________
4 a sharp
→ **drop (in)** / **decline (in)**

NO CHANGE

5 remain
6 be
→ **constant** / ________

SLOW/LITTLE CHANGE

Up
7 a growing → ________
8 a steady
9 a ________
→ **rise (in)** / **increase (in)**

Down
10 a steady
11 a gradual
→ **drop (in)** / ________

WORD STORE 5E | Verb–noun collocations

1 *be* in charge
2 ________ wired differently
3 ________ your niche
4 ________ on your strengths
5 ________ one true calling
6 ________ a vocation
7 ________ purpose

WORD IN FOCUS | *to*

_to_ after certain verbs, adjectives and _wh-_ words

Commit to taking on new challenges.
As we get older we tend to lose our imagination.
The most difficult task, the one you're most likely to put off until later.

_to_ + verb = infinitive of purpose

Let's stop to think about famous historical figures who were left-handed.

_to_ in phrases

to be honest, on a day-to-day basis

_to_ as a preposition (= as far as a particular point/limit)

The standard working day of nine to five has been replaced by flexitime.

_to_ in three-part phrasal verbs

He looks up to me.
Let's get down to work.

Word building

1 Complete the text with the correct form of the words in capitals.

Ghostwriters

Famous people, including models, [0] *musicians* and pop stars, are publishing more and more books these days. How can they write a whole book if, in [1] ________ , some of them can't write one sentence correctly? The answer is something publishers are quite [2] ________ about: ghostwriters. A ghostwriter is a writer for hire, who usually gets paid in [3] ________ . He or she does all or the [4] ________ of the work, but they are not usually credited as authors when the book is released. In some cases, they may get a thank-you note in the book if their contribution was [5] ________ important. Ghostwriters are quite enigmatic figures. They usually have to swear to keep their [6] ________ so we don't know much about them. Many ghostwriters work not only for celebrities, but also for [7] ________ , business people and fiction publishers. How would you feel if you made the [8] ________ that your favourite book was actually written by a ghostwriter?

MUSIC
REAL
MYSTERY
ADVANCEMENT
MAJOR
PARTICULAR
ANONYMOUS
POLITICS
DISCOVER

Key word transformation

2 Complete the second sentence so that it has a similar meaning to the first. Use between two and five words including the word in capitals. Do not change the word given.

0 She won't help you if you don't stop annoying her. **PROVIDED**
She'll help you *provided you stop annoying* her.

1 Jen got a degree. Now she's a manager. **WOULDN'T**
If Jen hadn't got a degree, ________________ a manager now.

2 I wouldn't take part in a protest unless it was peaceful. **IF**
I wouldn't take part in a protest ________________ peaceful.

3 The accused said he hadn't forged the document. **DENIED**
The accused ________________ the document.

4 You believed all his promises and now you're in trouble. **BE**
If you hadn't believed all his promises, ________________ in trouble now.

5 People should be responsible for their actions. **TAKE**
People ought ________________ for their actions.

6 To sum up, I think we had a very productive meeting. **THINGS**
All ________________ , I think we had a very productive meeting.

WORD STORE 6A | Truth and falsehood

People/Organisations can sometimes …

1 *distort* the truth
2 ____________ an agenda
3 ____________ the media
4 ____________/misinform people
5 ____________ fake news
6 ____________ with photos

You should …

7 ____________ the accuracy
8 ____________ facts
9 ____________ sources
10 ____________ your instincts
11 not ____________ a story at face value

WORD STORE 6B | Adjective–noun collocations

1 awash with / bombarded with → *information*
2 a clear / a long-term → ____________
3 for commercial / for political → ____________
4 on a daily / on a regular → ____________
5 a distinct / a gut → ____________
6 a newsworthy / an eye-catching → ____________
7 a reliable / a reputable → ____________

WORD STORE 6C | Adverbs

ADJECTIVE	ADVERB
1 alarming	*alarmingly*
2 close	____________
3 critical	____________
4 deliberate	____________
5 knowing	____________
6 remarkable	____________

WORD STORE 6D | Collocations

anonymous beliefs ~~commit~~ message protect raise statement

1 *commit* an offence
2 make a ____________
3 ____________ your identity
4 ____________ awareness
5 remain ____________
6 strong beliefs
7 underlying ____________

WORD STORE 6E | Photography

airbrush/retouch blurred/out of focus capture a (memorable) moment crop images ~~sharp/in focus~~ a lens pose (for a photo) a shot take a snap zoom in/out

1 *sharp/in focus* = clear
2 ____________ = unclear
3 ____________ = correct
4 ____________ = take a photo
5 ____________ = change photos' size/shape
6 ____________ = make larger/smaller
7 ____________ = a photo
8 ____________ = part of a camera
9 ____________ = take a photo in the right moment
10 ____________ = stand/sit in a special way

WORD IN FOCUS | *or*

or to talk about alternatives

There are different ways in which a story can be inaccurate or misleading.
Actors like their screen characters, or do they?

or – alternatives using *either* and *not*

Look for either a coupon or a code.
He can't read or write.

or to talk about two opposites

true or false
agree or disagree
for or against

Open cloze

1 Complete the text with one word in each gap.

The Internet of things

Although we like to think of the Internet [0] ___as___ a social network, it is mostly a network of machines. In fact, a few years ago the number of different devices connected to the net is believed to [1] ______ exceeded the number of human users. This phenomenon is [2] ______ as 'the Internet of things' and the number of online devices is still [3] ______ the rise.

Today almost any object, from your fridge to your car, can have [4] ______ to the Internet. Using a special application, you can check if you have enough tomatoes for a salad. And if you install a camera in your garage, you are [5] ______ to check – from any place on Earth – if your car is still there.

At the moment, many of the available applications offer you this remote control of your devices, but [6] ______ the near future, these devices will also take intelligent decisions for you (and without asking you first!). Some experts think it could [7] ______ risky. Imagine [8] ______ forced to eat healthy food by your fridge, which will do all your weekly shopping. What a scary thought!

Key word transformation

2 Complete the second sentence so that it has a similar meaning to the first. Use between two and five words including the word in capitals. Do not change the word given.

0 I hate it when people call me by my last name. **CALLED**
I hate ___being called by___ my last name.

1 Yesterday someone sent me the same spam advertisement ten times. **WAS**
Yesterday ______ the same spam advertisement ten times.

2 I didn't realise how much time I'd spent playing that game. **LOST**
I ______ while I was playing that game.

3 It was the rule at school to wear a grey uniform. **MADE**
At school we ______ a grey uniform.

4 Could you tell me what to do about this problem on my computer? **ADVICE**
Could ______ about this problem on my computer?

5 It took me a few days to understand how this device works. **FIGURE**
It took me a few days ______ this device works.

6 Most people think that wearable technology will soon be much more affordable. **BELIEVED**
It ______ wearable technology will soon be much more affordable.

WORD STORE 7A | Scientific research

1 award ___*a prize*___
2 coin a ____________
3 gain ____________
4 make a ____________
5 receive a ____________
6 recognise an ____________
7 see the ____________
8 win ____________

WORD STORE 7B | Prepositions after verbs and nouns

1 become an expert ___*in*___ sth
2 collaborate ______ sb
3 credit sb ______ sth
4 have access ______ sth
5 have an aptitude ______ sth
6 make reference/refer ______ sth
7 name sth ______ sb

WORD STORE 7C | Words in science

MATHS & COMPUTING

1 algorithm = ____________
2 calculation = ____________
3 equation = ____________
4 fraction = ____________
5 multiplication = ____________
6 division = ____________

CHEMISTRY

7 acid = ____________
8 base = ____________
9 element = ____________
10 molecular structure = ____________
11 radioactivity = ____________

PHYSICS

12 atom = ____________
13 electron = ____________
14 nucleus = ____________
15 relativity = ____________
16 velocity = ____________

WORD STORE 7D | Phrasal verbs

~~bring in~~ come out figure sth out go in for talk sb into sth throw sth in wind sb up

1 ___*bring in*___ = introduce sth
2 ____________ = enjoy, choose or do sth
3 ____________ = understand sth
4 ____________ = annoy or irritate sb
5 ____________ = include sth extra for free
6 ____________ = be released or be published
7 ____________ = persuade sb to do sth

WORD STORE 7E | Word families

NOUN	VERB	ADJECTIVE
1 advice	advise	*advisable*
2 benefit	benefit	____________
3 ____________	clean	clean
4 digestion	digest	____________
5 harm	harm	____________
6 ____________	medicate	medicinal
7 regulation	____________	regulatory
8 response	____________	responsive

WORD IN FOCUS | *on*

***on* as a preposition**

on your keyboard, on the Internet
It's not a good idea to store films and music on a laptop.

***on* as a dependent preposition**

I wish I was less dependent on technology.
These things have no effects on our bodies at all.

***on* in phrasal verbs**

We get on with each other.

***on* in phrases**

I'd not stare at a screen for hours on end.
It will become routine for doctors to keep an eye on their patients' microbiome.

Word building

1 Complete the text with the correct form of the words in capitals.

Dogs and the human brain

Human beings have trained animals to work for them and also used	
them as [0]*companions* for a long time. But which animal species did	**COMPANY**
the human race first manage to [1]__________ ? It was, of course,	**DOMESTIC**
the dog. Some experts claim it happened about 15,000 years	
ago, even before we settled down and became [2]__________ .	**FARM**
Although many people in the developed world consider dogs to be	
[3]__________ pets, the relationship between humans and dogs was	**PLAY**
initially different. Dogs helped us hunt for food and warned us of possibly	
[4]__________ situations. As everyone knows, the senses of smell and	**DANGER**
hearing that dogs have are [5]__________ superior to human abilities.	**DOUBT**
In return for this, dogs, unlike wolves, didn't have to worry about survival.	
Living with people, they were given food and [6]__________ . New	**PROTECT**
[7]__________ research suggests that both dogs and people had to pay	**SCIENCE**
a price for this perfect symbiosis. Dogs' brains seem to have shrunk	
by one fifth. Also, human attributes changed [8]__________ and our	**CONSIDER**
ancestors lost many of their own sensory abilities.	

Key word transformation

2 Complete the second sentence so that it has a similar meaning to the first. Use between two and five words including the word in capitals. Do not change the word given.

0 You really should sign up for the course now. **HIGH**
It's *high time you signed up* for the course.

1 I really don't want you to go there. **RATHER**
I __________ go there.

2 This is our first visit to this country. **NEVER**
We __________ this country before.

3 I find it surprising that no one has noticed this. **IS**
What __________ no one has noticed this.

4 It's a pity Luke didn't come with us. **HAD**
I __________ with us.

5 Most people don't know that there used to be a castle here. **AWARE**
Most people __________ there used to be a castle here.

6 The air pollution is worse in the city centre than here. **AS**
The air pollution here __________ in the city centre.

WORD STORE 8A | Environmental issues

biodegradable ~~**contamination**~~ **eco-warrior** **irreparable damage** **single-use plastics** **food chain**

1 *contamination* = pollution
2 ____________ = plastic that can be used only once
3 ____________ = somebody who is passionate about the environment
4 ____________ = irreversible, negative change
5 ____________ = broken down naturally by bacteria
6 ____________ = a series of living creatures, where each one eats the one preceding it

WORD STORE 8B | Landscapes

1

built-up area

2
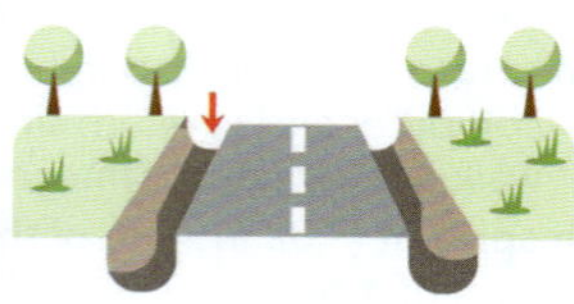
____

3

____

4

____

5

____

6

____

7

____

8

____

WORD STORE 8C | Animals

1 *breeding ground* = a place where animals have their babies
2 ____________ = when an animal no longer exists
3 ____________ = to be born by coming out of an egg
4 ____________ = not in the wild
5 ____________ = moving to another location
6 ____________ = the normal place for an animal to live
7 ____________ = having escaped from where it was kept
8 ____________ = to let an animal leave a place where it was kept
9 ____________ = a very successful group of animals

WORD STORE 8D | Word building

1 adolescent → a*dolescence* (noun)
2 competition → c____________ (adjective)
3 conceive → m____________ (noun)
4 deception → d____________ (adjective)
5 doubt → u____________ (adverb)
6 reputable → r____________ (noun)
7 resemblance → r____________ (verb)
8 value → u____________ (adjective – past participle)

WORD STORE 8E | Collocations

1 begin the *ascent*/descent (of a mountain)
2 ____________ poverty/hunger
3 a ____________ tale
4 life-threatening ____________
5 physically ____________
6 on a ____________ note
7 ____________ weather conditions
8 a storm is ____________
9 suffer ____________
10 be swept ____________

WORD IN FOCUS | *around*

***around* = approximately**

It has existed for around 100 years.
It is home to around 200 bird species.

***around* as a preposition**

around the house, all around the world
They love to play with their prey, kicking it around the playground.

***around* in phrasal verbs**

I don't want you hanging around the flat in the daytime.
Shop around for stores that encourage recycling.

PREPOSITIONS IN PHRASES

AT

at all times (1.7): *Children must be supervised at all times while in the park.*

at arm's length (6.4): *The first image taken in the same way as today, with the photographer holding the camera at arm's length, was in December 1920.*

at an auction (4.3): *Have you ever bought anything at an auction?*

at first sight (2.2): *When my grandfather met my grandmother, it was love at first sight.*

at least (4.1): *It will take at least three hours to get there.*

at lunchtime (1.2): *We couldn't stay in the classrooms at lunchtime – we had to go to the canteen.*

at night (3.1): *The town of Pontevedra comes alive at night and the atmosphere continues well into the early hours.*

at risk (5.3): *A lot of retail jobs are at risk.*

at the age of (1.4): *Chris built his first glider at the age of fifteen.*

at the concert (4.2): *What did Jamie say at the concert?*

at the door (4.2): *That's Jamie at the door, isn't it?*

at the end (3.7): *At the end, everybody burst into tears.*

at the end of (5.1, 8.4): *You're almost at the end of school and close to going on to further education./At the end of the film she is eventually rescued by a Japanese boat.*

at the famous auction house (4.4): *When the painting came up for auction at the famous auction house, it sold for £1.04 million.*

at the intersection (5.4): *It is at the intersection between seemingly unrelated ideas that innovation often happens.*

at the last minute (4.3): *We nearly missed our flight – we got to the airport at the last minute.*

at the main entrance (4.2): *He said he'd meet me at the main entrance.*

at the moment (3.4): *Where is he living at the moment?*

at the right price (3.6): *We want to find the right flat at the right price.*

at the roundabout (3.1): *Turn left at the first roundabout.*

at the same level (5.7): *Your arms should be at the same level as your desk.*

at the shopping centre (4.8): *I want to tell you about the incident that took place at the shopping centre.*

at the town hall (3.1): *Let's meet at the town hall.*

at the traffic lights (3.1): *She slowed down at the traffic lights by Sloane Street.*

at the weekend (3.2): *Who do you plan to see at the weekend?*

FOR

for a minute (4.2): *Can you look after my coat for a minute?*

for ages (2.2): *I've had the same phone for ages. It's time to change it now.*

for breakfast (3.4): *I have cereal for breakfast.*

for example/instance (4.4, 1.3): *You can paint the rooms different colours – for instance, the bedroom could be yellow, the bathroom blue, etc.*

for hours on end (7.6): *My brother usually stares at the screen for hours on end.*

for my eighteenth/last birthday (3.7, 4.2): *For my eighteenth birthday my parents took me on a trip to Greece.*

for six months (7.2): *What would happen in your home if all screens were banned for six months?*

FROM

from the start (2.8): *Attract the reader's attention from the start.*

IN

in ten minutes (3.5): *How to tidy your room in ten minutes?*

in a hurry (3.2): *You are always in such a hurry. Why don't you plan your days better?*

in a pile (3.5): *Why are your clothes in a pile in the middle of the room again?*

in advance (2.1): *Do I have to pay for the course in advance?*

in charge of (5.4): *Ed is in charge of promoting and reviewing gigs.*

in (one's) class (1.1, 8.7): *Your marks are good because you pay attention in class. / In my class, all the students turn off their phones in school time.*

in contrast (8.3): *House prices rose by 20 percent this year in contrast to last year when they dropped by about 15 percent.*

in decline (3.1): *It was a city in decline, polluted, with a lot of traffic accidents.*

in detail (5.1): *Can your grandma really recall her youth in detail?*

in fact (2.1): *Frank isn't a morning person. In fact, he loves sleeping long hours.*

in many/some/certain cases (3.8, 7.1): *Young people avoid certain courses, because in many cases they don't lead to an obvious career.*

in order to (3.8): *We sold our flat in order to buy a house in the suburbs.*

in other words (1.1): *Have you been living here all your life? In other words, for eighteen years?*

in place of (5.4): *In place of using an alarm clock, I had to ask mum to ring me at 6 a.m.*

in return (5.5): *Vikki's parents promised her a new computer and in return she agreed to take the dog for a walk twice a day for the next six months.*

in spite of (3.8): *In spite of the cost, many students prefer halls of residence.*

in summer (1.7): *In summer the temperatures can be quite high in this region.*

in terms of (5.8): *It's a mistake to think of Alaska only in terms of how cold it is there.*

in the twenty-first century (5.4): *You are the one who will thrive in the twenty-first-century workplace.*

in the age of (6.4): *For the most part, taking a selfie is harmless fun and normal behaviour in the age of social media.*

in the background (7.2): *Whenever I do my homework, my computer is always bleeping away in the background.*

in the bath (7.5): *Archimedes made his most famous discovery in the bath.*

in the city centre (3.1): *I'm standing in the city centre and I can't hear any cars!*

in the early hours of (6.2): *We decided to set off in the early hours of the morning to avoid the rush hour traffic.*

in the end (4.8): *His story didn't make any sense and in the end he admitted that it wasn't true.*

in the future (2.8): *She told us never to return to her restaurant in the future.*

in the passenger seat (1.6): *I saw a middle-aged man sitting in the passenger seat of the car.*

in the press (7.1): *Don't believe everything you read in the press.*

in the sales (4.1): *I never manage to pick up a bargain in the sales.*

in the same way (3.8): *He prepares for a gig in the same way an athlete does for a big sporting event.*

in the suburbs (3.1): *Don't you get bored living out here in the suburbs?*

in the wild (3.4): *The programme focuses on animals' behaviour in the wild.*

in time (1.6): *We arrived at the concert just in time, which was very lucky considering the amount of traffic in the city centre.*

in winter (1.7): *The last tour starts at 2:30 p.m. in winter and 3:30 p.m. in summer.*

INTO

into the early hours (3.1): *The town of Pontevedra comes alive at night and the atmosphere continues well into the early hours.*

ON

on arrival (3.7): *On arrival yesterday, the visitors were given a guided tour of the movie set.*

on average (1.4): *Every American owns seven pairs of jeans on average.*

on balance (3.8): *On balance, there are pros and cons to remaining in the family home while at university.*

on behalf of (4.8): *I am writing on behalf of my friends.*

on my way (1.5): *I usually buy some sweets on my way home.*

on purpose (5.4): *You've destroyed my dress on purpose!*

on social media (5.7): *I'm so busy on social media that I can't get down to any serious school work.*

on the border (3.1): *My grandparents live in a market town on the border of England and Wales.*

on the coast (3.1): *I used to live in a small village on the coast.*

on the ground (3.4): *The communications system is controlled by staff on the ground.*

on the outskirts (3.1): *He opened underground car parks on the outskirts of the city.*

on the website (1.7): *We haven't found any reference to the latest projects on the company's website.*

on time (6.2): *Don't be late – you have to be there on time.*

on top of (2.8): *On top of everything else, we now have extra classes every Saturday morning.*

TO

to be honest (1.6): *To be honest, I don't know what to advise you to do in this situation.*

to my mind (8.8): *To my mind, the benefits outweigh the drawbacks.*

to your left (1.6): *To your left you can see a new extension.*

UNDER

under any circumstances (4.7): *My parents are banned from using my phone under any circumstances.*

under no circumstances (8.5): *Under no circumstances are you allowed to enter the lab without my permission.*

under pressure (8.8): *The head teacher was under pressure to resign.*

WITH

with regard to (5.8): *We need to reconsider our policy with regard to immigrants.*

with sth in mind (1.8): *With your recent conduct in mind, I feel you should resign from being the student representative.*

WITHIN

within 500 metres (3.1): *There is a park within 500 metres of the school.*

within easy reach (3.1): *There is a play area within easy reach of our house.*

within walking distance (3.1): *They opened underground car parks within walking distance of the centre.*

WITHOUT

without (a) doubt (4.8): *Without doubt, the worst part of the whole incident was being humiliated in front of everybody.*

PREPOSITIONS AFTER NOUNS

access to (7.1): *Teenagers claim to need constant access to social media.*

aptitude for (7.1): *Ginny seems to have a real aptitude for painting.*

complaint about (4.8): *I'd like to make a complaint about the way we were treated.*

cost of (3.8): *In 2018/19, the average cost of renting a room in halls of residence in the UK was about £140 per week.*

decline/drop/increase/rise in (5.3): *There has been a sharp drop in the number of people commuting to work.*

effect on (2.3): *The accident had a terrible effect on Steve.*

enthusiasm for (5.8): *Considering her enthusiasm for the project, I'm sure we'll succeed.*

excuse for (3.5): *There is no excuse for an unmade bed.*

expert in (7.1): *Jill is an expert in EU funding.*

gift of (5.1): *Single-minded people have the gift of extreme focus. They know how to avoid distractions.*

home to (8.6): *The ocean is home to over half of all living species.*

love of (2.1): *John has a love of learning.*

love of your life (2.2): *Amelia never married because she had never forgotten Richard, who was the love of her life.*

be in love with (2.3): *He denied being in love with the actress.*

memory for (1.3): *I have a good memory for numbers and faces.*

network of (3.1): *The city has a reliable network of buses.*

point of view (7.8): *What's your point of view on global warming?*

range of (5.4): *The travel agency offered a wide range of destinations to choose from.*

reason for (2.7): *Please give me your reasons for applying for a job here.*

report on (6.4): *She was sent a report on the floods in Bangladesh.*

respect of (7.1): *She gained the respect of scientists.*

sense of (2.5): *Have you got a sense of humour?*

sort of (2.4): *What sort of ailments can these apps help?*

thought of (6.7): *The very thought of moving abroad brought me to tears.*

thousands of (4.3): *Every weekend thousands of people take their unwanted stuff to car boot sales.*

time for (5.7): *It's time for a radical shake-up of education in many regions of the world.*

urge to (1.4): *She felt an urge to paint, and overnight she became a talented abstract artist.*

PREPOSITIONS AFTER VERBS

accept into (3.6): *I can't believe we've both been accepted into the same university!*

accuse sb of (4.8): *A member of your staff accused me of stealing.*

add to (2.8): *If you add the pressure of schoolwork to household duties, you have a recipe for disaster.*

apologise for (5.5): *Although Rachel apologised for her misbehaviour, I still can't forgive her.*

apply for (1.8): *Only six people applied for the post, which was quite disappointing.*

associate with (7.7): *Most people associate GPS with giving directions when driving.*

bid for sth (4.4): *You can log on to a website to bid for a bargain.*

blame sb for (5.5): *Why are you blaming my son for starting the fight?*

burst with (2.5): *First-borns tend to be bursting with confidence.*

collaborate with (7.1): *During the late seventies, he collaborated with the legendary Muddy Waters.*

congratulate sb on (5.5): *My supervisor congratulated me on passing the exams with flying colours.*

consist of (7.7): *Her diet mainly consists of fruit and vegetables.*

contribute to (7.5): *Scholars in ancient China contributed to the advancement of mathematics.*

cope with (3.4): *Mum taught us about possible dangers and how to cope with them.*

die from (8.1): *A lot of animals died from starvation during the dry season.*

focus on (5.1): *In our test we're going to focus on brain activity.*

insist on (5.5): *My granny always insists on feeding me with sweets.*

interact with (7.6): *We interact with today's machines mostly by pushing buttons.*

judge by (1.6): *Judging by the examiner's reaction, I don't think she'll pass her driving test.*
lead to (2.3): *Space exploration might lead to the discovery of other planets.*
name after (7.1): *The baby was named after her maternal grandmother.*
object to (5.5): *The council objected to another shopping centre being built in the city.*
opt for (4.1): *We finally opted for the red paint in the kitchen.*
pose for (6.4): *Hannah looked so funny when she was posing for a selfie.*
prevent from (8.4): *Fire fighters are trying to prevent the fire from spreading any further.*
reason with (4.8): *We tried to reason with the guard, but he wouldn't listen.*
refer to/make reference to (7.1): *In her books she refers to her childhood.*
report on (6.7): *When are you going to report on the progress of the construction of the concert hall?*
roar with (2.7): *When was the last time you roared with laughter?*
sail across (3.2): *I admire my father who sailed across the Pacific when he was in his twenties.*
search for (7.1): *The fire brigade searched for the missing people, but they couldn't find anybody.*
specialise in (1.1): *Chris specialises in neurology.*
stare at (2.4): *Stop staring at me – I feel rather uncomfortable.*
stick to (5.4): *If you think your plan is good, then stick to it.*
struggle to (8.4): *Although the Kamkwamba family is struggling to survive, the parents do their best to focus on their children's education.*
sue sb for (5.5): *The customers decided to sue the supermarket for not paying attention to safety regulations.*
suffer from (7.4): *After falling off the horse, Dominic has been suffering from back pain.*
transfer sth to (4.2): *I've just transferred the money to your account so that you can buy yourself a new computer.*
treat yourself to (4.1): *Let's treat ourselves to some ice cream.*
warn sb against (7.3): *I warned you against buying a cheap laptop.*
welcome to (7.7): *Welcome fellow teens to my video blog.*

PREPOSITIONS AFTER ADJECTIVES

accompanied by (2.8): *Physical changes that happen during adolescence are often accompanied by emotional ones.*
accustomed to (2.5): *First-borns, who are accustomed to accepting rules, are better behaved at school.*
attracted to (2.3): *When my uncle saw his future wife for the first time, he was immediately attracted to her.*
awash with/bombarded with (6.1): *The Internet is awash with information that cannot be trusted.*
beneficial to (7.4): *Lots of bacteria are extremely useful and beneficial to our health.*
concerned about (4.2): *Some tourist destinations are concerned about more than just money.*
connected with (5.3): *There will be an increase in jobs connected with alternative energy.*
consistent with (6.4): *The results are consistent with earlier research.*
credited with (7.1): *She is credited with inventing the first computer algorithm.*
curious about (5.4): *A brainy person is curious about the world.*
dependent on (7.2): *We're all more and more dependent on technology in our lives.*
familiar with (8.6): *Are you familiar with the health and safety regulations in our factory?*
fed up with (5.7): *I've decided to give up social media (no, it's not a joke). I'm just completely fed up with it.*
important to sb (1.1): *Maintaining proper social relationships is very important to them.*
incapable of (1.3): *Rob was incapable of understanding how his wife felt.*
included in (3.8): *Is breakfast included in the price of the room?*
interested in (5.8): *Should students choose a degree based on what they are interested in?*
invited to (1.7): *You are invited to attend a reception in honour of the exchange group from Switzerland.*
involved in (2.6): *Our parents got really involved in the end-of-school play and they even made costumes.*
obsessed with (2.3): *Stop being so obsessed with cleanliness! A bit of dirt won't do any harm.*
passionate about (3.4): *Sally is passionate about music. She would like to be a conductor one day.*
popular with (3.1): *Why do you think fur is still popular with fashion designers and wealthy consumers?*
relevant for (5.3): *My brother has a hobby that has taught him skills that are relevant for his job.*
short of (5.8): *Young people tend to be short of money.*
suited to (5.4): *She explains how people like herself are suited to the modern workplace in three essential ways.*
surrounded by (8.8): *The whole island is surrounded by turquoise waters.*
unaware of (8.7): *Mike seems unaware of the trouble he's causing.*
unprepared for (6.2): *The pupils were unprepared for the questions that the teacher asked them.*
useful for (1.3): *Which method is most useful for memorising shopping lists?*

OTHER

according to (6.7): *According to recent figures, most students have part-time jobs.*
after a while (2.6): *We started talking and after a while I realised that we had met before.*
after all (7.7): *My mum received a phone call in which her boss told her that he couldn't extend her contract after all.*
aged fifteen to twenty-nine (6.4): *'Youth' is defined as people aged fifteen to twenty-nine.*
all in all (3.8): *All in all, I think experiments on animals should be banned.*
around 100 years (8.1): *Plastic has only existed for around 100 years, but it's everywhere.*
as a result (2.8): *As a result, whether it is playing sport or online games, we have time to enjoy ourselves.*
as a result of (7.8): *Frederic claimed that his eyes changed colour as a result of the traumas he had been through.*
be of interest to sb (1.1): *This course will be of interest to those working in the field of cultural studies.*
be of the opinion (5.8): *I'm of the opinion that public figures' private lives should not be reported in the papers.*
by the time (3.2): *By the time we go, I'll have been playing basketball for my school team for two years.*
contrary to (6.4): *Contrary to popular belief, a desert can be very cold.*
date back to (6.4): *The oldest existing selfie dates back to 1839 when photographer Robert Cornelius took a self-portrait photograph of himself.*
due to (7.4): *All the flights were cancelled due to bad weather.*
instead of (1.2): *Why don't you use honey instead of sugar?*
one by one (1.3): *You need to put the items in the basket carefully one by one.*
out of the blue (2.6): *It was going to be a nice day, but then it started raining out of the blue.*
put your heart into sth (5.1): *Identify what you're good at and then put your heart into doing those specific things.*
regardless of (2.8): *We'll go on the trip regardless of the weather.*
so on (1.3): *She was always disturbing her classmates and her homework was always late and so on.*
thanks to (3.4): *I managed to complete the project only thanks to your help.*

Use a dictionary to translate the phrasal verbs into your language.

back sth up (6.7) – ____________ : *The police officers are backed up by extra teams of people at the weekend.*
be caught up in sth (8.4) – ____________ : *A Spanish family were caught up in the tsunami.*
boss sb around (2.5) – ____________ : *Stop bossing me around! I'm not your servant!*
break down (5.6) – ____________ : *The car broke down in the middle of nowhere.*
break in (7.8) – ____________ : *Just as they were breaking in, Robert appeared at the bottom of the stairs.*
bring sth about (1.4) – ____________ : *A bang on the head has brought about changes in personality.*
bring in sth (7.3) – ____________ : *The police are going to bring in new security measures.*
bring sb up (2.5) – ____________ : *Parents who are bringing up their first child tend to be extremely protective.*
burn out (5.1) – ____________ : *It's a high-pressure job and you could burn out young.*
carry out (5.1) – ____________ : *The local newspaper carried out a survey on people's attitude to the council's policies.*
catch up with sb/sth (3.4) – ____________ : *I use my mobile every few weeks to catch up with friends.*
check up on sth (4.1) – ____________ : *Dustin called me to check up on some facts.*
clean sth up (3.8) – ____________ : *It took us ages to clean up the house after the party.*
clear out (5.7) – ____________ : *I need to clear out all the junk in my bedroom.*
come along (1.7) – ____________ : *Make sure all your staff come along to the meeting.*
come down to (5.7) – ____________ : *It all comes down to money in the end.*
come out (2.6) – ____________ : *His new novel is going to come out soon.*
come out of sth (1.4, 6.4) – ____________ : *Great news! Pete has come out of a coma. / The term 'selfie' comes out of the Australian habit of adding 'ie' at the end of words.*
come over (4.8) – ____________ : *You can come over any time you like.*
come up (5.2) – ____________ : *Don't worry, something better might come up.*
come up against sb/sth (5.7) – ____________ : *He came up against bullying from other boys and often got into trouble.*
come up with sth (2.1) – ____________ : *We still haven't come up with a name for our band.*
crack down on sth (6.7) – ____________ : *The government wants to crack down on terrorism.*
curl up (8.7) – ____________ : *Lynn curled up on the bed and fell asleep.*
cut down on (4.1) – ____________ : *You should cut down on the amount of chocolate you eat.*
deal with sb/sth (6.7) – ____________ : *I can't deal with so many problems at once.*
drift apart (2.2) – ____________ : *When John moved to another city, they drifted apart.*
drop out of sth (5.7) – ____________ : *If I dropped out of college, my parents would never forgive me.*
embark on sth (3.2) – ____________ : *Phil left the band to embark on a solo career.*
end up (4.3) – ____________ : *Lost luggage will eventually end up on a market stall.*
fall behind (with sth) (1.1) – ____________ : *You can go away at the weekend, but make sure you don't fall behind with your homework.*
fall for sb (2.3) – ____________ : *When you fall for someone, it's similar to hunger or thirst.*
fall out (with sb) (8.7) – ____________ : *Do you often fall out with your brothers and sisters?*
figure sth out (7.3) – ____________ : *The couple couldn't figure out which way to go.*
find sth out (4.4) – ____________ : *I'd like to find out what people think of me.*
get down to sth (5.1) – ____________ : *Let's get down to work.*
get on with sb (2.4) – ____________ : *I have always got on well with boys.*
get on with sth (5.1) – ____________ : *I need to get on with my project now.*
get out of sth (5.7) – ____________ : *How do you always manage to get out of cleaning the bathroom?*
get round to (5.7) – ____________ : *I need to go to the library, but I haven't got round to it yet.*
give away (4.7) – ____________ : *He managed to acquire shopping worth £500 for 4p, giving it all away to a charity.*
give sth up (5.7) – ____________ : *I've given up sweets.*
give up on sb (1.1) – ____________ : *The teachers gave up on him.*
go back (2.7) – ____________ : *I'll never go back to living in a tower block.*
go for sth (4.1) – ____________ : *I wouldn't go for a bracelet because I don't like wearing jewellery.*
go into (1.1) – ____________ : *Vivian wants to go into teaching.*
go in for (7.3) – ____________ : *I've never gone in for modern art.*
go off (4.8) – ____________ : *The thief ran away when the security alarm went off.*
go on (2.8) – ____________ : *Remember when you were little and school summer holidays seemed to go on forever?*
go on to (1.1) – ____________ : *You're keen to go on to higher education.*
go out (2.7) – ____________ : *Lights go out here at 11 p.m.*
go out with sb (2.3) – ____________ : *At the beginning, you're just attracted to somebody. Then you start going out with them.*
grow out of (5.7) – ____________ : *This app grew out of the simple idea that it's good to let people know if you're available.*
grow up (1.7) – ____________ : *I grew up in a rural area.*
hand sth in (1.1) – ____________ : *I always try to hand in my homework on time.*
hand sth out (6.6) – ____________ : *We need somebody to hand out invitations to the exhibition.*
hang on (5.6) – ____________ : *Hang on, I'm not ready yet.*
hang out (with sb) (4.8) – ____________ : *He usually hangs out with friends downtown.*
hear from sb (8.8) – ____________ : *Have you heard from Jane since she moved to another town?*
help sb out (6.7) – ____________ : *This loan will help us out.*
keep at sth (5.1) – ____________ : *I know it's hard, but keep at it! Don't give up!*
keep up with sb (5.7) – ____________ : *Davey isn't keeping up with the rest of the class in reading.*
kick back (7.6) – ____________ : *On Friday night I like to kick back and listen to some relaxing music.*
kick sb out (4.8) – ____________ : *Eve's parents kicked her out because she didn't want to contribute to the housework.*
knock sb out (1.4) – ____________ : *Ali knocked out his opponent in the fifth round.*
leave out (1.7) – ____________ : *You can leave out question 7.*
let sb down (5.7) – ____________ : *I dropped out of college and let my family down.*
log on (4.3) *You need a password to log on.*
look after (3.4) – ____________ : *I'd like to see more people look after the land.*
look back on sth (2.6) – ____________ : *One day you'll look back on adolescence as the best time of your life.*

look down on sb (5.7) – ____________ : *Kate looks down on everybody who doesn't have a university degree.*

look for (5.2) – ____________ : *You're exactly the person we're looking for.*

look forward to sth (6.7) – ____________ : *I'm looking forward to going away during the summer holidays.*

look out for sth (4.1) – ____________ : *Can you look out for a red handbag when you go shopping next?*

look up to sb (5.7) – ____________ : *Mary looks up to her older sister who is an authority for her.*

major in sth (1.1) – ____________ : *He majored in Psychology.*

make up for sth (5.7) – ____________ : *Jack lacks experience, but he makes up for it with hard work.*

map sth out (5.1) – ____________ : *Her parents have already mapped out her future.*

meet up (with sb) (2.2) – ____________ : *I'd like to meet up with you this afternoon.*

pass through (4.4) – ____________ : *Shortly after it was sold, the painting began to pass through a shredder hidden in the frame.*

pay sth back (6.2) – ____________ : *Lend me $200 today and I promise to pay it back next week.*

pay out for sth (4.1) – ____________ : *I paid out a lot of money for that car.*

pick sth up (5.1) – ____________ : *We picked up new surfing skills during our summer camp.*

pick up sth (4.1) – ____________ : *I never manage to pick up a bargain in the sales.*

point sth out (8.8) – ____________ : *The chairman pointed out that we haven't made much profit in the last few months.*

pour down (5.7) – ____________ : *The rain started to pour down.*

pull down (1.7) – ____________ : *They are pulling down the old hall next week.*

pull out (1.6) – ____________ : *Unfortunately, a car suddenly pulled out in front of me and we collided.*

put sth aside (4.1) – ____________ : *Ask the shop assistant to put the T-shirt aside while you think about it.*

put sb off (5.1) – ____________ : *Don't let the restaurant's decor put you off – the food is really good.*

put sth off (5.1) – ____________ : *Never put off until tomorrow what you have to do today.*

put up with sb/sth (5.7) – ____________ : *I don't know how you put up with all that noise.*

rely on sb/sth (3.4) – ____________ : *You can always rely on us for help.*

run sth down (5.7) – ____________ : *Don't leave it switched on – you'll run down the batteries.*

run out of sth (5.7) – ____________ : *We ran out of money halfway through our holiday.*

save up (4.7) – ____________ : *I've been saving up for months to buy this bike.*

scrape through (1.1) – ____________ : *I managed to scrape through the exam.*

send sth back (4.1) – ____________ : *She sent back the form immediately.*

set off for (1.2) – ____________ : *Mum usually makes me have something for breakfast before I set off for school.*

set off/out (3.2) – ____________ : *We need to set off now if you want to do some shopping before catching a train.*

set sth out (5.1) – ____________ : *Set out your objectives.*

settle down (1.1) – ____________ : *After an exhausting day, I needed to settle down and just be quiet for an hour or so.*

shake sth off (6.4) – ____________ : *I can't seem to shake off this cold.*

shine through (8.4) – ____________ : *The Impossible tells a captivating true story in which survival, society, family ties and human kindness all shine through.*

shop around (4.1) – ____________ : *It's a good idea to shop around before buying a new laptop.*

show up (6.7) – ____________ : *If you wear a green top, it doesn't show up against a green background and you appear as a floating head.*

sit in (1.8) – ____________ : *I sat in on staff meetings and coordinated a very successful sports day.*

split up (with sb) (2.3) – ____________ : *My aunt split up with her fiancé last week.*

spring up (4.1) – ____________ : *Fast-food restaurants are springing up all over town.*

stand up for sth (5.7) – ____________ : *It's time we stood up for our rights.*

step in (4.4) – ____________ : *The referee stepped in and stopped the fight.*

sum up (5.8) – ____________ : *His gesture summed up the situation.*

switch sth off (1.5) – ____________ : *Please, switch off your mobile phones in lessons.*

switch sth on (5.6) – ____________ : *I tried to switch the washing machine on, but it didn't work.*

take sth away (1.7) – ____________ : *Turn off your mobile phones, otherwise we will take them away from you.*

take sth back (4.5) – ____________ : *I took the jeans back because they were too tight.*

take off (about a career/business) (5.7) – ____________ : *My brother wanted to close down his business, but then it suddenly started taking off.*

take sth on (4.4) – ____________ : *I've taken on a challenge to run a marathon.*

take sth up (7.2) – ____________ : *My brother took up music seriously.*

talk sb into sth/doing sth (7.3) – ____________ : *Luke was happy when he talked me into buying a sat-nav.*

tell sb off (1.7) – ____________ : *Our neighbour told us off for being loud in the garden.*

throw sth away (8.1) – ____________ : *Do you still want this newspaper or can I throw it away?*

throw in (7.3) – ____________ : *Since I'm buying such an expensive computer, maybe you could throw something in for free.*

throw sb out (4.8) – ____________ : *The security guard noticed some underage girls in the club, so he threw them out.*

(be) tied up (5.7) – ____________ : *Mr Baker can't see you now,. He's tied up.*

turn sb/sth down (1.7) – ____________ : *They offered me the job but I turned it down, because I decided to set up my own business.*

turn sth off (7.2) – ____________ : *My laptop froze so I had to turn it off and on again.*

turn out (6.7) – ____________ : *It turned out Mike and I had the same hobbies.*

turn up (2.7) – ____________ : *Lots of fans turned up at Mark's graduation concert. There was hardly a seat left.*

wake sb up (6.2) – ____________ : *Please wake me up early tomorrow. I don't want to oversleep because I've got an important exam.*

warm up (5.7) – ____________ : *I can warm up the soup if you want.*

wind sb up (7.3) – ____________ : *You're constantly winding me up by telling me what to do.*

work sth out (5.5) – ____________ : *We need to work out how to get home from here.*

work towards (5.1) – ____________ : *Work towards finishing the job before you leave.*

zoom in on sth (6.4) – ____________ : *Please, zoom in on those people over there.*

zoom out (6.4) – ____________ : *The camera zoomed out and everything looked smaller.*

PREFIXES

Common prefixes

Prefix	Examples
anti- (=against)	anti-war, antisocial
bi- (=two)	bilingual
co- (=with, together)	co-worker, cooperate
de- (=sth is removed)	deforestation
down- (=become worse)	downturn
ex- (=former, before)	ex-partner, ex-boyfriend
hyper- (=extremely)	hyperactive, hypersensitive
inter- (=between)	international
macro- (=large)	macroeconomics
micro- (= extremely small)	micro-organism
mini- (=very small)	mini-break
mis- (badly, wrongly)	mismanage, misbehave
mono- (=one)	monolingual
multi- (=many/several)	multicultural
off- (=not the case)	off-colour
on- (=the place where)	onstage
out- (=beyond)	outdated
out- (=further, better than)	outweigh
over- (=too much)	overpriced, overactive
post- (=after)	postwar
pre- (=before)	pre-owned
pro- (=in favour)	pro-fairness
re- (=again)	reunite, remarry
self- (=done to/by yourself)	self-employed, self-esteem
semi- (=half or partly)	semicircle
sub- (=under, below)	subway, sub-standard
under- (=not enough)	under-performing
under- (=below, beneath)	underlying, underpaid
up- (=increase or improve)	upturn

Prefixes that give an opposite meaning

Prefix	Examples
dis-	disappear, disapprove
il-	illiterate, illogical
im-	impatient, immature
in-	inauthentic, incapable
ir-	irrational, irregular
non-	non-biodegradable
un-	unsupervised, unmade, undo

SUFFIXES

Noun suffixes

Suffix	Examples
-ion/-tion/-sion	explosion, illustration, conclusion
-ance/-ence	disappearance, violence
-ism	vandalism
-ise	expertise
-ment	recruitment, achievement
-ness	fairness, vastness
-ancy	vacancy, accountancy
-al	approval, withdrawal
-y	mystery
-cy	accuracy
-ty/-ity	stupidity, curiosity
-dom	freedom
-hood	adulthood, neighbourhood
-ing	handwriting, blessing
-ful	handful
-ship	leadership, apprenticeship
-th	strength, depth
-age	orphanage, marriage
-ics	economics
-sis	diagnosis, metamorphosis
-ure	pressure
-er/-or	campaigner, creator
-ian	mathematician
-ist	traditionalist, perfectionist
-ive	representative
-ant/-ent	applicant, adolescent
-ee	interviewee, nominee
-ess	happiness

Adjective suffixes

Suffix	Example
-ic	enthusiastic, iconic
-able/-ible	believable, accessible
-al	environmental, emotional
-ive	productive, disruptive
-us	anonymous, studious
-ing	challenging
-y	leafy, brainy
-ed	injured, ragged
-ate	passionate
-ful	painful, faithful
-less	pointless, useless
-ent/-ant	persistent, ignorant
-ly	friendly
-like	childlike
-ary	revolutionary
-ish	selfish
-ate	considerate
-ary	secondary
-ed	puzzled

Adverb suffixes

Suffix	Examples
-ly	surprisingly

Verb suffixes

Suffix	Examples
-ise/-ize (Am.E.)	familiarise, recognise
-en	deepen, frighten
-ify	justify, identify
-ate	domesticate, authenticate